SABBATAI ZEVI

THE LITTMAN LIBRARY OF
JEWISH CIVILIZATION

Dedicated to the memory of
LOUIS THOMAS SIDNEY LITTMAN
who founded the Littman Library for the love of God
and as an act of charity in memory of his father
JOSEPH AARON LITTMAN
and to the memory of
ROBERT JOSEPH LITTMAN
who continued what his father Louis had begun
יהא זכרם ברוך

'Get wisdom, get understanding:
Forsake her not and she shall preserve thee'
PROV. 4: 5

The Littman Library of Jewish Civilization is a registered UK charity
Registered charity no. 1000784

SABBATAI ZEVI

ৡ

Testimonies to a Fallen Messiah

ৡ

Translated, with Notes and Introductions, by
DAVID J. HALPERIN

The Littman Library of Jewish Civilization
in association with Liverpool University Press

The Littman Library of Jewish Civilization
in association with Liverpool University Press
4 Cambridge Street, Liverpool L69 7ZU, UK

www.liverpooluniversitypress.co.uk/littman

Managing Editor: Connie Webber

Distributed in North America by
Oxford University Press Inc., 198 Madison Avenue,
New York, NY 10016, USA

First published in hardback 2007
First published in paperback 2012

Catalogue records for this book are available from the
British Library and the Library of Congress

ISBN 978-1-906764-24-1

Publishing co-ordinator: Janet Moth
Proof reading: Kate Clements
Designed and typeset by Pete Russell, Faringdon, Oxon

Printed in Great Britain by
CPI Group (UK) Ltd, Croydon, CR0 4YY

Acknowledgements

꙳

NEARLY twenty years ago I undertook to prepare and publish extended English translations from the literature of the Sabbatian movement—the strange, enigmatic, sometimes scandalous messianic faith that crystallized around the apostate messiah Sabbatai Zevi. My book *Abraham Miguel Cardozo: Selected Writings*, published in 2001 by Paulist Press, was the first instalment of this project. The current volume is the second.

Many have helped me on this still unfinished journey. The generosity of the National Endowment for the Humanities (Travel to Collections programme), and of the American Philosophical Society, allowed me to spend much of the summer of 1989 in Israel, gathering texts for translation. Dr Etti Liebes, librarian of the Gershom G. Scholem Collection of materials on Jewish mysticism (National and University Library, Jerusalem), welcomed and oriented me to this extraordinary scholarly treasure-house, and helped me find there the materials I needed. Her husband, Professor Yehuda Liebes of the Hebrew University—one of the foremost Israeli scholars of Sabbatianism and kabbalah—generously took time to guide me through the often bewildering universe of Sabbatian thought.

At my home institution, the University of North Carolina at Chapel Hill, I was several times beneficiary of the financial support and intellectual fellowship of the UNC Institute for the Arts and Humanities, under the directorship of Professor Ruel W. Tyson. The Institute honoured me in the summer of 1990 with a faculty fellowship, in the autumn semester of 1992 with a Lyman Cotton Faculty Fellowship—supplemented by a generous grant from the Memorial Foundation for Jewish Culture, New York—and, in the spring semester of 1997, with a Chapman Family Faculty Fellowship. The drafts of the translations first took shape during these research leaves.

In 1994–5 the UNC Department of Religious Studies and the University Research Council funded a research assistant to help me edit and annotate my translation of Baruch of Arezzo's *Memorial to the Children of Israel* (the 'First Testimony' below). I was fortunate to have the services of Dr Pamela E. Hedrick—then a UNC graduate student, now assistant professor at Wheeling Jesuit University, West Virginia. The finished translation owes much to the information she diligently gathered for me, and to her thoughtful comments, queries, and suggestions.

For their help in obtaining copies of manuscripts of Baruch's *Memorial*, I am indebted to Israel Dubitsky and Rabbi Jerry Schwarzbard of the Jewish

Theological Seminary, New York; to Sally Giles, Stuart May, and Ilana Tahan of the British Library, London; to Doris Nicholson of the Bodleian Library, Oxford; and to Yael Okun and Benjamin Richler of the Institute of Microfilmed Hebrew Manuscripts, National and University Library, Jerusalem. Michael Glatzer and Dov Cohen of the Ben-Zvi Institute, Jerusalem, made available to me the Ben-Zvi Institute's manuscript of the *Memorial* (Ben-Zvi 2264), as well as the massive Sabbatian manuscript *Sefer yemot hamashiaḥ* (Ben-Zvi 2262) containing the 'Najara Chronicle'. Ms Heike Tröger, librarian of special collections at the University of Rostock (Germany), provided me with a copy of MS Rostock 36, the single known manuscript of Abraham Cuenque's biography of Sabbatai Zevi (the 'Fourth Testimony'). I am deeply grateful to them all—and most especially to Dr Richler, who patiently guided me in making use, from thousands of miles away, of the treasures of the Institute of Microfilmed Hebrew Manuscripts. It was he who called my attention to the existence of the Rostock manuscript, and thereby made possible my understanding of Cuenque's text and its pre-publication history.

The letters of Joseph Halevi (the 'Second Testimony') are translated from Hebrew texts published by the Bialik Institute, Jerusalem, as part of Isaiah Tishby's edition of Sasportas's *Tsitsat novel tsevi* ('Zevi's Fading Flower'). The Najara Chronicle (the 'Third Testimony') and the reminiscences of Abraham Cardozo (the 'Fifth Testimony') are translated from texts published by the Ben-Zvi Institute, in *Sefunot*, 5 (1961), 237–74, and *Sefunot*, 3–4 (1960), 217–18 respectively. For permission to publish these translations, I thank the Bialik Institute (and Ms Devorah Levinger), and the Ben-Zvi Institute (and Dr Michael Glatzer, the Institute's Academic Secretary).

Professors Elisheva Carlebach, Alan Corré, Benjamin Ravid, Joseph Shatzmiller, and Steven Wasserstrom graciously responded to my queries, putting their learning at my disposal for the interpretation of diverse points in the texts. My colleague Professor Yaakov Ariel, and Rabbi Hirsch Cohen and Jan-Erik Guerth (president, BlueBridge Books), provided me with materials of which I would otherwise have been unaware. I am particularly grateful to my old friend Professor Marc Bregman (now distinguished professor at the University of North Carolina at Greensboro) for his account of his 1971 visit to Sabbatai Zevi's supposed birthplace—and to Marc and to Yaakov Ariel for their friendship over the years. My friend and teacher Ms Sema Deeds, a native speaker of Turkish, kindly helped me understand and translate the Turkish words in the Najara Chronicle.

Professor Rachel Elior of the Hebrew University recommended to me the Littman Library of Jewish Civilization as a publisher for these translations, and put me in touch with Littman's managing editor, Connie Webber. I am so glad she did! Working with the people at Littman has been a true pleasure. Connie Webber, Ludo Craddock (Littman's Chief Executive Officer), and copy-editors Janet Moth and Lindsey Taylor-Guthartz gave my project their thoughtful and meticulous attention from beginning to end. I owe to Pete Russell the book's pleasing, eye-catching design. I could not have asked for finer partners than these in bringing my work to publication.

For their help preparing the index, I thank Nathan Hollister and his team of students from the Eno River Unitarian Universalist Fellowship (ERUUF) of Durham, North Carolina: Sam Baskir, Mary Deal, Dawn DelGaizo, and Vince Graffagnino.

My deepest gratitude goes, as always, to my wonderful wife of twenty-five years, Dr Rose Shalom Halperin. All through the two decades of this project, through the good years and the bad and now again the good, her love has been my support, my comfort, my delight. We both are grateful to ERUUF and its wonderful ministers, the Reverends Mary Grigolia, Don Southworth, and Sarah York, for giving us a nurturing spiritual home in which to learn and grow. And our debt to our old friend and adviser Steve Eubanks, for the help and good counsel that made this and so many other dreams possible, is greater than we can say.

Contents

❧

Note on Transliteration and Conventions Used in the Text

🐦

THE transliteration of Hebrew in this book reflects consideration of the type of book it is, in terms of its content, purpose, and readership. The system adopted therefore reflects a broad approach to transcription, rather than the narrower approaches found in the *Encyclopaedia Judaica* or other systems developed for text-based or linguistic studies. The aim has been to reflect the pronunciation prescribed for modern Hebrew, rather than the spelling or Hebrew word structure, and to do so using conventions that are generally familiar to the English-speaking reader.

In accordance with this approach, no attempt is made to indicate the distinctions between *alef* and *ayin*, *tet* and *taf*, *kaf* and *kuf*, *sin* and *samekh*, since these are not relevant to pronunciation; likewise, the *dagesh* is not indicated except where it affects pronunciation. Following the principle of using conventions familiar to the majority of readers, however, transcriptions that are well established have been retained even when they are not fully consistent with the transliteration system adopted. On similar grounds, the *tsadi* is rendered by 'tz' in such familiar words as barmitzvah. Likewise, the distinction between *ḥet* and *khaf* has been retained, using *ḥ* for the former and *kh* for the latter; the associated forms are generally familiar to readers, even if the distinction is not actually borne out in pronunciation, and for the same reason the final *heh* is indicated too. As in Hebrew, no capital letters are used, except that an initial capital has been retained in transliterating titles of published works (for example, *Shulḥan arukh*).

Since no distinction is made between *alef* and *ayin*, they are indicated by an apostrophe only in intervocalic positions where a failure to do so could lead an English-speaking reader to pronounce the vowel-cluster as a diphthong—as, for example, in *ha'ir*—or otherwise mispronounce the word.

The *sheva na* is indicated by an *e*—*perikat ol*, *reshut*—except, again, when established convention dictates otherwise.

The *yod* is represented by *i* when it occurs as a vowel (*bereshit*), by *y* when it occurs as a consonant (*yesodot*), and by *yi* when it occurs as both (*yisra'el*).

Names have generally been left in their familiar forms, even when this is inconsistent with the overall system; in particular, the name of Sabbatai Zevi and his family is spelt in the most widely used form.

INTRODUCTION

࿓

I

ON 16 SEPTEMBER 1666, a Jew from the Turkish city of Izmir was brought into the presence of Mehmed IV, sultan of the Ottoman empire. The sultan was perhaps the most powerful man on earth, although Louis XIV of France would have run him a close second. Certainly he was ruler of an empire which, although beginning its long decline, was still the greatest of the seventeenth-century world.

The sultan's captive was ruler of a realm of hope and dream. His name was Sabbatai Zevi. His Jewish followers, who were many—the majority of the Jews of the time—often preferred to call him Amirah, the Hebrew acronym for 'our Lord, our King, may his majesty be exalted'.[1] 'Messiah of the God of Jacob' was one of his less extravagant titles. For more than eighteen years, since the summer of 1648, he had been declaring himself messiah. Only in the past year and a half, however, had anyone listened.

Now Sabbatai Zevi was an international celebrity, the most notorious messianic claimant since Jesus of Nazareth. Jews everywhere were breathless for the expected news of how he would graciously, bloodlessly, receive the empire from the sultan and go on to establish his dominion over the earth. All over the Jewish diaspora redemption was the daily expectation, prayer and penitence and Torah study—to prepare the world for its imminent salvation—the daily routine. Those Jews who doubted Sabbatai's messiahship might, in places like Venice or Amsterdam, be lucky to escape with their lives.

The sultan, looking down from his latticed alcove,[2] would have seen a fleshy, bearded man of 40, perceived, at least by his followers, as radiantly handsome. Sabbatai Zevi would have looked up and seen or imagined— what? Certainly a man who held his life in his hands, who could destroy it at any moment and had every reason to do so. What the sultan, or the Turkish grandees who spoke in his name, threatened or promised to do to the helpless messiah, we cannot be sure. The sources on the encounter are many, their reliability doubtful. What we know is this: that when 16 September

---

[1] *Adonenu malkenu yarum hodo.*
[2] So Scholem, *Sabbatai Sevi*, 674–5, following Turkish sources.

1666 was over, Sabbatai had received from the sultan new clothing. He had received from him a turban, marker of his new identity as a Muslim. He had received a new name—Mehmed, the sultan's own name, the Turkish form of the name of the Prophet of Islam. To all intents and purposes the Jewish messiah had turned Muslim.

He did not cease to be the Jewish messiah, nor did many of his followers stop regarding him as such. That is the most fantastic, the most paradoxical feature of the whole incredible story. He lived ten more years, comporting himself as Jew and Muslim rolled into one, always and ever messiah. Even after his death, many kept on believing, longing for his Second Coming. The faith he founded survives, though in much attenuated form, to this day.

How did these things come to be?

II

The story of Sabbatai Zevi has been told time and time again, most definitively in Gershom Scholem's massive biography *Sabbatai Sevi: The Mystical Messiah*.[3] My aim in this book is to let the reader experience Sabbatai's life through the eyes and minds of his contemporaries—mostly, but not entirely, his devoted believers. The biographical sketch that follows is intended as orientation to the primary narratives.

Sabbatai was born in Izmir in 1626, on the fast-day of the Ninth of Av, which fell that year on 1 August. According to Jewish tradition, the Ninth of Av was the day on which both the First and Second Temples were destroyed, and which was ever after to be observed as a day of mourning and sorrow. In 1666, at the height of the messianic excitement, Sabbatai declared the fast abolished, transformed into a new festival, the 'Feast of Consolations' (*ḥag haneḥamot*), as if his birth on the Ninth of Av had redeemed the day and turned its mourning into gladness. Sabbatai's critics, of course, had a very different take on the symbolism of his having been born on this most 'ominous and unhappy day'[4] of the Jewish year.[5]

---

[3] In a superb English translation by R. J. Zwi Werblowsky (Princeton University Press, 1973). The Hebrew original was published in 1957. Recent book-length biographies include, in English, Freely, *The Lost Messiah*, and, in Hebrew, Shai, *Messiah of Incest*. Sabbatai's story has inspired numerous works of creative fiction; see Robert Alter, 'Sabbatai Zevi and the Jewish Imagination', and David Biale, 'Shabbtai Zvi and the Seductions of Jewish Orientalism'. One of the most recent is Lisa Goldstein's brilliant science fiction story 'Split Light'. (I thank Rabbi Hirsch Cohen for calling my attention to Alter's essay.)

[4] So the Ninth of Av is called by the contemporary Rabbi Menasseh ben Israel: Méchoulan and Nahon, *Menasseh ben Israel*, 148.

[5] A lampoon by the brothers Jacob and Emanuel Frances, composed after Sabbatai converted to Islam, declares the Ninth of Av 'appointed for a weeping unto all generations,

Izmir was at the time a bustling commercial centre thronged by European merchants, each group competing savagely against the others for the profits of trade with the East.[6] Sabbatai's father, Mordecai Zevi, made his living as an agent for a company of English merchants. This might lead us to speculate that, among the languages with which Sabbatai was familiar—above all, the Judaeo-Spanish that was the common tongue of the Sephardi diaspora—he may have had a smattering of English. It also suggests that, for all his unworldly and ascetic bent, he is likely to have been well aware of events in the world around him. A merchant did not survive in the cut-throat atmosphere of seventeenth-century Izmir without prompt and exact information on latest developments in the Ottoman court, the empire, the wider world. Surely any breaking news which Mordecai Zevi had not already gleaned from other sources would be told him by his employers. No doubt it would be passed along to Sabbatai as well.

Of his brothers Elijah and Joseph we will hear more in the texts translated below. Of his mother Clara we know practically nothing except that she died before he became famous, and that he was particularly attached to her.[7] The sources agree that he gave himself over to religious practices, often quite eccentric, from an early age. 'A son shall be born to Mordecai Zevi in the year 5386 [1625/6]', runs a 'prophecy' fabricated in 1665 by Sabbatai's follower Nathan of Gaza, 'and his name shall be called Sabbatai Zevi. . . . From the age of 5 or 6 he will submit his body like an ox to the yoke, like an ass to its burden, to serve the Lord.' The prophecy goes on to speak, in the most cryptic language, of a dream that 'will appear in flame' to the 6-year-old boy, 'burning his skin in the place of his genitalia'. Some sexual trauma is evidently hinted at here; we can only guess what it might have been.[8] Afterwards, 'dreams shall terrify him, yet he shall reveal none of this to anyone; and lust-demons shall attach themselves to him to cause him to stumble. They shall smite him, but he shall not give ear to them . . . and always they shall pursue him to lead him astray.'[9]

In later years Sabbatai Zevi was impotent. His first two marriages were dissolved because he could not or would not consummate them.[10] The biographer Baruch of Arezzo tells us he never made love to his third wife, the

---

because in it was born the foul and unclean Mehemed Kapici Bashi, formerly called Sabbatai Sevi' (Scholem, *Sabbatai Sevi*, 696).

[6] Goffman, *Izmir and the Levantine World*, 93–137.

[7] Goldish, *The Sabbatean Prophets*, 4. [8] Shai, *Messiah of Incest*, 106–10, 128–43.

[9] 'The Vision of Rabbi Abraham': text in Scholem, *In the Footsteps of the Messiah* (Heb.), 59–61; Sasportas, *Sefer tsitsat novel tsevi*, 157–60; see Werblowsky's translation in Scholem, *Sabbatai Sevi*, 224–6. Werblowsky and Shai seem to understand the subject of the verbs *yera'eh . . . veya'aseh* to be *shekhinta*; grammar seems to require that it be *ḥalom*.

[10] Scholem, *Sabbatai Sevi*, 124; Falk, 'The Messiah and the Qelippoth', 19–23.

notorious Sarah, until 'after he had put the pure turban on his head'—that is, become a Muslim.[11] He liked to believe, or at any rate to tell other people, that he had mastered the ancient skill of 'having sex with any number of virgins without causing blood'.[12] This apparently provided an explanation, more satisfying to Sabbatai's ego than the obvious alternative, of why his brides tended to remain virginal. There is clearly some connection, elusive but persistent, between Sabbatai's sexual pathology and his ascetic religiosity, as well as the charismatic power that captivated an entire generation.

For all his piety and asceticism, there was something demonic about the young Sabbatai. People in Izmir remembered, after he had become notorious, how in his early twenties he used to quote with reference to himself the biblical verse Isaiah 14: 14, 'I will ascend upon the heights of the clouds, I will be like the Most High.' Once, indeed, Sabbatai spoke these words 'with so special an emphasis that he imagined, was indeed convinced, that he was lifted into the air. He therefore dared once to ask his comrades whether they had not seen him being lifted up from the earth, and when they answered truthfully that they had not, he answered them: "You are not worthy of so glorious a sight, for you are not purified as I am".'[13]

The comic absurdity of this anecdote, transmitted by the contemporary Dutch minister Thomas Coenen, must not be allowed to obscure its sinister subtext. In their context in Isaiah, Sabbatai's words are spoken by the 'Morning Star', Lucifer. This archetypal rebel against God proposes to climb to heaven, to 'set my throne above the stars of God', to make himself God's equal. So, it would seem, Sabbatai intended, at least unconsciously. He thereby perhaps forgot—as Coenen gleefully reminds us—what, according to Isaiah, was the shining rebel's ultimate end. 'Thou shalt be brought down to Hell, to the uttermost parts of the pit.'

III

It was in 1648 that he first conceived himself to be the messiah. The Dönmeh—secret believers in Sabbatai Zevi, who kept the messianic faith alive down to the twentieth century under a thin veneer of Islam—preserved the recollection that, on 21 Sivan 5408 (11 June 1648), Sabbatai was anointed messiah by the prophet Elijah; he would then have been several weeks shy of his twenty-second birthday.[14] On that day, say the Dönmeh hymns, 'he

[11] See Baruch of Arezzo, *Memorial to the Children of Israel* (translated below), §§3, 21.

[12] Transmitted by Rabbi Benjamin Kohen: Tishby, 'R. Meir Rofé's Letters' (Heb.), 89.

[13] Coenen, *Ydele verwachtinge der Joden*, 9. I am grateful to Emeritus Professor Petrus Tax of the University of North Carolina for his help in reading and translating the Dutch text. Cf. the English version in Scholem, *Sabbatai Sevi*, 127.

[14] Texts in Benayahu, *The Sabbatian Movement in Greece* (Heb.), 288–9.

redeemed our soul',[15] 'the curse was transformed into blessing', and Sabbatai Zevi 'entered into his royal estate'.[16] Other traditions, less specific as to date, confirm that in 1648 Sabbatai passed a milestone in his messianic career.[17]

Jews had long expected great doings for the year 1648. The Zohar, the classic text of kabbalah (Jewish theosophical mysticism), had promised the resurrection of the dead for Year of Creation 5408, which began in the autumn of 1647 and ended twelve months later: '"In this year of Jubilee you shall return, each one to his own allotted portion" [Lev. 25: 13]; at the completion of the year of *this*, which has the numerical value 5408, you shall return each to his own allotted portion, that is to say his soul.'[18] As it happened, this 'messianic' year turned out to be one of the most abysmally awful years in all Jewish history. In the spring the Ukrainian Cossacks rebelled against their Polish overlords. The rebels had a particular hatred for the Jews, whom they slaughtered wherever they went. In the course of 1648 and 1649, tens of thousands of Jews were raped, tortured, and murdered in Poland and the Ukraine. Sabbatai was later to have an intimate personal connection with the massacres—his third wife, Sarah, was one of the survivors. But as of 11 June 1648 he could hardly have heard of them. The news was too recent, the distances too great.[19] Sabbatai could revel in his visionary anointing by the prophet Elijah without any inkling of the atrocities being committed in eastern Europe.

Meanwhile something momentous was happening much closer to home, in the Turkish capital of Constantinople. *This* news the merchants' agent's son must have heard within days or weeks; we can only guess at the imprint it left on his newly formed messianic consciousness.[20] Sultan Ibrahim, called 'Ibrahim the Mad', had ruled the Ottoman empire since 1640. His military failures, his corruption, and his brutal abuse of power had made him drastically unpopular. Early in August 1648 the Janissaries—the empire's professional military caste—received religious authorization to depose him as a tyrant. And so the most powerful man in the world was dethroned, imprisoned, and afterwards strangled. The Janissaries set his

[15] Attias and Scholem, *Sabbatian Songs and Praises* (Heb.), 77.

[16] Ibid. 92; Scholem, *Sabbatai Sevi*, 140–2.

[17] Scholem, *Sabbatai Sevi*, 138–50; Elqayam, 'Sabbatai Zevi's Manuscript Copy of the Zohar' (Heb.), 372–87.

[18] Zohar, i. 139*b* (*Midrash hane'elam*); Silver, *A History of Messianic Speculation in Israel*, 92, 138–9; Scholem, *Sabbatai Sevi*, 88–90.

[19] According to Joel Raba, the earliest written mention of the killing of Jews by the Ukrainian rebels dates from 6 June 1648 (*Between Remembrance and Denial*, 75). The first large-scale massacre, that at Nemirov, took place on 20 Sivan 5408, the day before Sabbatai's 'anointing'.

[20] Halperin, 'Sabbatai Zevi, Metatron, and Mehmed', 295–7.

6-year-old son 'on the throne of his father, and planting the *sargouch*, or imperial feathers, on his head, saluted him for emperor with loud acclamation'.[21] On 16 August the boy was solemnly invested with robe and turban in the traditional ceremonies at the mosque of Eyub, outside the walls of Constantinople.[22]

This was the beginning of the reign of Sultan Mehmed IV—the same Mehmed before whom Sabbatai Zevi was to stand eighteen years later, to be clothed in his turn with robe and turban.

IV

Sabbatai spent most of those eighteen years in exile. Early in the 1650s he was excommunicated by the Izmir rabbinate and driven from the city. He wandered to Salonica, to Constantinople, then back to Izmir. In 1662 he went to Jerusalem, then, on a fundraising mission for the Jerusalem Jewish community, to Cairo. There he attached himself to the court of the wealthy treasury official Raphael Joseph Chelebi, who later became one of his earliest and staunchest believers.

In 1664 he married for the third time. Sarah, his bride, was a woman with a reputation. 'I myself knew her when she was a Polish refugee in Amsterdam, some fourteen years ago [1655]', wrote Jacob Sasportas, an unemployed rabbi in Hamburg and a bitter and remorseless critic of Sabbatai and all his works:

She was a witless girl who used to deliver, to the general amusement, demented speeches about how she was going to be married to king messiah. She went off to Leghorn,[23] where, as Rabbi Joseph Halevi writes me, she made a practice of going to bed with anyone and everyone. Sabbatai Zevi got wind of the nonsense she spouted, and also that she was quite good-looking . . . and so he let [Raphael Joseph] in on some of his secrets—that he was king messiah, for example, and the woman in Leghorn his destined bride—and sent for her and made her his wife.[24]

Sasportas is plainly aware of, yet unmoved to any compassion by, the most salient fact about Sarah Zevi: she was a refugee from Poland. As a child, she lost her entire family in the massacres of 1648–9. The horrors she witnessed must have unhinged her permanently.

In the spring of 1665, about a year after his marriage, Sabbatai travelled from Cairo to Gaza. He went as a pilgrim, to pay court to a holy man named

---

[21] Rycaut, *History of the Turkish Empire*, 33.

[22] Hammer-Purgstall, *Geschichte des Osmanischen Reiches*, iii. 3, 319–24; Kinross, *The Ottoman Centuries*, 316–18.

[23] Livorno, a seaport on the west coast of Italy.   [24] *Sefer tsitsat novel tsevi*, 4–5.

Abraham Nathan ben Elisha Hayim Ashkenazi. This Nathan, though hardly more than 20 years old, was famous for his kabbalistic learning. He was still more famous for his uncanny ability to detect and identify sins his visitors had committed in present and past lifetimes, and to prescribe a 'mending' (*tikun*) for each one. And so Sabbatai 'repaired to Gaza in order to find a *tiqqun* and peace for his soul'—or, as Scholem puts it, 'as a sick man to the doctor of souls, who knew the hidden roots of every soul and who could prescribe to each its appropriate *tiqqun*'.[25]

The doctor's verdict was that Sabbatai was healthier than he knew: 'when R[abbi] Abraham Nathan beheld him, he fell to the ground before him, and . . . announced to him that he was a very exalted soul'.[26] Not only that: he was the messiah. For the past seventeen years Sabbatai had been intermittently declaring himself messiah; hardly anyone paid attention. Coming from Nathan, the same proclamation sounded different. 'Thus saith the Lord', Nathan cried in prophetic voice, 'behold your savior cometh, Sabbatai Sevi is his name'[27]—and this time people listened. A fire had been lit in Gaza. The flames spread, as if fanned by the desert wind, all over the Jewish diaspora.

V

The messiah and his self-chosen prophet were together in Gaza until the end of May. Then they parted. Nathan stayed in Gaza, composing and sending forth the messianic propaganda that was soon to circulate throughout Europe and the Middle East. (Scholem calls Nathan 'at once the John the Baptist and the Paul of the new messiah'.[28]) Sabbatai, meanwhile, began his travels.

His first stop was Jerusalem, then Safed in Galilee, then Aleppo. Jewish crowds, wild with excitement, clustered around him. Many went into a trance and 'prophesied'.[29] The prophetic 'message was always the same', says Baruch of Arezzo: '*Sabbatai Zevi is the messiah of the God of Jacob.*'[30] By September 1665 he had returned to his home town of Izmir.[31]

For nearly three months nothing happened. Sabbatai's psychic life was characterized by extreme mood swings, which we would now probably

---

[25] Scholem, *Sabbatai Sevi*, 214–15. The first quotation is from a letter written in the second half of 1665, quoted by Scholem and translated by Werblowsky.

[26] Ibid., quoting the same letter. [27] Ibid. 206. [28] Ibid. 207.

[29] Goldish, *The Sabbatean Prophets*, 89–129. [30] *Memorial*, §8.

[31] Baruch of Arezzo (*Memorial*, §6) claims that Sabbatai arrived in Izmir in the month of Kislev 5426, which began on 9 November 1665. But this is presumably an error, based on the fact that Sabbatai did nothing significant in Izmir until near the end of Kislev. For the earlier date, see Scholem, *Sabbatai Sevi*, 259.

consider symptoms of bipolar disorder (manic depressive illness).[32] When he was not in the grip either of his manic 'illuminations' or his hellish bouts of desolate depression, he tended to be quiet and passive in his behaviour. Then, early in December, the period of calm came to an end. On sabbath morning, 12 December 1665, Sabbatai and his mob of enthusiasts appeared before the doors of the Portuguese synagogue in Izmir, which had been locked against them. He demanded an axe; with his own hands he smashed his way into the synagogue. Once inside, he proceeded to harangue and ter- rorize the worshippers. He forced them to pronounce the sacred, always unspoken, four-letter Name of God. To his followers he distributed the kingdoms of the earth. His brother Elijah became sultan of Turkey that morning, his brother Joseph emperor of Rome.[33]

Sabbatai's demonic, 'Luciferan' side, which had long manifested itself in what contemporaries called his 'strange acts'—stunts like publicly marrying himself to a Torah scroll, or minor violations of the standard proprieties of Judaism—blossomed that morning into a display of exultant, violent, brutal despotism. People knew about the 'strange acts'; one could hardly hear about Sabbatai without knowing of them. In spite of the 'strange acts', or perhaps because of them, the people believed.

Hayim Benveniste, distinguished rabbi of Izmir, did not believe. But he didn't need a weatherman to know which way the wind was blowing. He made his obeisance—'Brethren, he is the true messiah; he and no other!'[34] Sabbatai in turn confirmed Benveniste, over his rival Aaron Lapapa, as chief rabbi of the city. Over positions like this, as opposed to the throne of Turkey or the emperorship of Rome, Sabbatai had begun to have some real influ- ence. All, or nearly all, the Jews of Izmir solemnly acknowledged Benveniste as their chief rabbi and Sabbatai Zevi as their king messiah. In the streets, men, women, and children alike took to falling to the ground, possessed by the spirit of prophecy, shouting out biblical and liturgical slogans in praise of God and His messiah. ('Hear, O Israel, the Lord is our God, the Lord is One! Blessed be the name of His glorious kingdom for ever and ever! Our king Sabbatai Zevi is already crowned! A mighty ban has been pronounced in heaven against those who do not believe!' etc., etc., etc.[35]) The cowed

---

[32] The diagnosis of 'manic-depressive psychosis' is made convincingly in Scholem, *Sab- batai Sevi*, 125–38, expanded from a psychoanalytical perspective in Falk, 'The Messiah and the Qelippoth', 5–29.

[33] Baruch of Arezzo, *Memorial*, §7; Scholem, *Sabbatai Sevi*, 396–405.

[34] Scholem, *Sabbatai Sevi*, 405. I follow Jacob Barnai's interpretation of Benveniste's motives in *Sabbatianism—Social Perspectives* (Heb.), 93–6. The responsum from Izmir, quoted in full and analysed in ch. 7 of Barnai's book, suggests some extremely unsavoury political manoeuvring behind Lapapa's removal and Benveniste's appointment (p. 158: *vehayah be'atsat ahitofel ... vehashamayim edi vesahadi ki ein yadi bama'al*).

[35] Baruch of Arezzo, *Memorial*, §8.

sceptic Hayim Peña came home, a few days after Sabbatai's invasion of the synagogue, to find his two teenage daughters among the prophets. With the eyes of the spirit the girls saw Sabbatai 'sitting on his throne in heaven with the crown of kingship on his head, and many other things. And when they finished speaking they called several times in sequence, "Crown! Crown!"'[36]

'Crown, crown' indeed. It was time for Sabbatai to take his royal crown, on earth as he had in heaven. On 30 December he set sail from Izmir for Constantinople, intending to remove the crown—the turban, that is—from the sultan Mehmed's head and put it on his own, and from the sultan's hands to receive the kingdom.[37] He arrived in the capital at the beginning of February 1666.

VI

Immediately he was thrown into gaol.

At first, wrote Paul Rycaut, the English consul in Izmir, the Turkish authorities imprisoned Sabbatai in Constantinople, in 'the most loathsom and darkest Dungeon in the Town'.[38] Later he was transferred to far more comfortable lodgings in the fortress of Gallipoli. There he was given considerable freedom. Surrounded by his followers and flatterers, he began to comport himself as though he were king already. From his cushioned prison he sent forth messianic edicts to the whole Jewish world. These included the decree, widely obeyed that summer of 1666, that the Ninth of Av should now be observed as a holiday, the 'Feast of Consolations, the nativity of our king and messiah Sabbatai Zevi . . . [God's] first-born son'.[39] He received delegations from communities as far away as Poland.

The Turkish gaolers pocketed their bribes from the visitors and did not try to interfere. Why should they? They had found, in Scholem's words, the goose that laid the golden eggs.[40] The foolish Jews were mad to have an audience with their messiah, and would pay for the privilege. Sabbatai's believers, in their turn, advertised the Turks' extraordinary complaisance as something miraculous. The fear of God must have fallen upon the Turkish officials; the sultan must have known that a greater king than he had arrived. It was only a matter of time before he would yield his power, and the messianic prophecies of Nathan of Gaza would begin to be fulfilled.

The elegant dance went on all summer long. In September the music abruptly stopped. Mehmed IV summoned Sabbatai to the old Ottoman

---

[36] Goldish, *The Sabbatean Prophets*, 118–24.

[37] Halperin, 'Sabbatai Zevi, Metatron, and Mehmed', 275–6. The equation of 'turban' (*mitsnefet*) with 'crown' (*atarah*) is made in Sasportas, *Sefer tsitsat novel tsevi*, 13, on the basis of Ezek. 21: 31.   [38] Rycaut, *History of the Turkish Empire*, 208.

[39] Baruch of Arezzo, *Memorial*, §15.   [40] Scholem, *Sabbatai Sevi*, 603.

capital of Adrianople (modern Edirne), where the sultan was currently holding court. Sabbatai arrived on the evening of 15 September. The next day he was brought into the sultan's presence.

Their encounter has already been described. Most sources claim that Sabbatai was given the choice between conversion to Islam or death, and chose conversion. This seems reasonable enough. But did he act out of fear, or out of some wild notion that he was in fact being offered the sultan's power, along with the turban and the name Mehmed—that the enthronement of Mehmed IV, eighteen years earlier, was now being replayed with himself as the hero?[41] Or perhaps both? In Baruch of Arezzo's account of Sabbatai's appearance before the sultan, translated in this volume, Sabbatai's apostasy is dismissed as a 'rumour', although it is acknowledged in the sequel. Baruch instead gives a scene of the transfer of royal insignia. An additional motif, dark and sinister, crops up persistently in some accounts of the meeting—that a mass pogrom against the Jews of Turkey was in preparation. The pogrom was either egged on by Sabbatai or prevented by him, depending on who is telling the story.[42]

Whatever the truth may have been, Sabbatai left the sultan's presence a different person from when he came in. Sabbatai knew this as well as anyone else. 'Now leave me be', he wrote to his brother Elijah eight days afterwards, 'for the Creator has made me into a Muslim . . . created me anew, according to His will.' He signed the letter as 'your brother, Mehmed *kapici bashi oturak*'[43] (these last words, according to Scholem, refer to the sinecure granted Sabbatai as honorary gate-keeper for the sultan[44]). A year or two later he wrote to his brothers, in a mixture of Judaeo-Spanish and Hebrew, and signed himself: 'Thus speaks the possessor of the Truth and the Faith, the *Turco*, the *Mezurman* ['Mussulman']'.[45]

VII

As Sabbatai the Jew he was a hapless member of a disempowered religious minority, which the Lord of the Universe had nevertheless chosen as His own. As Mehmed the Turk, the Mussulman, he could imagine himself a sharer in the power of the world's greatest empire. The last ten years of Sabbatai's life can be understood as a prolonged effort—reasonably successful,

[41] This is the argument in Halperin, 'Sabbatai Zevi, Metatron, and Mehmed'.

[42] See the versions of Baruch of Arezzo (*Memorial*, §16) and Joseph Halevi (first letter), translated below.

[43] See Halperin, 'Sabbatai Zevi, Metatron, and Mehmed', 274, and the sources cited there.

[44] Scholem, *Sabbatai Sevi*, 686.

[45] Text in Amarilio, 'Sabbatian Documents' (Heb.), 266–8; discussion in Liebes, 'Sabbatai Zevi's Attitude to his Conversion' (Heb.). I follow Liebes's interpretation of *Mezurman*.

given that the task was impossible—to be both, to prove to himself and the world that the two identities of Jew and Muslim can be fused in a single human being. Perhaps, at least at times, he wanted to bring the rest of his people with him into this double identity. He may have imagined this to be the Jews' true and authentic redemption. 'To the extent you can', warned Nathan of Gaza,[46] 'stay away from Amirah when he is in a state of illumination'—that is, one of his manic phases—'for when he is in a state of illumination he wants to convert everyone around him to Islam'.[47]

A vivid memoir of Sabbatai's doings in Adrianople for a few months in 1671, usually referred to as the Najara Chronicle and translated in full in this volume, will convey the paradox of Sabbatai's new life more powerfully than any paraphrase or analysis can do. Sabbatai is officially a Muslim, an honorary official of the Turkish court. For all practical purposes he talks, thinks, and behaves like the eccentric Jewish rabbi he always was. The Turks watch and do nothing, raising not the slightest objection, which strikes the author, Jacob Najara, as a divine miracle. Najara surely knows it is a capital crime in Muslim lands for a convert to relapse into his former religion; he surely knows what hideous penalties the Spanish Inquisition inflicts upon Catholic 'Judaizers' whose behaviour is not one-hundredth as obvious or egregious as Sabbatai's. Why, then, do the Turks see it and not intervene?

Why indeed? We can only guess. There are practically no contemporary Turkish sources on Sabbatai Zevi or the movement he founded; Turkish writers presumably did not think these matters important enough to waste ink upon. (The contrast with the profuse interest shown by contemporary European Christian writers, to whom the Sabbatian movement was fodder for their own millenarian fantasies, is very striking.) The best guess is that the sultan and his officials thought Sabbatai and his interfaith antics entirely harmless, and too amusing for anyone to want to stop them. The show could not go on for ever. It was halted at the beginning of 1673, when Sabbatai, whose offences against Muslim sensibilities had at last gone too far, was banished to the faraway coast of the Adriatic.[48] But while it lasted it was grand fun.

Every now and then Sabbatai tried to translate his nominal position in the sultan's court into something resembling real power. Writing in December 1671, Nathan of Gaza reports that Sabbatai felt himself treated

---

[46] Who was no longer in Gaza. Immediately after Sabbatai's conversion, Nathan set off on his own wanderings, bringing the gospel of the apostate messiah to the Jewish communities of Turkey, Italy, and Greece.

[47] From Israel Hazzan's commentary on the psalms of the midnight vigil liturgy, quoted in Scholem, 'The Commentary on Psalms from the Circle of Sabbatai Zevi in Adrianople' (Heb.), 94.   [48] Scholem, *Sabbatai Sevi*, 873–83.

disrespectfully by the rabbis of Constantinople. So off he went to the sultan, with the request 'that the Jews be handed over into his [Sabbatai's] power, that he might put them to the torture'. The sultan seems entirely to have ignored this revolting petition; Nathan, whose faith in his messiah remained absolute up to his dying day, is understandably shaken by it. A redeemer ought not to relish torturing the people he is supposed to be redeeming. Well, Nathan muses, 'let the Lord do what is good in His eyes, for we cannot fathom the secrets of the Merciful One. And we trust in the Lord that He shall open a great gate from the resources on high, to comfort us and bring us into the light.'[49]

Meanwhile, outside the sultan's court, the Jewish people had for the most part woken from their messianic dream. The awakening did not always come quickly. The German Jewish memoirist Glückel of Hameln reports that her father-in-law in Hildesheim had packed his trunks in 1666, in anticipation of a speedy journey to meet the messiah in the Holy Land. It took three years before he could reconcile himself to unpacking.[50] And a solid minority among the Jews, encouraged by Nathan and other propagandists, went on believing in Sabbatai Zevi.

They were not at the same pitch of eschatological ecstasy as in the summer of 1666. Such a state of mind cannot go on indefinitely. When the loyal Sabbatian and community fundraiser Meir Rofé writes (from Leghorn, later Hebron) to his friend and patron Abraham Rovigo (in Modena), he naturally passes on the latest information and gossip about 'the beloved', as he calls Sabbatai Zevi. But more mundane matters also occupy him. He requires a substitute to raise money in Italy on behalf of the Hebron community; he worries that the candidate Rovigo proposes is too mild-mannered, and does not have the hard-sell qualities a fundraiser needs 'to squeeze water out of stone'; he has already written to Samuel Aboab, chief rabbi in Venice, to see if he can find him anyone more suitable.[51] He nags Rovigo to please kindly send him tobacco—'not the English kind, but the sort from Foggia would be best, and if not then whatever you happen to have, for the tobacco here is expensive and bad and I can't live without it'.[52] Rofé's 'beloved' messiah was still alive; any day now he might cast off his gentile disfigurement, confute the unbelievers, and enact the redemption of Israel. In the meantime life went on.

---

[49] Amarilio, 'Sabbatian Documents' (Heb.), 264.
[50] *The Memoirs of Glückel of Hameln*, trans. Lowenthal, 46–7; pointed out in Carlebach, 'Two Amens that Delayed the Redemption', 244–5.
[51] Tishby, 'R. Meir Rofé's Letters' (Heb.), 97, 102–3.   [52] Ibid. 107.

VIII

And then, of course, the messiah died.

Born on the fast of the Ninth of Av, he died on the greater fast of the Day of Atonement (Yom Kippur), 17 September 1676—ten years almost to the day after he became Turk and Mussulman. He died far away from Izmir, from Jerusalem, from Adrianople, from any place he might have called home. The sultan had exiled him at the beginning of 1673 to Dulcigno (Ulcinj) on the Adriatic coast. There his wife Sarah had died in 1674, after which Sabbatai had married again, a much younger woman, Esther, the daughter of a Salonican rabbi named Joseph Filosoff. The widow returned to Salonica after Sabbatai's death, accompanied by his brother Elijah and his children by Sarah. Glowing legends, one of them repeated by Baruch of Arezzo (below), quickly surrounded the subject of his burial. Where he was really buried remains a mystery.[53]

His death was one more blow to the weary, disheartened, dwindling band of the faithful. They managed somehow to absorb it, as faithful folk will. Sabbatai was not really dead; rather, he had gone beyond the mythical river Sambatyon, there to dwell with the Lost Ten Tribes of Israel.[54] He would return, just as Moses did in ancient times, to redeem his people.

New messiahs, meanwhile, sprang up in Sabbatai's wake. The world had acknowledged Sabbatai to be messiah ben David, the messiah descended from David's royal house. But Jewish tradition made room also for a partner-messiah, 'messiah ben Joseph', who was normally expected to be messiah ben David's forerunner. What had become of *him*?[55] It was inevitable, after Sabbatai's apostasy, and still more after his death, that would-be messiah ben Josephs would appear. One of them was the brilliant, quirky, often outrageous Abraham Cardozo, a Spanish ex-Catholic returned to his ancestral Judaism, for whom Sabbatai had always been something of a disappointment.[56] The slightly pathetic Moroccan Joseph ibn Tsur was another.[57]

But the most successful of these new messiahs was Jacob Filosoff, later called Jacob Querido. He was the son of Joseph Filosoff, the young brother and perhaps also the lover of Sabbatai's widow Esther. With his father and his sister—who seems to have been the brains behind the movement—Querido gathered around himself hundreds of believers in his home town of

---

[53] There is evidence that, in the late 19th century, some of the Dönmeh made pilgrimages to what they thought was Sabbatai's grave in Ulcinj; Scholem, 'Where Did Sabbatai Zevi Die?' (Heb.; with an extremely useful addendum by Yehuda Liebes). Cf. Freely, *The Lost Messiah*, 243–57.   [54] Baruch of Arezzo, *Memorial*, §26.

[55] Elqayam, 'The Absent Messiah' (Heb.).

[56] Halperin, *Abraham Miguel Cardozo: Selected Writings*.

[57] Baruch of Arezzo, *Memorial*, §§27–8.

Salonica. Then, in imitation of his fellow-messiah, he converted to Islam in 1683. His followers converted with him en masse. Thus was born the Dönmeh, the bizarre Judaeo-Turkish sect that for more than three centuries continued to practise a secret Sabbatian Judaism beneath a veneer of Islam.[58]

Shabbtai Tzvee, Shabbtai Tzvee, no hay otro como ti. Shabbtai Tzvee, Shabbtai Tzvee, esperamos a ti ('Sabbatai Zevi, Sabbatai Zevi, there is no other like you . . . we wait for you').[59] So these mosque-attending, Ramadan-fasting Turkish Muslims continued secretly to pray for generations, in their seventeenth-century Judaeo-Spanish. The tradition has not quite died out. 'Every morning', wrote a reporter in 1999, 'one of the elders of the [Dönmeh] community, a 92-year-old *agon* [rabbi], ventures to the shores of the Bosporus, shortly before dawn, and recites . . . "*Sabetai, Sabetai, esperamos a ti.*"'[60]

In the absence of any identifiable tomb, Sabbatai's traditional birthplace in Izmir functioned as a shrine and place of pilgrimage. My friend Professor Marc Bregman visited it in 1971 and found it to be a third-floor room off a courtyard, in a building occupied by families of Gypsies. A former stable, part of the same building, had been used as a shrine. Many candles had been burned there; Professor Bregman remembers seeing a cascading sheet of coloured candle wax. The Gypsies told him, through an interpreter, that people would come to light candles and say prayers in some unfamiliar language. They told him of a young woman from New York who had given them a substantial sum of money to let her go into the third-floor room and stay there alone. She spent a long time there, crying loudly from behind the closed door. No one had the slightest idea who she might have been.[61]

IX

He is not an easy person to like, this flawed and fallen messiah. At times it is difficult not to detest him. Leave aside his Wild West antics in the Izmir

---

[58] Scholem, 'The Crypto-Jewish Sect of the Dönmeh'; Ross, *Acts of Faith*, 83–98; Nassi, 'Shabbetai Tzvi Lives'; Baer, 'Revealing a Hidden Community'; Temkin, 'Shabbtai Tzvi Would Be Proud'; Freely, *The Lost Messiah*, 231–42, 256–7; Baer, 'The Double Bind of Race and Religion'.   [59] Scholem, 'The Dönmeh Prayerbook of the Izmir Sect' (Heb.), 399.
[60] Temkin, 'Shabbtai Tzvi Would Be Proud', 36.
[61] Cf. Freely's description of Sabbatai's birthplace in Izmir, as it appeared in 1962 (*The Lost Messiah*, 7–9), and the description in Postal and Abramson, *The Landmarks of a People*, 236 (the description is repeated unchanged in the 1971 edition). I am immensely grateful to Professor Bregman for sharing his experience with me, and for referring me to Postal and Abramson's book.
[62] Specifically, the brutal beating of a sceptic by Sabbatai's enthusiasts in Venice: see Baruch of Arezzo, *Memorial*, §13.

synagogue, his enthusiastic endorsement of religious terrorism,[62] his hideous demand that the Constantinople Jews be handed over to him for torture. The account given by Jacob Najara of Sabbatai's circumcision of his 3-year-old son Ishmael is surely one of the most unwittingly horrific narratives in all literature.[63]

Imagine the scene from the perspective of its small victim. He is taken by force from his mother, hustled into an assembly of his father and a few dozen fellow-enthusiasts. There, without any anaesthetic or even comforting human presence, his penis is slashed, while a string of hymns and prophecies, unintelligible to the child, are chanted over him. His body has been turned into a prop in one of his father's dramatic extravaganzas.[64] Thus did Sabbatai Zevi habitually deal with the world: as a stage on which his private fantasies might turn into public performances. That is what happened for a few wild months in 1665–6, with all the Jewish people as actors.

But unlike Ishmael Zevi, dragged willy-nilly to his mutilation, the Sabbatian believers colluded enthusiastically in their abuse. The question for the historian is: why? Who was Sabbatai Zevi, what made him so extraordinary, that normally sober men and women should have streamed to become performers in his failed messianic drama?

It is not easy to say just who the man was, because his essence keeps changing. He takes on identities, from 'God's only begotten son' to Isaiah's 'Morning Star' to '*Turco*' and 'Mussulman', with all the zest and insouciance of a child playing make-believe. The people around him, and all who trust and believe in him, are left to pay the price. Perhaps in this very fluidity, this identity-shifting, lies the secret of his appeal. The seventeenth century was a time when the old self-identifications of the Jewish people were growing worn and cracked. How, for example, would a prosperous and well-acculturated physician or merchant in Rembrandt's Amsterdam fit into the identity of a persecuted and harassed exile, son or daughter of a nation without a land, under the perennial wrath of an offended God? Perhaps the man who could lead, through his example of taking on and discarding identities, to a broader, freer understanding of what it was to be Jewish might be presumed to be the redeemer of Israel?[65]

A century or two later, the descendants of Sabbatai's contemporaries would struggle with the problem of how they could be French and Jewish, German and Jewish, or American and Jewish, at the same time. But in Sab-

---

[63] See the Najara Chronicle below, at n. 52.

[64] The circumcision of Ishmael gives the impression of being a re-infliction, upon a helpless victim, of Sabbatai's own childhood sexual trauma (Shai, *Messiah of Incest*, 140, perhaps hints at this). On the short life and tragic fate of this unfortunate boy, see Halperin, 'The Son of the Messiah'.   [65] Halperin, 'Sabbatai Zevi, Metatron, and Mehmed'.

batai's time the redefinition of what a 'nation' was and what a 'citizen' needed to be, which made these questions possible, still lay in the future. If the Amsterdam merchant or physician wanted to become a full sharer in the rich civic life around him, he had to find a way to become Jewish and not-Jewish at the same time. Of course this was impossible; and impossible dilemmas demand mythic solutions. Even before the apostasy, Sabbatai's 'strange acts' hinted he might be the one to show the way.

Could this be why the Amsterdam community—the richest, freest, most comfortably situated Jewish community of the past 1,500 years—went wild for a man who promised to redeem them? Redeem them from what? Perhaps from the tension of self-definition created by these very advantages?

The Polish Jewish communities, still raw and bleeding from the Cossack massacres and the years of warfare that followed, did not have quite the same problems, which means that the 'identity' issue, if it is an answer, cannot be the only one. There probably is no single key to unlock the complex mystery of how a diverse, far-flung religious civilization could have agreed for a few fantastic months to pin its dearest ancient hope on a man so weak, so confused, so peevishly brutal as Sabbatai Zevi. This goes for the most obvious-seeming answer to the problem—that when people are in a state of deprivation and anguish they will listen to anyone who promises them relief. Jewish Amsterdam in the 1660s was neither deprived nor anguished; the 1660s on the whole were not a particularly bad time for the Jewish people; if it was the Polish and Ukrainian slaughters of 1648–9 that were determinative, as many scholars have thought, why was the messianic reaction to them so long in coming? It was not for lack of a messianic candidate. Sabbatai Zevi had been offering himself in this role ever since 1648, the year the massacres began. But for the next seventeen years hardly anybody paid attention. What made 1665 so different?

One difference, of course, was Nathan of Gaza. Perhaps it was neither Sabbatai by himself nor Nathan by himself, but something about the synergy of the pair, that managed to conquer the Jewish world with such speed and ease. Which brings us to Gershom Scholem's proposed solution to the riddle.

Scholem argued that the ground had been prepared for Sabbatianism by the prior spread of kabbalistic mysticism, particularly in its 'Lurianic' version.[66] By the mid-seventeenth century Lurianic kabbalah had become the normative theology of Judaism. Nathan's genius took this kabbalah to its

---

[66] Named after Rabbi Isaac Luria of Safed (1534–72), shaper of a new and innovative form of kabbalah that was rooted in the medieval kabbalistic texts but went substantially beyond them.

next logical step, which was to make the anarchic, quasi-demonic personality of Sabbatai Zevi—with its implicit rebellion against Judaism's religious proprieties, even the sacred law itself—the exact profile for the messiah.

Before the Creation, Isaac Luria taught, there had taken place a cosmic catastrophe called 'the shattering of the vessels'. Sparks of divinity had gone tumbling helplessly into the demonic abyss. There the Divinity must descend, to rescue its fallen fragments from the powers of darkness. Equate this 'abyss' with the impure realms of the gentiles, as the kabbalists tended to do, and there was a perfect ideological justification for the messiah's becoming a Muslim. It was not an act of betrayal, as the unenlightened might view it. It was a bold self-sacrifice, an imitation of God's own self-abasement. Sabbatai Zevi had plunged into the faecal sewer of gentiledom for the sake of ingathering the pure and holy sparks—a necessary prelude to redemption.

Unfortunately for Scholem's theory, there is strong evidence that Lurianic kabbalah was not the normative theology of seventeenth-century Judaism after all. At the time of Sabbatai's appearance it seems to have been an esoteric doctrine, studied by few and understood by fewer. It is possible even to argue that kabbalah became popular through the spread of Sabbatianism, not the other way round.[67] Yet Scholem's reconstruction has an intuitive, almost poetic, power that will not go away. Perhaps we can retain it in some form, as long as we do not insist on it as *the* answer. Perhaps we can also retain the suggestion of some early scholars, that Sabbatianism represented a revolt of the unlettered Jewish masses against the elite. Scholem tried to refute this view, on the grounds that the enthusiasm for Sabbatai Zevi cut across all social boundaries. The rich believed in him, as far as we can tell from the sources, no less than the poor. Yet does it follow that they believed for the same reasons as the poor? Perhaps the kabbalistic-ideology and social-conflict models will work for some of Sabbatai's believers and not for others, just as the 'desperation' theory will work for Poland and not for Amsterdam.

Another factor may be involved. Perhaps Jews everywhere—rich and poor, acculturated Amsterdam Jews and persecuted Polish Jews—were growing restive with the system of religious legalism that for centuries had defined them as a group. This antique legalism had directed, but also confined, their ethical and spiritual strivings. The age of Sabbatai Zevi was also the age of Spinoza's *Theologico-Political Treatise* (published in 1670), which bitterly inveighed against traditional Judaism's insistence that right and wrong are determined by divine command and not the inner compass of the

---

[67] Idel, "'One from a Town and Two from a Family'" (Heb.); Gries, *The Book as an Agent of Culture* (Heb.), 73–94.
[68] Spinoza, *Theologico-Political Treatise*, end of ch. 5 (trans. Shirley, p. 70).

rational soul.[68] Of course Spinoza was a heretic, of course he was an excommunicate. In the eyes of many he was an apostate and betrayer of his people. Yet some fifty years earlier the outwardly orthodox rabbi of Venice, Leone Modena (1571–1648), had composed under a thin veil of pseudonymity a savage attack on the rabbinic religious law.[69] More than one Jewish thinker seems to have felt Spinoza's discontent with the traditional religion, which might manifest itself in different ways.

'The law of Moses is a law of children', ran a freethinkers' slogan of early modern times, attributed (no doubt apocryphally) to the twelfth-century Arab philosopher Averroës.[70] Remarkably, Modena echoes this sentiment at the end of the preface to a book he wrote in 1614 or 1615, describing the rites and customs of contemporary Judaism.[71] He even finds it to be in conformity with the Bible:[72] 'However, very observable is the saying of That Great Person, though not by many rightly understood, (which yet is agreeable to that of the Prophet *Hosea, cap.* 11) *Lex Judaeorum, Lex Puerorum*: that is, *The Law of the Jews, is a Law of Children.*'[73] Can we imagine that, fifty years after Modena wrote these words, substantial numbers of Jews were aching to set aside this 'children's law', to become grown men and women in a dawning age of light—without, however, ceasing to be Jewish? That their enthusiasm for Sabbatai Zevi, with his 'strange' and persistent acts of defiance against Jewish law, expressed for them this inchoate, hardly articulate demand?

Certainly this was the direction taken in the eighteenth century by the Dönmeh, the secret Sabbatians of the Turkish empire. The most striking theme of their speculative, exegetical literature is the split they make between the 'Torah', the divine essence of Judaism, and the 'commandments', the negative and indeed demonic shell in which this essence has

[69] Fishman, *Shaking the Pillars of Exile.*

[70] *Lex Moysi, lex Puerorum; lex Christi, lex Impossibilium; lex Mahumeti, lex Porcorum* ('the law of Moses is a law of children, the law of Christ is a law of impossibilities, the law of Muhammad is a law of pigs'). Renan, *Averroès et l'Averroïsme*, 292–300; Retat, *Traité des Trois Imposteurs*, p. 9 of preface, p. 105 of text; Berti, Charles-Daubert, and Popkin, *Heterodoxy, Spinozism, and Free Thought*, 485.

[71] The book, though intended for King James I of England, was first published (in Italian, at Paris) in 1637, when James was already dead. It appeared in English translation in 1650.

[72] Hos. 11: 1: 'When Israel was a child, then I loved him.'

[73] Modena, *The History of the Rites, Customes, and Manner of Life of the Present Jews Throughout the World.* Cf. Rivkin, *Leon da Modena and the* Kol sakhal, 100.

[74] Telenberg, 'The Sabbatian Theology in Judah Levi Tovah's *Commentary on Genesis* (Heb.); Telenberg, Avayou, and Elqayam, 'A Translation of *Mirat bereshit tovah* from Ladino to Hebrew' (Heb.); see ibid. 338: 'The "shell" [*kelipah*, a standard kabbalistic term for the demonic forces] shall pass from the earth, as it is written, "I will remove the spirit of impurity from the earth" [Zech. 13: 2]. The "spirit" is Samael and "impurity" is Lilith, and the numerical value of their two names is equivalent to the 613 [commandments], which shall pass from

been encased.[74] 'The commandments have been abolished [*hamitsvot betelot*]', runs the Dönmeh credo. 'But the Torah shall remain for ever and for all eternity.'[75]

This dichotomy of 'Torah' versus 'commandments', so alien to anything in Judaism before the seventeenth century, could not possibly be made rationally and consistently. It was conceivable only in the realm of myth, and the fantastic forms of biblical interpretation in which the Sabbatians specialized. The time was not ripe for Reform Judaism, or for any of the secular or semi-secular Judaisms with which we are now familiar—including the secularized messianism called Zionism. The Torah and the commandments, the kernel and the shell, were inseparably fused. 'Inseparably'—unless one is the messiah, unless one is privy to the divine mystery of how the shell came to be, how it must be pried away. With his 'strange acts', the madcap messiah of Izmir conveyed the promise that he knew the secret, that he could be the people's guide.

The promise was a lie. A more inept guide than Sabbatai Zevi could hardly be conceived. He knew no secrets of any value—certainly not the most crucial secret, that of the private pathology that drove him to his 'strange acts' and to everything else he did. He led his believers into confusion, disillusionment, and sometimes despair.[76] The most gifted and independent-minded among them, Abraham Cardozo, could only look at Sabbatai in appalled wonder. Surely the man must be the messiah, Cardozo argued. For if he were not, he would be too great a sinner for the world to endure.[77]

If some global explanation must be found for why people were prepared

the earth.' The numerical equation, proposed here by the 18th-century Dönmeh theologian Judah Levi Tova, requires some juggling. But Tova's point is clear: the multiplex commandments of traditional Judaism are to be equated with the archdemons Samael and Lilith, the 'spirit of impurity' that is to be removed from the earth.

[75] Scholem, 'The Dönmeh Prayerbook of the Izmir Sect' (Heb.), 385; cf. the translation in id., 'The Crypto-Jewish Sect of the Dönmeh', 157.

[76] Carlebach, *Divided Souls*, 67–87.   [77] Halperin, *Abraham Miguel Cardozo*, 156.

to believe in Sabbatai Zevi, this one is as good as any.

FIRST TESTIMONY
Memorial to the Children of Israel

BARUCH OF AREZZO

ᛤ

INTRODUCTION

ABOUT THE AUTHOR of this earliest surviving biography of Sabbatai Zevi, *Zikaron livnei yisra'el* ('Memorial to the Children of Israel'), we know only what we can gather from his book. It is not much.

From the signature at the end of his preface we know his name was Baruch son of Gershon, and that he or his ancestors were from the town of Arezzo in Tuscany. He was related to the prominent Modena family of the Formigginis;[1] he proudly claims as his uncle 'the distinguished and accomplished gentleman Rabbi Samuel Formiggini', who helped Nathan of Gaza escape from a tight spot at Il Finale di Modena.[2] If we had any inclination to question Baruch's Italian origins, his habit of sprinkling his Hebrew with Italian words would settle our doubts.[3] So would the Italian provenance of the surviving manuscripts of his *Memorial*.[4] About what we would really like to know—how old he was when he wrote his book, what his life experience had been, what personal encounters he had with the Sabbatian movement and its leaders—he gives no clue at all.

His narrative covers the entire life of his messiah, from Sabbatai's birth on the Ninth of Av 1626 to his eventual 'concealment', which Baruch represents—not without some precedent—as a death followed by a resurrection.[5] Nathan's 'departure' is also mentioned, though in a very vague and ambiguous manner. The apostasy, whose character as apostasy is deliberately blurred, stands at about the midpoint (§16). The biography proper is preceded by a preface, in which Baruch sets out the aim and method of his book, as well as its intended audience. After this comes an opening section, which might (and perhaps once did) itself serve as preface, quoting rabbinic proof-

---

[1] '[T]he Formiggini family, who had their private synagogue at Modena, were court jewellers to the Este dukes, generation after generation, for two centuries' (Roth, *History of the Jews of Italy*, 376). The best-known scion of the family, the editor and publisher Angelo Fortunato Formiggini, committed suicide in 1938 by '[throwing] himself down from the cathedral tower of his native Modena', in despair at Mussolini's race laws (ibid. 530; *Encyclopedia Judaica*, s.v.).   [2] §19 below.   [3] See below, nn. 97, 198, 234.   [4] See Appendix 1 for details.
[5] See §26 below. I have divided the *Memorial* into sections, and provided titles for the sections, for the reader's convenience and my own. These divisions are not in the text itself.

texts to the effect that the messiah, like Moses before him, must go through a period of 'concealment' after his initial appearance.

As a sort of appendix to his book, after telling of the 'departures' of Sabbatai and Nathan, Baruch provides an account of the would-be messiah Joseph ibn Tsur, whose activities in Morocco date from a few years before Sabbatai's death (§§27–8). In the manuscripts, this appendix is set off from what precedes it by various graphic devices. There follows a series of concluding reflections and exhortations, more sombre and uncertain than their counterparts at the beginning of the book. It is hard to avoid the impression that Baruch's confidence in his messianic faith had waned between the beginning of his project and its completion. We will presently use this as a clue to the dating of the *Memorial*.

The book is written in clear and simple Hebrew, in a lively and appealing style. Especially in its early sections, it has a strong folkloric quality. In §10 Baruch begins to supplement his narrative with full verbatim quotations of contemporary documents, and he keeps up this practice to the end of the book. Many of these documents are also found in Jacob Sasportas's compilation *Sefer tsitsat novel tsevi* ('Zevi's Fading Flower'),[6] but there are others that survive only in Baruch's *Memorial*, whose preservation we owe to him.

The title, *Memorial to the Children of Israel*, has a curious background. It is taken from the Bible, as was typical of Jewish writings of the period.[7] Baruch tells us in the preface that it had already been used in 1668, by 'the luminaries of the Venetian rabbinate', as the title for their account of 'Nathan of Gaza and the things he said concerning Sabbatai Zevi . . . [which] they printed and disseminated throughout the Jewish diaspora'. He leaves the impression that this earlier 'Memorial to the Children of Israel' was a document very much like his own—a laudatory account of Sabbatai and Nathan, marred only by its excessive conciseness, a flaw which Baruch will now amend by reissuing the Venetian rabbis' work in expanded form, under the same title. This impression is, to put it mildly, misleading.

The original 'Memorial' was indeed, as Baruch says, printed and distributed by the rabbis of Venice in the spring of 1668. Written in the high-flown, often impenetrable Hebrew style called *melitsah*, it obliquely describes the rabbis' cross-examination of Nathan during his stay in Venice in April of that year. They concluded from their examination that he was addled rather than malignant and therefore ought not to be punished too severely; they contented themselves with extracting from him a confession that none of his so-called visions or prophecies about Sabbatai Zevi had any

[6] Published in a critical edition by Isaiah Tishby (Jerusalem: Bialik Institute, 1954).

[7] The phrase *zikaron livnei yisra'el* occurs in several biblical passages, of which Num. 17: 5 and Josh. 4: 7 are the most pertinent.

substance.[8] These, in brief, were the contents of the original 'Memorial to the Children of Israel'. Baruch's reuse of the title is clearly an effort to co-opt the authority of the Venetian rabbis in order to bolster the shaky credibility of his own *Memorial*. He may have gotten away with it, if only because the *melitsah* style of the original is so opaque that its readers cannot have had an easy time making out what it was trying to say.

Aharon Freimann, who published Baruch's *Memorial* for the first time in 1912, accuses the author of hypocrisy and deliberate deception in his choice of title.[9] In truth, it is not easy to think of any more benign explanation of Baruch's motive. Yet on the whole he gives the impression of being an honest, albeit naive and credulous, writer, trying to make sense for himself and his readers of the recent events that were 'the Lord's work, and mighty indeed' (preface), and praying the Lord God of truth to guide him in the path of truth as he writes (§2). For all his credulity he has not, like his more polished and sophisticated contemporary Abraham Cuenque, lost his basic grip on reality. Naturally he puts the best face possible on Sabbatai's interactions with Sultan Mehmed IV. But he never forgets that it is the sultan, and not Sabbatai, who has the power in that relationship. In this respect, the contrast between Baruch's work and Cuenque's is very striking.

As a source for the events of Sabbatai's and Nathan's lives, the *Memorial to the Children of Israel* must be used very critically. But it can be used, and not only for the wealth of primary material preserved in its quotations. As a window into the minds and hearts of the simple believers in Sabbatai Zevi in the years after his death—hungry for the straightforward redemption that was once promised them, respectful of but unswayed by the theological subtleties and heretical paradoxes of Nathan of Gaza, ever disappointed yet dogged in their faith—Baruch's composition has no equal.

When was the *Memorial* written?[10] Careful examination of the internal evidence suggests that it was composed in stages, and in at least two distinct 'editions'.

The book was begun very soon after the news of Sabbatai's death had become generally known, some time in 1677. Near the beginning (§1), Baruch quotes two passages from the ancient rabbinic midrash prophesying

---

[8] This episode is described, in terms far less complimentary to the 'luminaries of the Venetian rabbinate', in §19 of the *Memorial*. See also Scholem, *Sabbatai Sevi*, 764–70. The original 'Memorial' was published as an appendix to the collected responsa of Samuel Aboab, who was chief rabbi of Venice at the time: *Devar shemu'el*, 95*b*–96*b*; also in Emden, *Torat hakenaot*, 22*b*–24*a* (47–50; page numbers in parentheses refer to the 2nd edn, Lvov 1870). The most accessible text is in Tishby's edition of Sasportas, *Sefer tsitsat novel tsevi*, 263–7.

[9] Freimann, *Inyanei shabetai tsevi*, pp. X–XI.

[10] With what follows, compare the arguments in Scholem, 'Where Did Sabbatai Zevi Die?' (Heb.), 78 n. Scholem dates the book to 'between 1680 and 1685'.

that the 'Final Redeemer'—the messiah—will be 'concealed' for forty-five days before revealing himself once more. Forty-five days is not a very long time. If Baruch takes pains to highlight this prediction, it must be because he anticipates Sabbatai will quickly return from wherever he has gone following his resurrection. In the preface, too, Baruch expresses his confidence that 'events will soon be noised about the world that will stir us to fuller repentance than before, after which God will grant us a further redemption corresponding to the intensity of our repentance'. These 'events' are presumably the expected news of Sabbatai's reappearance, perhaps at the head of the armies of the Ten Lost Tribes of Israel.

Even near the end of the book (§26), Baruch continues to leave the possibility open that the messiah will be back soon. But the unpleasant alternative has begun to make itself felt. Sabbatai presently dwells with the Ten Tribes on the far side of the miraculous river Sambatyon, betrothed to the daughter of the lawgiver Moses, who lives once more on the other side of the river. 'If we are deserving, [Sabbatai] will return to redeem us immediately after the seven days of his wedding celebration. But if not, he will delay there until we are deluged by terrible calamities. Only then will he come to avenge us of our enemies and of those who hate us.' This uncertainty points to a time when the return has begun to take longer than Baruch originally expected, and the delay needs to be acknowledged and accounted for.

The end of §26, at any rate, needs to be dated to 1680. 'Rabbi Nathan Benjamin also departed a year or two later, having first announced he wanted to go and join our Lord. For, he said, he knew where it was he had gone' ('our Lord' is Baruch's standard designation for Sabbatai). Nathan of Gaza died on 11 January 1680. Oddly, Baruch writes after the name of the deceased the abbreviation *nun-resh-vav*, standing for *netareh raḥmana ufarkeh*, 'may the Merciful One protect and save him'—a pious wish invariably affixed to the names of people *who are still alive*. The oddity is explained when we realize that Baruch never says in so many words that Nathan has died, and wants quite strongly to believe it is not so. Nathan seems no longer to be on the scene; he is 'departed', no one knows for where; surely he cannot be dead? This would suit the early months after Nathan's death in 1680.

The concluding reflections (§29), following the story of Joseph ibn Tsur, take up the themes broached in the preface. But they have a defeated, defensive air that belies Baruch's earlier confidence. Not only was the penitential movement that accompanied Sabbatai's appearance a mere dress rehearsal for the full and complete repentance, as Baruch had indicated in his preface; it was fatally flawed as well. People then had 'repented only of their sins against God; of sins against their fellow-humans . . . they did not repent at all'. This, as our ancient rabbis have taught us, is no true repentance; when the messiah returns we must undertake to do better. The forty-five days of the messiah's 'concealment', meanwhile, have quietly metamorphosed into forty-five *years*, and the elderly are encouraged not to despair on that account of ever seeing the redemption. Plainly, some significant amount of time has elapsed since Baruch wrote §1.

Thus far the 'first edition' of the *Memorial*. Two of the manuscripts seem to represent a 'second edition', differing from the first in a number of respects.[11] Most noticeably, a fresh appendix has been added at the end: a letter from one Jedidiah Zarfatti, approving what Baruch has written and adding a series of observations on the date of the messianic redemption (§30). Zarfatti, unlike Baruch, is known to us from other sources.[12] He was a Sabbatian believer who arrived in Italy from Turkey around 1679 and spent the next few years travelling in Italy raising funds to ransom Jewish captives. It seems a fair assumption that he was more prominent than Baruch and had a longer history in the movement; Baruch therefore sent him a copy of the 'first edition' for his endorsement, and Baruch or someone else added that endorsement to the 'second edition'. From its contents, Zarfatti's letter can be dated to 1685. This gives the latest possible date for the 'first edition', as well as the earliest for the 'second'.

There are other differences. The 'second edition' inserts a new story into §23, in which the sultan responds to accusations against Sabbatai by saying: 'Leave him to do whatever he pleases. I have no power over him.'[13] This absurd detail, redolent of the stories with which Cuenque fills his biography of Sabbatai Zevi (written in 1692), points to the direction in which the biographical tradition was developing. If the 'second edition' is indeed the work of Baruch himself, and not some anonymous continuator, we must suppose that time and frustration had loosened his hold on reality: repeated disappointments must be compensated by more extravagant fantasies. On the other hand, the 'second edition' omits the *nun-resh-vav* formula ('may the Merciful One protect and save him') from the account of Nathan's 'departure'.[14] Baruch, or whoever is responsible for the revision, has finally faced the fact that Nathan is dead.

Most telling, the passage in the concluding reflections (§29) that describes and analyses the crucial flaw in the people's repentance is shifted in the 'second edition' from the end of the book to the preface.[15] The 'second

---

[11] The two manuscripts are London, British Library Add. 22096 (L$_2$), and Warsaw, Żydówski Instytut Historyczny LIV (W$_1$); see Appendix 1 for details. There is some reason to think the London manuscript may have been copied, by an 'unbeliever', from Warsaw or some similar text. A third manuscript, Cambridge University Library Or. 804 (C), seems to conflate readings from the 'first' and 'second' editions, but to keep to the broad outline of the 'first edition'.   [12] See below, n. 336.   [13] See Appendix 1 on p. 66, l. 8.
[14] See Appendix 1 on p. 69, ll. 1, 4.   [15] See Appendix 1 on p. 44, l. 22, and p. 76, ll. 9–23.

edition' thus makes it look as though Baruch had not discovered this flaw in the course of long, painful years of wondering why the messiah hadn't come back—as was in fact the case—but had known about it all along.[16]

THE TEXT

The *Memorial to the Children of Israel* remained in manuscript until 1912, when it was published for the first time in Aharon Freimann's collection of primary sources on the Sabbatian movement.[17] As he states in his introduction (p. XI), Freimann based his edition on a photostat of MS Oxford, Bodleian Library 2226 (Mich. 479). He also had access to the two Warsaw manuscripts, which were at the time in the library of the Jewish community of Vienna. He thanks Umberto Cassuto for having noted, in the margins of Freimann's proofs, variants from a fragmentary manuscript of the *Memorial* in the possession of the rabbinical academy of Florence. He does not appear to have seen the manuscript itself. What became of this Florence manuscript—whether it was destroyed in the Second World War or the flood of 1966, or whether it is present in Hebrew University's microfilm collection under a different name—I do not know.

Freimann notes variants from the Warsaw ('Vienna') and Florence manuscripts in the footnotes to his edition. He does not do this very consistently, and he often replaces the Oxford readings with those of the other manuscripts without saying so. He prints the Zarfatti appendix, presumably from MS Warsaw LIV, without indicating that it is absent from the Oxford manuscript that is supposed to be his base text. My impression is that, towards the end of the *Memorial*, he tends more and more to favour the Warsaw readings over those of MS Oxford.

Freimann's publication, useful as it has been for the past century, is thus no substitute for a real critical edition of the text. In the absence of any such edition, I have worked through the ten manuscripts of the *Memorial* represented in the Institute of Microfilmed Hebrew Manuscripts, Jewish National and University Library, Hebrew University of Jerusalem. In Appendix 1, I enumerate these manuscripts, note those variants that affect the meaning of the text, and in so doing present the evidence that led me to

---

[16] Three manuscripts (Jerusalem, Ben-Zvi Institute 2264 (J); Moscow, Russian State Library, Günzberg 528 (M_1); Warsaw, Żydówski Instytut Historyczny LV (W_2)) omit the preface. We may wonder if they do not reflect an edition of the *Memorial* prior to the 'first edition', in which §1 served as the preface. This is unlikely: the Jerusalem and Warsaw manuscripts both refer back to the preface ('as I have written above') in §29, showing it must have been in the texts from which they were copied. (The Moscow manuscript is incomplete.) Yet §1 is well suited to function as a preface, and it is entirely possible that it did stand at the beginning of an early draft of Baruch's book.　　　[17] *Inyanei shabetai tsevi*, 43–78.

my theory of the two 'editions' of the *Memorial*. In the translation, I have not tried to make consistent use of any one manuscript. Where the manuscripts differ, I translate the reading that seems to make the best sense or simply to flow the best, unless I see good reason to prefer some other reading.

An alternative translation of the early narrative portions of the *Memorial*, beginning in §2 and extending through the opening lines of §10, was published in 2001 by Matt Goldish.[18]

MEMORIAL TO THE CHILDREN OF ISRAEL

Concerning the event that took place in the days of Mehmet the Fourth, king of the Turks, from the year 5425 [1664/5] to 5436 [1675/6]

PREFACE

MANY worthy individuals from among our people's scholars have composed, for the benefit of the public, history books memorializing the events of the past. Such were Joseph ben Gorion, Joseph Hakohen, the author of *Shevet yehudah* ['The Rod of Judah'], Ibn Yahya, and many others.[19] In the year 5428 [1667/8] the luminaries of the Venetian rabbinate followed in their footsteps, on the subject of Master Nathan of Gaza and the things he said concerning Sabbatai Zevi. This may be seen from that *Zikaron livnei yisra'el* which they printed and disseminated throughout the Jewish diaspora.[20]

I realize, however, that one cannot get from this document a clear sense of what actually happened, inasmuch as the authors spoke of it in the fewest possible words. Hence I, insignificant though I am, have undertaken to pro-

---

[18] 'The Early Messianic Career of Shabbatai Zvi'.

[19] 'Joseph ben Gorion' was the supposed author of the *Yosipon*, a medieval Hebrew book of history and legend very loosely based on the ancient Jewish historian Josephus. Joseph Hakohen (1496–1580), an Italian Jewish historian, chronicled medieval Christendom and Islam, as well as persecutions of the Jews from the destruction of the Second Temple down to 1575. *Shevet yehudah*, written mainly by Solomon ibn Verga in the early 16th century and published in 1554, related stories of persecution from ancient and medieval times. Gedaliah ibn Yahya (1522–88) was author of *Shalshelet hakabalah* (The Chain of Tradition), a popular compendium of ancient and medieval Jewish history. See Waxman, *A History of Jewish Literature*, i. 419–21, ii. 469–79.

[20] See above, n. 8.

vide the public with a fuller narrative, such that all who have eyes to see and ears to hear can grasp the significance of this event—that it was the Lord's work, and mighty indeed it was. I have used the same title as the earlier text, *Memorial to the Children of Israel*, for this is the completion of that earlier 'Memorial'. I, too, shall write concisely. For if I were to seek to record everything that happened from the day that Master Nathan saw the prophetic vision as Ezekiel saw it, in the month of Elul 5425 [August/September 1665], to the day our Lord Sabbatai Zevi was concealed from us, in the month of Tishri 5436 [September/October 1675],[21] I would exhaust my time without having exhausted my subject.

It is well known that repentance is a necessary precondition for the redemption. So we read in the Torah portion 'Nitsavim':[22] 'It shall be, when you return to the Lord your God and grant Him obedience'—only then 'will the Lord your God turn your captivity' [Deut. 30: 2–3]. One must bear in mind that repentance and complete redemption do not happen all at once. Rather, one has a bit of repentance followed by a bit of redemption, then a bit more repentance followed by a bit more redemption, and finally a great repentance and the complete redemption. Thus wrote Rabbi [Isaac] Arama in the hundredth discourse of his book *Sefer akedat yitshak* ['Isaac's Binding'], drawing his evidence from the Scriptures.[23]

After Master Nathan saw his vision, Jews wherever they dwelt were roused to a general repentance, without a single sign or portent having anywhere been witnessed. There followed some small measure of redemption, namely that our messiah was revealed through the utterances of many prophets and prophetesses, and by other markers also, such that nearly all Israel believed in him. The gentiles all behaved towards the Jews in a very kind and loving way; despite the threat to their religion and their rule, they did not speak against the Jews or do them any harm. For 'mighty was their Redeemer, the Lord of Hosts His name' [Jer. 50: 34].

We now may trust in the Lord that events will soon be noised about the world that will stir us to fuller repentance than before, after which God will grant us a further redemption corresponding to the intensity of our repent-

---

[21] Baruch gives the wrong year; it should be Tishri 5437 (September/October 1676).

[22] Jewish liturgical usage divides the Pentateuch into fifty-four 'portions', each of which is to be read in the synagogue one week of the year, such that the Torah is read from beginning to end in the course of the year. 'Nitsavim' is the 'portion' that extends from Deut. 29: 9 to 30: 20.

[23] *Sefer akedat yitshak*, 5 vols (Pressburg: Victor Kittseer, 1849), v. 107*b*. This immensely popular work, by the 15th-century Spanish preacher and expositor Isaac Arama, is a series of 105 discourses on the Pentateuch, arranged according to the sequence of the biblical text (Waxman, *A History of Jewish Literature*, ii. 305–7). The hundredth of these discourses (v. 101*a*–108*b*), taking the beginning of Deut. 30 as its starting point, expounds the verses from the chapter Baruch quotes in his preface.

ance. Finally we shall all be stirred to a great repentance. Thus Scripture says: 'You will repent, and obey the Lord, and do all His commandments' [Deut. 30: 8]—and then 'the Lord your God will turn your captivity, and have mercy on you, and gather you again from all the nations . . . Though you be dispersed to the very end of the heavens, from there the Lord your God will gather you' [Deut. 30: 3–4]. And that will be the final redemption.

Jews are divided into three schools of thought with regard to this issue.

First, there are the exalted few who believe in the faith of our Lord Sabbatai Zevi, remain true to his covenant and maintain his word. Then there are those who utterly deny him and pour forth abuse against him, spouting errors against the Lord and His messiah. And there are those who doubt, yet maintain their silence and speak neither good nor ill.

I have no need to address the believers in this pure and holy faith, nor do they have any need of this *Memorial*. The power of the place from which their pure souls are hewn allows them to believe, without speaker or speech. Nor do I address myself to the unbelievers. This *Memorial* will give them no benefit, for they remain unworthy of benefit—as wrote the Faithful Shepherd, in the Torah portion 'Naso', on the verse 'if a man's wife should go astray' [Num. 5: 12].[24]

I intend this *Memorial*, rather, for the doubtful ones. From it they will learn the wondrous deeds of Him whose knowledge is perfect, which He has wondrously done for His people Israel—most specifically, that no harm has come on account of this matter to anyone called by the name 'Israelite'. They will undertake repentance, charitable deeds, Torah and good works, and will pray devotedly to the Lord their God that He may inspire them to be among the believers in our Lord's faith. Thus shall they merit great benefit. For our salvation is near at hand, our righteousness about to be revealed. Amen! So be His will!

Thus speaks that most insignificant man, seeker of his people's welfare—
Baruch, son of the honourable Rabbi Gershon of Arezzo, of blessed memory.

---

[24] The portion 'Naso' consists of Num. 4: 21–7: 89. By 'the Faithful Shepherd', Baruch intends the 13th-century kabbalistic text called *Ra'aya mehemna*, printed as part of the Zohar and named after the 'faithful shepherd' Moses, who is the chief speaker in the text. The reference here is to the portion of *Ra'aya mehemna* printed in the standard Mantua edition of the Zohar (iii. 124*a*–126*a*). This passage denies any share in the 'final redemption' to the 'mixed rabble' (*erev rav*)—a code phrase, taken from Exod. 12: 38, for the alien and unworthy element within the Jewish people, whom the Sabbatians identified with those who denied their messiah. We shall again meet the 'mixed rabble' in an epistle of Nathan of Gaza defending Sabbatai's conversion to Islam, which Baruch will quote in full (below, §18).

MEMORIAL TO THE
CHILDREN OF ISRAEL

[1. PROPHECIES OF THE MESSIAH'S 'CONCEALMENT']

In order that people may come to know and understand the event—the Lord's doing, mighty indeed—of the first manifestation of our Lord, our messiah, who is suited to his name and his name suited to him,[25] *crowned with Torah and with royalty, the holy rabbi Sabbatai Zevi, may his majesty be exalted! May he soon manifest himself a second time, and his glory then fill all the earth! Amen, amen!*

In *Midrash rabah* on the Torah portion 'Naso', chapter 11,[26] our ancient rabbis give the following interpretation of the verse, 'My beloved is like a gazelle' [*tsevi*; S. of S. 2: 9]:

> Just as a gazelle reveals itself, then again hides itself, so the First Redeemer [Moses] was revealed and then concealed. Rabbi Berechiah said in Rabbi Levi's name: Like the First Redeemer, the Final Redeemer will be revealed and then concealed. How long will he be concealed before he is again revealed? Rabbi Tanhuma said in the name of Rabbi Hama bar Hoshaiah: Forty-five days.

In *Midrash rabah* on Ruth commenting on the verse 'And he held out to her parched corn' (Ruth 2: 14),[27]

> Rabbi Berechiah said in Rabbi Levi's name: Like the First Redeemer, the Final Redeemer will be revealed and then concealed. How long will his concealment last? Rabbi Tanhuma said in the name of the rabbis: Forty-five days.

And the Zohar says frequently: 'He was revealed; then he was concealed; then he was revealed.'[28]

---

[25] In that the Holy Scriptures call him *tsevi*, 'gazelle'; see below.

[26] 'Naso' = Num. 4: 21–7: 89. Baruch quotes the rabbinic midrash *Numbers Rabbah* 11: 2, in somewhat abbreviated form. The full text of the midrash suggests that the allusion is to a rabbinic tradition that Moses was 'concealed' in Midian for three (or six) months, during the persecution described in Exod. 5: 10–19.   [27] *Ruth Rabbah* 5: 6.

[28] I am not aware of any such passage in the Zohar or anywhere else. The verbs *itgaleya itkaseya itgaleya* are found in sequence in Zohar, iii. 146*b* (a supposed quotation from *Sifra ditseniuta*; cf. ii. 178*a*), but with a meaning entirely different from that which Baruch attributes to them.

[2. SABBATAI'S EARLY YEARS]

I shall now begin to record, as concisely as possible, certain events that befell our Lord from his birth down to the time he was concealed from us. I rely on what I have seen in trustworthy written sources, as well as what I have heard from truthful and honourable individuals who cannot be suspected of falsehood. The testimonies confirm one another, such that the true facts may be discerned. And may the Lord God of truth guide me in the path of truth!

On the ninth day of Av, in the year 5386 [1 August 1626], a son was born to Mordecai Zevi and given the Jewish name Sabbatai. He had one older brother, named Elijah, and a younger brother named Joseph. As the child Sabbatai grew and matured he was brought to school, and he began to learn, and showed great passion for God's Torah. Upon reaching manhood he conducted himself in an ascetic manner, piously and most holily.

One day he was studying Torah with the rabbis—among them the saintly and humble Rabbi Moses Pinheiro, currently resident in Leghorn[29]—when he began to weep most bitterly. 'Why are you weeping?' the rabbis asked. To which he answered: 'I know I am the messiah, and that against my will I will perform strange acts against the Lord and His Torah, and therefore do I weep.' And they were all amazed.

Afterwards he set forth from his native city Izmir and went to his own land, the glorious land.[30] There also he studied Torah day and night. The rabbis, perceiving his piety and fidelity, sent him to Egypt to collect funds for the Jewish communities in the Land of Israel. Then he returned to Jerusalem.

[3. THE STORY OF SABBATAI'S BRIDE]

Now there was a certain Jew in the Ashkenazi lands[31] to whom a baby girl was born. The gentiles carried her off by force while she was small, and converted her and gave her into the care of an exceedingly rich gentile woman. This woman had only one son. When the boy and the girl grew up she

---

[29] On Pinheiro, see Scholem's article in the *Encyclopedia Judaica*, and *Sabbatai Sevi*, 110, 114–15, 140, 144, 486–9, 722–4, 761, 890.

[30] That is, the Land of Israel, called in Dan. 11: 16, 41 'the glorious land' (*erets hatsevi*— which can also be translated 'the land of Zevi'. Hence the Holy Land is Sabbatai Zevi's 'own land'. Baruch either does not know or prefers not to mention that Sabbatai was excommunicated and expelled from Izmir, and that he spent nearly ten years wandering before he reached Palestine.

[31] *Erets ashkenaz*, referring to the central and eastern European lands of the German- (= Yiddish-) speaking Jews. Here the reference is to Poland, and to the Cossack massacres of 1648–9.

wanted to marry them to one another, and to give them all her money and possessions and all that she had.

One night—the very night before they were to go to the church to be married by the bishop of the city, as was the custom—the girl's father, dead some two years, appeared to her in a dream. 'Woe to you!' said he. 'And woe to your soul! What have you done?'

When the girl heard her father's voice she wept and cried aloud. 'My father, my father!' she said. 'What can I possibly do? I am in their power; they give me no liberty to go anywhere.'

'Now listen to me,' her father said to her. 'Put on this leather garment[32] I am giving you, and go this night to the graveyard. Stay there. The Lord will be your confidence; He will keep your foot from the snare.'[33]

Thus she did. In the morning, when the people of the town went there to bury a certain Jew, they saw the girl wearing that garment. On it was plainly written: THIS WOMAN WILL BE THE MESSIAH'S WIFE. At once they took the girl and spirited her from place to place and from city to city, by way of Venice, finally bringing her to Leghorn.

There she stayed a long time, until a ship arrived on its way to Egypt. During this time she delivered prophecies of the future, all of which came true. When the worthy scholar Rabbi Isaac Halevi Valle[34] heard about these things and the truth she spoke, he himself went to talk with her. He asked her to tell him the root of his soul, and about other things which ought not to be recorded. She answered his questions, and he knew for certain that what she said was true. The mistress of the house then said to the rabbi in the girl's presence: 'Do you know, sir, what this girl says? She says she will be the messiah's wife!'—to which the girl gave no reply.

The people of Leghorn sent her to Egypt, to the care of the high Egyptian dignitary, the honourable Rabbi Raphael Joseph Chelebi, who was finance minister to the king.[35] He received her with great honour; he told

---

[32] *Malbush shel or*. The allusion to the 'garments of skin' (*or*) with which Adam and Eve clothed themselves (Gen. 3: 21) is presumably deliberate. A Christian Hebraist, Johannes Braun, wrote in 1698 how the Jews claim that 'the wife of that new impostor, Sabbathi Zebi, got the coat of skins that Eve made almost six thousand years ago. Embroidered with many names of saints and patriarchs and adorned with letters of gold, it was by a stupendous miracle lowered down from heaven into a field to which she was led naked by the spirit of her father who had been a Jew while she herself only knew she was born a Christian' (Goldish, *The Sabbatean Prophets*, 89–97; cf. Scholem, *Sabbatai Sevi*, 193–5). The story Braun heard is very different from the one given by Baruch, but the common motifs are evident.

[33] Quoting Prov. 3: 26.

[34] Presumably the Isaac Halevi Valle whom Meir Benayahu mentions as a rabbi from Modena, author of an unpublished commentary on the *Shulḥan arukh*, teacher of the Sabbatian Abraham Rovigo (Benayahu, *The Sabbatian Movement in Greece* (Heb.), 253).

[35] On Raphael Joseph Chelebi and the position he held in the Egyptian government, see Scholem, *Sabbatai Sevi*, 177–8; Hathaway, 'The Grand Vizier and the False Messiah'.

her he wanted to marry her to one of his friends and settle great wealth upon her. But she was unwilling. She must go to Jerusalem, she told him, for there was her destined match. So he sent her to Jerusalem, accompanied by a certain upright and honest Jew.

When they arrived in the midst of Jerusalem, she caught sight of our Lord. 'See that rabbi, among his fellow-rabbis!' she said to the Jew who was with her. 'He is my intended.' Meanwhile our Lord raised his eyes and saw the girl, and said to his companion rabbis: 'That young lady coming towards us is my intended; blessed is she among women!'

And so they were betrothed, and they were wed. Yet he never made love to her until after he had set the pure turban on his head, and then she bore him a son and a daughter. But all this we shall relate presently, with God's help.

[4. NATHAN OF GAZA]

In the year 5425 [1664/5] Rabbi Abraham Nathan, son of the honourable Rabbi Elisha Ashkenazi, was living in Gaza—about 22 years old, married, with children. One day, about the time of the Purim festival,[36] there came to him a great illumination in the course of which he came to know the secrets of others' consciences and the sins they had committed. One by one he summoned them, saying to them: 'I know you have done such-and-such a sin, in such-and-such a place, on such-and-such a day.' They all would admit the truth of what he said, whereat he would prescribe for them a mending [*tikun*] for their souls. His reputation spread in those parts, with the result that many people came to Gaza to consult with him about their souls' mending.

Many rabbis came, even from Jerusalem. Among them was Rabbi Israel Benjamin, grandson of the divine kabbalist Rabbi Israel Benjamin the Elder.[37] To him Master Nathan said: 'Go to the graveyard. There you will find an old man holding a dipper of water, a scarf draped over his shoulder. Take the dipper from him and pour water over his hands, and recite the verse that begins "Grant atonement to Your people Israel" [Deut. 21: 8].'[38]

He went to the graveyard; he found nothing. He went back to Master Nathan and told him: 'I went there and found no one.' 'Go back again', said he. Back he went, and found an old man with a dipper of water in his hand.

[36] The festival ordained in the book of Esther, to celebrate the deliverance of the Jews of ancient Persia from a planned massacre. Purim 5425 would have fallen on 1 March 1665.

[37] On the elder Israel Benjamin (*c.*1570–1649), a very prominent Jerusalem kabbalist, see the article in the *Encyclopedia Judaica*; on his grandson, and the episode recounted here, see Scholem, *Sabbatai Sevi*, 263–5.

[38] '"Grant atonement to Your people Israel, whom You have redeemed, O Lord; and do not place [the guilt for shedding] innocent blood in the midst of Your people Israel." And they shall be granted atonement for the blood.'

He took the dipper from him, and poured water to wash his hands. He recited the verse, 'Grant atonement to Your people Israel.' To which the old man responded: 'You are granted atonement for the blood.'[39]

He returned to Master Nathan. 'I have done all that you instructed me', he said. Whereupon Master Nathan told him that the old man was the prophet Zechariah,[40] and that the spirit of the man who killed Zechariah had been reincarnated in Master Israel Benjamin. Now he had performed the appropriate mending, and the entire Jewish people had been granted atonement for the great crime of Zechariah's murder.[41]

[5. NATHAN'S VISIONS]

Some time after this, Master Nathan told the rabbis of Gaza that for the Lord's sake they must show great honour to Rabbi Sabbatai Zevi upon his returning to Gaza, for he was a most venerable man of God. Rabbi Jacob Najara[42] accordingly prepared for him a room with bed, table, chair and lamp, and royal decorations.

When [Sabbatai] arrived, they all went out to greet him and received him with great honour. They brought him to [Najara's] house and prepared a dinner in celebration. When they were finished eating they gave Master Nathan the cup of blessing.[43] [As Nathan was reciting the grace,] when he got to the section 'the Merciful One', he recited: 'May the Merciful One bless our Lord, our king, our messiah Sabbatai Zevi.' At which [Sabbatai] cried out: 'Be silent!'

---

[39] Based on the last words of Deut. 21: 8 (above).

[40] That is, Zechariah son of Jehoiada, a Judaean prophet in the time of the First Temple, whose martyrdom is described in 2 Chron. 24: 20–2. This murder became the subject of lurid rabbinic legends, which declared countless Jewish children to have been slaughtered at the time of Nebuchadnezzar's capture of Jerusalem as punishment for the crime. See Blank, 'The Death of Zechariah in Rabbinic Literature'. (Matt. 23: 35 alludes to this episode, but confuses Zechariah with the Second Temple prophet of the same name.)

[41] The details of the episode, and their relation to Deut. 21: 1–8, suggest an alternative interpretation. Deuteronomy prescribes for a case where a corpse is found in an open country, its murderer unknown. The elders of the nearest city (*zekenim*, the word translated 'old man' in this text) are to take a calf down to a running brook and there break its neck. They must then 'wash their hands over the calf . . . and say, "Our hands did not shed this blood, and we were not aware of it. Grant atonement to Your people Israel . . . " And they shall be granted atonement for the blood.' It would appear from this that the 'elder' who must wash his hands is a representative of the Jewish people, and perhaps also Israel Benjamin's alter ego, who had committed the ancient murder. Cf. the variants published in Haberman, 'On the History of Anti-Sabbatian Polemic' (Heb.), 210; Wilensky, 'Four English Pamphlets' (Heb.), 170.

[42] Rabbi of Gaza from 1660 onwards (Scholem, *Sabbatai Sevi*, 202). We will meet him again as the author of the Najara Chronicle.

[43] Thereby inviting Nathan to say the grace after meals.

When the Shavuot festival arrived,[44] Master Nathan invited the rabbis of Gaza to spend the night studying Torah with him. About midnight, Master Nathan went into a deep trance.[45] He stood up, walked back and forth in the room, recited the entire tractate *Ketubot* by heart.[46] He ordered one rabbi to sing a certain hymn, then did the same to another. While this was going on, all the rabbis became aware of[47] a pleasant aroma, wonderfully fragrant, like the smell of a field the Lord had blessed.[48] They went looking in the surrounding houses and alleyways for the source of the aroma, but found nothing. All the while [Nathan] was jumping and dancing around the room. He stripped off one piece of clothing after another, until he was down to his undergarment. Then he made a great leap and fell flat onto the floor.

When the rabbis saw this, they tried to help him to his feet. But they found him lifeless as a corpse. The honourable Rabbi Meir Rofé[49] was present, and he felt his wrist the way physicians do and announced that he had no pulse. They laid a cloth over his face, as one does—God protect us!—for the dead.

But a short while later they heard a very low voice. They removed the cloth from his face and saw that a voice was emanating from his mouth, though his lips did not move. *Be careful,* [the voice] said, *of My son, My beloved, My messiah Sabbatai Zevi.* Then it went on: *Be careful of My son, My beloved,*

---

[44] The festival commemorating the giving of the Torah on Mount Sinai. It had become the custom in pietist circles to spend the entire night of Shavuot studying Torah. The date was 19 May 1665.

[45] *Tardemah*, the word used in the Bible for the 'deep sleep' in which divine revelation is granted to Abraham (Gen. 15: 12), and to lesser mortals as well (Job 4: 13, 33: 15). In Gen. 2: 21, Eve is fashioned from Adam while he is in a state of *tardemah*.

[46] A tractate of the Mishnah. On the significance of this detail, see Goldish, *The Sabbatean Prophets*, 63–71.

[47] Literally, 'heard'. (So all the manuscripts, despite the obvious inappropriateness of the reading. See also the textual note to p. 47, l. 17.)

[48] The language is taken from Gen. 27: 27. The allusion may be significant: the Zohar (i. 142*b*) applies this verse to the Shekhinah, the 'field of apples', the feminine element in the deity. The purpose of the all-night Shavuot vigil, in the kabbalists' eyes, was to adorn this feminine element for the coming day's wedding to the divine masculine, 'the Blessed Holy One'. Cf. also Goldish, *The Sabbatean Prophets*, 65.

[49] Hebron scholar, son of the distinguished talmudist and kabbalist Hiya Rofé of Safed, and principal of Abraham Pereira's Hesed Le'avraham yeshiva in Hebron. We have already met him in the Introduction, section VII. He travelled extensively to collect money for the Hebron Jewish community. On one of these fundraising missions he met Rabbi Menasseh ben Israel in Amsterdam, where he told the credulous Menasseh the tale of an hourglass kept at the door to a mosque in Aleppo, whose sands ran six days of the week but rested on the sabbath (Méchoulan and Nahon, *Menasseh ben Israel*, 136–7). Rofé was to become a member of Sabbatai's inner circle, and to remain a devout believer all his life; Tishby, 'R. Meir Rofé's Letters' (Heb.), 74–6. Baruch gives Rofé's name as *harofe*, 'the physician'. Evidently he assumed it was a professional title rather than a family name, and he reports Rofé's behaviour accordingly (Scholem, *Sabbatai Sevi*, 219).

Nathan the prophet. Thus did the rabbis come to realize that the aroma they smelled had emanated from that same spark of spiritual holiness that had entered into Master Nathan and spoken these words.

[Nathan] then gave a great sigh.[50] He began to shake himself. His companions helped him to his feet and asked him how this had befallen, and what it was he had said. 'I have no idea at all', he replied. So the rabbis told him what had happened, at which he was astounded.

Another night they gathered with Master Nathan to study all night, he sitting in one room and the rabbis in another. He had instructed them, 'Do not eat anything.' As they began their studying, he emerged from his room and said: 'One of you has eaten.' And one rabbi indeed admitted he had absently eaten a plum that had been in his pouch. An hour later he came forth once more. 'One of you has had an emission!' he said. And so it was.

His ability to divine these matters correctly won Master Nathan their deep and unanimous respect. His reputation spread even among the Turks; they became like the dumb, unable to speak a word.

It was afterwards revealed to Master Nathan in a dream vision that he must undertake a fast of several days' duration, for he was about to experience a great illumination. This he did. On Sunday, 25 Elul 5425 [5 September 1665],[51] he secluded himself in one room, with the rabbis in another, adjoining room. On Monday, after the morning prayer, a great illumination came upon him.

He saw the light God had created during the six days of Creation, by which he could see from one end of the world to the other. He saw the vision seen by Ezekiel the prophet.[52] He saw the following letters inscribed in supernal lights: *Thus saith the Lord: Behold your saviour cometh, Sabbatai Zevi [his name]*. Some sort of angelic being became embodied in him and compelled him to utter this message. He heard a herald proclaim in the Celestial Academy: *In another year, and a few more months, the kingdom of the house of David will become manifest and visible.* By the ever-living God he swore this was true, that he had indeed seen this vision, that, moreover, he had read

---

[50] See the textual note to p. 47, ll. 18–19. Matt Goldish's translation, 'he rested a great rest' ('The Early Messianic Career of Shabbatai Zvi', 476) is based on the corrupt reading given by Freimann.

[51] The date is problematic. 25 Elul 5425 fell on Saturday, not Sunday, and, as Scholem (*Sabbatai Sevi*, 268–9) and Goldish (*The Sabbatean Prophets*, 192 n. 9) point out, there are other grounds for believing this vision took place in the spring of 1665 rather than the early autumn. But see the textual note on this passage (p. 47, l. 27), and also Appendix 3.

[52] The vision of the Divine Chariot (*merkavah*) described in Ezek. 1, which had long been a focus of attention for Jewish mystics.

some very ancient book in which was written: *In the year 5386* [1625/6], *a son shall be born to Mordecai Zevi, and his name shall be called Sabbatai; and he shall subdue the Great Dragon*—and so on.[53]

People came to Gaza from all over, to seek mending for their souls. Even from distant lands they sent him letters to this end. In order to test his accuracy, they sent him the names of many who sought mending, one of these being dead and another a nursling at his mother's breast. For all of them he prescribed mendings. When he got to the man who had died, he wrote opposite his name: 'His death has atoned for him.' For the nursling he wrote: 'Without sin.' Thus did they come to realize that what he said was true and dependable.

[6. FROM GAZA TO IZMIR]

From Gaza, our Lord set out for Izmir, the city of his birth.

He passed through Jerusalem, where dwelt Rabbi Hayim[54] who did not believe in him. The community officials there went to the *cadi*—that is, the [Muslim] judge of the city—and laid a charge against [Sabbatai], to the effect that they had sent him to Egypt to collect funds. Now, they said, they wanted an accounting from him. So the *cadi* sent a servant to summon our Lord, and he came.

Upon seeing him, the *cadi* was seized with trembling. He showed him great honour; he invited him to take a seat higher than the *cadi*'s own; they talked together for about half an hour. Afterwards [Sabbatai] asked permission to ride a horse in the city;[55] permission was at once granted. He circled all Jerusalem on the outside seven times, riding on horseback, and then returned to the city. No one knew what his purpose was.

Then he departed Jerusalem for Aleppo, which is [the biblical] Aram-Zova.[56] There the Jews received him with great honour. He had already acquired a reputation as the messiah; the Jews said so quite openly. Yet not the Turks nor even the *pasha*—the city's governor—spoke a word of protest.

---

[53] The quotation is from 'The Vision of Rabbi Abraham', an apocalyptic text which Scholem believes to have been composed by Nathan himself some time in the spring of 1665 (*Sabbatai Sevi*, 224–33, which includes a full translation). See above, Introduction, n. 9.

[54] See the textual note. The variant 'Rabbi Hagis' makes excellent sense; the Jerusalem rabbi Jacob Hagiz is known to have been a strong opponent of Sabbatai Zevi. But it is found only in W_2, the most careless and least reliable of the manuscripts. In a marginal note in his personal copy of Freimann's book (now in the Scholem Collection of the National and University Library, Jerusalem), Scholem raises and dismisses the possibility that the Hebron rabbi Hayim Abulafia may be intended. Cf. *Sabbatai Sevi*, 358 n. 52. On Hagiz and Abulafia, see below, Fourth Testimony, nn. 64 and 93.

[55] Normally prohibited to Jews in Muslim lands.   [56] Mentioned in 2 Sam. 10: 6.

It was as though they were dumb; they could not speak, for great trembling had fallen upon them.

He reached Izmir in Kislev 5426 [9 November–8 December 1665]. There, too, he was received with great honour. He went to the home of his brothers, Masters Elijah and Joseph. There also, the *pasha* and the *cadi* and all the Turks knew perfectly well that the Jews believed him to be the messiah. Not one of them raised a voice in complaint.

So there he dwelt, a king in his palace. Many Jews came to kiss his hands, as was their practice with great men. Those who were not of our people came also to pay their respects, such that his doors were never closed day or night for all the gentiles bringing him their wealth and offering him their service.[57]

His brother Rabbi Elijah, who did not believe him to be the messiah, became alarmed at this. Perhaps it might bring calamity upon the Jewish community of Izmir—indeed, upon all the communities under the Turkish king's rule? Better this one man die, he thought, than that all the communities be lost. So one day, finding [Sabbatai] alone in a room, he approached him with his sword drawn, intending to strike. But our Lord set his eyes upon him and trembling seized him. He collapsed before him as though dead, and could do him no harm.

[7. STRANGE DEEDS]

It was after this that [Sabbatai] began to do things that seemed strange. He would pronounce the Sacred Name precisely as it was written.[58] He ate animal fat.[59] He did other things contrary to God and His Torah, and pressed others to do the same wicked deeds.

On Thursday, the third day of Hanukah,[60] he went in the morning to the Algazi synagogue, dressed in royal robes. He began to sing the hymns with such melody that the entire congregation was astonished at the melodies of his hymns.[61] On Friday Rabbi Galante appeared there, testifying truly that he certainly was the messiah.

---

[57] Alluding to Isa. 60: 11.

[58] The four-letter Name of God *YHVH*, which Jews traditionally will not speak aloud.

[59] *Ḥelev*, a type of intestinal fat used in the ancient Temple sacrifices, forbidden for human consumption on the basis of Lev. 7: 23 and its rabbinic elaborations.

[60] 27 Kislev 5426 (5 December 1665), which, inconveniently, fell on a Saturday rather than a Thursday. Baruch's dates are evidently confused. See Scholem, *Sabbatai Zevi*, 384 n., 386 n. (but cf. also Appendix 3, below).

[61] Baruch does not make clear what there was about the melodies that so astonished them.

Then, that sabbath, he recited petitionary prayers[62] at great length and afterwards went off to the Portuguese synagogue. Many of those who worshipped there did not believe in him, and therefore had barred the synagogue doors. He fell into a terrific rage. He sent for an axe, and, sabbath though it was, hacked away at the doors until they opened them.

They were reciting the Nishmat prayer[63] as he entered the synagogue. He told them to stop right there. He began to chant petitionary prayers, and went on doing so until the time for the Amidah prayer[64] had passed. 'Today', he told them, 'you are released from the obligation of saying the Amidah. Just recite the Shema, without benedictions.'[65] He then produced a printed text of the Pentateuch from his pouch, declared it to be holier than the Torah scroll, and launched into the Torah reading.

His elder brother Master Elijah—who, as we have said, had wanted to kill him—he called to the Torah as though he were of priestly descent, and made him king of Turkey. His second brother he called as Roman emperor. He called to the Torah many men, and women as well,[66] granting them royal status. Each did he compel to pronounce the Divine Name as written.

The next day those who disbelieved in him denounced him to the *cadi*, the city judge, on account of these wicked deeds. The *cadi* summoned him, but, upon his appearance, was seized with trembling and showed him great honour. Then he sent to summon the men who had denounced him. They feared for their lives, and fled into hiding.

These strange deeds notwithstanding, his reputation as the hoped-for messiah spread everywhere. So did Master Nathan's reputation as a true

---

[62] *Bakashot*, hymns recited in traditional Sephardi communities before the start of the regular sabbath morning prayer service.

[63] The prayer of the sabbath morning service that begins *nishmat kol ḥai tevarekh et shimkha*, 'the spirit of every living being shall bless Thy Name', and comes directly before the benedictions accompanying the Shema.

[64] A series of benedictions, recited while standing, that constitutes the indispensable core of every Jewish worship service. 'There is no service without the Amida' (Idelsohn, *Jewish Liturgy and its Development*, p. xv)—until Sabbatai burst into the Izmir synagogue and blithely proclaimed one.

[65] The Shema is a string of three biblical passages—Deut. 6: 4–9, 11: 13–21, Num. 15: 37–41—that convey the central principles of Judaism. In the synagogue service the Shema is preceded and followed by a series of liturgical benedictions. Sabbatai decrees that the congregants are to recite the Shema but skip the benedictions, he having already used up the time with his petitionary prayers.

[66] The words 'and women as well' occur in four manuscripts, two of them representing the 'second edition'. They reflect Sabbatianism's strong tendency to grant equality to women, in a way unheard of in Judaism down to very modern times. (Women are traditionally not supposed to be called to the synagogue lectern, to recite the blessings that precede and follow readings from the Torah.) See the important study by Ada Rapoport-Albert, 'On the Position of Women in Sabbatianism' (Heb.).

prophet. Nearly all Jews believed in him, without the confirmation of any miraculous sign. The Christians and the Turks were quite aware of this. Yet not one of them spoke a word of protest, for the Lord's terror had fallen upon them.

The Jews throughout the diaspora, for their part, were stirred to great acts of penitence. A 'mending',[67] to be recited day and night, was dispatched from the Land of Israel; it was printed in Mantua and in that great centre of Jewish learning, the city of Amsterdam. Many undertook protracted fasts, extending from one sabbath day to the next. Day and night they stood in the synagogues—men, women, and children alike—reciting prayers and imploring God's forgiveness and mercy. Along with this they performed ritual immersions and did acts of charity. Mass penitence on such a scale had, without the slightest doubt, never been done before, even in the days of Mordecai and Esther.[68]

Shops were closed. People gave only a bare minimum of time to their business. All this was witnessed by Christians and Muslims alike. Yet they did not speak an ill word against the Jews. On the contrary, they showed them the greatest friendliness and affection.

In the month of Shevat [7 January–5 February 1666][69] our Lord donned royal robes, embroidered with fine gold. In one hand he held a copy of the Pentateuch, in the other a golden sceptre, as the great emperors do. He went forth from his house, followed by about five hundred Jews.

Through the main street, through the major thoroughfares of Izmir they went, loudly proclaiming: 'Long live the king our lord! Long live our lord the king!' The Turks saw and heard everything but did not say a word. Rather, they threw themselves to the ground in abject prostration. Even when the *pasha* and the *cadi* and the city officials became aware of what was going on, not one of them made any protest. Nor did they do the slightest harm to the Jews, either to their persons or their property.

[67] *Tikun*: in this context, a liturgy of biblical psalms which, recited with the proper kabbalistic 'intentions', would effect the needed 'mendings' in the damaged world of divinity and smooth the way for the redemption. See Halperin, 'The Son of the Messiah', 152–9.

[68] When there was everywhere 'great mourning for the Jews: fasting, weeping and lamentation, sackcloth and ashes spread out for many', and Queen Esther herself, and all the Jews of Shushan with her, abstained three days from food and drink (Esther 4: 3, 15–17).

[69] In fact, Sabbatai had already left for Constantinople at the end of December 1665. Baruch presumably wants to keep him in Izmir through January, in order to square the legend that the sea voyage was preternaturally swift (below, §9) with the fact that Sabbatai did not arrive until early February.

[8. THE PROPHESYING]

Afterwards the prophesying began. It fell upon many men, women, and children, in Izmir, Constantinople, Aleppo, and other places.[70] The message to which they testified was always the same: *Sabbatai Zevi is the messiah of the God of Jacob.*

This was the manner of prophesying in those days: people would go into a trance[71] and fall to the ground as though dead, their spirits entirely gone. After about half an hour they would begin to breathe and, without moving their lips, would speak scriptural verses praising God, offering comfort. All would say: *Sabbatai Zevi is the messiah of the God of Jacob.* Upon recovering, they had no awareness of what they had done or said.

Izmir produced more than one hundred and fifty prophets, of whom the following were the most distinguished: our Lord's wife, the wife of Jacob Peña, the wife of Vana, the wife of Jacob Sarrano, the wife of Jacob Benveniste, the wife of Jacob Capua, Rabbi Daniel Pinto, Joseph Halevi, Solomon son of the honourable Rabbi Daniel Valencin, Joshua Morletto, Samuel Bonomo, Moses Safami, Elijah Bonseñor, and a certain orphan.[72] The prophets of Aleppo were Master Isaiah Hakohen, Moses Galante, Daniel Pinto, the wife of Yom Tov Laniado, the wife of Rabbi Nissim Mizrahi, the daughter of Rabbi Abraham Simhon, and about twenty other prophets and prophetesses.

The following was the prophecy of Abraham, son of the honourable Rabbi Jacob Jeshurun (Izmir, 4 Shevat 5426 [10 January 1666]):

> Lord, I have heard tell of You! The Lord is king, the Lord was king, the Lord will be king for ever and ever! Hear, O Israel, the Lord is our God, the Lord is One! Blessed be the name of His glorious kingdom for ever and ever! Our king Sabbatai Zevi is already crowned! A mighty ban has been pronounced in heaven against those who do not believe! The Lord is guardian of Israel; our prayers have been heard! A song of ascents: from the depths I have called You, Lord! Great joy! Blessed be he who is alive! They have brought a crown for our Lord the king! Woe to the unbeliever; he is under the ban! Joy to anyone living in this time! A song of ascents: happy are they who fear the Lord! Let him make great joy! Give

---

[70] See Goldish, *The Sabbatean Prophets*, 101–29. The full participation of women in the 'prophesying' is a marker of their new status among Sabbatai's followers; see above, n. 66.

[71] *Tardemah*; see above, n. 45. Goldish observes that the popular Sabbatian prophecy follows the pattern set by the experiences of Nathan of Gaza (*The Sabbatean Prophets*, 109–10).

[72] The reference to 'a certain orphan' seems very odd as a conclusion to this list of named individuals. But it is attested by all the manuscripts. Perhaps, as Pamela Kinlaw has suggested to me, the family name Yatom ('orphan') is intended?

ear, Lord, have mercy on me! They have already given him the crown!
His kingdom is eternal! Rabbi Sabbatai Zevi reigns, seated on his royal
throne! Hear O Israel! Precious are the Jews in the eyes of God! Rejoice,
ye righteous, in the Lord! Praise the Lord, for He is good! God is true,
Moses is true, his Torah is true, Sabbatai Zevi is true! Great joy! You open
Your hands![73] The Lord is God! Sabbatai Zevi reigns; he sits on his
throne! Hear O Israel! A song of ascents: when the Lord returned Zion's
captivity![74] Great joy to the Jews! The Lord is God! Happy is the man
who fears the Lord! How great are His signs, how mighty His wonders!
When the Lord returned Zion's captivity! Great joy! Praise the Lord, for
He is good! Praise the God of heaven! The Lord is king, the Lord was
king! Woe to the unbeliever! Our Lord king reigns! Lord, righteousness
is Yours! Great joy! A song of ascents: when the Lord returned Zion's
captivity! They have done homage to the Jews; the star of our kingdom
has risen! Praise the Lord for He is good, His mercies endure for ever!
Have mercy on me, Lord, lift me up! From my troubles I called to the
Lord! Blessed be he who comes in the Lord's name! May the Lord answer
you on the day of trouble! Praise the Lord for He is good (three times)!
The Lord is strong and mighty for ever! The king sits on the throne of
mercy! The Lord of hosts sits on His royal throne! The Lord will fight
for you! The Lord is the king of glory, *selah*! The Lord is strong and
mighty; may His kingdom be exalted! True! true! true! Save me, Lord, in
Your mercy! Joy to the Jews! Save me in Your mercy (three times)! Praise
the Lord for He is good! Blessed be His glorious kingdom for ever! Hear
O Israel! You will light my lamp (twice)! Great is the Lord, much to be
praised! The evil impulse is no more! Lord, hear my prayer! Praise the
Lord for He is good . . .

All these words of truth did he speak, repeating everything four or five
times.

[9. CONSTANTINOPLE: THE MESSIAH ARRESTED]

When our Lord set forth from Izmir to Constantinople, to see the Turkish
king, he travelled by ship in the company of four rabbis. One of these rabbis,
he said, possessed the soul of Jehoshaphat [king of Judah]; a second, that of
Zedekiah king of Judah. The two others had the souls of kings of ancient
Israel. A second ship accompanied theirs.

[73] Alluding to Ps. 145: 16: 'You open Your hand and satisfy every living thing with favour.'
[74] The opening of Ps. 126.

A great storm arose at sea, threatening to destroy the ships. Realizing this, our Lord set one foot upon the ship's mast, and something like a pillar of fire appeared there. In hardly more than a moment they found themselves at Constantinople. But the ship that accompanied theirs sank beneath the waves, and to this day no one knows where it lies.

Now, the Jewish leaders in Constantinople had anticipated his arrival by going to the grand vizier, the king's second in command.[75] 'Our Lord', they said, 'you should be aware that a certain one of our people is on his way here, claiming to be the messiah. We ourselves do not believe in him. Consider what you ought to do.'

Upon hearing this, the vizier ordered that our Lord be seized and confined in a prison where the royal prisoners were kept. He was there two days and a night. During that time he received a great illumination, so that his face shone like torchlight and the night was as bright as day wherever he happened to be. Afterwards the vizier summoned [Sabbatai] to appear before him and before the *mufti*, the official set in authority over the Turks' religion. Entering their presence, our Lord was told by a certain rabbi who accompanied him to 'bow and prostrate yourself before the officials. That is the customary practice.'

'Be silent,' our Lord replied. 'I know what to do.'

He was not willing to prostrate himself before them, nor did he show deference or anxiety in their presence. 'Tell me which language I am to speak with you', he said to the vizier. 'I am conversant with them all.' The vizier tried four or five languages, ending with Arabic. [Sabbatai] answered in all of them. The vizier was so pleased with him that he was not willing to execute him, for all that he merited execution. He ordered him conveyed to a certain house in the royal court, where he dwelt unharmed and at his ease.

[10. VENICE ENQUIRES OF CONSTANTINOPLE]

News of these events spread through Italy, above all the city of Venice. The overwhelming majority there believed that 'the Lord had looked after His people to give them bread' [Ruth 1: 6], namely the bread of salvation. The rabbis and community leaders assembled and agreed to perform a mass penitence, the like of which had certainly never been done in that city. Afterwards they dispatched a courier to Constantinople, to enquire of the rabbis there whether the good tidings of our redemption and salvation were indeed true. Similarly, if it was all a 'castle in the air'[76] they must tell them honestly. And if the matter was in doubt, in what direction did their judgment incline?

[75] Fazil Ahmed Köprülü, vizier from 1661 to 1676.

[76] Literally, 'a tower flying in the air' (*migdal hapore'ah ba'avir*). The expression is taken from BT Ḥag. 15*b*, *San*. 106*b*.

The response was that *Rabbi Sabbatai Zevi was the true Redeemer, and that entertaining doubts about him was tantamount to doubting the Lord God Himself.* This may be seen from the text of the correspondence, quoted here in evidence:[77]

TO THE WORTHY RABBIS, and so forth:[78]

In these days of ours, when wherever one turns one finds the world divided—split into parties and factions by the multitude of vague and wild rumours of salvation that flood upon us, promising our redemption, to which some give credence while others are opposed and doubtful— our natural course is to seek the truth from those who know and will say it. This is, after all, no trivial matter of profit or loss. The entire world is troubled, deeply confused, and—God forbid!—exposed to danger.[79]

Therefore, at the urgent request of our entire community and its leaders, we have resolved to come before you as supplicant wanderers, to seek with these few words of ours the pearls of your wisdom. If this is indeed a day of good tidings—proclaim them to us! Spare no detail; apprise us of any new development. And if this rumour should prove to be a 'castle in the air', then let us together determine the fittest way to quiet our communities and comfort them in their disillusionment, that their lot may be a pleasant one when God's appointed time shall arrive.[80] Though it delay, we must wait for it with a patience that never ends. This is to our advantage; this is our proper course.

One thing more we beg of you, our great sheltering oaks: if the matter is in doubt, tell us in what direction your judgment inclines.

All Israel looks to you for the truth.[81]

In all sincerity,
The members of the General Academy of the city of Venice,
8th day of Second Adar, of the year,
'The kingdom *shall be* God's' [15 March 1666].[82]

---

[77] These two letters—the query from Venice and the reply of the Constantinople rabbis— are quoted somewhat more fully in Sasportas, *Sefer tsitsat novel tsevi*, 109–11.

[78] Thus does Baruch abbreviate the flowery address to the rabbis of Constantinople with which the letter originally opened (quoted in full in Sasportas, *Sefer tsitsat novel tsevi*, 109).

[79] By 'the entire world' the writers intend the Jews of the diaspora, upon whom the messianic agitation may bring the gentiles' anger and retaliation.

[80] The writers' implied concern—a very reasonable one—is that people's disillusionment with the failure of these messianic hopes may lead them to abandon the Jewish messianic hope altogether, and to despair of Judaism.

[81] In Sasportas's text, this is followed by a few more sentences of flowery praise for the rabbis of Constantinople, which Baruch has chosen to omit. Sasportas also lists, after the date, the names of the signatories: Jacob Halevi, Moses Treves, Moses Zacuto, Joseph Valensi, Solomon Hai Saraval (Scholem, *Sabbatai Sevi*, 501). On Zacuto, see below, n. 200.

[82] The quotation is from Obad. 21. The stressed word *vehayetah* (corresponding to the

This is the answer they received from the rabbis of Constantinople:[83]

TO THOSE ENTHRONED UPON THE LOFTY SEATS OF THE LEARNED, and so forth:

The splendid design of Torah and testimony, holily indited by your pen,[84] has reached us. You enquire about the goat's hair that Rabbi Israel the Jerusalemite, son of the honourable Rabbi Abraham,[85] purchased here in Constantinople. Some of his relatives have disputed the matter, claiming he had been negligent, he had ignorantly purchased unacceptable merchandise, and he had wasted their money.

We have thoroughly investigated Rabbi Israel's transaction here in Constantinople. We find that, to the contrary, his merchandise is of the most excellent quality, acceptable the world over. Anyone who casts aspersions on it will be held accountable. Merchants with long experience in commerce judge that the ensuing profit will be great. It will be necessary, however, to wait for the great fair which, God willing, will take place in the coming year 5427 [1666/7]. The merchandise is bound then to fetch[86] a high price, with the gracious assistance of God the First and Ultimate Cause.

These matters have received our most diligent attention. We have established clearly and beyond any doubt that Master Israel is in the right. It is your responsibility, O 'priests',[87] to carry out properly what needs to be done. May the Lord establish harmony among the contending parties; may they take thought of their actions, and no longer entertain any suspicions. For Rabbi Israel's dependability is beyond all question.

In order that the truth be placed beyond doubt, we have written this and signed it—

English 'shall be') has the numerical value 426; it is therefore used to designate the year 5426. This method of dating documents, by quoting a significant biblical verse and stressing one or more words in it, was very common among Hebrew-writing Jews of the 17th century. We shall meet it again more than once.

83 On this letter, see Scholem, *Sabbatai Sevi*, 505–6.

84 In plain language: your letter.

85 'Rabbi Israel' is presumably symbolic of the Jewish people, which has 'bought' the new messiah and now wonders if it has made a mistake. I do not know why 'goat's hair' (*notsat ha'izim*) is used to represent Sabbatai Zevi. Can there be an allusion to the goatskins in which Rebecca dresses Jacob, so he will seem to be Esau (Gen. 27: 16)? If so, this will be an eerie foreshadowing of Sabbatai's apostasy.

86 *Tizkeh vetimakher*; the first of these two verbs does double duty, indicating through its numerical value that the 'great fair' will take place in the year 5427. The 'fair' is, of course, Sabbatai's glorious manifestation as messiah and ruler of the world.

87 Alluding to Mal. 2: 1.

In the week of the Torah portion 'I will give peace to the land,
and you shall lie down unafraid' [Lev. 26: 6], on the thirty-third
day of the counting of the Omer [23 May 1666],[88] here in
Constantinople.

All this is absolutely true, correct, authoritative, and binding.

[1] Yom Tov, son of the honourable Rabbi Hananiah ibn Yakar;

[2] Moses Sagis;[89]

[3] Moses Galante.

[4] Everything written above is true and authoritative, correct
and binding, good and right, as is the action taken by Rabbi Israel.
'The worthy are in great glory; the righteous man is upright in an
upright faith'—thus speaks the servant of my masters, Abraham
Yakhini my name.[90]

[5] Caleb, son of the honourable Rabbi Samuel of blessed
memory.

[6] Righteousness and truth have joined together in the case of
Rabbi Israel. His deeds are the Lord's deed; anyone who doubts
him is as though he had doubted God Himself—this is the
opinion of the insignificant Nissim, son of the honourable
Rabbi Hayim Egozi, who signs in the week of the Torah portion
'I made you walk with heads high' [Lev. 26: 11].

---

[88] The two dates seem inconsistent. The thirty-third day of the Omer—the fifty-day
period from the second day of Passover to the Shavuot festival—is 18 Iyar, which fell that year
on Sunday, 23 May. But the Torah portion 'Behukotai', which contains Lev. 26: 6 (and 26: 11,
quoted below), would have been the sabbath reading in the synagogue the day before, and the
week *ending* 22 May would have been considered the 'week' of that portion. We can hardly
suppose the fault is Baruch's, since Sasportas's text here is exactly the same. I see no way to
resolve the difficulty.

[89] Sasportas gives the name as 'Moses ibn Shanji'.

[90] Abraham Yakhini (1617–82) was a preacher in Constantinople, a devout and lifelong follower of Sabbatai Zevi. Sasportas (*Sefer tsitsat novel tsevi*, 110) accuses Yakhini of having composed this response on his own, and then forged the signatures of other rabbis who had not
seen it and would not have approved it if they had. Be this as it may, Yakhini and Nissim Egozi
are clearly the most enthusiastic partisans. Not content with just signing their names, as the
others do, they reiterate the letter's message with mini-homilies of their own. Yakhini's slogan—'The worthy are in great glory', etc.—is a Hebrew jingle, *shelemim berov tifarah, yashar
tsadik be'emunah yesharah*, in which the initial letters of the words spell 'Sabbatai Zevi'. (The
last three words suggest Hab. 2: 4, *tsadik be'emunato yibyeh*, 'the righteous shall live by his
faith', which became a watchword of the Sabbatian movement—not least because its initial
letters spell 'Zevi'.)

[11. THE MESSIAH IN CAPTIVITY]

The vizier gave the Jews permission to come speak with our Lord while he dwelt in the royal court. On the authority of the king and his nobles, and on pain of the most extreme penalties,[91] it was proclaimed that neither man nor woman might do any harm to anyone called by the name of Israelite. Surely the kindnesses of our God are not exhausted, nor do His mercies fail!—that He made the vizier so pleased with our Lord that he not only held back from harming him, but did such great good to all the people of Constantinople.

Obliged by royal command to go to the city of Candia[92] to battle, the vizier summoned the leaders of the Jewish community. 'I must go to war', he told them, 'and I am concerned that some calamity may follow upon the sheer numbers of people coming into town to see this Zevi. I should like, therefore, to send him to the castle of Gallipoli'—this being one of those strongly fortified places where it was the practice to keep great nobles in custody. The vizier personally escorted him from the city.

So our Lord dwelt in great honour in his 'tower of strength'.[93] God made the superintendent of the tower to be kindly disposed toward him, to such an extent that he became [Sabbatai's] servant. ('I am serving two kings', he used to remark.) Men, women, and children, of our people and of other peoples as well, came from all over the world to see him, talk with him, do obeisance to him, kiss his hands. His fame as messiah had spread everywhere. From every land, Italy excepted, Jews sent him their embassies.

When the Jewish communities in Poland became aware in what honour our Lord was held, they dispatched as emissaries five worthy rabbis, well-known pietists and ascetics: Rabbi Eliezer of Krotoschin, Master Mordecai the Mediator,[94] Master Jacob Naschauer, Master Isaiah the Reprover,[95] Master Judah of Kamenetz. He received them seated upon a carpet of silk and gold. He was dressed in a white robe, interwoven with gold, and a shawl

---

[91] Literally, 'to be torn to pieces, one's house reduced to rubble' (Dan. 3: 29).

[92] The capital, and largest and most important city, of the island of Crete; modern Iraklion. The Turks had been battling the Republic of Venice over Crete ever since 1644. In May 1666 the vizier Ahmed Köprülü departed to begin the campaign against Candia, as described here. The following winter and spring he spent strengthening the Turkish fleet, as mentioned in Joseph Halevi's second letter, translated below. The siege began in May 1667, and in September 1669 the city was at last taken. See Gökbilgin and Repp, s.v. 'Köprülü', 260.

[93] *Migdal oz*, from Prov. 18: 10: 'The name of the Lord is a tower of strength; the righteous runs into it and is raised up high.' The Sabbatians regularly applied this designation to the fortress of Gallipoli, thereby transforming it from Sabbatai's prison into his castle (Scholem, *Sabbatai Sevi*, 460).

[94] *Shtadlan*, a community official with the function of representing the Jews to the non-Jewish authorities. [95] See Scholem, *Sabbatai Zevi*, 600.

with the four ritual fringes. His 'cap of salvation' was on his head.[96] He wore another garment called '*manto* of *velluto*' ['mantle of velvet']—white, sable-trimmed, of great value.[97]

They had intended to remain standing while they spoke with him. But our Lord bade them be seated, and they obeyed. They saw his face shining like the face of Moses,[98] for he was then experiencing a great illumination. They gave him the letters sent by their communities, and told him all the ills that had befallen them. Thereupon our Lord lifted his eyes to heaven and prayed to God, and they heard his voice like a lion's roar. 'I will be with you', said he, 'and will save you from your troubles.'

He asked whether there was a prophet in their country; they said there was not. 'Yes there is,' he said to them, 'and his name is Master Nehemiah. Tell him he must present himself to me. You will find him in such-and-such a place.'

Thus it happened: they found him in the very place our Lord had told them. 'I know', Master Nehemiah said to them, 'that when you came into our Lord's presence you found him sitting on the floor, surrounded by many rabbis studying Torah with him. In his arm he held a small Torah scroll, and he had two other Torah scrolls in a chest. Before him you saw a box upon which lay two books, tractate *Ḥulin* [of the Talmud] and the Zohar. He had in front of him a large piece of glass which he used to cool off his intense heat.[99] For he is like a fiery angel, and his face shone with such intensity that you sat yourselves four cubits away from him. And he is the handsomest man in all the world.'

They admitted it had been precisely as [Master Nehemiah] described.

Before the emissaries left [Sabbatai], they asked whether the messianic woes[100] were indeed to take place. He answered: 'Be satisfied with what you have received.' They asked him when the redemption would come, and he refused to say. It is possible he himself does not know, for the day of God's vengeance is known to God and to none other.[101] But he did tell them he had

---

[96] The phrase *kova yeshuah* is from Isa. 59: 17, where *kova* means 'helmet' rather than 'cap'. Here perhaps the reference is to Sabbatai's distinctively Jewish headgear (regularly called *kova* in our sources), which he will later replace with a Muslim turban.

[97] Baruch uses four Italian words in this paragraph: *tappeto* ('carpet'), *manto* ('mantle'), *velluto* ('velvet'), *zibellino* ('sable').

[98] Referring to Exod. 34: 29–35, where Moses' face shines from his contact with God, so that Aaron and the rest of the Israelites can hardly approach him.

[99] Cf. below, n. 80 on the Najara Chronicle.

[100] The catastrophes that are to afflict the world immediately before the messiah's arrival.

[101] Isa. 63: 4, as expounded in BT *San. 99a*. Cf. Matt. 24: 36, Mark 13: 32: 'No one knows concerning that day and hour, not even the angels in heaven or even the Son, but only the Father.'

been crowned in the year 5408 [1647/8], not by an angel or a seraph or a messenger, but by God Himself.[102]

[12. WHAT HAPPENS TO DISSENTERS]

Two rabbis from Izmir, joined by five other persons, sent to Constantinople a letter slandering our Lord over the strange acts he had performed. The rabbis of Constantinople accordingly convened. They prepared a letter, signed by fifty-four rabbis,[103] in which the accusers found themselves excommunicated. The text of the letter, here quoted in full, will demonstrate that all those rabbis believed with perfect faith that our Lord was the true Redeemer.[104]

To the judges of the Diaspora, jurists of profoundly critical bent,[105] the worthy and honourable Rabbis Aaron Lapapa and Solomon Algazi:

We write to express our dismay over the letter you sent us, and to pronounce our judgment upon it. You have seen fit to believe the worst about an angel in human form—the form that is God's own image[106]— on account of certain acts that on the surface seem peculiar but in truth are marvellous. Incredibly, you seem hardly to consider that *he* might be the one to know the appropriate priorities.[107] We know perfectly well, moreover, that the events themselves have undergone such embellishment that there is more exaggeration than fact in the telling of them. We

---

[102] On Sabbatai's transforming experience in 1648, see above, Introduction, section III.

[103] The letter is actually signed by twelve rabbis, with an appendage, signed by forty-two prominent Jews of Constantinople, reinforcing the provisions of the rabbis' letter. Baruch chooses to regard all the signatories as 'rabbis'.

[104] Quoted also in Sasportas, *Sefer tsitsat novel tsevi*, 133–5. Sasportas's readings often differ slightly from Baruch's, but few of the variations affect the meaning. Naturally Sasportas dismisses the document as a Sabbatian forgery; Scholem agrees that at least a few of its signatures may not have been genuine (*Sabbatai Sevi*, 415–17).

[105] A slightly malicious play on the complimentary phrase *lanim be'umkah shel halakhah*, 'dwelling in the depths of the halakhah' (BT *Meg.* 7b, *San.* 44b), with a jab at the 'critical' (i.e. complaining) propensities of the two rabbis named. It will not be forgotten that Aaron Lapapa was Hayim Benveniste's competitor for the chief rabbinic position in Izmir, whom Benveniste had pushed aside the previous December with Sabbatai Zevi's support (above, Introduction, section V). The letter to Constantinople, which has not survived, was Lapapa's revenge.

[106] *Akh betselem*, a compressed allusion to Gen. 1: 27, Ps. 39: 7, and Mishnah *Pirkei avot* 3: 14. (The manuscript evidence overwhelmingly favours *akh* over Freimann's *af*, although final *kaf* and final *peh* are often difficult to tell apart.)

[107] That is, the messiah would be in the position to know which commandments might be set aside—temporarily? permanently?—in order to further the divine agenda to which only he is privy.

ourselves, God be thanked, do not lack the wit to distinguish essential facts from embellishments fabricated for their shock value.

This is not how men like you ought to behave! You bring the Torah into public disgrace, as people wonder how the exemplary rabbis of Israel could have brought themselves to concoct libellous accusations against such a holy angel, such a prince of the Torah as [Sabbatai]. Among the co-signers with you reverend gentlemen, moreover, are men whom we know to be utterly godless, lawless, brutal, mad for controversy, all but illiterate. You would have done well to emulate the pure-minded men of ancient Jerusalem, who never would sign any document without knowing their co-signatories.[108] They certainly would not have associated themselves with public nuisances like Abraham Canton, Mordecai Ezra, and Isaac Barbina,[109] nor would they have lent their prestige to such an assemblage. Our sages' maxim, that hatred will drive a man to act beneath his dignity,[110] seems to us admirably to suit this case.

We therefore, by decree of the angels and on the authority of the holy ones on high,[111] do excommunicate all the signers of that letter, with the exception of the two worthy rabbis [Lapapa and Algazi] specified at the beginning of this document. They shall be excommunicate, they shall be banned, they shall be under all the curses written in the book of the Torah, until such time as their ungodly hearts shall become submissive, and they reverently come to seek the Lord and David their king.[112]

Mountains of Israel! The opportunity is now yours to set right what these men have perverted. You must grant the lawless no more freedom to speak heresy.[113] For it is our solemn duty to pursue unto destruction those who, in their arrogance and contempt, speak abusively of the righteous.[114] If we do nothing, we shall ourselves be found sinners. What,

---

[108] BT *San.* 23*a*; cf. Mishnah *Git.* 9: 8.

[109] Sasportas gives the names as 'Abraham Boton, Mordecai ben Ezra, and Isaac bar Maimon'; cf. the textual note to p. 54, l. 6. Clearly these were prominent Jews in the Izmir community who opposed Sabbatai Zevi. Scholem remarks that their names 'are those of well-known and respected families' (*Sabbatai Sevi*, 416 n.).

[110] *Genesis Rabbah* 55: 8 (ed. Theodor-Albeck, 592–3), cf. BT *San.* 105*b*. The writers insinuate that Lapapa and Algazi are so driven by hatred and malice for Sabbatai, that they are prepared to lower themselves in ways they would otherwise never consider.

[111] Following Dan. 4: 14.

[112] Following Hos. 3: 5. By 'David their king' the writers mean the messiah Sabbatai, descendant of David.

[113] The language is drawn from Deut. 13: 6 and Jer. 28: 16, 29: 32. In all these passages the 'heretic' is punished by death.

[114] Following Ps. 31: 19, a favourite slogan of the Sabbatians. The 'righteous' in this passage is of course Sabbatai Zevi.

then, shall we say when God rises up? When He examines us, how shall we answer Him?

Surely you are endowed with God's wisdom to remove all obstacles, to keep divisions from spreading among the Jewish people. If because of their unfaithfulness these men cannot believe, then let them at least keep silent, and speak no more in their unbearable insolence.

'Happy is he who waits patiently' [Dan. 12: 12]. Yet we, thank God, shall make the ascent [to Jerusalem], and with our own eyes shall witness the Redeemer's advent and the building of our holy shrine![115]

Signed in Constantinople, in the week of the Torah portion 'Holy shall you be' [Lev. 19: 2], in the year of *saved*
[20–26 Nisan 5426 (25 April–1 May 1666)].
There shall be peace.[116]

[1] Yom Tov, son of the honourable Rabbi Hananiah ibn Yakar;

[2] Moses Benveniste;

[3] Isaac Elnekave;

[4] Abraham Yakhini;

[5] Moses Brudo;

[6] Caleb, son of the honourable Rabbi Solomon Teshuar;[117]

[7] David Anaf;

[8] Nissim Egozi;

[9] Moses ibn Jamil;

[10] Hayim Shoshan;

[11] Abraham Brudo;

[12] Eliezer Gershon.

---

[115] Former generations were obliged to 'wait patiently', as Daniel advises (cf. BT *San.* 97*b*). But this no longer applies to us, who have the messiah in our midst, and for whom it is only a matter of time before we are returned to the Holy Land.

[116] The Hebrew word *nosha*, 'saved' (from Deut. 33: 29, 'Who is like you, people saved by the Lord?'), has the numerical value 426. It therefore serves as an auspicious designation for the year 5426. The Torah portion 'Kedoshim', opening with the equally auspicious words 'Holy shall you be', was read on sabbath, 26 Nisan of that year. The closing sentence apparently alludes to Mic. 5: 4, and the messianic prophecy of which it is part.

[117] Texeira, perhaps? Sasportas gives the name as 'Caleb, son of the honourable Rabbi Samuel Qeshu'ah[?]'; we have met him, as 'Caleb, son of the honourable Rabbi Samuel', in the list of signatories in §10, above. (Yakhini, Egozi, and Yom Tov ibn Yakar also appear on the earlier list.)

Anyone who questions the action of this court, and its certification by the rabbis of the diaspora whose signatures are affixed above, is to be considered as though he were questioning God Himself. As the earthly court has agreed upon it, so has the Heavenly Court: the seventy-one-member Sanhedrin in the Palace of Merit, the Twelve Princes, the seven who are the King's inner circle.[118]

Let us now, who wear the crown of the divine faith and who tremble at God's word, arm ourselves to harass and to destroy those sinners who speak abusively of that Righteous One who is 'the foundation of the world'.[119] In their passion for the derogatory, they do not content themselves with vicious talk, but must turn their efforts towards spreading their malice in writing. Yet who could possibly raise his hand against God's messiah and remain guiltless?[120]

Shall they go on speaking heresy against the holy one of Israel, against that beloved Man—Adam, David, and messiah in one—created in the divine image?[121] Then we shall concentrate all our resources toward bringing them here in chains and destroying them utterly, as our rabbis[122] have directed us. Or shall they wholeheartedly repent their evil ways, and seek the Lord and David their king?[123] Then the rabbis may perhaps revoke their excommunication,[124] and stretch forth their arms to receive back the penitent.

May God Almighty show you mercy, and may we see the king's beauty with our own eyes.

---

[118] In the Zohar (ii. 251a), the 'Palace of Merit' is the fourth of the heavenly palaces, where 'all the world's judgments are decided: all the merits and all the sins, all the punishments and all the good rewards for those who keep the Torah'. The seven angels 'who are the King's inner circle' appear under a different designation in the midrash *Pirkei derabi eli'ezer*, ch. 4. They and the 'twelve' are mentioned together in the mystical text *Heikhalot zutarti* (Schäfer, *Synopse zur Hekhalot-Literatur*, no. 372; trans. in Halperin, *The Faces of the Chariot*, 391).

[119] Prov. 10: 25, normally applied to Yesod, the divine phallus of kabbalistic theosophy, which brings together God's masculine and feminine aspects. The Constantinople rabbis have already made Sabbatai Zevi 'an angel in human form'; here, as Yesod's earthly manifestation, he begins to take on qualities of divinity. In the next section, we shall see this apotheosis carried to grotesque lengths.   [120] Following 1 Sam. 26: 9.

[121] Mishnah *Pirkei avot* 3: 14. The writing of the word *adam* ('man') indicates it is intended as an abbreviation: *ADaM*, the kabbalistic acronym for 'Adam, David, Messiah', who all shared the same soul (see Scholem, *On the Mystical Shape of the Godhead*, 214). I have translated accordingly.

[122] That is, the Constantinople rabbis who had signed the earlier part of the document. See the textual note to p. 54, l. 29.   [123] Hos. 3: 5. 'David their king' is, as above, Sabbatai Zevi.

[124] Literally, 'the tongue of the sages brings healing' (Prov. 12: 18), understood as in BT *Eruv.* 64b, *Ned.* 22a.

To which, in the week of the Torah portion 'Justly shall you judge your neighbour' [Lev. 19: 19], with broken and contrite hearts, we affix our signatures.

[1] Jacob de Leon [2] Judah Hakohen [3] Joseph Kimhi
[4] Hayim d'Avila [5] Hayim Mevorakh[125] [6] Israel Pesach
[7] Joseph Volesir [8] Hayim Canarbon [9] Joseph Bon Roi
[10] Daniel Sid [11] Abraham Uzziel [12] Samuel Sid
[13] Sasson Bon Roi [14] Samuel Canarbon [15] Solomon Galimidi[126]
[16] Joseph Kohen [17] David Rosanes [18] Abraham Baruch
[19] Israel Ya'ish [21] Aaron Halevi [22] Eliezer Narvoni
[20] Philomomeno[?]
[23] Abraham Cavazon [24] Judah Rosanes [25] Menahem Brudo
[26] Hayim Kimhi [27] Isaac Baruch [28] Moses Rosanes
[29] Moses Alaton [30] Abraham Canarbon [31] Moses Kohen
[32] Abraham Jeshurun [33] Jacob Nuñes [34] Isaac de Leon
[35] Jehiel Alguades [36] Moses Aboab Soria [37] Hayim Halevi
[38] Elijah Hakohen[127] [39] Mordecai Caleb [40] Moses Jeshurun
[41] Judah Sharaf [42] David Samson

[13. WHAT HAPPENS TO DISSENTERS— CONTINUED]

While our Lord was in his 'tower of strength', the castle of Gallipoli, a Venetian named Moses ben Nahmias happened to be there and came to do homage. He told [Sabbatai] that many of the Jews in Venice were believers in his faith. Indeed, they had beaten one man severely for speaking ill [of Sabbatai], even though it had been the sabbath at the time.

In response to this, our Lord commanded the worthy Rabbi Samuel Primo[128] to compose a letter to the people of Venice. He did so, and gave

[125] Who, as Tishby points out, turns up some fifteen years later among Abraham Cardozo's disciples in Constantinople (*Sefer merivat kodesh*, in Freimann, *Inyanei shabetai tsevi*, 17 n. 2).

[126] Later to become Cardozo's patron (Halperin, *Abraham Miguel Cardozo*, index). For the possible Cardozan connections of Joseph Volesir [7] and Abraham Uzziel [11], see the textual note to p. 55, ll. 2–13.

[127] Cardozo's disciple in Izmir, ten years later? (See Halperin, *Abraham Miguel Cardozo*, index.) But if so, he must have been very young in 1666.

[128] One of the more intelligent and ruthless of Sabbatai's followers, who served in the movement's heyday as his personal secretary. Later, despite his extreme and unreconstructed Sabbatian views—that Sabbatai Zevi was divine and indeed the current Ruler of the Universe,

Master Moses the letter to be transmitted to the learned and venerable rabbis of Venice. The letter was written and signed by Rabbi Primo, and by our Lord's own pure hand.

And this is what the letter said:[129]

On the forty-first of the Torah's reckoning,[130] in the week of the Torah portion 'It flows with milk and honey, and this is its fruit'[131] [13–19 June 1666]—

At the 'tower of strength' that is the Lord's name, into which the Righteous runs and is raised up high[132]—

I heard 'hymns sung from the edges of the earth'[133] when this man—the honourable Rabbi Moses Nahmias of Venice—came here to tell his tale in the presence of the man set over all the ranks of heaven and earth, his heart meditating wisdom, the messiah of the God of Jacob.[134] This is our Lord, king of kings, 'God our righteousness',[135] Sabbatai Zevi—may his glory be exalted, may his eternal kingdom speedily be raised up.

This man [Nahmias] made bold proclamation of the strength of Venice's holy congregation: how they were fired with zeal to stamp out the iniquity and do away with the sinfulness of the man who spoke heresy against our righteous messiah, other than whom there is no [messiah]. They beat that man to death,[136] thereby giving no heed to the distinction between sacred and profane; for that day was the holy and venerable sabbath.

I now come to address those men—distinguished, virtuous in the eyes of God and of our Lord king—who have done this noble deed. Thus speaks our Lord king: *There is no finer sanctification of the sabbath than that which those men have performed.*

the God of traditional Judaism having 'withdrawn into His root above'—Primo would become a prominent, outwardly orthodox rabbi in Adrianople. He used his considerable power to persecute Cardozo, who detested him as a heretic. Primo's noxious letter to Venice, here quoted by Baruch, is entirely in character for him. He died in 1708. (Rubashov, 'The Messiah's Scribe' (Heb.); Halperin, *Abraham Miguel Cardozo*, 51–3, 90–4.)

[129] Sasportas evidently intended to include this document in his *Sefer tsitsat novel tsevi*, but the page containing it has for some reason disappeared. Tishby prints it in his edition of Sasportas (pp. 128–9), on the basis of the *Memorial*.

[130] I do not know what this means. See the textual note to p. 55, l. 20, for a full discussion.

[131] Num. 13: 27.   [132] Prov. 18: 10. The 'Righteous', needless to say, is Sabbatai Zevi.

[133] Following Isa. 24: 16, which represents the content of those 'hymns' as *tsevi latsadik*, 'Glory to the Righteous!' Sabbatai's followers took both 'Righteous' and *tsevi* as specific references to Sabbatai Zevi.   [134] Following 2 Sam. 23: 1.

[135] The name of the Davidic messiah, according to Jer. 23: 6, 33: 16.

[136] *Hiku oto nefesh*; contrary to the impression given by Baruch, that the 'sinner' was badly injured but survived.

Speedily and soon may he save you, and us as well! Rejoice and be glad in the Lord your God and in your righteous messiah, for this will come to pass very soon. Circulate this document as widely as you can; rejoice, and bring joy to others with you. Proclaim the good news of salvation and comfort everywhere the king's word and his faith can reach, and hold tight to the fortress of repentance. Help each other; exhort one another to stand firmly with God's Torah and the faith of our righteous messiah. Our Lord king will give wealth and honour and nobility to you all, and most especially to those righteous men who beat to death him who rebelled against the Lord of the world [Sabbatai].[137] *They kept the sabbath strictly and well, for our Lord king is himself the sabbath.*[138]

All these pronouncements were spoken by the king of the world [Sabbatai] himself. He spoke also messages of comfort which neither pen nor paper can contain. Let the fear of him be ever with you, his faith always before your eyes. Rejoice and be glad in your king and saviour, who redeems your souls and your bodies in heaven and on earth, who resurrects your dead, who rescues you from the pain of gentile oppression and from the judgments of hell. The tongue cannot utter this; the pen cannot convey even the smallest hint of it. For there is none who can grasp the greatness of THE ALMIGHTY ONE[139]—our Lord, our Redeemer, our Saviour in one.

Signing on king messiah's authority—praying you may live in tranquil security, that you may gaze upon the king in his beauty, that what you see may gladden your heart as you gaze upon the Lord's goodness and visit His Temple—

The lowliest and most submissive servant of the
messiah of the God of Israel,

The insignificant Samuel Primo.

Heartiest congratulations and good wishes to you, for you have done repentance—the essential act of faith—and I must give full reward to all of you who believe with perfect faith, men, women, and children alike.

---

[137] The following initials *yod-resh-heh* (*yarum hodo*, 'may his majesty be exalted'), found in all the manuscripts, show that the 'Lord of the world' is not God but Sabbatai Zevi.

[138] Compare, with appropriate distinctions, Matt. 12: 8, Mark 2: 28, Luke 6: 5. The name 'Sabbatai' is taken from 'sabbath'; in kabbalistic symbolism, both the sabbath and the Righteous One can be identified with the divine potentiality of Yesod (the divine phallus), and therefore with each other.

[139] Following Job 11: 7, but spelling out each letter of the divine name Shaddai ('the Almighty') such that the total numerical value becomes equal to that of 'Sabbatai Zevi'. (Cf. below, n. 171. This is a standard technique of kabbalistic exegesis.) The apotheosis of Sabbatai grows wilder and wilder.

From the Lord of Peace—
And from me, Israel your Father, the bridegroom coming
forth from his chamber, husband of the beloved and
precious Torah, the lovely and gracious Lady[140]—
The man raised on high, the Messiah of God,
the exalted Lion, the exalted Gazelle[141]—

Sabbatai Zevi.

[14. PRAYER FOR THE KING]

Those times witnessed a great penitential movement throughout all the provinces of the Turkish domain. Not only that: on sabbaths, and indeed on every day, a special prayer invoking God's blessing[142] was offered for our Lord in the synagogues. The entire congregation would stand as the cantor uttered his name. All this was known to the Turks. Yet they did not say a word, for the Lord's dread had fallen upon them.

This is the text of the prayer the people recited:

He who gives victory to kings and dominion to princes, whose own kingdom is everlasting—

The great, the mighty, the terrible God, King of kings of kings, the Blessed Holy One, the incomparable—

He who removes kings and establishes them, who covenanted with His servant David to establish his royal throne for ever—

May He bless and preserve, assist and exalt, raise to the loftiest heights our Lord and king the holy rabbi, the Righteous and Redeemed One,[143] SULTAN SABBATAI ZEVI, MESSIAH OF THE GOD OF JACOB! (May his glory be exalted and his kingdom uplifted!)

---

[140] A string of kabbalistic allusions identifying Sabbatai with Tiferet, the central masculine aspect of the deity. Sabbatai's description of himself as 'husband of the beloved and precious Torah' is presumably linked with his penchant for marrying himself to the Torah scroll, or otherwise treating it as a lover (Scholem, *Sabbatai Sevi*, 159–60, 400–1). What is striking about Sabbatai's postscript to Primo's letter, apart from its megalomania, is its apparent obliviousness to the event that had called forth the letter—the brutalization of the Venetian sceptic. Was Sabbatai even aware of what had happened?

[141] Aramaic *tavya*, corresponding to Hebrew *tsevi*, 'gazelle'.

[142] Literally, 'a *mi sheberakh*', the prayer offered on sabbaths on behalf of the congregation and its officers. The reference here is to the prayer immediately following the *mi sheberakh*, beginning 'He who gives victory to kings . . .', which invokes divine blessing and protection upon the secular authorities under whose rule the Jews live. The Turkish Jews' recitation of this prayer—not to mention their use of the title 'Sultan' for Sabbatai Zevi!—amounted to a declaration that Sabbatai and not Mehmed IV was now their legitimate ruler.

[143] *Tsadik venosha*; from the messianic prophecy of Zech. 9: 9.

To him is given dominion, glory, and royalty. All peoples, nations, and tongues shall obey him. His dominion is eternal and shall never pass away, nor shall his kingdom be destroyed. His horn shall rise in glory; the crown of his God is upon his head.[144] Kings shall stand up when they see him, princes prostrate themselves—for the sake of the Lord who is faithful, the Holy One of Israel who has chosen him.

May his name endure for ever! Let his name wax great before the sun![145] By him all nations shall bless themselves, and shall call him happy. Joyously shall we witness the building of our holy and glorious Temple, the sanctuary established by God's own hands. So may it be His will! And let us say: *Amen.*

[15. THE FAST ABOLISHED]

Afterwards our Lord decreed that the Ninth of Av be observed as a great festival, in every place to which his authority extended.[146]

When the decree reached Constantinople the people of the city, believers though they were, were in doubt whether to take such a grave step. So their rabbis poured out prayers and petitions before the Lord their God, begging Him to show them the path they must take and the thing they must do.

They all then assembled. They prepared two slips of paper, on one of which was written *FESTIVAL* and on the other *FAST*. They put them in a jar; they summoned a boy and told him to pick out one of them and hold his hand high. So he did—and out came *FESTIVAL*. Back went the slips of paper into the jar. Again the boy pulled one out—*FESTIVAL*. A third time they put the slips into the jar; out came *FESTIVAL*.

Some of those rabbis, in addition, propounded this as a question to be answered through a dream.[147] The answer their dreams gave was *FESTIVAL*. And thus it was that, in that year 5426, the Ninth of Av [10 August 1666] was celebrated [in Constantinople] as a festival.

From Salonica—that great centre of Jewish learning, home to about 60,000 Jews—they sent a courier to our Lord in the 'tower of strength'. The message was that they would not celebrate the day as a festival unless he performed some miraculous sign before the courier's eyes. 'This is the

---

[144] Quoting Ps. 112: 9 and Num. 6: 7.

[145] Ps. 72: 17, applied to the messiah in BT *San.* 98*b*.

[146] See the Introduction, section II.

[147] *She'elat ḥalom*, a method of divination going back to the Middle Ages. The questioner 'would purify himself before going to sleep, and then ask *she'elat ḥalom* ("a question asked of a dream"), believing that his question would be answered by the nature of the dream that he was about to have' (*Encyclopedia Judaica*, s.v. 'Visions', by Joseph Dan).

miraculous sign I shall give you,' said our Lord to the courier—'that without any miraculous sign at all, they shall celebrate a festival!'

And so it was. There, too,[148] they kept the day as a festival the like of which had never before been celebrated, with fine clothes and tasty foods and plenteous melodies. So the Jews did in Adrianople, Sofia, Izmir, and many other places. And they went to the synagogues to recite the prayers our Lord had ordained for them.

This is the decree our Lord sent to Sofia:[149]

Blessed and exalted be God's name for ever! Amen!

The day after my great sabbath,[150] which is that of my brethren and my people, dwellers of the city A-Tower-of-Strength-Is-the-Lord's-Name, and all who happen to be there—

Tuesday, twenty-fourth day of Tamuz the most eminent of months [27 July 1666], in the week of the Torah portion 'They set forth from Rithmah and camped in Rimmon-perez' [Num. 33: 19],[151] Day Eight of the Restoring to Life of my spirit and my light, which befell on the festival of the Seventeenth of Tamuz[152]—

O my brethren! my people! my faithful folk of Sofia—men, women, children alike—and of every province to which the king's decree and authority extend! Abundant peace to you from the Lord of Peace, and also from me, His only-begotten son king Solomon![153]

---

[148] That is, in Salonica as well as in Constantinople.

[149] Quoted also in Sasportas, *Sefer tsitsat novel tsevi*, 129–31.

[150] Mentioned also at the end of Joseph Halevi's first letter (translated below). Halevi complains that Sabbatai 'ordained that sabbath be observed on Monday instead of Saturday, starting out with Monday, 22 [23] Tamuz, which he called the "great sabbath"'. In his note to *Sefer tsitsat novel tsevi* (p. 76) Tishby plausibly suggests that 23 Tamuz was picked as 'great sabbath' because it was the seventh day of the week that began on the Seventeenth of Tamuz, the day of the restoration of Sabbatai's 'spirit and light' (below). See Scholem, *Sabbatai Sevi*, 613–33.

[151] On the significance of this verse for Sabbatai and his followers, cf. Halperin, *Abraham Miguel Cardozo*, 261.

[152] *Yom tov* is made to bear the double meaning of 'festival' and 'seventeenth day' (the numerical value of *tov* is 17). The 'festival' of the Seventeenth of Tamuz was a traditional fast-day, commemorating the breaching of the walls of Jerusalem by Nebuchadnezzar. Like the Ninth of Av, it is turned into a holiday to mark the coming of messianic times, in fulfilment of the prophecy of Zech. 8: 19. Sasportas, in a note on this passage, explains that Sabbatai 'said he received the holy spirit on 17 Tamuz', and that, by 'the restoring to life of my spirit', he meant he had been endowed with prophecy (*Sefer tsitsat novel tsevi*, 130). The Dönmeh continued for decades, if not centuries, to celebrate the day as 'the first day of Amirah's illumination, and the restoring to life of his spirit and light' (Benayahu, *The Sabbatian Movement in Greece* (Heb.), 288).

[153] Sasportas's text reads 'beloved son' for 'only-begotten son' (*yedido* for *yeḥido*). In calling himself 'King Solomon', Sabbatai alludes no doubt to the rabbinic midrash that explains 'King Solomon' in Song of Songs as 'the King to whom peace belongs'—namely, God. (See

I hereby decree that the above-mentioned date, namely the Ninth of Av,[154] is to be observed by you as a great feast and a great rejoicing. Celebrate it with fine foods, sweet drinks, a multitude of illuminations, a plenitude of music and song. For it is the birthday of Sabbatai Zevi your king, supreme over all the kings of the earth.

With respect to the prohibition on labour, and in all other respects, you shall observe it as a full holy day. With your finest clothing, and with holy-day liturgy, you shall observe it as a full holy day. You are entirely permitted, however, to bid a gentile perform even a labour forbidden on biblical authority,[155] and you are entirely exempted from the prohibition on instrumental music. And this shall be its prayer formula: *In Your love, O Lord our God, You have given us festivals for our joy, holy days and festive times for our delight: this Feast of Consolations, the nativity of our king and messiah Sabbatai Zevi, Your servant, Your first-born son — granted in love, a holy convocation, memorial to our redemption from Egypt.*[156]

Five people shall read the week's Torah portion out of a ritually proper Torah scroll, going as far as the words 'the slopes of Pisgah'.[157] The reading shall be accompanied by the blessings appropriate for a full holy day. The reading from the Prophets[158] shall be the passage beginning, 'Thus says the Lord: The people who survived the sword have found favour in the desert', and extending through the words 'I will remember their sin no more'.[159]

---

e.g. *Song of Songs Rabbah* 3: 19: *hamelekh shelomoh — hamelekh shehashalom shelo*. On the kabbalistic extensions of this interpretation, see Moses Cordovero, *Pardes rimonim*, 'Sha'ar erkhei hakinuyim', s.v. *melekh*; Daniel C. Matt's note to Zohar, i. *29a*, in *The Zohar: Pritzker Edition*, i. 170.) Here Sabbatai distinguishes himself from God his 'father' and, in the same sentence, identifies himself with Him.

[154] The reference to 'the above-mentioned date' is odd; the Ninth of Av has been mentioned in Baruch's narrative, but not in the decree itself. Sasportas's text has: 'the approaching Ninth of Av'.

[155] As opposed to those activities the Torah permits to be done on holy days, but which are forbidden by the ancient rabbis. The playing of musical instruments belongs in the latter category.

[156] A variant on the standard formula used as part of the Amidah prayer (see above, n. 64) on Jewish holidays; Birnbaum, *Daily Prayer Book*, 591–2. On Passover, for example, one would say: 'In Your love, O Lord our God, You have given us ... this Feast of Unleavened Bread, the time of our freedom ... memorial to our redemption from Egypt.' The 'Feast of Consolations' thus takes its place among the traditional festivals of the Jewish calendar.

[157] That is, from Deut. 3: 23 (the beginning of the Torah section that would have been read during the week of the Ninth of Av) to Deut. 4: 49.

[158] That follows the Torah reading on sabbaths and festivals.

[159] Jer. 31: 2–34—including, perhaps significantly, a prophecy of God's 'new covenant' with the Jewish people.

You shall pray the festival 'additional service' that takes the place of the additional sacrifice [in the ancient Temple]. As the Torah scroll is returned to its place [in the synagogue ark], recite the psalm 'You are the fairest of humankind' [Ps. 45], loudly and clearly and with sacred melody. Insert among the hymns, between 'He who sits under the Most High's protection' [Ps. 91] and 'Sing to the Lord a new song' [Ps. 96], the 132nd psalm, 'Remember on David's behalf, Lord, all his suffering' through 'his crown shall shine upon him' [Ps. 132: 1–18], and the psalm that begins, 'When the Lord restored Zion's captivity' [Ps. 126]. Recite also the full complement of festival psalms [Pss. 113–18], with full benediction.

On the eve of the festival, you shall declare it holy as you would any festival, reciting the blessing, [*Blessed are You, O Lord our God, king of the universe*], *who has kept us alive* [*and has sustained us, and has permitted us to see this day*]. The formula of sanctification shall be the same as the prayer formula: *You have given us . . . this Feast of Consolations, this festal day, this holy convocation, the nativity of our king and messiah Sabbatai Zevi, Your servant, Your first-born son.* The evening service shall begin with Psalm 89, 'Maskil of Ethan the Ezrahite' through 'a faithful witness in the sky, *selah*' [Ps. 89: 1–38]. This same psalm shall be inserted also among the hymns, between 'Remember on David's behalf' [Ps. 132] and 'When the Lord restored Zion's captivity' [Ps. 126].

This day shall be a memorial for you, a great festival for all eternity; it is an eternal sign between me and the Jewish people.[160] Obey me,[161] and you shall eat what is good and enjoy what is succulent. Give ear and come to me. Listen—and your spirit shall be restored to life. And I will make with you an eternal covenant: the gracious deeds of David, which may be relied upon.

So speaks David, son of Jesse,
who strikes terror into the kings of the earth[162]—
The man raised up over all blessing and hymn,
messiah of the God of Jacob,
exalted Lion and exalted Gazelle—

Sabbatai Zevi.

[160] Following Exod. 31: 17, where God speaks these words of the sabbath. Sabbatai's use of the verse is one more indication he has identified himself with God.

[161] Following Deut. 11: 13, a verse that would have been familiar to most Jews through its liturgical use as part of the Shema. Here again God is the speaker.

[162] Said of God, in Ps. 76: 13. The irony of this boast, in light of the sequel, will not be missed.

[16. SABBATAI BEFORE THE SULTAN]

In the month of Elul 5426 [1–29 September 1666], the Turkish king dispatched an officer with his troop to the fortress [Gallipoli] to summon our Lord to appear before him. At every town along the route where there were Jews living, [Sabbatai] would ask the officer to 'wait for me, for I desire to pray in this synagogue'. The officer would stand by the door guarding him.

When the Muslims and Christians[163] of Adrianople heard the king had summoned our Lord, they assumed his head was about to be cut off and all the Jews to be murdered, it having become common knowledge that the king had sentenced the city's Jews to death.[164] They sent emissaries to Constantinople to do that same dreadful deed there. They sharpened their swords and awaited [Sabbatai's] arrival, all ready to work their will upon the Jews.

Our Lord, however, did not arrive until two days after they had expected him. He arrived in the evening, too late to receive an audience. The next morning he stood before the king. 'Peace be upon you', he said; and he received the answer 'Upon you be peace', in the Turkish language.[165]

A certain eunuch, one of the king's intimates, stepped forward carrying a robe the king had worn. Another eunuch held the king's turban. With these garments they clothed [Sabbatai], calling him by the king's own name Mehmed.[166] The king decreed a large sum for his daily allowance.

Thus it was that the rumour spread he had changed his faith and become a Muslim. The city remained quiet; the Jews were saved. Our Lord asked the king to revoke the murderous orders decreeing the extermination of the Jews in Constantinople. This the king granted without hesitation. The couriers set forth urgently at the king's command; [the prior orders] were cancelled; not a single Jew came to harm on this account.[167]

By no means are the Lord's kindnesses a thing of the past! He who performed for His people so great and notable a miracle as this, cannot have ceased to show them mercy.

[163] Literally, 'the Turks and the uncircumcised'.

[164] Three manuscripts—the two representing the 'second edition', and the eclectic Cambridge manuscript—read: 'the king having sentenced the city's Jews to death, as became known afterwards'. The 'first edition' reading makes better sense in context; if it only 'became known afterwards' that the sultan had sentenced the Jews to death, why were the Muslims and Christians already sharpening their swords?

[165] It is not clear whether Baruch represents both Sabbatai and the sultan as speaking Turkish, or only the sultan.

[166] Baruch thus transforms Sabbatai's apostasy into something quite different: his investiture as deputy or successor to the sultan (Halperin, 'Sabbatai Zevi, Metatron, and Mehmed'). As we go on we will see other, seemingly contradictory, efforts to make sense of the apostasy.

[167] Contrast the account of the near-pogrom in Joseph Halevi's first letter, translated below.

[17. NATHAN'S JOURNEYS BEGIN]

When word reached Rabbi Nathan at Gaza—him whom our Lord had called 'Benjamin'[168]—that [Sabbatai] had set the pure turban upon his head, he knew for certain that our Lord had handed himself over to the demonic[169] in order to extract from it the sparks of holiness. Abraham had done the same when he married Hagar the Egyptian. So had Jacob, when he married Laban's daughters. So had Moses, when he married the daughter of Jethro the 'Kenite', the 'nest', that is, of impurity.[170] And thus it had been incumbent upon [Sabbatai] to do, in order to mend the world through the dominion of SHIN–DALET–YOD.[171]

So [Nathan] departed from Gaza, accompanied by more than twenty rabbis from the Land of Israel—stalwart, God-fearing men—to go see our Lord.

As he passed the town of Safed (God soon restore it!), there came to greet him and do him obeisance the holy saint, the divine kabbalist, the most aged and reverend Rabbi Benjamin Halevi, together with his son Rabbi Solomon.[172] They conferred with him at some length. Afterwards they wrote as follows to the principal men of the Norzi and Sullam families in Mantua:

---

[168] On Nathan's new name, see Scholem, *Sabbatai Sevi*, 364.

[169] Literally, 'shell', a kabbalistic term for the realm of the demonic. See the discussion of the fallen sparks in the Introduction, section IX.

[170] Baruch calls Moses' father-in-law Jethro 'the Kenite', on the basis of Judg. 1: 16 and 4: 11, and derives this word from *ken*, 'nest'. His further interpretation of this 'nest' as that of 'impurity' (i.e. the demonic) is drawn from Zohar, i. 54*a*—which applies it to Cain—combined with i. 28*b*. Baruch presumably has the interpretation via kabbalistic or kabbalistically influenced writers such as Moses Cordovero (1522–70) and Isaiah Horowitz (1565–1630), who use, as the Zohar does not, Baruch's phrase *kina demasavuta*. See Cordovero's comments on the zoharic passage in Abraham Azulai, *Or haḥamah*, i. 48*c* (top), and Cordovero's *Sefer pardes rimonim*, i. 70*b*, which foreshadows the Sabbatian belief that the divine must descend into the impure realm of the gentiles in order to redeem the 'sparks' there imprisoned. Cf. also Horowitz, *Shenei luḥot haberit*, *Toledot adam*, 'Beit yisra'el', iii. 17; ibid. 'Beit david', 27.

[171] Spelling out Shaddai, 'the Almighty', so that the numerical value of the names of its three letters is equivalent to that of 'Sabbatai Zevi'. Cf. above, n. 139.

[172] Safed had been, in the previous century, a major centre of kabbalistic learning and innovation. Benjamin Halevi of Safed was one of the most highly regarded and influential kabbalists of his time, in part through his disciple Moses Zacuto (below, n. 200). He visited Mantua in 1659, where he worked closely with the prominent Norzi and Sullam families; apparently he maintained ties with them for years. On him and his son Solomon, see Yaari, *Mystery of a Book* (Heb.), 51–75; Scholem, *Sabbatai Sevi*, 369–70, 478–9.

Safed, thirty-third day of the counting of the Omer,[173]
5427 [12 May 1667]

We have already written at length about our redemption at the hands of
our King Sabbatai Zevi. Your Worships therefore must remain true to
this faith, whatever you may hear to the contrary. Exalted mysteries,
which cannot be put in writing, are involved in the matter. Suffice it to say
that I spoke with Master Nathan the prophet, and he demonstrated it to
me as clear as sunlight. To one who wishes to hear (as the proverb says) a
few words are enough.

Benjamin and Solomon Halevi

As Master Nathan drew near Adrianople and the people of the city
became aware of his approach, they recalled what had happened to them
when our Lord came there: they had nearly been massacred. They consequently dispatched four or five rabbis to meet him and tell him they did not
want him coming there, that his presence was too dangerous. They, and the
rabbis of Ipsola, excommunicated him and forced him to depart. So he went
with Rabbi Samuel Gandoor to the land of Morea,[174] travelling at the direction of his spirit-guide[175] from one town to the next, from one place to the
next.

In the year 5428 [1667/8], he travelled from the province of Ioannina[176]
to Corfu, and remained there a few days. While he was there he received a
letter from Rabbi Joseph Zevi, who dwelt in the town of Zante. He
responded as follows:

[18. NATHAN'S EPISTLE TO JOSEPH ZEVI][177]

To that gentleman of high degree, offspring of noble
family—all enwrapped in praise is he—the honourable
Rabbi Joseph Zevi:

---

[173] The fifty-day period from the second day of Passover to the Shavuot festival.

[174] The Peloponnese, the southern peninsula of Greece. On Gandoor, and his travels with
Nathan, see §19 below, and Scholem, *Sabbatai Sevi*, 213–14, 718–48, 770–81.

[175] *Magid*: a supernatural entity—perhaps an angel, perhaps the spirit of a departed saint—
that attaches itself to an individual and serves as his mentor, guide, and revealer of secrets. The
phenomenon is discussed in Werblowsky, *Joseph Karo: Lawyer and Mystic*, esp. 76–83. Cf. the
magidim of Abraham Cardozo (Halperin, *Abraham Miguel Cardozo*, index s.v. 'Spirit-guide')
and the *magid* of Joseph ibn Tsur, below.

[176] A district of north-western Greece, directly across from the island of Corfu (Kérkira).

[177] Quoted, with minor variations, in Sasportas, *Sefer tsitsat novel tsevi*, 260–2. Sasportas
claims to have acquired the text at second hand, from an unbeliever who tricked Nathan into
loaning him a copy, and then prepared his own copy for the benefit of the anti-Sabbatian

(After the formal greetings:[178]) I have received your letter, and from it I understand how passionately you yearn to know about the Lord [Sabbatai], whom we seek and expect each and every day, each and every hour, each and every minute. He is the great sabbath; he is the holy sabbath; from him spring the supernal wisdom and holiness. He is the Power of the Supernal Crown, which designation corresponds to his name and his surname.[179]

You may rest assured—this one thing will I swear by His holiness, by the great and holy power of the Cause of all causes: that he is the messiah, and none other, and beside him Israel has no Redeemer. Though indeed he has set the pure turban on his head, his holiness is not thereby profaned. God, who will not lie, has sworn to this by His right hand. This is one of God's own secrets, and no one versed in the mysteries of the Torah will find cause for astonishment therein.

On the surface, to be sure, I can find nothing of this hinted in the Torah. Yet we have seen, among the words of our ancient rabbis, remarks on these subjects so astonishing that the full intent of even a single utterance is beyond our ability to fathom.[180] The great luminary Maimonides has testified, similarly, that not until the event itself will these [messianic] utterances be understood.[181] Nevertheless, anyone with eyes, ears, and a brain should be able to find [in what has already transpired] evidence for the truth of these utterances—at least to the extent of restraining himself from speaking falsehoods against the holiness of the sabbath [Sabbatai Zevi]. For there can be no doubt that anyone who speaks out against him is possessor of a soul inherited from the 'mixed rabble'.[182]

camp. Scholem, *Sabbatai Sevi*, 741–7, argues that the letter's recipient was not Sabbatai Zevi's brother Joseph (as both Baruch and Sasportas seem to have believed), but a Sabbatian kabbalist named Joseph Hamiz.

[178] Given in full in Nathan's original letter, but omitted by the copyists as being of no general interest. For an example of what these 'formal greetings' might have been like, see Joseph Halevi's first letter to Sasportas, below.

[179] 'Supernal Crown' (*keter elyon*) is a standard designation for Keter, the highest of the kabbalistic system of divine potentialities. The phrase 'Power of the Supernal Crown' has the same numerical value as 'Sabbatai Zevi'. Cf. Liebes, 'Sabbatianism and the Bounds of Religion' (Heb.), 9–10.

[180] Presumably referring to the passages from *Ra'aya mehemna* and *Tikunei zohar* that Nathan proceeds to quote. Although these texts are now supposed the work of an anonymous kabbalist about the year 1300 (see below), Nathan will have regarded them as rabbinic in origin.

[181] Maimonides, *Mishneh torah*, 'Hilkhot melakhim', 12: 2: 'no one will know how these [messianic] events are to transpire, until they do transpire'.

[182] On the *erev rav*, the 'mixed rabble', see above, n. 24. This 'rabble', according to rabbinic tradition, accompanied the true Israelites out of Egypt and were responsible for their sins in

We find convincing evidence for this in the matters revealed by the holy Faithful Shepherd [Moses], on the Torah portion 'Naso'.[183] Anyone who has studied this book [*Ra'aya mehemna*] is familiar with the claims Moses makes on behalf of the True Redeemer, which he formulates as though he were speaking of himself—since, in fact, he and the Redeemer are one and the same. And thus does [Moses] speak of being 'profaned for the sins of the people[184] . . . I suffer terribly. . . . Of me Scripture says, "[God] placed his grave with the wicked" [Isa. 53: 9]. They are quite unaware of me; among the iniquitous "mixed rabble" I am considered as a dead dog, stinking among them.'

This passage is, as is well known, a revelation of events to come. We can hardly interpret it to mean that it is on account of the torments he must suffer that the speaker will be considered 'like a stinking dog'—for is it at all conceivable that the great men among us could regard a righteous man in torment as the equivalent of a stinking dog? We may well wonder, moreover, why those people who do not know the speaker are on that account called 'wicked'. Yet this will cause no astonishment once we grasp why they are called 'mixed rabble'. Surely, one might think, the designation 'mixed rabble' is relevant only to the time of Moses.[185] How is it that these people, more than any other Jews [of the present time], are linked to that ancient 'rabble'?

The reason, beyond any doubt, is that they have inherited an evil soul, plentifully imbued with the Serpent's filth. At the present time, to be sure, they are righteous. They are nonetheless designated 'wicked', just like those souls that are designated 'wicked' in the next world. They themselves have indeed not sinned. Yet in accord with the measure of bitterness and filth with which their souls are infected, and which they have left unmended, they are brought to speak falsehood and error—unwilling, for all the clear evidence already available, even to suspend judgment

the wilderness, including the worship of the Golden Calf. According to the kabbalists, they are the originators of the souls of the ungodly Jews of the present time.

[183] The reference is to the pseudepigraphic composition *Ra'aya mehemna* (Faithful Shepherd) written about the year 1300 in apparent imitation of the Zohar, and printed in standard editions of the Zohar. The 'faithful shepherd' of the title is Moses, who is the chief speaker in the text; Nathan assumes the authenticity of this attribution. In the passage quoted (Zohar, iii. 125b–126a), 'Moses' applies to himself Isaiah's famous prophecy (ch. 53) of the 'suffering servant'. Nathan understands Moses as a 'type' of the true messiah, Sabbatai Zevi, and supposes that Moses therefore speaks of Sabbatai's sufferings as though they were his own.

[184] Alluding to Isa. 53: 5, 'He was profaned for our sins'—the standard Sabbatian prooftext for the messiah's 'profanation' in Islam. Cf. the very similar argument in Abraham Cardozo's *Epistle to the Judges of Izmir*: Halperin, *Abraham Miguel Cardozo*, 121–30, 138–44.

[185] When the 'mixed rabble' accompanied the Israelites out of Egypt (Exod. 12: 28).

until they see how matters turn out. The rich and the miserly, not coincidentally, are the ones who hold this opinion.[186]

There can be no doubt about what the Faithful Shepherd has
revealed: [the messiah] *is destined to perform strange deeds, on account of
which he will be considered as though he were a dead dog.* This is what we see
happening today, among certain people who have chosen no longer to
trust in the Lord.

Yet another clear proof may be found in the sixtieth of the *Tikunei
zohar*,[187] which speaks of 'one who is good on the inside, yet *his garment is
evil*; this is the one whom Scripture calls "poor, riding on an ass" [Zech. 9:
9]'.[188] There is no need to take this passage in any but its most literal
sense. When the text says 'his garment is evil', it means just that. [The
messiah] is to wear 'evil clothing', namely the turban he has put on.

That is why the Bible calls him 'poor, riding on an ass'. There would
surely be no need for Scripture to call him 'poor' in the sense of lacking
money. Is his purpose, after all, to enrich the world? The meaning,
rather, must be this: *On account of the 'evil clothing'* [the messiah] *will be
compelled to wear, he will be in a state of 'poverty' in the sense of lacking Torah,
'poverty' in the sense of not performing the commandments.* (Wherever the
word 'poor' occurs in the Bible, this is its meaning.)

Nor is it possible to say that 'his garment' is a [metaphorical] reference to the body.[189] Careful scrutiny of the text's language will reveal
that, up to this point, when it has meant to speak of a person's body it has
said 'his body'. Why—if not in accord with the interpretation we have
just given—should it now shift its terminology to talk of 'his garment'?

When the text [of *Tikunei zohar*] goes on to say, 'There is one who is
evil on the inside, yet his garment is beautiful', you may see its application
among those people who dress in Jewish clothing, which is indeed beautiful—yet they are filled with foulness. The relevance of the phrase 'his

---

[186] The anti-Sabbatian community leaders, of whom Nathan understands the *Ra'aya
mehemna* to prophesy, are considered 'wicked' even though in their present life they are not
notoriously sinful. The souls incarnated within them have sinned in past lives—as in Moses'
time—and they have not undertaken their souls' mending. This explains, as Nathan goes on
to say, why these people oppose the messiah.

[187] A series of interpretations of the beginning of Genesis, written (like the *Ra'aya mehemna*)
in imitation of the Zohar, yet, unlike the former, printed as a distinct work. *Ra'aya mehemna*
and *Tikunei zohar* are normally supposed to have the same author (see Giller, *The Enlightened
Will Shine*, 1–6). It is hardly surprising they share the doctrine, so important to Nathan, of the
suffering and rejected redeemer.

[188] The biblical verse Zech. 9: 9 plainly refers to the messiah, and was so interpreted by the
talmudic rabbis.   [189] Since, after all, the body is a 'garment' for the soul.

garment is evil' to the issue under discussion [that is, Sabbatai Zevi's donning Muslim garb] is consequently beyond dispute.

Tikunei zohar elsewhere states, along the same lines: 'In him was to be fulfilled the scriptural verse, "He was profaned for our sins" [Isa. 53: 5] — he was made, on their account, [from one who was holy] into one who is profane.'[190] Anyone with any intelligence will realize that 'profane' must refer specifically to someone who has left the Jewish people. For the Bible repeatedly calls the Jewish people 'holy', in expressions like 'a holy nation' [Exod. 19: 6], 'holy shall you be' [Lev. 19: 2], and many others of this kind.

Again in the same vein, the author of *Sefer torat ḥakham* ['A Scholar's Torah'], on the Torah portion 'Noaḥ',[191] quotes the Zohar's testimony that 'he [the messiah = Moses] is destined to be made profane among the gentiles'.[192] The expression 'made profane' points inescapably to a person who *renders himself profane*, who *mingles himself* with the gentiles, who *gives up* what he once was *in exchange* for becoming something else. (For *profaning* is in fact a term denoting *exchange*. Hence the usage, 'The second tithe may not be *profaned* [in *exchange* for an unmarked coin].'[193])

---

[190] Nathan quotes the twenty-first *tikun* of the *Tikunei zohar*. The context of the passage, omitted by Nathan, is important for his argument. Moses, we are told, begged God 'erase me from Your book' to atone for his sinful people (Exod. 32: 32). 'That was why the Faithful Shepherd was destined to be present in the final exile, where the Scripture, "He was profaned for our sins" . . . was to be fulfilled in him.' (Cf. the very similar passage in *Ra'aya meḥemna*, Zohar, iii. 280*a*). This prophecy of Moses' 'second coming' during 'the final exile' is, Nathan argues, fulfilled in the person of Sabbatai Zevi.   [191] Gen. 6: 9–11: 32.

[192] *Sefer torat ḥakham* is a collection of sermons on the Pentateuch, published in 1654 by Hayim Hakohen of Aleppo, a disciple of the great Safed kabbalist Hayim Vital. In the course of an extended argument that Isaiah 53's prophecy of God's 'suffering servant' refers to the messiah, Hayim Hakohen twice quotes—or, rather, slightly misquotes—a passage from *Ra'aya meḥemna* that applies Isa. 53: 5 to Moses, and suggests that Moses was 'made profane' in order to atone for the sins of Jeroboam (*Sefer torat ḥakham*, 18*a* and 18*b*, quoting Zohar, iii. 276*b*, cf. 277*b*). Hakohen thus lays the foundation for Nathan's argument that (1) Isaiah 53 refers to the future atoning sufferings of Moses, and (2) that this 'Moses' is to be equated with the messiah. (The parallel with the Christian interpretation of Isaiah 53, as a prophecy of the atoning suffering of Jesus, is self-evident. Cf. Scholem, *Sabbatai Sevi*, 54–5.)

[193] Mishnah *MS* 1: 2. Nathan's argument may be laid out as follows. When the Mishnah speaks of *profaning* the 'second tithe' of Deut. 14: 22–7—that is to say, removing it from the realm of the sacred and making it accessible to profane use—it takes for granted that this 'profanation' will take place by an act of *exchange*. (The tithe is *profaned* by *exchanging* it for legitimate coinage. The Mishnah prohibits the use of unmarked coins for this purpose.) When, therefore, *Ra'aya meḥemna* (following Isa. 53: 5) predicts the *profanation* of Moses/messiah, it means that he will *exchange himself* for something other than what he had been. It prophesies, in other words, that Sabbatai Zevi will *exchange* his Jewish self for his Muslim self.

Rabbi Simeon ben Yohai reveals the very same thing, in the Zohar on the Torah portion 'Bereshit':[194] that 'Moses was transformed, among the "mixed rabble", into "an object of horror and contempt" [Deut. 28: 37].'[195] Recall that Rabbi Isaac Luria has revealed the First Redeemer [Moses] and the Final Redeemer [the messiah] to be one and the same, for their souls were carved from the same source;[196] recall also that [the same passage from Zohar *Bereshit*] says it is in the 'final exile' that [Moses] will become 'an object of horror and contempt'. *Does it not then become quite certain that this 'horror and contempt' derive from his having taken on the turban?* A righteous person could not otherwise become 'an object of horror and contempt', even to the most depraved among Jews.

And [Rabbi Simeon ben Yohai] also says: 'I adjure you . . . that you reveal him [the messiah = Moses] before the rabbinic scholars . . . that he be profaned no more.'[197]

It is plain what conclusion we are to draw. Our 'sabbath' [Sabbatai Zevi] is in no way profaned through his wearing of the turban. He acted as our ancient rabbis declared he must, compelled to this by the sins of the Jewish people. His fate is just like Queen Esther's. She ate forbidden foods. Yet righteous Mordecai declared it was not in vain that Ahasuerus took her to his bed, for it was through her that redemption came.

Thus it shall be now, God willing. Our enemies shall see and be ashamed; those who scheme against us shall know humiliation. But those

---

[194] Gen. 1: 1–6: 8.

[195] Zohar, i. 28*b*, slightly misquoted (and, I think, misinterpreted). Simeon ben Yohai, a 2nd-century rabbi, was long assumed to be the principal author of the Zohar.

[196] Isaac Luria (1534–72) was the greatest of the Safed kabbalists. I do not know which, if any, specific passage in the voluminous Lurianic writings Nathan has in mind. The equation of the 'First' and the 'Final Redeemer', drawn from midrashic passages like those Baruch quotes in §1 (above), had become a commonplace by Nathan's time. See e.g. Isaiah Horowitz's *Shenei luḥot haberit*, 'Va'etḥanan', *Torah or*, ch. 3 (v. 102–4 in the Jerusalem 1993 edn), quoting an extended passage which Horowitz attributes to 'the kabbalist Rabbi Hayim [Vital], the outstanding student of Rabbi Isaac Luria'. Here the themes of the 'mixed rabble', Moses' degradation and humiliation, his return in subsequent incarnations, and the messianic interpretation of the fifty-third chapter of Isaiah—'this is Moses, who is also the messiah'—are combined in ways very suggestive of Nathan's epistle. Cf. also Halperin, *Abraham Miguel Cardozo*, 152–3.

[197] An elliptical quotation from *Ra'aya mehemna*, Zohar iii. 282*b*: Rabbi Simeon ben Yohai adjures the prophet Elijah to 'reveal him [Moses] before the leaders of the rabbinic scholars. Let them become aware of who he is; let him be profaned no more. For Scripture says of him, "He was profaned for our sins" [Isa. 53: 5].' Moses, as throughout this epistle, is a 'type' of the messiah Sabbatai Zevi, who has undergone the 'profanation' of Islam on behalf of the sins of the Jewish people. The Jewish religious leaders ('rabbinic scholars') have yet to become aware of his messiahship.

who look expectantly to him [the messiah] shall taste supreme delight. Higher and higher shall he lift their souls, just as Moses our Master lifted up the souls of those who followed him in the wilderness.

The reasons for all this must not be revealed, far less written, other than to expert kabbalists. All will soon be revealed, God willing. This is, God willing, a prophecy not for the remote but for the immediate future. Blessed is the one who waits patiently! He shall be the one to arrive.

O my brothers! All my brothers, my companions, faithful ones of Israel who contemplate these matters in eager and fearful expectation! I call upon you to remain strong and take heart. Do not let yourselves become cowed or intimidated. Return to the Lord your God with all your heart and soul, and give thanks to His great name. For without any doubt we are about to see what our fathers never saw, nor their fathers before them.

Some may say I am offering nothing but empty consolation, since I do not presently have the power to demonstrate this through any miracle. No matter. I shall not cease to comfort those sorrowing souls whom this affair has set all a-tremble, and who, in their yearning for God's nearness, turn to me for the truth. For my sake and for theirs shall the Lord be glorified—yes, and for the sake of all the poor and humble Jewish folk, oppressed and persecuted for God's holy name, and for the sake of His Torah as well. Speedily and soon shall we witness this joy!

> Corfu, 25 Shevat 5428 [7 February 1668],
> Nathan Benjamin.

[19. NATHAN IN VENICE]

From Corfu, [Nathan] travelled by sea to Venice. He arrived at the quarantine hospital[198] there shortly before Passover.

As soon as they heard he had arrived, the leading rabbis of Venice imposed a sentence of excommunication upon any man or woman who should show him hospitality, or even talk with him. The worthy Rabbi Samuel Aboab[199] subsequently paid him a visit. 'Why have you come?' he said to him. 'I need to make one thing clear to you: you are not setting foot in this city. If you do, you will cause a disaster.'

---

[198] Baruch uses the Italian word *lazzaretto*, referring to the building on the isle of Lazzaretto Nuovo, in the Venetian lagoon, where sea travellers suspected of being infected with the bubonic plague were temporarily confined (Panzac, *Quarantines et Lazarets*, 198–9).

[199] 1610–94; chief rabbi in Venice, a strong opponent of Sabbatianism. (Yet we have seen him, a decade or so later, on reasonably good terms with the Sabbatian Meir Rofé: Introduction, section VII).

'And there is one thing', Rabbi Nathan retorted, 'that I must make absolutely and thoroughly clear to *you*. I am travelling towards a certain place, at God's command, in order to benefit the entire Jewish community. I am not going to suffer any harm, nor will you, nor will any Jew whatsoever. If you do not want me in your town, I will not trouble myself about you.'

The day before Passover [26 March 1668] he received another visitor, quite otherwise minded. This was Rabbi Moses Zacuto—accomplished scholar, divine kabbalist, truly faithful soul.[200] They spent a long time in conversation. As [Zacuto] left, he remarked to the effect that 'I have read the Zohar for the past thirty-eight years, but I do not understand it as that rabbi does.'[201]

Two highly placed gentile officials happened to chance upon that rabbi [Nathan]. Radiant with wisdom, he made the most favourable impression upon them. They brought him to their home in Venice, where he was nobly entertained for two days and one night. They then conveyed him to the Jews, who, at these potentates' demand, were compelled to receive him against their will.[202]

On Monday, the nineteenth day of the Omer [15 April 1668],[203] they forced him to issue a confession that all he had professed was without substance. His confession, craftily worded, ran as follows:

Inasmuch as the noble rabbis of Venice have instructed me, to wit—

That, although I have asserted I saw the divine chariot[204] just as Ezekiel the prophet saw it, and the accompanying prophetic message declared Sabbatai Zevi to be the messiah,

[200] Zacuto (1620–97) was a very prominent and influential Venetian kabbalist, and also a reasonably talented poet whose works show the influence of Dante. Baruch's portrayal of him, as open-minded and mildly sympathetic, is grounded in reality. Zacuto was initially favourable to Sabbatai's messianic claims, and, even after rejecting them, never lost respect for Nathan's kabbalistic learning and creativity. See Benayahu, *The Sabbatian Movement in Greece* (Heb.), 122–32; Scholem, 'Rabbi Moses Zacuto's Attitude to Sabbatianism'. Cardozo claims to have studied with both Aboab and Zacuto in the late 1640s (Halperin, *Abraham Miguel Cardozo*, 111).   [201] Was this a compliment? Baruch plainly thinks so.

[202] Why should the non-Jewish authorities in Venice have cared whether the Jews admitted Nathan to their ghetto or not? The account of the episode given by Sasportas (*Sefer tsitsat novel tsevi*, 263) suggests that their motive may have been to keep the Jews' autonomy within proper bounds. According to Sasportas, Nathan's supporters in Venice went as informers to 'a certain wicked gentile official' and accused the Jews of 'wanting to seize dominion for themselves' by not admitting Nathan. The gentile sent for the Jews' 'prophet' to see what sort of person he might turn out to be, and, despising him, sent him off to the ghetto.

[203] Baruch must have the date wrong: 15 April 1668 (the nineteenth day of the Omer, the fifty-day period between Passover and Shavuot) fell on Sunday (but cf. Appendix 3). The account given by the Venetian rabbis themselves—the original *Memorial to the Children of Israel*—has the hearing take place on the night of Monday, the thirteenth day of the Omer (Sasportas, *Sefer tsitsat novel tsevi*, 265). This would be Monday, 9 April. (Cf. Scholem, *Sabbatai Sevi*, 766, which mistakenly gives the Hebrew date as 'the Twelfth of Omer'.)

[204] The *merkavah*; see above, n. 52.

Nevertheless I was misled, and the vision devoid of any substance—
I have conceded the truth of their opinion, and declared my prophecy
concerning Sabbatai Zevi to have been without substance,

alef–gimel,[205] Nathan Benjamin.

They used their thugs and bully-boys to 'persuade' him of this. But he
tricked them in return, in the writing of his signature. Where they expected
him to sign, 'I, Nathan Benjamin', he wrote [in place of *alef–nun–yod,*
spelling the word *ani,* 'I'] the letters *alef–gimel*—these being the initials of
ones gamur, 'under absolute duress'![206]

While it was still night, they put him in a small boat with Rabbi Samuel Gandoor, along with a certain Venetian of the 'Satan' family, so they could say
they had sent him off with Satan.[207] But God was with him, for the Lord
protects all His pious folk, and no harm came to him even though Satan was
standing by his side to accuse him.

They sent him to Il Finale di Modona[208] with a letter addressed to the
distinguished and accomplished gentleman Rabbi Samuel Formiggini, who
was my uncle. For God's sake, the letter requested, [Nathan] must be conveyed to Florence quickly and secretly. For the Christians had become
aware of his arrival through the newsletters that had been printed, and there
was reason for concern lest the Pope's agents apprehend him and carry him
off to Rome in chains.

As his boat pulled into Il Finale, on the Panaro River, the two banks of the
river filled with Christians. They took up the chant 'the Jews' messiah!' at
the top of their lungs. The Jews found themselves in considerable danger,
these people being at once a doltish folk and a cunning one.[209] The gentleman Master Samuel thereupon produced two horses, one for Master
Nathan and the other for Master Samuel Gandoor, with a Christian servant
to run before them. 'Ride these horses', he told them, 'and you will be safely
on your way.'

---

[205] The significance of these two Hebrew letters will be explained in the next paragraph.

[206] That is: '[Signed] under absolute duress, Nathan Benjamin.' The letters *alef–gimel* do
bear some resemblance to *alef–nun–yod,* and could perhaps be mistaken for them by a very
careless reader. This reads nevertheless like an ingenious bit of apologetic, invented to cover
up the embarrassment of Nathan's having so cravenly recanted.

[207] Baruch evidently refers to some Venetian family whose name sounded more or less like
'Satan'. (A Jewish family? Or was the man a non-Jew, hired by the Venetian rabbis to travel
with Nathan and Gandoor?) Professor Benjamin Ravid, who was kind enough to discuss the
passage with me by email, suggests tentatively that 'Seta', 'della Setta', or 'Saitta' might be
intended.

[208] Modern Finale Emilia, on the Panaro River, 22 miles north-east of Modena. The town
had a Jewish community in the 17th century.

[209] *Am naval vehakham,* a play on Deut. 32: 6.

So they did, and they rode away to safety. When the crowds along the river saw how handsome the man[210] was and what fine clothing he wore, God set it in their minds to think well of him. They quietened down; their chanting ceased; not one of them made a sound. Like Lot's wife, they all became as pillars of salt.

[Nathan] travelled safely and smoothly to Bologna, to Florence, and to Leghorn on the sea coast. There he stayed a long time, studying Torah day and night with the local rabbis. The unbelievers in Venice spread the rumour he had fled the Turkish lands because the Turk[211] had wanted to kill him, and that was why he drifted from place to place, not knowing where to find refuge. God silence those lying lips, taunting the righteous with their arrogant mockery![212]

[20. NATHAN'S TRAVELS, CONCLUDED]

After [Nathan] had been in Leghorn for a considerable time, he summoned the gentleman Rabbi Moses Capsuto.[213] 'I should be grateful to you', he said to him, 'if you would go with me to Rome. It was for this purpose, to carry out a great mending [*tikun*], that I came to these regions.'

'I will', he replied.

They accordingly made their journey, going safely and returning safely. What [Nathan] did and what he said there, I do not know; if I did know, I would not record a word of it.

From Leghorn he went to Ancona. There he stayed more than three weeks, in close consultation with the local rabbis and with the blind rabbi,[214] reporting on the mission he had performed [in Rome]. This being done, he travelled to Ragusa and thence back to the Turkish lands[215]—thereby showing he had not fled from them, contrary to what the unbelievers claimed.

While aboard the ship, he wrote the following letter to the gentleman Caleb Hakohen:[216]

[210] Nathan? The servant? Or perhaps Samuel Formiggini himself?

[211] That is, the 'Grand Turk', the sultan.

[212] Following Ps. 31: 19. On the 'rumour', compare the end of Joseph Halevi's first letter (below): 'Towards the fraud of Gaza, however, the king remained implacably furious, and he dispatched orders for his arrest. For the king understood clearly that it was he who had instigated the entire affair.'

[213] On Moses Capsuto, and this whole mysterious episode, see Scholem, *Sabbatai Sevi*, 771–4.   [214] Whom Scholem identifies as Rabbi Mahallelel Halleluyah (ibid. 775–6).

[215] Crossing the Adriatic from Ancona, on the east coast of Italy, to Ragusa (Dubrovnik) on the Dalmatian coast.

[216] Scholem identifies Hakohen as 'one of the leading believers in Sofia or Corfu' (*Sabbatai Sevi*, 765). The reading of three of the manuscripts points to Corfu. I am not clear if there exists any information on him beyond what may be gathered from this passage.

(After the opening salutations:[217]) I hereby lodge a most vigourous protest, before you and before all pious and faithful Israelites, against the duress to which I was subjected in the Italian lands. I know you[218] have already heard the appalling reports of how foully the Venetians treated me—how, in order to boost their prestige among the Jewish public, they forcibly extracted from me an agreement that I would do their will and pleasure. I now directly inform you of this. One may pay attention or not, as one pleases.

For there is not one bit of truth in all their claims and in all their juridical acts. You need only winnow them, and the wind will carry them off; the storm wind will scatter them. I, meanwhile, will rejoice in the Lord and take pride in the Holy One of Israel.

Who has seen such a thing? Who has heard the like?—That these men, wholly worthless in their Creator's sight yet imagining themselves without peer in all Jewry, should compose baseless fictions of having 'thoroughly investigated this case and found it without substance'. As if they were in sole possession of the machinery for testing gold and purifying silver!

What I said to them was this: *I do not at present have the power to perform any miraculous sign. I am going to a certain place to carry out my Creator's will,*[219] *and the entire Jewish community will benefit from it. No Jews will have any need for sackcloth or lamentation, any more than they have had heretofore.* They listened to what I said, then ruled it 'without substance'. So much for their 'thorough investigation'.

But this did not satisfy them. They had to force me to affirm their claims in writing. Anyone with brains will perceive how I tricked them, thereby fulfilling the scriptural injunction to 'treat the decent person with decency' and so forth.[220] They dictated my words to me; I gave my agreement. The document[221] and the juridical act represent nothing but what they dictated to me, in a matter concerning which dictation has no legitimacy. It was, in fact, a pack of lies.

They tormented me for their pleasure. Had God not taken pity on me, they would have driven me to my grave. It was He who frustrated their schemes and made nonsense of their plotting. In all their verbal diarrhoea there was not one particle of solid matter.[222]

---

[217] See above, n. 178.   [218] 'You', here and in the next sentence, is plural.

[219] Referring apparently to his trip to Rome.

[220] 2 Sam. 22: 27. The biblical verse goes on: 'and outmanoeuvre the trickster'. It is, of course, this latter part of the Scripture that Nathan prides himself on having fulfilled.

[221] Of Nathan's confession, extracted from him by the 'thugs and bully-boys' of the Venetian rabbis.   [222] A repellent image drawn from BT *San.* 64a.

But God granted me the admiration and affection of many faithful and reliable friends. He helped me, giving me the strength and fortitude to reach the destination for which I longed, there to perform my Creator's will. And now, God be praised, my plan has gone from conception to reality.[223]

God saw my poverty. He saw how I suffered in the course of my journeying, and how I sacrificed myself in order to sanctify Him and do His will. Consequently, not even a dog threatened any harm to me—nor to any Jew at all—even after the news of my arrival had spread among the Christians.

As for me, I am resolved to remain at my post, encouraging and fortifying all who await God's salvation. Do not lose confidence! Do not let yourselves be cowed or intimidated by the facile, pretentious chatter of those who taunt the righteous with their arrogant mockery. For, God willing, the good news I have preached to you is near at hand.

I could not write you a proper letter, given I am on board ship. But, with God helping 'from another place'[224] I will bring you joy, and announce to you the good news of our redemption and our ransom. For what I have told you is true and reliable, well founded and enduring.

Nathan Benjamin.

[Nathan] set out for the land of the Morea.[225] He travelled its length and breadth, visiting, at the inspiration of his spirit-guide,[226] the towns of Patras and Navarino.[227] He went then to Salonica, where he was received with great honour. Nearly everyone there believed in the truth of his message, for they recognized the divine wisdom with which he was graced.

Afterward he went to Adrianople, where our Lord dwelt, and also the rabbis who had travelled with him from Gaza. There also he was received with great honour, in spite of his having earlier been put under a ban prohibiting him from entering the city, as we have written above. From there he went to Kastoria,[228] where he stayed a long time.

---

[223] More oblique hints at the 'mending' Nathan performed in Rome.

[224] Alluding to Esther 4: 14, 'relief and salvation will come to the Jews from another place'—that is, from God.   [225] Above, n. 174.

[226] Above, n. 175. This reads almost like a repeat of the earlier passage.

[227] Modern Patrai and Pilos.

[228] In northern Greece, close to the border with modern Macedonia. In Kastoria there was a substantial Jewish community, many of them Sabbatian believers. Scholem dates Nathan's arrival in Kastoria to the early summer of 1669 (*Sabbatai Sevi*, 779–80).

[21. THE MESSIAH AS MUSLIM]

We return now to the narrative of our Lord's doings.

After he had put the pure turban on his head, he made love to his Ashkenazi wife.[229] She conceived; she bore him a son. On the eighth day he circumcised the infant with his own hands, with wine and blessings recited in a loud voice.[230] He did this in full view of the Turks. He gave the baby the name 'Ishmael Mordecai'.[231]

His wife later bore him a daughter, whom he named ———.[232]

From Izmir he summoned his elder brother Rabbi Elijah Zevi, who, as we have earlier related, once tried to kill him. [Elijah] appeared before him in Adrianople, his eldest son with him. He ordered them to set the pure turban on their heads, in the manner of the Turks, and they obeyed at once.[233] So he did with many of the rabbis who were with him.

Nearly every day he would go to the mosque[234]—their prayer-house—where he would pray before the Lord his God and perform great acts of mending.[235] While he was there he was approached by envoys from very distant parts, a sixteen-month journey[236] from Constantinople. They came from the territory of the Uzbeks, near the kingdom of China and Great Tartary.[237] They told the following story.

---

[229] See above, n. 31.

[230] Following the Cambridge manuscript. Baruch's point is that wine was part of the ceremony—which it would not have been at a Muslim circumcision—and that the Hebrew blessings were chanted loudly and without shame.

[231] That is, he performed the circumcision in accordance with Jewish rather than Muslim practice, giving the infant a name that symbolized his dual identity as a Muslim ('Ishmael') and as a Jew placed at the centre of non-Jewish power ('Mordecai'). Baruch's account of the circumcision is legendary, if not fabricated; contrast the eyewitness report of Jacob Najara (below). On Ishmael Zevi, see Halperin, 'The Son of the Messiah'.

[232] All manuscripts unaccountably leave a blank where the girl's name ought to be. With one possible exception (below, n. 294), I am not aware of any other source that even mentions Sabbatai's daughter. There is something very mysterious here, and I have no idea how to resolve it.

[233] This episode took place in February 1671. It is recounted in more detail in the Najara Chronicle (below).   [234] Baruch uses the Italian word *meschita*.

[235] *Tikunim*—kabbalistic-magical rites and formulas intended to repair the damaged fabric of the universe. See Halperin, *Abraham Miguel Cardozo*, 36, 74–6.

[236] Or, 'six-month' (according to three manuscripts).

[237] 'Great Tartary' is an early modern designation for an enormous stretch of northern Asia east of the Ural mountains, very roughly corresponding to what is now called Siberia. The Jewish community of Uzbekistan goes back at least to medieval times. On the geographical terms in this passage, cf. Rapoport-Albert, 'On the Position of Women in Sabbatianism' (Heb.), 161 n.

In Elul 5425 [12 August–9 September 1665], people arrived in Maragheh[238] from Pamos,[239] claiming there were prophets and prophetesses among them. One prophetess, Rebecca by name, had offered many predictions to prove her claims, all of which had come true. She told how she had seen Elijah and Rabbi Nissim[240] in the company of the messiah son of David. Both men said to her: 'This is the messiah, son of David.' She told, further, that on the sabbath before Passover [28 March 1665] she had been shown the messiah son of David wearing black clothing. The messiah, she said, must remain isolated from all his friends, and he must dress himself in Muslim garb.

They sent five emissaries throughout the world, and more prophets and prophetesses began to appear in various places. All conveyed the prophetic message: *There is a messiah in the world.*

From Ethiopia came four other envoys, seeking an audience with our Lord. When they realized how our Lord was dressing himself, they donned that same [Muslim] clothing and went to him in the mosque. They wanted to kiss his hands, as one does with great princes, but he would not let them. In their land as well, they said, there were prophets and prophetesses. The envoys bore letters from the Jewish community of Baghdad, recommending them and attesting to the truth of their report.

Yet our Lord did not want to make any response to them, for he was at the time in a state of eclipse.[241] Nevertheless, in order to please the envoys, he gave them a sealed letter to the effect that they had found the man of whom the prophets in their homeland had prophesied, and that they had found him in his present condition.[242]

Certain vicious and dishonest people slandered two rabbis in our Lord's presence, claiming that they entertained doubts about his faith. [The rabbis] wrote to him in their own defence, and our Lord responded as follows, in the manner of a father to his dear child:

---

[238] In Azerbaijan in north-western Iran, across the Caspian Sea from Turkmenistan and Uzbekistan. The Jewish community there goes back to medieval times. On the reading 'Maragheh', see the textual note to p. 64, l. 3.

[239] Attested, in slightly variant spellings, in all the manuscripts. I do not know what place is intended.

[240] I do not know who 'Rabbi Nissim' might be. Perhaps Nissim ben Jacob (ibn Shahin), well known in the 17th century as the author of the popular *Ḥibur yafeh meḥayeshuah* ('Book of Comfort')?

[241] *Hester panim*, literally 'concealment of the [divine] face'. The reference is to one of Sabbatai's depressive phases, as opposed to his manic 'illuminations'.

[242] Thus confirming that the envoys had indeed found him dressed and acting as a Muslim, as they would certainly report upon their return.

To my brothers and friends, who love my king and my God, the Lord God of Truth—the worthy Rabbi David Yitshaki and the noble Rabbi Benjamin Argevan[243]—God preserve them, and grant them life and happiness in the land:

(After an invocation of 'abundant peace between me and you':[244]) I desire you to know that my warm affections have been stirred up towards you. 'One rebuke', the Bible tells us, 'makes more impression upon a person of understanding than a hundred beatings do upon a fool' [Prov. 17: 10]; and so it has been with you.

My reason for rebuking you was that I heard you were wanting in the exalted faith. That would not have been appropriate. Be strong and valiant, rather, in the truth of the Lord God of Truth, most fearsome of divinities! This is the truth that is concealed from all living creatures, yet destined to be revealed to earthly and heavenly beings alike, by His servant whose name is like his Master's.[245] 'What is His name? What is His Son's name, if you know?'[246]

Let the heavens be glad and the earth rejoice! Let it be said among the nations, 'The Lord reigns'![247] Thus you and I are reconciled together. Your souls shall rejoice in the Lord and take pleasure in His salvation. Once again shall I entrust my sacred deposit[248] to your care, until, by virtue of it, your minds shall become fully and radiantly enlightened in this exalted Faith. And I pledge to you the peace that the Lord God of

---

[243] David Yitshaki was a prominent jurist of Jerusalem, a passionate believer in Sabbatai Zevi—he once publicly declared faith in Sabbatai's messiahship to be as essential to Judaism as belief in 'God's unity and His Torah'—who may or may not have had second thoughts in his later years, as this story perhaps suggests. Benjamin Argevan, whose name appears in other sources as 'Rijwan' or 'Rejwan', was an intimate friend of Sabbatai's, supposedly the only man who ever accompanied him to the bathhouse. See Scholem, *Sabbatai Sevi*, 245, 489–90, 852–4, and 'Rabbi David Yitshaki and his Attitude to Sabbatianism' (with the important notes of Yehuda Liebes), and the sources cited there.   [244] See above, n. 178.

[245] A phrase used in the Talmud (BT *San.* 38*b*) for Metatron, the 'Lesser YHVH', a near-divine being 'whose name is like his Master's'. The talmudic passage applies Exod. 23: 21, 'My name is in him', to Metatron; Rashi, commenting on the biblical verse, explains that Metatron has the same numerical value as Shaddai, 'the Almighty'. But Sabbatai Zevi also partakes in the name Shaddai, as we have already seen (above, nn. 139, 171). Thus, like Metatron, he is a 'servant whose name is like his Master's'. At the end of the letter, in his signature, Sabbatai will give a new and startling twist to this idea.

[246] Prov. 30: 4. Kabbalistic speculations on this passage applied it to the potentialities within the divinity, but also at times to the exaltation and near-divinization of human beings. See Zohar, ii. 197*a–b*, iii. 279*b* (*Ra'aya mehemna*); Cordovero, *Sefer pardes rimonim*, 'Sha'ar erkhei hakinuyim', s.v. *mah*; *Wisdom of the Zohar*, ed. Tishby, i. 221.   [247] Following Ps. 96: 10–11.

[248] Referring presumably to the 'Mystery of God's Divinity', known only to the messiah and those lucky few to whom he is willing to teach it.

Israel has promised to His people and His pious ones—namely, those within my faith.

> Thus speaks your brother ME'EMET[249]
> —the faith of the Lord God of Truth.
> This is the gate of the Lord—ZEVI.[250]

[22. THE LETTER OF SOLOMON KATZ]

While he was in Adrianople our Lord wore ritual fringes and phylacteries. He studied Torah with the rabbis, prayed in the synagogue, and performed all the commandments just as he had done previously. The great illumination that had been his in the castle of Gallipoli came back to him. Afterwards he was left in a state of eclipse; yet after a short time the illumination would return. And so it continued, until the time of his final concealment when he was in Dulcigno, as we shall presently relate.

There follows the report of one who saw him for a full week in a state of great illumination—the text of a letter written from the province of Volhynia to his brother by the worthy Rabbi Solomon Katz (son-in-law of Rabbi Sender, beadle of [. . .]),[251] upon his return to Volhynia from Adrianople:

MY DEAR BROTHER—

I wrote to you several times before I left for Adrianople. From Adrianople also I have written to you, courtesy of an elder there named Master Zerah. I have written as well to the Jewish community of Jaslowicz, and to the great rabbi of Brody. In these letters I have provided truthful accounts of what I had (thank God!) the privilege of experiencing with our Lord, our righteous messiah, and also with Rabbi Nathan the true prophet and with the most distinguished rabbis of our time, currently in our Lord's company.

[249] Sabbatai's name is now 'Me'emet [Mehmed] Zevi'. It is 'like his Master's' name, in that Me'emet incorporates the Hebrew word 'truth' (*emet*), and Sabbatai has reminded us no fewer than three times in this letter that his God is 'the Lord God of Truth' (*adonai el emet*). It is again 'like his Master's', in that Sabbatai now has the sultan for his master and shares with him the name Mehmed. Jewish God and Muslim king thus shade into one another in Sabbatai's mind, and he is bonded simultaneously to both. (Is this the meaning of 'my king and my God', in the letter's salutation?) See Halperin, 'Sabbatai Zevi, Metatron, and Mehmed', 278–86.

[250] Interpreting 'Zevi' in accordance with Ps. 118: 20, 'This is the Lord's gate; the righteous shall enter it': the opening letters of the words *tsadikim yavo'u vo* ('the righteous shall enter it') are also the three letters of 'Zevi' (*tsadi, yod, beit*). Sabbatai Zevi is thus himself 'the gate of the Lord', into which the 'righteous'—we have already seen that this word had special meaning for Sabbatai and his followers—must enter.

[251] I cannot identify the town mentioned here. See the textual note to p. 65, l. 2.

I was privileged, thank God, to see the king's face as though in a clear shining mirror, on the occasion of the great festival that extends from the Ninth to the Fifteenth day of Av [16–22 July 1671].[252] There we witnessed, thank God, the most awe-inspiring sights. For he is a man who inspires awe; all his actions are true; he is beyond any doubt the true Redeemer.

For more than eight weeks I was in his presence continuously, day and night. (For it must be understood that when the great light is upon him he does not sleep, beyond an occasional half-doze.) His face was like a shining mirror, like the sun rising in brilliance. Time and time again, thank God, I was privileged even to pray in his company.

We eagerly anticipate that in the near future these matters will be fully clarified, and the hidden secrets made plain. Those who heap copious ridicule upon the righteous will then be put to shame. So it has come to pass just now. A treacherous conspiracy was hatched, great wealth was expended thereon, and he was betrayed to the royal power. Yet the plotters found themselves on their knees before him, begging and pleading, their evil intent abandoned. The righteous does truly live by his faith,[253] while the blasphemers are now very sorry indeed. Make no mistake: the time is close at hand when his glory will be revealed to the whole world, with the entire Jewish people watching.

To make a long story short, dear brother: for more than twelve years I was rabbi for the community of Buda (that is, Ofen Stadt),[254] issuing legal rulings. They would not have wanted to let me leave them, were it not for the great fire they suffered, and also that I wanted to make the pilgrimage to see our Lord.[255]

---

[252] The letter is dated 18 Av 5432 (11 August 1672). If Baruch is right, and Solomon Katz wrote the letter after his return from Adrianople, the events described in it must have taken place the summer before (since one could hardly get from Adrianople to Volhynia in three days). But it seems odd that Katz would have waited so long to write to his brother about events that had so stirred him. It seems at least possible that Baruch is mistaken, that the letter was written from Adrianople immediately after the events, and that 'the Ninth to the Fifteenth day of Av' is equivalent to 2–8 August 1672. In either case, it is clear that the period 9–15 Av is the 'full week' to which Baruch refers. The Ninth of Av, as we have plentifully seen, was a traditional fast-day turned into a festival at Sabbatai's bidding; 15 Av appears in the Mishnah (*Ta'an.* 4: 8) as a merry time in which the girls danced in the vineyards and challenged the boys to pick out their mates. (On the reading 'Fifteenth', see the textual note to p. 65, l. 8.) [253] Hab. 2: 4; see above, n. 90.

[254] Later to become part of Budapest. 'Ofen' was the German name for the town.

[255] This strange little paragraph sounds very much as if Katz had been dismissed from his post—perhaps precisely because of his attachment to Sabbatai Zevi—and is trying to put an acceptable face on it.

I saw things in our Lord's synagogue that were too awe-inspiring to speak about or to record in writing. I conversed also with our messiah's brother, his senior by some few years, the distinguished and exceedingly wealthy rabbi.[256] He told me all that his brother had done and all that had befallen him, from his youth to the present day; I wrote everything down. He told me [Sabbatai] is clearly King David in person. Other things also did I see, thank God.

I had the privilege of delivering a sermon in the great synagogue of the Portuguese community of Adrianople. Rabbi Nathan was present along with all the rabbis, of which our Lord was well aware. At length our Lord himself arrived, for on account of my sermon they had not prayed with him, all coming instead to the Portuguese synagogue. I preached to the unbelievers, to such effect that the arch-unbeliever Rabbi Denan,[257] who was present in the synagogue, was in spite of himself put in fear of our Lord. (He indeed has already come to regret his unbelief but cannot admit it publicly, inasmuch as he is the leading instigator of blasphemy against God and His messiah.)

To make a long story short, dear brother, here is how matters now stand: all who plotted against our Lord are dead. Meanwhile he grows more powerful each day, for he has now revealed himself to all the Turks as the messiah. You must therefore take pains, dear brother, as I have written you many and many a time—for I know you are a God-fearing man—to pray devotedly that you may be among the believers in our Lord's faith. Thereby you shall come to deserve rich reward, inasmuch as faith in this matter is greater than the entire Torah. (The name 'Zevi' and the word 'faith', you will observe, share the same numerical value.)

Let these few words suffice, in lieu of the many I might have written. Only this, in conclusion: we are obligated to believe that God has come to look after His people. This is our king and our Lord, the true messiah. Let him draw near! Our eyes shall see the king in his beauty, for the sake of God's great and holy name.

Solomon, son of the holy Rabbi Leib Katz,
leader of public worship for the Lublin community,
18 Av 5432 [11 August 1672].

---

[256] Elijah Zevi. Cf. the beginning of §21 above.

[257] Scholem identifies him, I am not sure on what basis, as 'Rabbi Jacob Danon' (*Sabbatai Sevi*, 845). A weird little notation, preserved in a notebook of the Sabbatian Abraham Rovigo, speaks of 'Rabbi Denan in Adrianople' having died 'a strange death while eating', apparently some time in the mid-1670s (Sonne, 'New Material on Sabbatai Zevi' (Heb.), 57–9). Sonne suspects he may have been poisoned by the Sabbatians.

[23. THE BANISHMENT OF SABBATAI ZEVI]

The Ashkenazi woman[258] who had been our Lord's wife died. He thereupon sought in marriage the daughter of the worthy Rabbi Aaron Magueres[259] of Sofia, who had continued devoutly to believe in him despite his wearing the pure turban.[260] [Magueres] was willing to marry her to him. But the girl was not yet worthy. She therefore died before she could be sent off to him, along with [Magueres'] brother who was to have accompanied her.[261]

It happened afterwards that the Turkish king waged war upon the king of Poland. He laid siege to the large, mightily fortified city of Kamenets-Podolski, and he subdued it.[262] Our Lord, meanwhile, went to Constantinople together with the rabbis who wore the green turban.[263]

When the unbelievers in Constantinople saw them, they went to the *kaimakam*—that is to say, the king's second in command[264]—and lodged a complaint. 'Even though that Zevi has converted, he goes on acting as a Jew! He goes to synagogue wearing ritual fringes, with phylacteries on his head, and he prays along with the others!'

[The *kaimakam*] at once ordered him to be brought into his presence, and he questioned him on this matter.

---

[258] See above, n. 31.

[259] See textual note to p. 66, l. 6. The name is given in other sources (such as the Najara Chronicle, below) as 'Majar' or 'Mayar'. The modern scholarly literature normally uses the form 'Majar'.

[260] Baruch is mistaken. Sarah's death, and the subsequent death of Sabbatai's new bride (whose name was also Sarah), happened after Sabbatai's banishment to Dulcigno, not before. Baruch was evidently unaware that Sabbatai had *twice* sought the daughter of Majar/Magueres in marriage: once in 1671, when he was briefly divorced from Sarah (as reported in the Najara Chronicle), and a second time in 1674, after his banishment and Sarah's death. Baruch *did* know, apparently, that Sabbatai had been in Adrianople when he originally sought to marry Majar's daughter. It was natural, therefore, for him to have conflated Sabbatai's original suit of Majar's daughter with his resumption of it after Sarah's death, and to have transferred all these events to the time before the banishment. See the account of this episode near the end of the Najara Chronicle, below.

[261] Three manuscripts insert here an additional story. See the textual notes to p. 66, l. 8.

[262] 27 August 1672. The campaign had been undertaken in support of the Ukrainian Cossacks and their rebellion against the Polish Crown. Kamenets-Podolski, in the Ukraine, was a major border fortress.

[263] That is, who had converted to Islam. Baruch's reference to the colour presumably reflects the significance of green for the Muslims; non-Muslims in the Ottoman empire were prohibited from wearing it (Shaw, *The Jews of the Ottoman Empire and the Turkish Republic*, 79). Joseph Halevi's second letter (below) similarly speaks of Sabbatai's 'leek-green turban'. More normally, however, the sources represent it as having been white.

[264] Actually the grand vizier's deputy, who, in Sabbatai's time, functioned as the effective governor of the city of Constantinople.

'It is so', he said.

'You have pronounced your own judgment', the *kaimakam* responded. 'You have no choice but to die.'[265]

They gaoled him in the place where they kept the king's prisoners. But the *kaimakam*, well knowing how [Sabbatai] had fared with the Turkish king, was afraid to put him to death. So he sent him to Adrianople to the sultana— that is, the queen mother—along with his confession and the order for his execution. He wrote to her that she should deal with [Sabbatai] at her discretion.

When our Lord arrived in Adrianople, he was put under guard pending the sultana's verdict. She also was afraid to have him executed, for the Lord his God was with him and he had the king's friendship. So she wrote to her son the Turkish king, informing him of all our Lord had done and of the death sentence the *kaimakam* had pronounced against him. Would [the king] now instruct them as to what must be done?

When the Turkish king received this message, he wrote at once to his mother: 'Be very careful of that man. Do not put him to death; do him no harm whatever. Not one hair of his head must fall to the ground until I am safely back from Kamenets.'

Upon returning to Adrianople the king summoned our Lord to appear before him. 'What is that you are carrying under your arm?' the king asked him.

Our Lord replied: 'It is the Torah of Moses.'

The king thereupon ordered that he be given a substantial present. He set him free, only commanding him, 'From time to time you must come to do obeisance before me.'

When this news reached the grand vizier, he dispatched to the king a certain member of the nobility, bearing with him the *kaimakam*'s letter and the execution order. The king took the letter and tore it into pieces before the nobleman's eyes, leaving him in a state of humiliated grief.

The nobleman told the vizier what had happened. The vizier, realizing this was a matter of major importance, went in person to the king.

'My lord king!' he said to him. 'It is contrary to our religion and faith that a Jew, having once abjured his religion, should go back to practising Judaism as before and performing all the Jewish precepts in full public view. If you are unwilling to have him executed, then at least send him to a distant place where he can live out his life and do whatever he pleases.'

The king granted him permission to do this. They sent our Lord to

---

[265] As an apostate from Islam.

Dulcigno, on the border between the territories of Islam and of Christendom.[266] There he remained until the day he was concealed from us.

[24. EVENTS IN DULCIGNO AND KASTORIA]

While he was at Dulcigno our Lord sent a message to the great scholar and divine kabbalist Rabbi Joseph Filosoff, president of the rabbinical academy at Salonica, proposing marriage with his daughter.

The rabbi was agreeable to the marriage. The community officials and power brokers of Salonica, however, were not. They removed him from his rabbinical post and cut off his salary. 'I know what I am about', he told them. 'This is the Lord's doing.'

And thus he did. He sent the girl, along with his son. The wedding was held in Dulcigno, and our Lord took her in marriage in accordance with the religion of Moses and Israel.[267]

In the year 5735 [1674/5] an envoy appeared in Kastoria, where Rabbi Nathan was then living. He had been sent by our brother-Israelites from the other side of the river Gozan, also known as 'Sambatyon'.[268] He bore with him a letter for Rabbi Nathan.

Ever since the year 5733, said the letter, the river Sambatyon had turned placid. This remarkable phenomenon had set them to speculating: surely

---

[266] Modern Ulcinj, on the western seacoast of the Balkan peninsula—then, as now, at the border between Muslim Albania and Christian Montenegro.

[267] That is, in a Jewish and not an Islamic ceremony. It is clear from Filosoff's poem in honour of his daughter's wedding that the girl's name was Esther, not Jochebed as claimed in Sabbatian tradition (Benayahu, *The Sabbatian Movement in Greece* (Heb.), 27–32, 365–6). Filosoff's 'son', left unnamed here, was presumably the infamous Jacob Querido, who several years later was to lead his followers into mass conversion to Islam and thus to become founder of the strange sect of the Dönmeh—outwardly Muslim Turks, secretly Sabbatian believers. See the Introduction, section VIII.

[268] The Ten Lost Tribes of Israel, according to 2 Kgs. 17: 1–6, were exiled to 'Halah and Habor, the river Gozan, and the cities of the Medes'. An ancient Jewish legend declares that these tribes still survive, hidden from the rest of the world by a wondrous river, Sambatyon (here equated with the Gozan), which 'is full of sand and stones, and on the six working days of the week, they tumble over each other with such vehemence that the crash and the roar are heard far and wide. But on the Sabbath the tumultuous river subsides into quiet' (Ginzberg, *Legends of the Jews*, iv. 316–18, vi. 407–9). In messianic times, according to popular belief, the Ten Tribes would emerge to rejoin their Jewish kinsfolk—hence the importance of the detail that the Sambatyon, whose raging had kept the tribes isolated for centuries, had become tranquil (below). Belief in the tribes' imminent appearance played an important role in the fantasies of the Sabbatians themselves, and of the European Christians who found them so fascinating. See Scholem, *Sabbatai Sevi*, index, s.v. 'Ten Tribes'; Goldish, *The Sabbatean Prophets*, 27–34, 151–60.

some great and holy event must be taking place in the world. So they had prayed to the Lord their God for enlightenment, and had received their answer when the holy spirit settled on a certain young boy. He had told them our Lord's name and the name of his town, and also the name, and the name of the town, of the true prophet Rabbi Nathan. The letter went on to enquire of [Nathan] what action they must take.

The envoy had also a second letter which he was to give to our Lord. He accordingly went to Dulcigno, by way of Durazzo,[269] and delivered it into the pure hand of our Lord himself. What it may have contained, no one knows. For only a short time afterwards our Lord was concealed from us, as we shall relate.

The envoy was dressed in the garb of the Muslims and spoke their language,[270] as well as Aramaic and Hebrew. He reported that their king was named Daniel, and that the tribe of Reuben was eager to set forth on its way. They have arrows, swords, and spears, but are without firearms.[271] They recite the Shema with the 'eternal love' benediction, just as we do, but in reciting the Eighteen Benedictions they diverge slightly from our practice.[272] He gave also the names of the places where they are encamped.

All the time our Lord lived in Dulcigno, he alternated between states of illumination and of eclipse. This lasted until the year 5736 [1675/6],[273] when a great and wholly unprecedented illumination came upon him.

[In this state,] he went one day to the house of the *moḥan*, the place where the great nobles take their leisure.[274] He thereby aroused the indignation of thirty-six brutal, violent fellows from among the Turks. They came armed, planning to assault him. When he heard the great commotion they were making he stepped forth, a small stick in his hand. He struck them over the head and they all fled, desperately seeking a place to hide.

[269] Modern Durrës on the Albanian sea coast, south of Ulcinj.

[270] Arabic? Or Turkish? See the textual note to p. 67, l. 17.

[271] This sentence is nearly identical with a passage in an English pamphlet, published in London in 1665, describing the Israelite hordes said to be on the move in North Africa: 'they are armed with Swords, Spears and Bows, and no fire-Arms are found amongst them' (Wilensky, 'Four English Pamphlets' (Heb.), 161; see also Goldish, *The Sabbatean Prophets*, 153).

[272] On the Shema, see above, n. 65. 'Eternal love' is a benediction, beginning 'With eternal love have You loved Israel Your people', recited before the Shema in the evening prayer service—and, in the Sephardi and Italian liturgies with which Baruch would have been familiar, the morning service as well (Idelsohn, *Jewish Liturgy and its Development*, 90). The 'Eighteen Benedictions' are the same as the Amidah (see above, n. 64).

[273] Two manuscripts give '5735'. The reading '5736' seems the more plausible.

[274] The reading *moḥan* is attested by nearly all manuscripts. I have not been able to identify the word.

One night at midnight he climbed upon the tower wall, there to pronounce his wondrous mendings along with their mystical 'intentions'.[275] The men guarding the walls heard his voice. More than one hundred and fifty of those cutthroats approached from all sides, their swords drawn. He saw them coming. Yet he did not show the slightest fear of them, nor did he budge from there until all his mendings were completed. He then rebuked them; at his reprimand trembling overcame them. They threw themselves down before him, begging and pleading. With lutes and drums they escorted him home in great honour.

As Passover approached he prepared his unleavened bread. The *pasha*, the *cadi*, and the city notables came to serve him, attending to the cakes of dough to make sure they would not rise. Like slaves they submitted to his rule. And thus he came to believe that the time for Redemption, for his second manifestation before all the world, was at hand.

He accordingly sent off letters to his relatives and friends, as follows:

[25. EPISTLES OF SABBATAI ZEVI]

This is the text of the letter he sent to his father-in-law, the accomplished scholar Rabbi Joseph Filosoff:

To my lord, man of God — you who are Joseph, appointed ruler of the earth, provider for all the people of the earth — you who are Saul, God's chosen one — you who are Mordecai son of Jair son of Shimei son of Kish, my right-hand man:[276]

In the name of the Lord of Hosts I announce to you good tidings: that I, your son-in-law Jethro, will come to you soon! With me will be my wife, Michal Hadassah (most blessed of women!) who is Esther, my sister my lover my dove my pure one, and, with her, her two sons Ishmael and

---

[275] That is, the thoughts that are to accompany the spoken words and performed actions of the 'mendings', in order to give them their proper effect. Scholem suggests the 'tower wall' might have been the minaret of some local mosque (*Sabbatai Sevi*, 914). This would certainly explain the Turks' fury. But the context seems more to point to some spot along the town's fortifications.

[276] Compressing biblical allusions to Elisha (2 Kgs. 4: 16), Joseph (Gen. 42: 6), Saul (2 Sam. 21: 6), and Mordecai (Esther 2: 5). Filosoff is called 'Joseph' because that is his real name, 'Saul' because King Saul's daughter Michal became King David's wife and Sabbatai identifies himself with David, 'Mordecai' because Mordecai was the surrogate father of Esther, which is the name of Sabbatai's new wife. The biblical Esther was of course the bride of the gentile potentate Ahasuerus, with whom it would appear Sabbatai also identifies himself. (So Scholem's marginal note, in his copy of Freimann's *Inyanei shabetai tsevi*.) That this letter is the work of a lunatic goes almost without saying.

Abraham (blessed be they to the Lord!).[277] You shall then rejoice in the
Lord and take pride in the Holy One of Israel, while the eyes of the
wicked—enemies of God, enemies of His messiah—shall wear away in
frustration. They shall have no refuge, and their hopes shall turn to
grief.[278]

> Thus speaks the man raised up over all blessing and hymn,
> who rises above nobilities—the messiah of the
> God of Judah and Israel.[279]

TO MY BRETHREN AND FRIENDS, ALL THE FAITHFUL FOLK OF
THE CITY OF SOFIA—MAY THEY BE PRIVILEGED TO SEE GOD'S
SALVATION, TO BE EYEWITNESSES TO HIS RETURN TO ZION![280]

I am sending an angel before you [to bring you good tidings]. He will tell
you all my honour in Egypt, and something of what he has seen. Be careful of him: obey him, and do not rebel against anything he tells you on my
authority.[281] For when God arises to judge, and the Lord of hosts is

---

[277] Following Exod. 18: 6, but with 'Jethro' turned from the father-in-law into the son-in-
law of the person being addressed. Filosoff's daughter Esther is 'Michal' because she is married to 'King David' (2 Sam. 18: 20, 27–8) and 'Hadassah' because Esther is also named
Hadassah (Esther 2: 7). The string of endearments applied to her is taken from S. of S. 5: 2.
Ishmael Zevi is identified as her son, his real mother 'the Ashkenazi woman' (above, §21)
apparently having been blotted from the collective memory. (May we suspect Esther had
some part in this?) About 'her' other son Abraham we know nothing, unless Benayahu is correct in identifying him with the 'Abraham Zevi' who was killed in Salonica in the summer of
1697 (*The Sabbatian Movement in Greece* (Heb.), 167).

[278] Sabbatai promises, in other words, that he will soon come to Salonica in triumph.
Filosoff will then have revenge on his enemies in the city, the men who had forced him from
his rabbinical position and cut off his salary (Benayahu, *The Sabbatian Movement in Greece*,
31–2). Nothing of the sort ever happened, and Filosoff's career as religious leader was about
to undergo a twist that could not have been foreseen by Sabbatai or by himself (above, Introduction, section VIII).   [279] A pastiche of 2 Sam. 23: 1, Neh. 9: 5, Isa. 32: 8.

[280] A fuller version of this letter, preserved at Aleppo into the 1930s and copied from the
original manuscript by Israel's second president Yitshak Ben-Zvi, is published by Israel's third
president Zalman Rubashov (Shazar) in 'Sabbatian Documents from Aleppo'. A third version,
addressed to Sabbatai's followers at Arnaut-Belgrade, has survived in what seems to be Sabbatai's own handwriting: Amarilio, 'Sabbatian Documents' (Heb.), 238–9, 249–50. It seems
fairly clear that it was intended as a circular letter, sent to at least two places, which could be (as in
the Arnaut-Belgrade version) appended as a postscript to letters dealing with other matters. It
also seems clear that, as Rubashov says, Baruch has censored his version of the letter, reasonably judging that the megalomaniac blasphemy of the original would not sit well with his
readers. The version of the letter published by Rubashov is dated Monday, 23 Nisan, in a year
that must be 5436 (because there is no other suitable year in which 23 Nisan would have fallen
on Monday); that is, 6 April 1676. I have restored in brackets the words Baruch censored from
the original. See Appendix 2 for full translations of the three surviving versions, and also the
discussion in Halperin, 'Sabbatai Zevi, Metatron, and Mehmed', 292–4.

[281] The language is drawn from Exod. 23: 20–2, which an influential talmudic passage (BT

exalted in judgment, I will not forgive your sins. [And who is the God who can save you from my power? For apart from me there is no God.[282]]

But if you obey him and do all he tells you, I will surely arise and fill your treasuries.

Thus speaks the man raised up on high
[above the heights of the Father],[283]
exalted Lion and exalted Gazelle,
messiah of the God of Israel and Judah—
[SABBATAI ZEVI MEHMED].

TO MY BROTHER, MY COMPANION, MY DEAR FRIEND, THE NOBLE AND HONOURABLE RABBI JOSEPH KARILLO[284]— MAY HE BE EYEWITNESS TO GOD'S RETURN TO ZION!

Come to me, for God has made me lord of all Egypt! Come down to me without delay![285] Bring with you your two friends and colleagues, the honourable Rabbi Isaac Haver, may he be privileged to see God's salvation, and the honourable Rabbi Abraham Ohev, may he be privileged to see God's salvation.

Thus speaks the man raised up over all blessing and hymn, who
rises above nobilities—the messiah of the God of Judah and Israel.

San. 38*b*) interpreted as referring to the near-divine angel Metatron. Sabbatai identified himself with Metatron (above, n. 245); the parallel 'Arnaut-Belgrade' version makes it likely that the 'angel' of whom he speaks is none other than himself. Here Sabbatai takes on the roles both of the angelic messenger and of the God who 'sends' that messenger. The phrase 'all my honour in Egypt' is drawn from Gen. 45: 13, where the speaker is Joseph. We can only guess at the significance of 'Egypt' for Sabbatai, here and in the next letter; cf. Scholem, *Sabbatai Sevi*, 841–2; Liebes, 'Sabbatai Zevi's Attitude to his Conversion' (Heb.), 276–8 n. 69 (*On Sabbatianism*, 280–1 (endnotes)).

[282] The words in brackets combine Dan. 3: 15 (spoken by the heathen tyrant Nebuchadnezzar!) and Isa. 44: 6. No wonder Baruch thought it better to omit them.

[283] A blasphemous distortion of Isa. 14: 14, twisting אעלה על במתי עב, 'I will ascend above the heights of the clouds', into אעלה על במתי אב (*alef* in place of *ayin* as the first letter of the last word), 'I will ascend above the *heights of the Father*'. Sabbatai is not merely God; he is something superior to God. The demonic, 'Luciferian' element of his personality, which we have seen in his youth (Introduction, section II), here bursts forth a few months before his death, almost hair-raising in its insane thirst for power.

[284] One of Sabbatai's early followers, who converted to Islam in 1671 at Sabbatai's urging. We will meet him again in the Najara Chronicle and in the reminiscences of Abraham Cardozo (below). See Scholem, *Sabbatai Sevi*, index. About Karillo's two 'colleagues' we know nothing, unless, as Scholem suspects (ibid. 917), one of them is to be identified with the 'Ali Chelebi' who appears in Cardozo's story (see the notes on Cardozo's reminiscences). Their two surnames mean respectively 'friend' and 'lover'—the biblical Abraham is called God's 'lover' in Isa. 41: 8—and, although both names are entirely possible, the collocation of the two seems suspicious. I suspect 'Haver' and 'Ohev' may be symbolic rather than real persons.

[285] Following Gen. 45: 9—part of the same speech of Joseph's that Sabbatai draws on in the preceding letter.

[26. 'CONCEALMENT']

At the beginning of Tishri 5437 [8 September–7 October 1676][286] he summoned his brother Master Elijah, his wife, and the rabbis who were with him. He addressed them as follows:

'You must clearly understand I am going to depart from among you on the Day of Atonement, at the time of the concluding service. Carry me then to the cave I have prepared for myself by the seashore, in the "valley"'—by which he meant the border between Christendom and Islam[287]—'and on the third day let my brother Master Elijah come to the cave.'

On the Day of Atonement [17 September], at the time of the concluding prayer service, he departed. They did as he had ordered them. They carried him into the cave, then went their way.

On the third day his brother set out for the cave. At the cave's entrance was a great dragon, and it would not allow him to enter. Said Rabbi Elijah to the dragon: 'My brother ordered me before his departure to come to this cave on the third day. If you permit me to enter, I will do as he told me. Otherwise I will go home.'

So the serpent allowed him to enter. He looked all around him, but our Lord was not in the cave. Nor was there anything else there; but the entire house[?] was filled with light.[288]

It became known afterwards that our Lord had journeyed to our Israelite brethren, the ten 'tribes of the Lord'[289] on the far side of the River Sambatyon, there to wed the daughter of Moses our Teacher who lives on among them. If we are deserving, he will return to redeem us immediately after the seven days of his wedding celebrations. But if not, he will delay there until we are deluged by terrible calamities. Only then will he come to avenge us of our enemies and of those who hate us.

A certain rabbi from the land of Morea saw our Lord in the town called Malvasia.[290] That very week, [our Lord] told him, he would be on

---

[286] The correct year is given in three manuscripts; others, mistakenly, '5736'.

[287] Treating the Hebrew word *gai*, 'valley', as though it were composed of the initials of *gevul edom* [*ve*]*yishma'el*, 'border of Christendom and Islam'. 'The valley' presumably alludes to Deut. 34: 6, where God buries Moses in 'the valley [*gai*] in the land of Moab . . . and to this day no one knows where he is buried'—a hint that Baruch and his contemporaries did not claim to know the spot where Sabbatai's body had been laid?

[288] The reference to 'the entire house' seems out of place—one would expect, 'the entire cave'—but is attested by all the manuscripts. See the textual note to p. 68, l. 27, for a fuller discussion.   [289] Ps. 122: 4.

[290] Modern Monemvasia, just off the south-eastern coast of the Peloponnese. Malvasia was famous in early modern times for its sweet 'malmsey' wine, named after the town. (George, duke of Clarence, was supposedly done to death in 1478 by being 'drowned in a butt of malmsey'; Shakespeare made the future Richard III take the blame.)

his way to Great Tartary,[291] which is the proper route to the River Sambatyon.

Rabbi Nathan Benjamin also departed a year or two later,[292] having first announced he wanted to go and join our Lord. For, he said, he knew where it was he had gone.

These are but the smallest and most inadequate hints of that which was wrought by our Lord Sabbatai Zevi, messiah of the God of Jacob, and by Rabbi Nathan Benjamin the true and righteous prophet.

Now we shall briefly narrate some of the deeds of the faithful young man Joseph ibn Tsur, who was messiah son of Joseph.[293]

[27. THE STORY OF JOSEPH IBN TSUR][294]

On the night of Rosh Hashanah of the year 5434 from the Creation [11 September 1673], a spirit-guide appeared, neither in a dream nor in a waking

---

[291] Above, n. 237.

[292] The vagueness of the language, coupled with the blessing *nun-resh-vav* added after Nathan's name ('may the Merciful One protect and save him', used for people who are still alive), suggests that, at least originally, Baruch wanted to give the impression Nathan had not died. See the textual note to p. 69, l. 4, for a fuller discussion. In reality Nathan died in Üsküb (Skopje), Macedonia, on 11 January 1680, more than three years after Sabbatai: Scholem, *Sabbatai Sevi*, 925–7.

[293] 'Messiah ben Joseph' figures in rabbinic and early medieval traditions as a forerunner of the messiah proper, 'messiah ben David'. Often he is expected to die in battle against the gentiles, after which messiah ben David will complete the work he has begun. See above, Introduction, section VIII; Halperin, *Abraham Miguel Cardozo*, 40–2.

[294] Baruch's account of Joseph ibn Tsur is the fullest we have. Jacob Sasportas, himself of North African origin, devotes a paragraph to Ibn Tsur at the end of *Sefer tsitsat novel tsevi* (pp. 368–9), in which he seems to claim that Ibn Tsur expected, as messiah ben Joseph, to take Sabbatai Zevi's daughter as his wife. (Is this the mysterious daughter mentioned earlier by Baruch? See above, n. 232.) Cardozo mentions Ibn Tsur, along with Nathan of Gaza, among those who were led astray by false revelations and 'wrote heresies' (Halperin, *Abraham Miguel Cardozo*, 289). Elie Moyal draws upon an unpublished manuscript of 'Kabbalistic Interpretations of Master Joseph ben Tsur', compiled by Ibn Tsur's follower Daniel Bahlul and preserved in the Schocken Library in Jerusalem (MS 91); I have not seen the manuscript. See Moyal, *The Sabbatian Movement in Marroco* [sic] (Heb.), 116–25; Scholem, *Sabbatai Sevi*, 895–8; Hirschberg, *A History of the Jews in North Africa*, ii. 247–51.

state,[295] to a certain young man[296] in the city of Meknes in the land of Barbary.[297] His name was Joseph ibn Tsur, and he was wholly unlettered, yet God-fearing nonetheless.

[The spirit-guide] brought him the good news that the Redeemer had come. It forced him to his feet. It gave him a purificatory bath with the water of a single pitcher, which flowed so copiously he was obliged to change his clothes. He was shown, in heaven, our Lord and king Sabbatai Zevi. 'This man', he was told, 'is the true Redeemer, messiah son of David. Rabbi Nathan Benjamin is a true prophet. And you are messiah son of Joseph.'

The angel Raphael revealed to him an alphabet that went as follows:

ANI MELEKH HA'OZ SATAḤ DARAG PAKATS SHABAT TSAMAKH NOF[298]

This, [Raphael] said, was the sequence in which it[299] was revealed at Sinai. The letters became jumbled after the Israelites made the golden calf, which is why our current alphabet is in a different order. Using this alphabet, [Joseph] learned the whole Torah with its exalted mysteries; among all the scholars of the Maghreb he had no equal.

It was further revealed to him that the date of the End is hinted in the Torah and the book of Daniel. It is hinted in the Torah, in the verse that begins 'I call to witness [ha'idoti] against you this day' [Deut. 4: 26]. The date is calculated as follows: The letter heh of ha'idoti represents '5000';[300] the let-

---

[295] On the 'spirit-guide', see above, n. 175. But if Ibn Tsur was neither dreaming nor awake when he saw the 'spirit-guide', what other options are there? One is tempted to emend velo behakits to ela behakits, 'not in a dream but rather in a waking state'. This is an easy emendation, but if we make it here we must also make it in the letter of the anonymous Jew of Salé (below, §28), and in neither place does it have any manuscript support.

[296] Baḥur. If the word is used here to mean 'bachelor', as Moyal thinks (Sabbatian Movement, 117), this would give a special poignancy to Ibn Tsur's fantasy that he was destined to marry Sabbatai Zevi's daughter.

[297] North Africa, particularly the territories of Morocco and Algeria. Moyal points out (ibid. 116) that at the time of Ibn Tsur's appearance Meknes had just risen to considerable importance, having been picked by the Moroccan ruler Mulay Isma'il as his new capital and built up in grand style, in imitation of Louis XIV's Versailles.

[298] 'I am the King of Might satah darag pakats sabbath tsamakh nof.' These nine words contain the twenty-two letters of the Hebrew alphabet, plus the five special forms used at the ends of words, in an order that differs greatly from the standard sequence. It is surely significant that 'sabbath' appears in the seventh position, after three meaningless clusters of letters. (Daniel Bahlul, according to Moyal, quotes Ibn Tsur as identifying this 'sabbath' with Sabbatai Zevi.) Tsamakh nof, if read aloud (with the final kaf pronounced like ḥet), could possibly have been understood to mean something like 'foliage has sprouted'. On the manuscript variations with regard to this 'alphabet', see the textual note to p. 73, l. 8.

[299] The alphabet? The Torah?

[300] Heh would normally stand for 'five' in numerical calculations of this sort. But the practice of writing heh in dates, to indicate the first five millennia of the world's existence, was very common in this period.

ter *tav* is '400'; the letter *ayin* is '70'. Afterwards David will come, as indicated by [the remaining letters of *ha'idoti*, namely] *dalet* and *yod*.[301] The same date is indicated in the story of the Binding of Isaac, where God brings Abraham tidings of salvation at the time of the binding, saying to him: 'Now [*atah: ayin-tav-heh*] I know', and so forth [Gen. 22: 12]. And this was what our ancient rabbis had in mind when they said: 'If the Jews are deserving, I [God] will speed their redemption; if not, it will come in its appointed time [*itah: ayin-tav-heh*]', that is, in the year 5470.[302]

The date is hinted in Daniel, in the verse 'You shall rest [in your grave], then arise to your lot at the end of days' [Dan. 12: 13]. *Hayamin* ['days'] indicates the year 5435 [1674/5], in accordance with the previous system of calculation.[303] It is similarly hinted in the Psalms [40: 4]: 'He set a new song in my mouth: praise [*tehilah*] to our God.'[304]

Learned men, skilled kabbalists, came to speak with him. They came from Fez, the great centre of Jewish learning—from Marrakesh, Tetuan, Salé, and other places. They recognized clearly the divine source of his wisdom. From the Zohar, from Daniel, and from the Creation narrative of Genesis, he demonstrated to them that Israel's true Redeemer is our Lord Sabbatai Zevi, and that the redemption would take place on the eve of Passover 5435 [10 April 1675], after the elimination of the leaven.[305]

'Ask from your spirit-guide', the rabbis said to him, 'some miraculous sign to validate your claim.' He replied: 'What greater sign could you ask than this—that you knew me beforehand as one who could not so much as

---

[301] Standing for *david yavo*, 'David will come'. The letter *yod* occurs twice within *ha'idoti*, but is apparently counted only once. The numerical values presupposed by this exegesis are those of our current, 'jumbled' alphabetic sequence; the angelically revealed rearrangement seems to have had no effect on them. (The same is true, according to Moyal, of the numerical calculations in Daniel Bahlul's manuscript.)

[302] Baruch quotes the Talmud, BT *San.* 98*a*, which interprets the seeming contradiction in Isa. 60: 22, 'I am the Lord; in its appointed time I will speed it.' The three letters of 'its appointed time', *ayin-tav-heh*, are understood to indicate the year 5470 (1709/10). It would appear from what follows, and from what is said in §§29–30 below, that 5470 is indeed the 'appointed time' for the redemption. But if the Jews are 'deserving'—that is, if they undertake the sort of penitence to which the Sabbatian prophets called them—God will 'speed' the redemption to arrive thirty-five years earlier. On this passage, see Benayahu, *The Sabbatian Movement in Greece* (Heb.), 197 (which, however, mistakenly attributes Baruch's words to Jedidiah Zarfatti; see below, §30).

[303] That is, taking the opening letter *heh* as indicating '5000' and the remaining four letters (*yod-mem-yod-nun*) as adding up to 435. But those four letters in fact add up to 110, and I see no way to make the arithmetic come out right. See the following note.

[304] One of the two *hehs* of the word *tehilah* (*tav-heh-lamed-heh*, 'praise') is understood as '5000', the *tav* as '400'. The *lamed* and the remaining *heh* are added to get 35.

[305] The ritual act, performed the day before Passover, of destroying or disowning any leaven that happens to be in one's possession.

read Rashi,[306] and now I am revealing to you exalted mysteries of which you never had any inkling? And I will walk, if you like, through the main street of this town proclaiming Sabbatai Zevi to be the messiah of Israel, and you will see that no harm will come to me, to you, or to any other Jew.'

In consequence, many rabbis who had spoken ill words against our Lord came greatly to regret what they had done. They set their evil opinion behind them and are now believers in his faith. Throughout the land of Barbary a penitential movement was stirred up, even greater than the one that had accompanied our Lord's initial revelation. Meanwhile the patriarch Abraham revealed to [Ibn Tsur] that the redemption should properly have come ten years earlier. But the exile had been extended in deference to our Lord's prayers, in order that the Jewish people might be spared the woes that were to precede the messiah's coming, and that the unbelievers—who had been sentenced to death in heaven—might escape their doom.

The spirit-guide also explained the reason why our Lord had set the turban on his head. This was in order that he might become an object of ridicule, and thus bear the messianic woes on behalf of the entire Jewish people. [The spirit-guide] added that it served yet another purpose: to attract the sparks of holiness that had become embedded in the gentile nations, amid the 'shells'.[307] The messiah having thus come into the shells' domain, these sparks of purity would enter into him. For in our messiah they would have discovered a kindred spirit, and would thereby be awakened [to their true essence][308] and would cling to him.

But why, it may be asked, did he become a Turk and not a Christian? The answer is that the Turks had already incorporated all the sparks of holiness that were present in Christendom. (This is the hidden meaning of the verse, 'He will raise a standard for the gentiles, and gather the scattered of Israel' [Isa. 11: 12].[309]) And how did the Turks come to have all those sparks trapped within them? Through the Turkish king's practice of selecting young boys by lot, as his tribute from the Christians, and converting them to Islam.[310] By God's will the lot would choose only those boys possessing holy sparks.

[306] The medieval scholar (1040–1105) whose Bible commentary was one of the 'first-grade' subjects of traditional Jewish education. Any Jewish man who could not read the Bible with Rashi was considered ignorant indeed.

[307] Kabbalistic terminology for the demonic powers.

[308] The language is taken from BT *Eruv. 9a, AZ 73a, Bekh. 22a*; cf. Rashi on *AZ 73a*.

[309] Apparently understood to suggest that 'the scattered of Israel' are to be gathered via the gentiles.

[310] Baruch alludes to the practice of the 'devshirme', the levy imposed by the Ottoman sultans upon the Christian communities of the Balkans. The Janissaries, the elite corps of the Turkish military, were recruited from among the boys taken in the Devshirme. So were the pages and administrators in the sultan's palaces. See Lewis, *Everyday Life in Ottoman Turkey*, 25–7.

The consequence was that all the sparks of holiness have become embedded within the Turkish king; and that is why [Sabbatai] became a Turk. This
is a great wonder indeed. Rabbi Isaac Luria, of blessed memory, hints at it in
his writings.[311]

[28. CORRESPONDENCE CONCERNING JOSEPH IBN TSUR]

There follows the text of a letter sent by Rabbi Abraham ibn Amram to
Rabbi Benjamin Duran, Tuesday, 9 Shevat 5435 [5 February 1675]:[312]

To that splendid judge, that learned man, that
scholar bred of noble clan—the honourable Rabbi
Benjamin Duran (in the city of Algiers):

I must inform you, sir, that fresh reports arrive here daily from Meknes
concerning this young man, and the interpretations and secret revelations of which he speaks. I could not restrain myself when I realized what
was happening. It is essential, said I, that I go see it for myself.

So I took the Zohar and some other books, and travelled there to ask
him about certain obscure passages in the Zohar, intending to remain
until Passover. I discovered the young man to be humble and God-fearing, possessor of every good quality. When I told him, 'I have come to
learn from you the incomprehensible mysteries of the Zohar', he replied:
'I am astonished at Your Worship! For my own part, I do not even know
Rashi, and I do not know even a single verse of the Bible beyond what is
revealed to me.'

The first night I spent there I stayed awake past dawn, in the company
of two rabbis from the town of Alcazar. He told us the most delightful
things, exalted mysteries concerning the End. He spoke in a manner
lucid and brilliant, and, were he the possessor of three or four mouths, he
could have spoken with them all. He gave the impression of a full water-
skin with a narrow mouth; when one wants to bring forth what is inside it,
one turns it upside-down and its contents all come pouring out. So it is
with that young man.

[311] See the Introduction, section IX. All the manuscripts but one have *vekhuleh* ('and so
forth') at the end of this sentence. Perhaps Baruch intends by this to convey that he might, but
has chosen not to, quote the actual passages from the Lurianic writings.

[312] The Duran family had been prominent in Algiers since the end of the 14th century. A
part Hebrew, part Judaeo-Arabic letter from Palestine, dated 16 October 1684, makes mention of 'the judge Rabbi Benjamin Duran' in Algiers (Aranov, *A Descriptive Catalogue of the
Bension Collection*, 82). I have no information on Abraham ibn Amram.

He told us things we cannot put in writing, since they cannot be understood except in face-to-face conversation. He used his fingers to expound them, doing his calculations on his knuckles and the joints of his hand. The outcome of these calculations was that the End is to arrive, God willing, this coming Passover, as Your Worship will see from the pamphlet I shall send presently.

I asked him, 'Can you not enquire [of your spirit-guide] concerning these recondite passages of the Zohar?'[313] He replied: 'I do not know who it is that speaks with me. I see nothing and I say nothing. What happens is that my lips speak and the utterance comes forth from them, and this is the voice I hear.'

'But could you not enquire nonetheless?' I asked.

He responded: 'My senses no longer function [at the time of revelation], and I do not know whether I am in heaven or on earth'. He tries to open his eyes but cannot; it feels to him as if they were weighted shut with lead. He said many things with his own mouth and afterward insisted to me: 'I never said that!'

I asked if it were true he is messiah son of Joseph. 'That is what they tell me', he answered. Since birth he has had on his arm a mark shaped like a lily, from the first joint of his little finger to his forearm.[314]

I came from there, to make a long story short, in the most excellent spirits. It was clear to us he was not possessed by a ghost or a demon, God forbid, for his demeanour was exceedingly calm and rational, and all his conversation was of the divine Unity. Moreover, he fasts continually.

I asked him to perform some miraculous sign. 'What could be more miraculous', he replied, 'than what you now see? I once knew nothing even about the Bible, and now I speak of the ten *sefirot* and the kabbalistic mysteries. I am not telling you to anticipate a redemption that is one year away, or two years. Wait two months only; then you will no longer need to ask questions.

The text of a letter sent by Rabbi Jacob Aboab to Rabbi Solomon Halevi:[315]

[313] Which Ibn Amram had gone to ask about in the first place.

[314] A marker of some supernatural destiny, presumably. Sabbatai Zevi was reported to have had a 'messianic' birthmark in the shape of a lion on his left arm: Scholem, 'The Commentary on Psalms from the Circle of Sabbatai Zevi in Adrianople', 98–9.

[315] Aboab was rabbi in Tetuan, Morocco, subsequently (in the 1680s) president of the rabbinic court there. See Moyal, *The Sabbatian Movement in Marroco* (Heb.), 124–5. It is not clear whether this 'Solomon Halevi' is the same as the kabbalist who met Nathan at Safed in 1667, in the company of his distinguished father (above, §17), and who in 1675 was travelling through the Balkans into Hungary on a fundraising mission for the Palestinian communities (Yaari, *Mystery of a Book* (Heb.), 61).

The lads are with me until such time as Your Worship should arrive, God willing.[316] I do not want, moreover, to dispatch them with these good tidings until I see how matters turn out. The long and the short of it is that this preacher[317] of Meknes says our God's messiah will definitely reveal himself the eve of this coming Passover—amen! so may God do, for the sake of His name!—and that he is our Lord King Sabbatai Zevi.

Jews from here have travelled to [Meknes] and have seen him. He speaks hidden secrets, previously unknown and unheard of, and he provides the reasons for each. His best news was that the messianic woes are not going to happen, our exile having been extended for that reason.

Copy of a letter sent by a certain Jew of Salé to his brother in Leghorn, 24 Elul 5435 [15 September 1675]:[318]

We trust in our blessed God that soon we shall be redeemed!

Be aware, my honoured brother, that from the beginning of the year 5434 there has appeared here [in Morocco], in the place called Meknes, a Jew named Master Joseph ibn Tsur who has spoken prophecies. He was an unlettered man, all his life God-fearing, with no knowledge of Torah whatsoever. On the night of Rosh Hashanah 5434, a spirit-guide came to him, neither in a dream nor in a waking state,[319] and declared to him the good news that the Redeemer had come. It forced him to his feet; it gave him a purificatory bath with the water of a pitcher he was in the habit of keeping by his pillow at night. The water flowed so copiously he was obliged to change his clothes.

In that night [he and the spirit-guide] studied the entire Torah, with mysteries so great there was not a single rabbi in all the Maghreb who could best him on any subject whatever. Many of these mysteries even the late, great Rabbi Joseph, who died in the month of Kislev, was unable to penetrate.[320] The spirit-guide's revelations prompted all the people of the Maghreb, small and great alike, to undertake a penitential movement that was greater by far than the penitence in Sabbatai Zevi's time.

The rabbis questioned this prophet about what the spirit-guide had told him, that the messiah would reveal himself after midnight on the eve

---

[316] We can only guess at who these 'lads' are and why Aboab is keeping them with him.

[317] *Magid*, the same word that is normally used for the 'spirit-guide'. But here the reference seems to be to Joseph ibn Tsur himself.

[318] Six days before the beginning of the new year 5436.   [319] See above, n. 295.

[320] I do not know who the 'late, great Rabbi Joseph' might have been. By 'Kislev', the writer might intend either Kislev 5434 (10 November–9 December 1673) or Kislev 5435 (30 November–29 December 1674).

of Passover 5435. All the Jewish communities of the Maghreb had gathered in their homes that Passover eve, in a state of continual expectation;
yet, for our many sins, [the messiah] was delayed and did not arrive. The
prophet answered, on the spirit-guide's authority, that it was compelled
thus to happen on account of the plenteous sins of the Jewish people. For
the sake of the anguish the prophet suffered in that he had been shown up
as a liar, those sins had now been forgiven.[321]

Now he says the spirit-guide has told him he is messiah son of
Ephraim—Sabbatai Zevi being messiah son of David—and has shown
him many oblique and mysterious passages [in the sacred writings] that
point in this direction. His face, meanwhile, shines with such radiance
that not a single rabbi can look upon it. He therefore has a sheet hanging
in the room where he sits as a partition between him and the rabbis, and
they speak with him from the opposite side of the curtain.[322] He studies
Torah day and night, profound mysteries are revealed to him daily, and
one great rabbi, to whom Elijah appeared while he was awake, has said
this prophet's face resembles Elijah's. He says, whenever asked, that the
redemption is very near indeed.

We trust in our blessed God that in [this coming] year 5436 our
redemption shall be manifested, in accord with the secret hints given by
the patriarchs,[323] such that [you and I] may hope to see one another in
Jerusalem this very year! All the forced converts[324] in the Maghreb are
now performing great acts of penitence, fasting for days on end, and giving alms. They have made for themselves special finery, and are in a state
of continual readiness for the journey to Jerusalem. With God's help shall
we witness this, and our hearts rejoice.

Do please write and send me some good news from your part of the
world, about Sabbatai Zevi, his prophet [Nathan], or the like. This shall
be our comfort.

[29. CONCLUDING REFLECTIONS]

The young man, acknowledged as God's true prophet, died after that. True,
redemption had not arrived when he said it would. Yet all knew clearly that
this was God's doing, and no one is entitled to question His decisions.

[321] Surely one of the more remarkable excuses in the long history of failed prophecy!

[322] *Me'ahorei hapargod*, used in the Talmud for revelations granted from behind the heavenly curtain that separates God from His angels.

[323] Abraham, for example (above, §27).

[324] *Anusim*, normally used for those Jews forced to convert to Catholicism in 15th-century
Spain, and for their descendants.

Who is there, after all, who has taken part in God's privy council? Who has listened to His plan and understood it? His is the measure of human events; surely He will show us marvels and speed our salvation. Amen! so be His will.

Final repentance and final redemption, as I have written above, will not come all at once.[325] Rather, we shall perform some slight penitence and experience some slight redemption, followed by increased penitence and increased redemption, until at length both repentance and Redemption shall be complete.

At the time of our messiah's first appearance, there indeed sprang up a penitential movement encompassing the entire Jewish people. But it is essential to grasp that this repentance was incomplete. For people repented only of their sins against God; of sins against their fellow-humans—with a very few exceptions in the Ashkenazi lands[326]—they did not repent at all. And our ancient rabbis have declared that 'the Day of Atonement can effect no atonement for the wrongs one person does to another, until the injured party is appeased'.[327]

Proof that the repentance was incomplete may be found in this: nowhere throughout all Italy did we hear of anyone saying to anyone else, 'Here are the hundred *scudi* I stole from you'—or even some more trivial amount. (Yet the Torah insists that 'he must return whatever it was he stole', and so forth [Lev. 5: 23].) No one repented of such things as exploiting one another, injuring one another, insulting or cursing one another, or the like; hence their repentance could not be complete. When our messiah appears for the second time, however, we must perform a complete penitence, covering our sins against our fellows as well as those against God. The Lord, whose hand is always stretched out to welcome the penitent, will then accept our repentance. This, God willing, will be the ultimate Redemption.

Therefore, my brethren and friends, be bold and steadfast, and let this *Memorial* ever be your guide. Stand firm within the fortress of perfect penitence. For our salvation is near at hand, our righteousness about to be revealed.[328]

O ye worthy rabbis of Israel! Solid pillars, upon whom rests the house of Jacob! Now that God has revealed all this to you, you must listen carefully to what I say and let it be your wisdom and consolation. Read this *Memorial*

---

[325] Referring back to the preface.   [326] Above, n. 31.   [327] Mishnah *Yoma* 8: 9.
[328] The two manuscripts L₂,W₁, which I believe to represent a 'second edition' of Baruch's *Memorial*, transfer these four paragraphs (from 'Final repentance and final redemption . . .') to the end of the preface. See my introduction to the *Memorial*, and the textual notes.

through two or three times. Then study carefully what is said on this subject in the Zohar and the *Tikunei zohar*,[329] in the *midrashim* and the utterances of our [ancient] rabbis, in our true and righteous prophets. You will arrive at the clear understanding that it was our true Redeemer who revealed himself for the first time in the year 5426 [1665/6]. You will know for certain that the word of the Lord indeed came to Rabbi Nathan Benjamin, and also to the young man of Meknes, Master Joseph ibn Tsur. True, their predictions about the time of the redemption went unfulfilled. Yet we can hardly declare them liars. Rather, it was thus decreed from heaven; and many of the greatest and most monumentally learned scholars, ancient and modern alike, have similarly gone astray and become hopelessly confused on this subject. (So the learned Ibn Yahya demonstrates in his book.[330]) Why? Because 'the day of vengeance is in My heart' [Isa. 63: 4], and the angels themselves do not know when it is to be.

We must look toward God's mercies, that soon [the messiah] will reveal himself once more, when God shall again settle His holy spirit upon him. It will not be as it was the first time, when everything transpired as though in a cloudy mirror, and all was therefore open to doubt. No; the Lord's spirit shall now 'rest upon him: a spirit of wisdom and understanding, a spirit of counsel and might, a spirit of knowledge and fear of God' [Isa. 11: 2]. In a clear, sparkling mirror shall all this take place, and all the peoples shall see his glory.

O ye elderly! Aged folk, well advanced in years! Do not be frightened or disheartened by our rabbis' dictum in *Midrash rabah*, that following his appearance our messiah will be concealed from us forty-five years.[331] Do not on that account despair of seeing the Redemption. For thus speaks the Lord: 'I am the Lord; in its appointed time I will speed it.'[332] Granted that the final End is 'appointed' for the year 5470 [1709/10]—that is, the year *ayin–tav–heh*[333]—nevertheless 'I will speed it'—I will not wait until all those years have elapsed.

---

[329] Above, n. 187.

[330] No doubt referring, as Freimann says in his note on this passage, to the stories of false messiahs and calculations of the end that Ibn Yahya attaches to his account of Maimonides (*Sefer shalshelet hakabalah*, 32b–35b). On Ibn Yahya, see above, n. 19.

[331] Above, §1; but the rabbinic sources, and the quotations from them given above, speak of 'forty-five days' and not 'forty-five years'. When Baruch began to write the *Memorial*, the news of Sabbatai's death was still fresh and it was possible to believe he would return after forty-five days—permitting, no doubt, a certain amount of leeway—as the ancient sages had prophesied. By the time Baruch wrote this passage, that had plainly become impossible. He therefore chose to interpret the midrash's 'days' as 'years', and now seeks to evade the depressing implications of this calculation.

[332] Isa. 60: 22; see above, n. 302.

[333] Spelling *itah*, 'its appointed time'.

God acted similarly [with regard to the Israelites' enslavement] in Egypt. He had indeed declared: 'They will serve [the Egyptians], and they will oppress them four hundred years' [Gen. 15: 13]. Yet in fact they remained in their exile only 210 years, that being the numerical value of the word *redu*, 'go down' [Gen. 42: 2]. Thus will it be in our days, God willing. Consider further: our ancestors in Egypt merited this, even though they had to their credit only two commandments, the Paschal sacrifice and the circumcision. We, by contrast, have God's entire pure and perfect Torah with its 613 commandments. Shall we not, God willing, merit the same?

Therefore, house of Israel, you must all stand firm within the fortress of penitence and good deeds. You must help one another in God's Torah and in the faith of His messiah, for faith in the Redeemer is a most essential principle. The Jews were redeemed from Egypt only on account of their faith— as it is written, 'The people believed'[334]—and the believers in this pure and holy faith have the strength of a lion, who reduces [all around him] to a state of terror.[335] And all who babble blasphemy against God and His Messiah will pay for it.

God grant our eyes shall witness the king in his beauty, in his proper form, in his splendour! God grant we see our holy and splendid Temple rebuilt, and the priests offering sacrifice and the Levites chanting hymns and the lay folk drawn up in their corresponding orders! Amen! so be His will.

[30. ADDENDUM: THE COMMENTS OF JEDIDIAH ZARFATTI][336]

I have seen all you have written, and it is very fine indeed. The assertion, however, that the messiah is to be concealed for forty-five years,[337] would be wholly unthinkable even if it were not for Rabbi Nathan's prophecy on his deathbed that the final End will come in the year 5452 [1691/2]. At this time the dead will be resurrected and the Temple rebuilt.

---

[334] Exod. 4: 31, as interpreted in midrash *Exodus Rabbah* 23: 5.

[335] The final words of this sentence are difficult, and the manuscripts differ considerably among themselves. See the textual note to p. 77, ll. 13–15, for details.

[336] This section is found only in the two manuscripts representing the 'second edition' of Baruch's *Memorial* (see the textual note, and the introduction to this translation). Baruch evidently gave a copy of his original *Memorial* to his fellow-Sabbatian Zarfatti, who arrived in Italy from Turkey around 1679 and, over the next few years, travelled around Italy raising money to ransom Jewish captives (Benayahu, *The Sabbatian Movement in Greece* (Heb.), 75, 411–14). Either Baruch himself, or some anonymous continuator of his work, found Zarfatti's response so useful he decided to incorporate it within the 'second edition'.

[337] Made by Baruch in the preceding section.

I must call your attention also to the holy Zohar's treatment (at the end of the section on the Torah portion 'Va'ethanan') of the biblical verse, 'For the evening shadows are extending' [Jer. 6: 4]. Here the Redemption is discussed at some length. "'It shall be in the end [of days]" [Isa. 2: 2]—*be'aharit*, "in the end", is to be taken in its most exact sense.'[338] Calculate the numerical value of the word *be'aharit* ['in the end'], and you will find it comes to 1620.[339]

With this in mind you will understand what the Zohar goes on to say: 'What is the measure of this "shadow"? Six and a half handbreadths, equivalent to the measure of [the shadow of] an ordinary man.' Now, the calculation I have just proposed will define the Zohar's measure of 'six and a half handbreadths', of which three years yet remain before the coming of our messiah. (Our calculation assumes the destruction of our holy Temple, may it soon be rebuilt, as its starting point.)[340]

Allow me to tell you further of a most extraordinary experience I had with a certain bishop, a great expert in astronomy.[341] He remarked to me: 'God seems to take precious poor care of you in this interminable exile of yours, which has lasted 1617 years so far.[342] Would you care to explain to me why?'

'The measure', I said to him, 'remains yet to be filled.'

'And how much will it take to fill that "measure"?'

I told him this was a secret tightly wrapped in obscurity, God's heart having concealed it even from His own mouth.[343]

---

[338] Zohar, iii. 270*a*, freely quoted and very freely reinterpreted. When the Zohar speaks of the 'most exact sense' of the word *be'aharit*, it intends the theosophical symbolism of the word. Zarfatti, by contrast, takes the 'exact sense' to be the word's numerical value.

[339] Understanding the *alef* of *be'aharit* as equivalent to 1,000; the remaining letters add up to 620. (The manuscripts' *aharit* must be emended to *be'aharit* in order for the calculation to work.)

[340] This very complex and elliptical argument may be set forth as follows. Just as the destruction of the Temple and the subsequent 'day' of exile were preceded by shadows—it is of these 'shadows' that Jeremiah complains, 'Woe is me . . . for the evening shadows are extending' (Jer. 6: 4)—so the new day that follows the exile will begin with a 'shadow'. Thus far the Zohar, which adds: 'The "day" plus the "shadow"—this is the end of the exile.' The 'day', in accordance with Ps. 90: 4, is 1,000 years long. The 'shadow', as defined by the Zohar, is 'six and a half handbreaths', which Zarfatti takes to mean six centuries plus a fraction of a century. So the exile will last 1,600 years, plus some fraction of a century; Zarfatti's calculation of the numerical value of *be'aharit* allows us to specify its duration as 1,620 years. Since (according to the Jewish chronographers of early modern times) the Temple was destroyed in 68 CE, it follows that the exile will end and the messiah arrive in 1688—which Zarfatti asserts to be three years in the future. The rebuilding of the Temple and resurrection of the dead, prophesied by Nathan of Gaza, are presumably to happen at a later stage.

[341] Or astrology?

[342] Which, counting from 68 CE, would bring the date of the conversation to 1685.

[343] Following the exposition of Isa. 63: 4 in BT *San.* 99*a*. Cf. above, n. 101.

'Yet you may infer it', the bishop said to me, 'from analysing the reasons behind your laws. Your penalty of flogging, imposed upon someone whose sin merits it, consists of "forty strokes and no more" [Deut. 25: 3]. When you sinned against God in the desert and made the golden calf, He condemned you to spend forty years in the desert, "one year for each day [of your sin]" [Num. 14: 34]. You may calculate the length of your current exile by multiplying forty times forty.'[344]

'That comes to 1,600 years', I said. 'And they are already behind us.'

'Not at all', said he. 'The forty-first [period of forty years] is the [time of] hoping, in which you await [the messiah] daily until 41 × 40 years have passed.'[345]

So said the bishop, and there seems considerable justice in his argument.

A short time afterwards I was hunting up a passage in a midrash anthology in preparation for a sermon, and I found that what the bishop said was in accordance with our ancient rabbis. This is how the rabbis put it: 'Whenever God has punished Israel, it has been by multiples of forty, as it is written, "Forty days, one year for each day" [Num. 14: 34]. In their final exile, too, they will be punished by a multiple of forty.'[346]

There is more I would like to write, but the dreadful diseases from which I suffer have sapped my strength. I pray God grant me complete recovery. Amen! so be His will.

I shall come to you like a river of peace abounding, and our eyes will gaze upon the king in his beauty. Amen!

So writes the weary wanderer, the outcast exile,
in bitterness and grief and aching everywhere—
Jedidiah Zarfatti.

---

[344] The logic (less than rigorous) seems to run as follows: Num. 14: 34 attests a mathematical relationship between duration of sin and duration of punishment. We may infer from this a parallel relationship between past and present punishments. The forty years' wandering in the desert may be considered a single 'stroke' imposed upon a sinful people. Since the Torah's laws are intended to communicate the ways of God, the limitation of 'strokes' to forty suggests that the exile will last no more than 40 × 40 = 1,600 years.

[345] In other words, the exile should have ended in 1668; from then until 1708 the Jews may be expected to live in daily anticipation of their messiah. (The bishop could easily have got the impression, from observing Sabbatians like Zarfatti, that this was indeed the case.) In 1708, presumably—in the bishop's expectation, if not Zarfatti's—they will give up hope and accept that their messiah has already come in the person of Jesus. One gets the impression the bishop is not altogether friendly, and may be more interested in parodying the Jewish methods of calculating the End than in imitating them. If so, Zarfatti has missed this entirely.

[346] I do not know the midrash Zarfatti is quoting.

SECOND TESTIMONY
The Letters of Joseph Halevi

☙

INTRODUCTION

FOUR LETTERS from Rabbi Joseph Halevi of Leghorn are preserved in the book *Sefer tsitsat novel tsevi* ('Zevi's Fading Flower'), Jacob Sasportas's dossier of materials on the Sabbatian movement in its heyday.[1] One of these letters, the earliest, was written by Halevi to an Alexandrian 'believer' named Hosea Nantawa at the beginning of November 1666, when the rumours of Sabbatai's apostasy had begun to spread.[2] It is a prolonged howl of triumphant rage, an 'I told you so' from a man who had always loathed Sabbatai Zevi and now saw himself vindicated, which Halevi copied and sent to his fellow-sceptic Sasportas for his delectation. The other three letters—dated, respectively, the last week of November 1666, 16 February 1667, and 27 March 1667—are reports addressed to Sasportas himself.[3]

About Halevi we know surprisingly little. From his letters, and from the framing narrative of *Sefer tsitsat novel tsevi*, we can gather he was rabbi and preacher in the newly thriving port city of Leghorn (Livorno), whose Jewish community was then some decades old. Yet Renzo Toaff's massive history of the Jewries of seventeenth-century Pisa and Leghorn contains not a single mention of him.[4] He wrote, as a learned rabbi would be expected to do, pre-sumably on religious subjects other than Sabbatai Zevi. What these were we do not know. 'I intend, if God favours us, to bring my complete works to press', he told Sasportas.[5] But God did not favour Joseph Halevi, at least not in this regard. No published writings of his are known, and perhaps this has something to do with the obscurity that seems to surround him. We shall see presently that there may have been other factors involved.

Halevi was a brilliant Hebrew stylist. He wrote his letters burning with anger against Sabbatai and his believers—'these nincompoops, these credu-

---

[1] Published in a critical edition by Isaiah Tishby: *Sefer tsitsat novel tsevi* (Jerusalem: Bialik Institute, 1954). The title Sasportas gave his book is a learned pun on Isa. 28: 4, *tsevi* both meaning 'beauty' and being part of Sabbatai Zevi's name.

[2] Ibid. 186–97. The letter is dated to the week of 2–8 Heshvan 5427 (31 October–6 November 1666).   [3] Ibid. 169–74, 247–51, 255–6.

[4] *La Nazione Ebrea a Livorno e a Pisa (1591–1700)*. The Joseph Halevi who was fundraiser for the Hebron Jewish community, and who presented his credentials at Pisa in 1669 (ibid. 84), was surely not our Joseph Halevi.   [5] In his first letter, below.

lous imbeciles'—in pungent, at times scarifying prose. Often he is offensive in his vituperation, his bitterness, his undisguised thirst for revenge. He is never boring. The first two of his surviving letters to Sasportas give a supremely vivid portrait, almost photographic in quality, of what it was like to be Jewish and sentient in 1666 and early 1667, when news of the messiah's apostasy had begun to leak out but had not yet been fully confirmed. These are the two letters translated here.[6] According to one contemporary report[7] Halevi also composed a book on Sabbatai, unpublished like the rest of his writings. The book is lost, as is his letter to Sasportas telling of the bedroom antics of Sabbatai's intended bride.[8] This is regrettable—they would have made lively reading.

The value of Halevi's letters as historical sources cannot be over-estimated. The first, from November 1666, gives one of the earliest as well as most compelling accounts of Sabbatai's conversion to Islam. The second conveys the various expedients by which the believers of Leghorn resisted or reinterpreted the indigestible news; these foreshadow the more sophisti-cated and carefully developed rationalizations that Nathan of Gaza and Abraham Cardozo would begin to offer a year or two later. Several of Halevi's *bêtes noires* appear in this second letter: 'the physician Rabbi Isaac Nahar', Raphael Supino ('a boiling cauldron frothing over with badness'), and the 'deluded numbskull' Moses Pinheiro, a companion of Sabbatai's from eighteen years back and still his devoted believer. Ironically, Toaff's history reckons Nahar, Supino, and Pinheiro among the rabbis active in Leghorn in the seventeenth century, along with the anti-Sabbatians Jacob Hagiz, Immanuel Frances, and Sasportas.[9] Only Halevi is missing.

In *Sefer tsitsat novel tsevi*, Sasportas tells a strange story about Isaac Nahar. This Amsterdam physician and kabbalist set forth in the middle of March 1666, together with the wealthy philanthropist Abraham Pereira—who also makes an appearance in Halevi's second letter—to pay homage to their messiah in the Holy Land. In Leghorn, Nahar made a stop. Realizing 'that nearly everyone there was a believer, he made a great display of the intensity of his own faith [in Sabbatai Zevi] and thus won their support against Rabbi Joseph Halevi, who was an unbeliever. He stayed on there, certain he would be appointed their rabbi, ingratiating himself all the while by gathering

---

[6] Halevi's third letter (*Sefer tsitsat novel tsevi*, 255–6) is very little more than a hasty summary of the second, made in the mistaken belief that Sasportas had not received the earlier letter.

[7] From the poet Immanuel Frances (1618–1710), cited in Tishby's note on *Sefer tsitsat novel tsevi*, 5, and Scholem, *Sabbatai Sevi*, 933.

[8] Mentioned by Sasportas in *Sefer tsitsat novel tsevi*, 5; see above, Introduction, section IV.

[9] All but Pinheiro are in Toaff's listing of thirty-two rabbis (*La Nazione Ebrea*, 343–58); for Pinheiro see the index.

small crowds and preaching to them. They eventually offered him a salary of two hundred *grossos* per year. He has been there ever since, about two years now.'[10] Toaff confirms that Nahar appears in 1669 as superintendent of the Leghorn Talmud Torah (Jewish religious academy), and claims, without citing his sources, that Nahar served as rabbi there from 1671 to some time after 1686.[11]

Sasportas represents Nahar as a thoroughly slippery character, who had 'been manoeuvring all along for the position' at Leghorn, and a few years earlier had hypocritically persuaded Sasportas not to accept the job when it was offered him.[12] ('God pay him back for what he did!') Initially, it would seem, Halevi was charmed by the learned and versatile visitor from Amsterdam. He appears in the November 1666 letter as 'our friend Rabbi Isaac Nahar'; his support is invoked against false rumours impugning Halevi's integrity. By February 1667 the 'friendship' has gone sour. It is easy to imagine what must have happened in the interim. The truth had dawned on Halevi that Nahar was angling for his job.

'If [Nahar's] aim in coming here [to Leghorn] was to make himself supreme authority, to preach, to deliver legal rulings—if so, I can tell you, he is pouring out his energies for nothing.' So Halevi assures Sasportas, towards the end of his second letter. Halevi's confidence, unfortunately, was not very well founded. In his third letter to Sasportas, dated 27 March 1667, he seems to have a chill sense of which way the wind is blowing. 'Everyone who has believed [in Sabbatai Zevi] is here the people's darling and enjoys their esteem; not so those who have disbelieved.' He is a frightened man. 'I beg Your Worship to say nothing of our communications on this subject in Amsterdam, for whatever is said there comes by letter here. But keep all our exchanges a tightly guarded secret.'[13]

'Uno dei più considerati rabbini della città' ('one of the most respected rabbis of the city'). This is how Toaff describes Isaac Nahar.[14] Joseph Halevi, meanwhile, seems to have vanished entirely from the collective memory of the Leghorn Jewish community. Purged from the record, perhaps, by the victorious Nahar? We are unlikely ever to know. Yet some memory of this

---

[10] *Sefer tsitsat novel tsevi*, 57. From Sasportas's account we know that Nahar and Pereira left Amsterdam some time after February 1666; the more precise date can be gathered from other sources (Scholem, *Sabbatai Sevi*, 529–30). On Nahar, see also Scholem, pp. 488, 522, 761.

[11] *La Nazione Ebrea*, 353, 371. Scholem makes the contrary claim, also without citing any source, that Nahar went back to Amsterdam in 1668 (*Sabbatai Sevi*, 761).

[12] Sasportas assures us he never really wanted to be rabbi in Leghorn anyway, but much preferred a rival offer from London. It was Sasportas's bad luck that the Great Plague of 1665 broke out not long after he had taken up the London position, and he found himself jobless once more.   [13] *Sefer tsitsat novel tsevi*, 256.   [14] *La Nazione Ebrea*, 371.

clear-sighted, passionate, and supremely eloquent man has come down to us through his letters to his friend Sasportas, and for this we may be grateful.

THE TEXT

The material that became *Sefer tsitsat novel tsevi* survives in two versions.[15] One of these, a manuscript formerly owned by the Berlin Hochschule für die Wissenschaft des Judentums,[16] seems to be Sasportas's own autograph. It is not, however, *Sefer tsitsat novel tsevi* as Sasportas intended it to be published, but a notebook into which Sasportas transcribed the correspondence he sent and received, along with other relevant documents. Only later did Sasportas shape these materials into a book, providing them with a narrative framework, here and there touching up the original texts to show himself as more courageous and confidently outspoken against the Sabbatians than he really was.[17] The finished work is, or rather was, represented by a single manuscript, formerly in the possession of the Israelitische Kultusgemeinde in Vienna, which A. Z. Schwarz described in his catalogue as having been written in 'Spanish-rabbinic' script of the seventeenth or eighteenth century.[18]

During the Second World War the Nazis confiscated the manuscripts of the Vienna Kultusgemeinde, and no one knows what became of *Sefer tsitsat novel tsevi*.[19] Schwarz had made a copy of it, however, and in 1954 Isaiah Tishby used this copy (his MS A) as the base text for his critical edition of the book, from which my translations are taken. Tishby entered the readings from Sasportas's notebook (MS B) in his critical apparatus. Where the two differ significantly in the Halevi letters—which does not happen very often—I invariably follow the MS B readings. These may be trusted to represent something close to what Halevi originally wrote, without Sasportas's editorial interference.

A small but telling example: early in the first letter, according to MS A, Halevi speaks of 'our friend, the late Rabbi Solomon Abudarham' (*kaf-mem-heh-resh, shelomoh abudarham, zayin-lamed*, literally 'Rabbi Solomon Abudarham of blessed memory').[20] In MS B, however, the abbreviation attached to Abudarham's name is *nun-resh-vav*, 'may the Merciful One guard and save

---

[15] Besides the later abridgment *Kitsur tsitsat novel tsevi*, published at Amsterdam in 1737 and again at Altona in 1757.

[16] Brought to America in 1936 by Joseph Gutmann, and currently located at Yeshiva University in New York (MS 1251). See Richler, *Guide to Hebrew Manuscript Collections*, 16–17.

[17] Tishby, introduction to *Sefer tsitsat novel tsevi*, 39–44; Scholem, *Sabbatai Sevi*, 566–9, 577.

[18] Schwarz, *Die hebräische Handschriften in Österreich*, 92 (no. 142).

[19] Richler, *Guide to Hebrew Manuscript Collections*, 196, 250. [20] *Sefer tsitsat novel tsevi*, 170.

him', used exclusively for people who are living. The explanation is not far to seek. When Halevi wrote his letter in 1666, Abudarham was still alive. When Sasportas redacted the letter for publication, sometime in the course of the next two years,[21] Abudarham had died. Sasportas altered the text to reflect the new reality.

LETTER 1
To Jacob Sasportas of Hamburg,
21–27 November 1666

TO OUR WESTERN LIGHT, OUR SCHOLAR, MORE EXCELLENT THAN A PROPHET—OUR WORTHY RABBI, ADMIRABLE JUDGE, MAN OF LEARNING AND OF NOBLE BIRTH—THE HONOURABLE RABBI JACOB SASPORTAS, WHOSE LIGHT, PLEASE GOD, SHALL NEVER DIE OUT:[22]

Peace, peace, to him who is distant and him who is near!—to you who are distant from my sight, yet ever near in my heart and my thoughts. Your letter has arrived, bearing the good news that all is well with you and you are in fine health, and I pray God you may ever flourish and prosper most splendidly.

Let the skies bear witness: if I had all the money in the world, it could not give me more satisfaction than I have when I reflect that our friendship has survived all the cares that afflict me, despite our never yet having met face to face, beyond what our friend Rabbi Solomon Abudarham has told me about you. I never fail to ask about you whenever some traveller passes through our town, and the good Lord alone knows the grief I felt when Rabbi Isaac Palache brought me news of all your misfortunes. I devoutly hope your sorrows and ours will soon be at an end, and you will again find the happiness you once knew.[23]

A full year has passed since we began to receive letters from Alexandria, from Egypt, from the Holy Land, from Syria and from all Asia, announcing that

---

[21] Tishby's introduction, *Sefer tsitsat novel tsevi*, 34–9.

[22] The Talmud speaks of the 'western light' as holding a special place among the seven lights of the Temple candelabrum. Its flame was a token of the divine presence in Israel (BT *Shab.* 22*b*), and its occasional dying out was an omen of the Temple's destruction (BT *Yoma* 39*a*). Halevi uses this image to make graceful allusion to Sasportas's North African ('western') origin.

[23] When Sasportas was a dazzling young scholar in the Maghreb—president in his twenties of the rabbinical court at Tlemcen—and not a learned but under-employed wanderer through the cities of Europe.

our redemption was at hand. This good news was brought us by a brainless adolescent from Gaza, Nathan the Lying Prophet, who, not satisfied with proclaiming himself a prophet, went on to anoint king of Israel a coarse, malignant lunatic whose Jewish name used to be Sabbatai Zevi.[24]

All Jewry invoked this man as 'our king', 'our saviour', 'our redeemer', 'Israel's one and only saviour'. Our leaders were as bad as anyone: those rabbis, I mean, who wrote to us that we ought to believe in him as in God's unity and Moses' Torah, who called him by such names as 'the Lord our righteousness', 'king of kings of kings', 'Almighty',[25] 'God', and so many more titles of this kind it would take days to record them. Every mangy outcast declared himself a prophet, edifying the people with prophetic lies.

Once the delusion had begun to flourish in this country, I found myself presented with the demand that I preach to the people on the subject of repentance. Very well, I preached—not in private, but in full public view, and I did not mince my words. If they wanted to repent, I warned the people, they must do it for its own sake. Did they imagine repentance consists of fasting and penitential prayers? Hardly! Rather, they must disgorge their loot, give back the money they stole from one another, put an end to their meaningless grudges; they must stop drinking the gentiles' wine and shaving off their sidelocks, running after gentile women, and so forth. It is no true repentance otherwise, I told them, and the Lord will not find it acceptable. The rabble did not like *that* very much, I can assure you! Least of all did they like my demand that they return the money they had stolen, since it is not very easy to give back money that has already been spent.

For they had put their trust in the letters that had been arriving from many different places, promising them that every true believer is assured of the next world. Their prophet of Gaza had written that the messiah is able to justify even the most abandoned sinner, and has sovereign power to bring even his infamous executed predecessor[26] into a blessed afterlife. He has by the same token power to damn even the purest saint, with the result that the unbeliever—who dare not even ask for some miracle in proof of his mission—can have no share in the next world, even if he has Torah and good deeds to his credit. And everyone in the world believed this libertine trash as though it were the Torah of Moses.

It was against this that I preached to the people. The unbeliever, I told them, is under no disadvantage whatsoever. Torah and good deeds are what

---

24   This is the letter's first hint at Sabbatai's apostasy.
25   Shaddai; see nn. 139, 171 on Baruch of Arezzo.
26   That is, Jesus. Halevi refers in this paragraph to Nathan's epistle to Raphael Joseph Chelebi (September 1665), which was very widely circulated and quoted in the months that followed. See Scholem, *Sabbatai Sevi*, 272.

counts: he who has them to his credit is assured of the next world, and he who does not is headed straight for hellfire. We do not believe as do the gentiles, I told them, who think that a human being is capable of saving souls.

Hardly was this past, before the 'prophesying' began among the worthless scum of our land. People would pretend to go into a swoon, fall to the ground, babble sundry inanities, and predict the future.[27] All our dull-witted dunces, of course, believed them. 'Prophets of the Lord', they called them; praised be the Lord, they said, that He has come to look after us, giving us a prophet of our very own. They dared even to preach insubordination against the rabbis of the Mishnah and Gemara.

Faced with this, I found myself seized by an indignation that could not be suppressed. I stepped forward boldly and preached a public sermon on the prophecy of Gideon.[28] I laid out for them the stages of prophecy and wisdom; I explained that a prophet must engage in solitary contemplation, abstracting his intellect through all the stages and all the worlds. I showed how prophecy came upon the prophets, and how it was that a prophet might delude himself into thinking he had achieved true prophecy when all he had was the illusion thereof. I analysed the source of such errors, and the tests a prophet must apply to his prophecy to discover whether or not it was illusory. I explored profound questions of this sort, basing my arguments upon the Zohar and the Gemara.

The wealthy and enlightened folk responded to me with praise and congratulations. I had made clear to them, they said, that in all the land there did not exist a single prophet. But the reaction of the empty-headed rabble, once they grasped that I had totally refuted their faith in the prophet and his messiah, was something else again. They waxed mightily indignant and launched against me an unending stream of verbal abuse.

Since they had no way to get back at me, either for what I had said about repentance or for what I had said about prophecy, they took a different tack. They sent letters everywhere, whining about how I had blocked their repentance by telling them their fasting and prayers would accomplish nothing unless they also gave up their grudges and ill-gotten gains, and so on and so forth; my sermon about prophecy, moreover, had demoralized the faithful. But nowhere did these accusations provoke anything beyond ridicule, and no one even bothered to respond to them.

[27] The reader may judge, from the more detailed account of the 'prophesying' given by Baruch of Arezzo (§8), the extent to which Halevi's acid summary of it is justified.

[28] Judg. 6: 11–24. Gideon is visited by an angel of the Lord, but is extremely cautious and circumspect about his experience. At first he demands proof his visitor is truly an angel; then, convinced this is so, he is seized by pious dread. Halevi presumably used Gideon's example to rebuke his contemporaries' heedless claims to prophecy. (Cf. his letter to the Sabbatian Hosea Nantawa, quoted in *Sefer tsitsat novel tsevi*, 188–9.)

In light of their failure, the scoundrels tried yet another course. They concocted the libel that the rabbis of Izmir had imposed punishment upon me,[29] and they dispatched this libel to all distant parts, never daring, meanwhile, to speak a whisper of it here at home.

That is the rumour you have heard. It never had any factual basis whatever—not in Izmir, not in Constantinople, not anywhere. Any rabbi, nonetheless, who truly merits his title of 'sage'[30]—I am not talking about those so-called 'sages' of ours, who have nothing 'sage' about them, who are engaged upon nothing more nor less than the wrecking of God's vineyard[31] —I cannot grasp how anyone of normal human intelligence could possibly conceive that the rabbis of one city could agree to excommunicate the rabbis of another. Such a decision would have been null and void even if the rabbis of the former town were the ranking scholars of their times, and those of the latter were by comparison unlettered louts. (They surely cannot have forgotten what happened to Resh Lakish, in the third chapter of *Mo'ed katan*![32]) And since in reality they are not privy to any divine wisdom hidden from the likes of us, it is doubly null and void. For I intend, if God favours us, to bring my complete works to press, and then they will see clearly enough who is superior to whom.[33]

The long and the short of it, as our friend Rabbi Isaac Nahar[34] will write to you, is this: the alleged 'excommunication' never was; it never happened; it does not bear even a symbolic relation to anything that ever happened. It is pure fabrication, concocted by the malice of the believers, who knew perfectly well that everything I said was true and were about to burst with rage

---

[29] That is, excommunication. Sasportas (*Sefer tsitsat novel tsevi*, 138) reports the rumour as follows: the Jews of Amsterdam and Hamburg received copies of a letter, originally sent to Halevi from Palestine by Shalom ben Joseph (see below), claiming that 'only one out of a thousand' Jerusalemites believes in Sabbatai's messiahship. The Sabbatians promptly claimed 'that Rabbi Joseph Halevi had doctored the letter on account of his lack of faith. They also said that he [Halevi] had publicly announced it was all a delusion, that he had denounced both messiah and prophet, and that when his statements had come to the attention of the rabbis of Constantinople, they excommunicated him.'

[30] *Hakham*, 'sage', is the Sephardi designation for a rabbi.

[31] The Jewish people, following Isa. 5: 7.

[32] The 3rd-century rabbi Resh Lakish (according to BT *MK* 17a) frivolously excommunicated a man whom he found stealing figs. The man retorted by excommunicating Resh Lakish; it was this latter excommunication, not the one pronounced by Resh Lakish, that was upheld. The rabbi had, in other words, made improper use of the weapon of excommunication—against someone who may well have been an 'unlettered lout'—and it therefore boomeranged upon him.

[33] Halevi's rambling, embittered harangue against his rabbinic contemporaries strongly suggests that the reports of his excommunication were not quite as baseless as he would have Sasportas believe.

[34] The 'friendship' was to sour fairly quickly; see the introduction to Halevi's letters above.

over it. For they could not endure that I had dared to bring their whole structure crashing down. Most people the world over, after all, had maintained it. The noble, the wealthy, the learned, had everywhere written in its support. Why, even the gentile scholars had admitted it was true, and all their rulers had given it credence! How could I possibly have imagined all of them were wrong?

I am still trying to find out who the people were who authored those libels. When I do, rest assured, I will have full power to harass them, to eliminate them, to sweep them away like the shit they are.

As to the matter of Rabbi Shalom ben Joseph's letter,[35] the truth is that he has followed the current fashion of playing the hypocrite, saying one thing and thinking another. The letter he sent me was precisely the one you read, which Rabbi Isaac Nahar copied from the original; all the Amsterdam people currently here [in Leghorn] have recognized his signature on it. He then turned around and wrote the exact opposite to Amsterdam.

I am not going to trouble myself to provide witnesses, since the truth has already come to light, and Rabbi Isaac Nahar has written to his brother about it. Those counterfeits are going to know soon enough who the real counterfeit is. I, who never set any stock by that lunatic?[36] Or those damned fools themselves?—'capable', as the Bible says, 'of believing in anything whatever' [Prov. 14: 15]—even in some brainless adolescent.[37] Did it never once cross their minds to ask what possible motive I would have for forging a letter in Master Shalom's name? For I did not base my opinions upon letters, but only upon the teachings of our ancient rabbis, may their memory be a blessing.

Meanwhile, what of the destroying demon himself, Spirit-of-Lies Sabbatai Zevi[38] (may his name and memory be blotted out)? This is the story:

---

[35] Referring to the letter (above, n. 29) in which Shalom ben Joseph told Halevi that only one out of a thousand Jerusalemites believed in Sabbatai's messiahship. Shalom, a retired schoolteacher from Amsterdam who travelled to the Holy Land in 1665, had at the same time written to his home city in quite a different vein. In that other letter, Shalom told how he had gone with Nathan of Gaza's father to Egypt, where Raphael Joseph Chelebi had received them in style. He gave a glowing report of Nathan's international reputation as scholar and prophet; he described how Gaza was given over to festivities, the Jews there believing that Sabbatai had gone to Constantinople to receive the sultan's submission and his crown. It is easy to see how the contrast between this letter, and the one forwarded to Amsterdam by Halevi, provoked the suspicion that the unbelieving Halevi had tampered with the latter's text. See *Sefer tsitsat novel tsevi*, 136–8; Scholem, *Sabbatai Sevi*, 354–8, 363–4.

[36] That is, Sabbatai Zevi.   [37] That is, Nathan of Gaza.

[38] 'Spirit of lies' (1 Kgs. 22: 22–3) and 'Sabbatai Zevi' have the same numerical value in Hebrew.

He had dispatched, as you well know, a demented edict to every town far and near that his emissaries could reach, demanding the Ninth of Av be turned into a celebration,[39] accompanied by the formula (in the sanctification ceremony and the [Amidah] prayer) *You have given us . . . this Feast of Consolations . . . the nativity of our king . . . Sabbatai Zevi, Your first-born son, Your beloved.*[40] And so they did.

On 4 Elul [4 September 1666], while he was imprisoned in the fortress of Gallipoli, there appeared a certain rabbi from Poland, bent on discovering the truth of the matter.[41] He spent three days with him in the tower. The moment he came out, this rabbi repudiated his Judaism and told the gentiles everything. The Jews were savagely beaten and expelled that very day, and a detailed report on the proceedings went off to the king in Adrianople.

On 23 Elul [23 September],[42] the royal emissaries arrived. They took [Sabbatai] to Adrianople to appear before the king.

'Who are you?' the king asked him. 'I am a Jewish rabbi', says he. 'Are you the messiah?' asks the king. 'No, my lord', says he. 'Then why do the Jews do you royal obeisance?' asks the king. 'The prophet from Gaza anointed me and treacherously encouraged me', says he, 'and now the Jews want to declare me king against my will.'

The king sentenced him to death.

But then a certain physician intervened, who formerly had been a Jew himself but had been forcibly converted at the king's orders. 'If you have any power whatever to perform a miracle', he told [Sabbatai], 'now is the time for it.'

'I have no power at all', he said.

'The king has condemned you', the physician told him, 'and you have only two choices. Either convert or die.'

He thereupon began grovelling on the ground before the king, begging that he might be allowed to take refuge in the king's religion. He threw his cap onto the ground and spat on it.[43] He insulted the Jewish faith and profaned our God, in full public view.

So the king took him under his protection. He changed his name for the worse, calling him Mehmed Kapiji—'royal doorkeeper', that is—and fixing his salary at 150 *esperos* a day.

---

[39]   See the Introduction, section II; Baruch of Arezzo, *Memorial*, §15.

[40]   The full text is given in the *Memorial*, §15.

[41]   His name is given in other sources as 'Nehemiah'. On this whole peculiar episode, see Scholem, *Sabbatai Sevi*, 658–68.

[42]   Apparently an error for 13 Elul (13 September). See Tishby's note ad loc., and Scholem, *Sabbatai Sevi*, 672–4.

[43]   Symbolizing, through his Jewish headgear, his repudiation of the Jewish religion.

The king was by now pretty much placated. But the apostate was not yet satisfied. He produced the letters sent him by the communities he had duped and showed them to the king, as evidence that the Jews were bent upon making a king of him. The king flew into a rage, and decreed the total extermination of all Jews in his empire above the age of 7. Those younger than 7 were to be made into Muslims.

These murderous orders had already been prepared and sealed when two of the empire's notables appeared before the king. They fell at his feet and begged to pacify him. His ancestors, they said, would not have destroyed an entire nation on account of one criminal, and neither must he. The queen mother also took pity on God's people and interceded with her son on their behalf. At length he yielded, abandoned his cruel plan, and drew up a writ of amnesty.

But even this was not the limit of the apostate's vindictiveness. His next step was to blame the rabbis for having incited his activities, with the result that the king dispatched orders for their execution. But they, too, had their intercessors, and they received the king's amnesty. Towards the fraud of Gaza, however, the king remained implacably furious, and he dispatched orders for his arrest. For the king clearly understood that it was he who had instigated the entire affair.[44]

And now, sir, will you kindly convey a message from me to these nincompoops, these credulous imbeciles? Tell them I do not forgive them one bit of the slander they heaped upon me, and that I beseech Almighty God to take it out of their hides in this world and the next. Season after season shall grind remorselessly upon them, while God pays them back for the humiliation they caused me.

But tell them, all the same, not to lose hope. For Mehmed their saviour has now returned to his schooldays, a pupil now of the Muslim religion. Yes, indeed: the king has enrolled him in one of their abomination-houses,[45] there to receive instruction in their faith. He will no doubt study hard, and will grow to be quite a scholar. He will then come to save them, and raise

---

[44] This last assertion, according to Tishby, is found in no other source (though Halevi's second letter also alludes to it). Sasportas must have had his qualms about it, for, editing Halevi's letter, he softens it: '*it is said* that he sent orders for his arrest as the instigator of the entire affair, *but whether this is true remains unclear*'.

[45] *Beit to'avotam*, a standard derogatory term for churches and mosques. Scholem quotes a similar report from the contemporary British consul Paul Rycaut: Sabbatai 'passed his time devoutly at the Ottoman Court, educated at the Feet of the learned *Gamaliel* of the Turkish Law . . . *Vani* Effendi. . . . To this Master *Sabbatai* was a most docile scholar, and profited, as we may imagine, beyond measure in the Turkish Doctrine' (*Sabbatai Sevi*, 727).

them to the spiritual level of their prophet—his master, whose name he bears—their prophet Muhammad.[46]

Just this week I sent off a packet of letters to Rabbi Isaac Del Prado in Amsterdam, courtesy of the noble Rabbi Isaac Bueno.[47] It contained a copy of the letter we received from Alexandria, from a leading believer named Hosea Nantawa, trying to induce us to join the new faith. It contained also my response to that letter, which included my reactions to the letter the Gazan prophet sent us here in Leghorn.[48] The noble Rabbi Isaac Del Prado has ordered a copy made and sent to you, inasmuch as your letter reached me just as the courier was departing and I did not have time to reply. (I should mention that I did not want it known I was the author of the response, and therefore composed it as though it were being written in Venice.[49])

I am a little concerned, however, that Rabbi Del Prado may not have got round to having the copy made, and that you consequently may not yet have received it. I am therefore sending you a fresh copy—considerably expanded, as you will observe—by way of Venice.

We now have reports, based on reliable sources who had actually been present in the fortress of Gallipoli, that the Polish rabbi who abandoned his Judaism was acting from pious motives. He had come to realize, it seems, that [Sabbatai] was bent on the wholesale destruction of the Jewish faith. He had already ordained that the sabbath be observed on Monday instead of Saturday, starting with Monday, 22 Tamuz, which he called the 'great

[46] A savage parody of Sabbatai's claim to bear, like the semi-divine Metatron, the name of his divine Master. (See above, n. 245 on Baruch of Arezzo.) 'Mehmed' is the Turkish form of the name Muhammad.

[47] Both men, according to Tishby's note ad loc., served at various times in the 1650s and 1660s as governors of the community religious school (Talmud Torah) of Amsterdam. I do not know whether or how Isaac Bueno was related to the Amsterdam physician Ephraim Bueno (d. 1665), subject of Rembrandt's *The Jewish Doctor*.

[48] Following Tishby's interpretation. Tishby suggests that 'the letter the Gazan prophet sent us here in Leghorn' refers to Nathan's epistle to Raphael Joseph Chelebi, which was circulated throughout the diaspora (above, n. 26). Nantawa's letter and Halevi's response to it (presumably with the 'expansions' mentioned in the next paragraph) are both preserved in *Sefer tsitsat novel tsevi*, 155–60, 186–97.

[49] Why? Perhaps because Halevi's 'response' to Nantawa is in fact one long stream of gleeful, ferocious insult, written at the beginning of November 1666, right after Halevi first heard the news of Sabbatai's conversion to Islam. He might reasonably have feared the Sabbatians would still be in a position to take reprisals. He therefore hid behind the mask of an anonymous 'believer in the God of Israel and the Torah of Moses . . . who hates the idiot believers [in Sabbatai Zevi], signing [plural!] here in Venice' (*Sefer tsitsat novel tsevi*, 197; Scholem, *Sabbatai Sevi*, 759, is misleading on this point).

sabbath'.[50] He planned, similarly, to shift God's festivals from their appointed dates: to observe the Day of Atonement on Thursday this year,[51] and so forth. The rabbi realized that he could not simply tell people not to obey [Sabbatai], given that there were more than five thousand Jews—sometimes as many as ten thousand—who had come a forty-day journey to pay homage to him, and that his word had absolute sway over them. He was afraid they would kill him if he tried. He converted to Islam, therefore, in order that he might have an opportunity to reveal what was going on, and thereby to prevent a plague, worse than the heresies of Zadok and Boethus,[52] from spreading among us.

This, at any rate, is what they write us from Izmir. True enough, it is not sufficient motive to abandon one's faith and turn one's back on God. Still, they say he acted with pious intent, and he has by now returned to his native land.[53]

There is more I would like to say, but I do not want this letter to become any longer than it already is. I will write again presently. In the meantime, let us pray God to allow us to witness His goodness, the true and authentic consolation of Jerusalem—and the wreck and annihilation of the wicked rebels.

Written in the year 5427, week of the Torah portion 'Esau went to Ishmael and took Mahalath to wife' [Gen. 28: 9],[54] by—

Your faithful friend,

Joseph Halevi

---

[50] See above, n. 150 on Baruch of Arezzo. '22 Tamuz' is a mistake, as Tishby observes, for 23 Tamuz.

[51] Instead of Saturday, when it properly would have fallen.

[52] Legendary figures of Second Temple times, from whom the heretical sects of the Sadducees and the Boethusians were believed to have derived (*Avot derabi natan*, ch. 5).

[53] Where, presumably, he would be free to return to Judaism. Cf. Sasportas, *Sefer tsitsat novel tsevi*, 345–6.

[54] 23–9 Heshvan 5427 (21–7 November 1666). The biblical passage reads, in full: 'Esau went to Ishmael and took to wife Mahalath, daughter of Ishmael son of Abraham, sister of Nebaioth, in addition to his other wives.' Halevi's selection of this verse to designate the week's Torah portion perhaps reflects the reports that Sabbatai ('Esau') had not only gone over to Islam ('Ishmael'), but had married a Muslim woman ('daughter of Ishmael'; see *Sefer tsitsat novel tsevi*, 198, 202, 304) in addition to Sarah. He perhaps implies a demonological subtext for Sabbatai's behaviour; in rabbinic and kabbalistic tradition, Mahalath—whose name suggests the idea of 'disease'—appears as a demon or a demon's mother.

LETTER 2
To Jacob Sasportas, 16 February 1667

To the worthy rabbi, admirable judge,
man of learning and of noble birth,
the honourable Rabbi Jacob Sasportas:

All your letters have reached me. I am only now responding, and hope you do not attribute this to any neglectfulness on my part. I have suffered most dreadfully for the past several days from an illness in my throat, and have endured a continuous string of bleedings, one right after the other, which left me entirely without strength until at last God took pity and restored me to health.[55]

There is another reason I did not want to answer you immediately. I had been hoping that any day now ships would arrive from Izmir, with confirmation of the initial reports of how the scoundrel Sabbatai Zevi had become an apostate. But as it happens we have not had a single ship put in [from Izmir] for the past three months, thanks to a major interference in our sea traffic: the [Turkish] king has seized all the Christian ships to be found there and sent them to Candia.[56] The consequence has been that our faithful idiots have begun once again to incite rebellion against God and His messiah, once again to declare the true messiah to be Sabbatai Zevi.

The people are now split into a number of factions. The first group simply denies he apostatized at all. It is pure slander, they say. What really happened, they say, is that upon seeing him the king hugged and kissed him and placed the royal crown on his head. He also placed atop [Sabbatai's] cap a leek-green turban,[57] and thus arose the impression he had converted. Among the numbskulls who maintain this viewpoint, its outstanding representative is a certain Pereira:[58] an Amsterdam gentleman now resident in

---

[55] The same traditional remedy of bloodletting was applied, more than a hundred years later, to a similar illness of George Washington. Washington, unlike Halevi, did not survive his treatment (Cousins, *Head First*, 154–6).

[56] For the war against the Venetians. See Baruch of Arezzo, *Memorial*, §11.

[57] On the colour of the turban, see Baruch of Arezzo, *Memorial*, §23.

[58] Abraham Israel Pereira, one of the richest merchants in Amsterdam. A former Marrano, he was a pious philanthropist given to founding and supporting yeshivas, institutes of higher Jewish learning: the Or Torah yeshiva in Amsterdam in 1656 (in collaboration with the physician Ephraim Bueno, whose portrait Rembrandt had painted) and the Hesed Le'avraham yeshiva in Hebron in 1659 (with none other than Meir Rofé as its principal). In 1666 he published an inspirational volume in Spanish entitled *La Certeza del Camino* (The Certainty of the Way). Its publication at that date, as Scholem says, 'cannot have been accidental' (*Sabbatai Sevi*, 530). Pereira was and remained a raptly enthusiastic Sabbatian. Upon leaving

Venice, from which place he dispatches his pernicious tracts to our local simpletons. Others write in the same vein from Verona and elsewhere.

The second faction is willing to grant the possibility that he may indeed have converted. But, if so, he had a hidden purpose: to acquaint himself with the Turkish imperial treasury and the sources from which it derives. The empire, after all, is eventually to come under his rule; he needs therefore to become familiar with its workings.

The third faction finds sacred mysteries, too numerous to count, in the apostasy. It is part of the divine plan: he must enter among the 'shells'[59] in order to make himself their master, and he therefore wears them as his garment. This theory finds its most distinguished representative in Rabbi Raphael Supino,[60] who has managed to gather around himself a crew so disreputable you would think Jephthah's cronies were back in a fresh incarnation.[61] They meet in his house, where he preaches, or rather brays, to them on this topic. (Their messiah, I have pointed out to them, is in the position of the proverbial camel who tried to get himself horns, and instead got his ears cut off.[62] The 'shells' are now *his* masters, and he has so mixed himself up with them that they are all one.) [Supino] has also composed a number of hymns, each one a small torment, in honour of his king—may the two of them be tormented together! Imagine a boiling cauldron frothing over with badness,[63] and there you will have Raphael Supino.

Rabbi Isaac Nahar has been considerably influenced by him, but belongs essentially to the first school.

The fourth faction argues that, even if perchance he may be said to have apostatized, it was not really he who did so, but only his shadow. The real

Amsterdam in the spring of 1666, he 'offered to sell a Countrey-house of his worth Three thousand pound *Sterling*, at much loss, and on this Condition, That the Buyer should not pay one farthing till he be convinced in his own Conscience, That the *Jews* have a King' (ibid. quoting a contemporary English pamphlet).

[59] That is, the demonic powers. See the Introduction, section IX.

[60] Cf. Toaff, *La Nazione Ebrea*, 355. Ironically, Supino and Sasportas were old friends, having been together in 1655 in England, where they had both attached themselves to Manasseh ben Israel's misson to Cromwell on behalf of Jewish readmission (Roth, *A Life of Menasseh ben Israel*, 250–1). There Supino made a rather good impression on the chaplain of the Tuscan envoy, with whom he argued religion (Ifrah, *L'Aigle d'Amsterdam*, 216; cf. Katz, 'Menasseh ben Israel's Christian Connection', 128–9). Supino's relations with Sasportas became strained, understandably, over their differences concerning Sabbatai Zevi, but appear afterwards to have recovered. See Scholem, *Sabbatai Zevi*, 347, 760–2.

[61] Referring to Judg. 11: 3: 'worthless fellows collected around Jephthah, and went raiding with him' (Revised Standard Version).

[62] The Talmud (BT *San.* 106a) quotes this proverb to make the point that someone who seeks more than he ought is likely to be deprived of what he has; thus it was that the biblical Balaam lost his life (Num. 31: 8). The analogy between Sabbatai and the ancient villain Balaam is not likely to be an accident.   [63] The image is drawn from Jer. 1: 13–14.

'him' had ascended on high, concealed from human sight. (Which prompted me to observe, tongue in cheek, that Rav was right: meat that has been out of our sight *is* forbidden.[64])

And the fifth group insists he never apostatized—he is still Jewish. He defended himself before the Turkish king, they say, by arguing that he was acting in accordance with the prognostications of the Gazan prophet, whom the king has now summoned.[65] He has, in any case, been brought back to the fortress of Gallipoli.

Aside from these theories, all of them equally idiotic, the professional liars have begun afresh to circulate their literature. They claim the Turkish king has made [Sabbatai] his generalissimo, and has sent him to the Polish campaign with 200,000 troops. Satan Ashkenazi of Gaza,[66] after all, had prophesied he would avenge upon Poland the blood of its Jewish martyrs, and that prophecy is now coming true. He has, they assure us, performed all manner of amazing miracles, too numerous to count.

Those who keep faith with the true Torah, of course, are unswayed by this treacherous bluster. They know perfectly well that the letters from Izmir describing the apostasy are accurate, and that they have been confirmed by letters to Venice from Constantinople and Adrianople. A ship put in here about a month ago, bearing a letter from Aleppo which confirmed that Sabbatai had apostatized.

This week, however, we received a packet of letters from Alexandria via Tripoli, dated 12 Heshvan [10 November 1666], and not one of them made the least mention of this or suggested it had made any impression on the writers. The only exception was a letter from Professor Raphael Joseph,[67] declaring that anyone who says Sabbatai apostatized is a damned liar, that he is the true messiah, he is our redeemer,[68] etc. etc. Our imbeciles, with the support of Rabbi Isaac Nahar, find in this fresh justification for clinging to their miserable faith. The people in Tripoli had sent a courier to Alexandria to find out if they were going to fast there on the Tenth of Tevet [6 January

---

[64] The 3rd-century scholar Rav forbids the eating of meat that has been out of one's sight, lest unkosher meat might have been substituted for the original (BT *BM* 24*b*, *Ḥul. 95a*). Halevi's rather ponderous joke represents Sabbatai as the 'meat': having been 'concealed from human sight', he is now 'forbidden' to all good Jews.

[65] See above, at n. 44.

[66] Not exactly a slip of the pen for 'Nathan Ashkenazi'. Nathan had made this prediction in his epistle to Raphael Joseph Chelebi (Scholem, *Sabbatai Sevi*, 273, 287–8).

[67] Raphael Joseph Chelebi (above, Introduction, section IV). Halevi gives him the Arabic title *mualim*, 'teacher'.

[68] Reading *vego'alenu* for the manuscripts' *umigo'alenu*. Otherwise we would have to understand, 'he is the true messiah, dispatched by our [divine] redeemer'. But 'redeemer' (*go'el*) is almost invariably used in the Sabbatian literature to refer to Sabbatai himself.

1667];[69] the response was they were planning to celebrate it as a feast-day. Let us pray their food has turned to snake poison in their guts.

I continue to await the arrival of a ship from Izmir. I will then send you a full report of what happened in Izmir and what it really means.[70]

With regard to the issue of the priestly blessing, there is something I need to let you know.[71] While I was ill, all my colleagues from the yeshiva came to visit me at my sickbed, Rabbi Isaac Nahar among them. They began by asking me about halakhic issues of all sorts, but it was really the priestly blessing they had come to talk about. He[72] raised it as a hypothetical question. Suppose some sound practice were to be instituted erroneously: ought we to discontinue it? No, I told him, we ought not to discontinue it; but I could not quite grasp how a sound practice might come to be instituted erroneously.

He then explained what he was driving at, and produced a copy of the enquiry that had been sent to our yeshiva,[73] along with the response they had composed. They had, it turned out, already discussed the issue and come to their decision—that the priestly blessing is *not* to be discontinued—before they even saw me. Our most senior colleague had affixed his signature, and they had left a space for mine. Would I be so kind as to sign?

Could this not wait, I asked him, until I recover my health, so I can go to the yeshiva and sign it there? No, no, says he, the matter is urgent; the rifts within the community must be healed; delay is most definitely not to be advised.[74] So there I was, pressured to sign, so weak I could barely keep my arms and legs steady. Only afterwards did your letter arrive. By then the document had already been drawn up and signed, and there was no way to revoke it.

[69] Another of the traditional fasts commemorating the destruction of the Temple and the events leading up to it; like the others (the Seventeenth of Tamuz, the Ninth of Av), it was declared abolished by Sabbatai and his followers.

[70] *Kol mah she'era be'izmir vesod hama'aseh shehayah.* I am not at all sure what Halevi has in mind. If he is thinking of the apostasy, as the beginning of this letter might lead us to imagine, why does he speak of it as having happened 'in Izmir', and not in Adrianople or Gallipoli?

[71] Influenced by the messianic excitement, the Jewish community of Amsterdam had established the practice of having men of priestly descent recite the threefold blessing of Num. 6: 24–6 over the congregation each sabbath—not just on festivals, as had been the prior (and nearly universal) custom. After news of the apostasy spread, the priestly blessing became a hot issue between the sceptics and the faithful, the former wanting to abolish what they perceived as the Sabbatians' innovation. Since December 1666 Sasportas had waged a single-minded and slightly fanatical campaign for the abolition of Amsterdam's weekly blessing (*Sefer tsitsat novel tsevi*, 210–47). Hence Halevi's apologetic and defensive tone.

[72] Nahar, presumably.   [73] From Amsterdam.

[74] The language is taken from BT *Ber.* 40a, in accordance with Rashi's interpretation.

And, to be perfectly frank, I personally cannot see how it would be right to demand of [the Amsterdam Jews] that they discontinue their custom, now that they have initiated it.[75]

It is, after all, the universal consensus that the recitation of the priestly blessing fulfils no fewer than three of the Torah's positive commandments. This is acknowledged even by those who dispute Rabbi Manoah's opinion (as quoted in *Beit yosef*, §128)[76] and assert that the *failure* to recite the blessing will constitute no transgression at all, as long as the *kohanim*[77] have not actually been summoned to do so. True enough, the Torah does not lay the responsibility for its fulfilment on the *kohanim* themselves. That is why the Bible's ambiguous 'say to them' [Num. 6: 23] is represented by the Targum[78] as commanding the *kohanim* to say the blessing only 'when they are bidden to do so'. Yet surely the community is under some obligation to give the *kohanim* their opportunity to perform the commandments appropriate to them. The effort this requires of the community is trivial; and one ought not to seem less than virtuous through carrying out only virtue's minimum demands.

Another consideration argues yet more strongly in this direction, and it is this: our ancient rabbis were prepared to condone one person's committing a minor violation in order to spare another person from committing a major one. Rabbi Judah the Patriarch lays down this principle in the third chapter of *Eruvin*,[79] when he declares it acceptable for a scholar to commit a trivial offence (i.e. offering the priestly tithe from produce that has not been gathered to one spot) in order to prevent an unlettered person from committing a serious offence (i.e. eating untithed produce). Rabbi Judah the

---

[75] The legal discussion that follows need not be grasped in all its details, especially since—as Halevi admits at the close of his exhaustive and exhausting argument—it is nothing more than a rationalization for what was in any case a *fait accompli*.

[76] *Beit yosef* is the massive commentary by Rabbi Joseph Karo (1488–1575) on the 14th-century code *Arba'ah turim* of Jacob ben Asher, which for Halevi and his contemporaries was a fundamental source of religious law. 'Rabbi Manoah' is the 14th-century legal scholar Manoah of Narbonne, whom Karo quotes to the effect that one of the three relevant commandments is indeed transgressed if a man of priestly descent does not take the initiative and pronounce the blessing over the congregation, even without being summoned to do so. This, says Karo, is not the consensus of the legal authorities ('those who dispute Rabbi Manoah's opinion'). *Tur orah hayim*, §128 (Vilna, 1900 edn, p. 111*a*), the passage beginning *vekhatav harav rabi manoah*.

[77] The technical term for Jewish men whose family tradition claims for them descent from the ancient priesthood.

[78] The ancient Aramaic translation of the Pentateuch, treated by Jacob ben Asher in the course of this discussion—and, consequently, by Halevi and his colleagues—as an authoritative interpretation of the text.   [79] BT *Eruv.* 32*a–b*.

Patriarch himself declares this principle legally binding, and Maimonides rules accordingly in the tenth chapter of his 'Laws of Tithing'.[80]

We may go yet further. A minor violation is permissible, not only when it will prevent a major violation, but even when it will make possible the performance of a positive commandment. The Talmud makes this clear, in the following passages . . . [81]

The issue that lies before us is far more clear-cut. For it goes without saying that the usage under discussion involves no hint of a violation, and can occasion only blessing. Surely we would think it appropriate to give the *kohanim* the opportunity to perform their distinctive commandment, even where this would require taking some pains. Where it involves no inconvenience whatever, shall we not approve? Even if the usage were not already in place, surely we would favour instituting it. Now that it is in place, shall we demand that it be stopped?

True, the practice owes its existence to lying, deceiving rumours. But nothing follows from this. It is no worse than doing a commandment for the wrong reasons. Rabbi Eleazar ben Azariah's maxim remains valid: 'We should never hesitate to study [Torah or perform virtuous actions, even if our motives are wrong]. From doing these things for the wrong reasons, we will progress to doing them for the right reasons.'[82] Sooner or later everyone will forget how the practice of saying the priestly blessing each sabbath came to be instituted.[83] They will assume that, like the same practice in the Maghreb, it was done for the sake of the blessing itself.

It was none other than the glorious author of *Beit yosef*[84] who, expressing his astonishment over Rabbi Jacob Moellin's efforts to uphold his own local custom,[85] concluded by declaring: 'I have only admiration for the Jews of the Land of Israel and of Egypt, who recite the priestly blessing each and every day.' People everywhere let their behaviour be ruled by the opinions of this man, the great Rabbi Joseph Karo. Why, then, must Sabbatai Zevi's idiocies compel us to cheat ourselves of these blessings? To cheat the

[80] Referring to Maimonides's 12th-century code *Mishneh torah*, 'Hilkhot Ma'aser', 10: 10.

[81] There follows a close analysis, omitted from the translation, of four talmudic passages that seem to make this point: BT *Pes.* 58b–59a, *Git.* 38b, *Pes.* 88b, *Eruv.* 103b.

[82] BT *Pes.* 50b. Halevi abbreviates the quotation, which he could assume Sasportas already knew by heart; I supply the missing words.

[83] According to the article 'Birkat Ha-kohanim' in Werblowsky and Wigoder (eds), *Oxford Dictionary of the Jewish Religion*, the practice is observed to this day in the Spanish-Portuguese congregation of Amsterdam. But its origins have not been forgotten.

[84] Above, n. 76. The quotation that follows is from *Arba'ah turim*, 'Orah hayim', §128 (p. 115b), the passage beginning *katav ha'agur*.

[85] That the priestly blessing be spoken only on festivals. Moellin (1360–1427) was a German talmudist, normally referred to by the initials of his name, 'Maharil'.

kohanim of their opportunity to perform three of the Torah's command-ments? To let our faith be lost—as Rabbi Akiba says to Zonin in the fourth chapter of *Avodah zarah*[86]—on account of these imbeciles?

But surely the priestly blessing must be recited in a state of joyfulness? And surely, now our apostate 'messiah' has become a destroying devil,[87] all our joy must necessarily be turned to sorrow? True enough—but only for those stupid fools who had convinced themselves, even as they groped in darkness, that they had emerged from the ruins into the light. For intelligent folk, who know and understand the Torah, it is just the opposite. Their sor-row turned to joy. They praised God, who, by paying the scoundrel back exactly as he deserved, had vindicated His name's holiness in the sight of all. Our ancient rabbis were proven right: anyone who pronounces God's name the way it is written indeed has no share in the future life.[88]

This, at any rate, is my opinion. I see no reason to extend this discussion, which is gratuitous in any case. For, to judge from the letter that Rabbi Isaac Nahar showed me, the Amsterdam community stands firmly by its practice. They show no sign of abandoning it.

As far as I can see—returning now to our subject—the craziness is back at its old level of intensity. Thanks to the letters from Alexandria, the imbeciles have recovered their former faith, and they tell the most amazing tales of the wonders performed by their Destroyer.

I cannot resist passing along a particularly choice story, reported in one of the Alexandrian letters. No sooner had Sabbatai Zevi appeared before the king, it seems, than the king threw himself to the ground and began grovel-ling before him. He ordered that [Sabbatai] be taken to the baths and after-wards given a new suit of clothes. When [Sabbatai] stepped out, he found a crowd of about thirty thousand people waiting to see him. So he puts his hand in his pocket—which had been perfectly empty, remember—and starts pulling out gold coins to toss to the crowd. By the time he is finished, all thirty thousand of them have more gold than they can possibly carry, and need to hire animals to bring the treasure home. Our nitwits have swallowed this tale with great delight and go about repeating it to each other, which amuses me no end.

Letters continue to arrive from other places, with more miraculous stor-ies than I can count, and the whole affair continues to gain ground just as it did before.

---

[86] BT *AZ* 55*a*.

[87] *Mashiaḥ*, 'messiah', and *mashḥit*, 'destroyer', sound somewhat alike.

[88] Mishnah *San.* 10: 1. Pronouncing the sacred four-letter name of God was one of Sabbatai's notorious 'strange acts'; see Baruch of Arezzo, *Memorial*, §7.

You wrote me that I should not show people the legal decision concerning the priestly blessing. Well, I have done just that, and particularly to the physician Rabbi Isaac Nahar. (He is one of our leading believers, still perfectly convinced that the Turkish king set his royal crown on the apostate's head.) If his aim in coming here was to make himself supreme authority, to preach, to deliver legal rulings—if so, I can tell you, he is pouring out his energies for nothing.[89]

Praise the Lord, whose kindness never fails to amaze! It is now Wednesday, 22 Shevat [16 February 1667], and a ship has just put in from Izmir with news that has turned the believers' faces so dark you would think they had sat on the stove too long!

All the reports we had received are now confirmed. He did indeed apostatize, pure and simple, along with his whore of a wife. He eats forbidden meats for the sheer joy of transgressing.[90] His current name is Mehmed Effendi.

The news left his enthusiasts depressed and demoralized, each of them slinking off alone. I happened to encounter the physician Rabbi Isaac Nahar, and took the opportunity to enquire about the nature of that crown his messiah wears. Is it a crown of *roses*? I asked him. Or perchance of *nettles*?

And yet. There is one deluded numbskull, a Rabbi Moses Pinheiro, one of Sabbatai Zevi's companions from the old times;[91] eighteen years ago, in fact, he was persecuted and soundly beaten at Izmir along with his messiah. This Pinheiro, hearing the reports that Sabbatai is the messiah, now sets out for Izmir and finds him an apostate. So he writes to us as follows: 'I have a letter from my beloved brother, who is the very substance of my heart. He writes that he is to all appearances severely ill. Yet the illness is not as bad as it seems. For its cure it requires but an alteration,[92] and the light will again shine forth. That is his doctor's prescription'—his 'doctor' being Satan of Gaza.[93] Thanks to this dispatch, our imbeciles manage still to cling to their hopes. But they are about as effective as dogs who have lost their bark.

[89] Which I take to mean 'Nahar is *not* going to get my job' (see my introduction to the Halevi letters). I have the impression that Halevi intended to continue this tirade against Nahar, but was interrupted in the middle by the good news from Izmir.

[90] Following the talmudic distinction between the sinner who eats forbidden meats 'out of appetite for them', and the vastly worse sinner who eats them purely in order to anger God (BT *AZ* 26*b*). In another talmudic passage (BT *San.* 103*b*), one of the wicked kings of antiquity has sex with his own mother, not because he derives any pleasure from it, but solely 'to outrage my Creator'. This is the company among whom Halevi enrols Sabbatai Zevi.

[91] See Baruch of Arezzo, *Memorial*, §2.

[92] *Hamarah*, 'alteration', is the word regularly used for apostasy from Judaism.

[93] aka Nathan of Gaza.

One thing, at any rate, is now perfectly clear. All of the previous letters, which solemnly urged upon the people the necessity for faith, were motivated by one solitary passion: money. I will send more details in a subsequent letter. I must cut this short for now: I am very pressed for time; the quantity of verbiage currently being generated, moreover, inspires in me a certain fondness for brevity. I will write at greater length presently.

This, in the meantime, do I ask of our blessed God: that He act speedily, swiftly, to send us our true redeemer. In our very lifetimes, may Judah find salvation and Israel live in security! May we see our enemies paid back in full—most especially that damned scoundrel,[94] who caused the Jewish people no end of troubles, wasting their money on travel[95] and so forth.

> Written in Leghorn, in the week of the Torah portion
> 'The man who started the fire must pay in
> full for the destruction it caused' [Exod. 22: 5],[96] by—
>
> Your humble correspondent,
>
> Joseph Halevi.

[94] Sabbatai Zevi.

[95] It is worth reflecting that, if Nahar had not set forth from Amsterdam to pay homage to Sabbatai, he would not have darkened Halevi's door in Leghorn.

[96] 19–25 Shevat 5427 (13–19 February 1667). The relevance of the biblical quotation to the subject of Halevi's letter is almost painfully obvious.

THIRD TESTIMONY
The Najara Chronicle

§°

INTRODUCTION

IT WAS JACOB NAJARA's famous grandfather who was responsible, indir-
ectly, for his having known Sabbatai Zevi. The brilliant and much-admired
poet Israel Najara, born in Damascus around 1555, lived a wandering,
irregular life that brought him eventually to Gaza.[1] There he served as
rabbi, as did his son Moses and his grandson Jacob after him. Thus it was
that Jacob Najara was rabbi in Gaza when Sabbatai Zevi arrived there in the
spring of 1665 for his fateful meeting with the young prophet Nathan.
When Nathan revealed in his Shavuot night trance that Sabbatai Zevi was
the messiah, Sabbatai was staying as a guest in Najara's home.[2]

Israel Najara's soul had yearned passionately for God, his heart just as
passionately for the redemption of his people. 'O God of glory and greatness!' he cried out in the best-known of his poems.[3] 'Save Your flock from
the mouth of the lions! Bring Your people out from the midst of exile!' Now,
two generations later, the poet's grandson had played host to the man, proclaimed messiah by God's inspired prophet, who promised to do just that.
From that time forth Jacob Najara was a believer. When his messiah converted to Islam, he kept on believing.

And so in 1671 Najara travelled to Adrianople, where his former guest
was now a minor appendage to the sultan's court, to pay a visit of his own. By
his own account, he arrived there at the end of January. We do not know how
long he stayed; his narrative of the visit is incomplete, and its end, as well as
some of its middle, is missing. The surviving portion of the text, at any rate,
extends into the second week of June 1671. In this 'Najara Chronicle',[4] we
have what amounts almost to a diary of four months of Sabbatai's life as a
nominal Muslim, recorded by an eyewitness observer. In its vividness and

---

[1] Zinberg, *A History of Jewish Literature*, v. 94–106; *Encyclopedia Judaica*, s.v. 'Najara, Israel
ben Moses'.

[2] Baruch of Arezzo, *Memorial*, §5; cf. Scholem, *Sabbatai Sevi*, 217. The various manuscripts of Baruch give the name as Nayar or Nagyar.

[3] 'Yah ribon olam', still chanted around the sabbath table in traditional Jewish households.

[4] This conventional designation for the text is based on the title Najara himself gave it:
'Chronicle [*divrei hayamim*] of the events that befell here in Adrianople'. *Divrei hayamim* is the
Hebrew title of the biblical books of Chronicles.

immediacy, and its close-up view of the enigmatic messiah, Najara's text has no equal.

What are we to make of this messiah? At times he seems a divided, tormented soul, split between the Judaism he could not leave behind him and the Islam he could not cease to profess without forfeiting his life. More often he comes across as manipulative and duplicitous, enjoying his access to the sultan and the power that gives him to 'summon' rabbis from other towns, issue commands and 'decrees', barge into synagogues and hijack the services at his pleasure. He gives the impression of cultivating some private eschatology in which Islam, and the act of converting to Islam, do have a real and important role—but not quite the role that his Turkish patrons, the sultan Mehmed and the court preacher Vani Effendi, would have assumed it to possess. As always, he is utterly without empathy, oblivious to the needs or even the existence of any human being but himself.

Najara's chronicle, or at least the portion of it that survives, oscillates between the poles of Sabbatai's 'illuminations' and the corresponding 'eclipses' of his light. When Najara arrives in Adrianople, on 28 January 1671, Sabbatai is just emerging from a persistent 'eclipse' that has lasted more than a year. In the days and weeks that follow he discourses to Najara (who refers to himself throughout the chronicle in the third person, as 'this rabbi') on the need for nearly the whole of the Jewish people to enter through the 'gate' of Islam. He commands his brother and his nephew to 'take on the turban', that is, convert to Islam; they obey. He divorces his wife Sarah, complaining he has been a 'slave' for the six years of their marriage and now it is time to be free, blaming her for his persistent sense of being a leper.[5] (Later he will take her back, and she will follow him loyally into his exile.)

With Vani Effendi's collusion, Sabbatai manages to extract his 3-year-old son Ishmael from Sarah's custody. Promptly he has the boy circumcised in a ceremony that is patently Jewish rather than Muslim, he himself reciting the blessings and the unconverted rabbi Najara doing the cutting. He invites the Muslim grandees of Adrianople to the ceremony, but in such a way that they are misled into showing up on the wrong day. Najara assures us over and over that the Turks know that Sabbatai still behaves as an unconverted Jew,

---

[5] The same manuscript that preserves the Najara Chronicle also contains a letter from Nathan of Gaza, claiming Sarah had twice tried to poison her husband (Amarilio, 'Sabbatian Documents' (Heb.), 263). It is unclear how seriously we are to take this claim. Nathan had never liked Sarah Zevi; as far back as 1665 he was fantasizing about how Sabbatai would take the 13-year-old daughter of the resurrected Moses as his true wife, relegating poor Sarah to the position of servant-girl (Scholem, *Sabbatai Sevi*, 273–4). No doubt he was prepared to believe, or invent, the worst about her.

and do not seem to object. Yet it is clear, from the story of Ishmael's circumcision, that there were times when Sabbatai preferred them not to be watching too closely.

The central episode of the Najara Chronicle is a religious disputation between Sabbatai and a selected contingent of rabbis, conducted in the (mostly uncomprehending) presence of the sultan himself. Najara tells the story in the most vivid and at times suspenseful manner; parts of it, unfortunately, have fallen victim to a lacuna in the middle of the text. The Jewish disputants are summoned months in advance from the cities of Constantinople, Sofia, and Brusa; four men arrive from Constantinople, three from Brusa; the former contingent includes Meir Rofé, the Hebron fundraiser who—at least if Baruch of Arezzo is to be trusted—was among the observers of Nathan of Gaza's Shavuot eve ecstasies in 1665. These seven are joined by Joseph Karillo of Adrianople, and apparently Najara himself. As the sultan watches from his *kafes*, his latticed alcove, Sabbatai debates with the rabbis, instructs them in the secret knowledge of God, and invites them to embrace Islam. Only afterwards do they become aware the sultan has ordered the royal executioner to 'fall upon' anyone refusing the invitation.

The entire episode has the smell of the Jewish–Christian disputations of the later Middle Ages, in which a prominent rabbi or group of rabbis would be forced publicly to debate with some learned apostate under the Church's aegis, the expected outcome being a Christian victory and the mass conversion of the Jews. 'These are the greatest rabbis of the Jewish people . . . if these convert, all the Jews will convert'—so Sabbatai assures the sultan, and we might almost be hearing the voice of a medieval apostate such as Nicholas Donin or Pablo Christiani. Yet there is something different here. Sabbatai is playing a double game, conspiring with his supposed antagonists to orchestrate what is in effect a theatrical performance for the sultan. At one point he coaches his fellow-actors on how to play their parts.[6] Plainly he has an agenda of his own, very different from that of the sultan or Vani Effendi; his ultimate purpose is far from clear. In the number of participants involved—Sabbatai and nine rabbis—there is a peculiar echo of the *Idra rabah*, a section of the Zohar in which Rabbi Simeon ben Yohai assembles nine of his colleagues and reveals to them the innermost secrets of the divinity.[7] Was it part of Sabbatai's intention to stage a re-enactment of the *Idra*? Unsettlingly, three of Ben Yohai's fellow-rabbis die in the course of hearing his revelations, and it may have been Sabbatai's intent that not all his debating partners survive their experience.

[6] See below, at n. 88.
[7] Zohar, iii. 127*b*–145*a*. The beginning and end of *Idra rabah* are translated in *Wisdom of the Zohar*, ed. Tishby, i. 155–9.

The incident left a deep imprint on the collective memory of the Sabbatians. It figures prominently in the hagiography of Sabbatai Zevi written twenty years afterwards by the Hebron fundraiser and *littérateur* Abraham Cuenque (translated below, as our fourth testimony). Cuenque may have got the details from his colleague Meir Rofé, who was present at the scene. But he recasts them in his own highly creative manner, bringing out in multiple ways the parallel with *Idra rabah*.[8]

Abraham Cardozo, who in 1671 was nowhere near Adrianople, also remembered the disputation. He remembered the men who under pressure had been faithful to Judaism, and those who treacherously abandoned it. In a letter written near the end of his life, in the first years of the eighteenth century, he claims to have met the three Brusan rabbis in their home city in 1681. 'These were the three who went to Adrianople at Rabbi Sabbatai [Zevi's] summons, who were among the rabbis who were in the Turk's presence yet did not wish to put on the turban [convert to Islam].' Apparently they were still loyal to Sabbatai's memory; they wanted Cardozo's opinion of Nathan's doctrine that Sabbatai was destined to become a deity—which for Cardozo was rank heresy. (Cardozo was not much impressed by the three rabbis' intelligence. But then Cardozo was seldom impressed by anyone's intelligence but his own.[9])

Thirty years after the event, the memory of Joseph Karillo and Abraham Gamaliel, the two rabbis who did 'put on the turban', still rankled. Cardozo complains, in another letter of about 1700, that Sabbatai 'had no call to induce anyone but himself to put on [the turban]'. He fondly imagines that Sabbatai privately shared his feelings, that he 'spoke well of those rabbis who would not wear the turban when he pressed them to do so in the Turkish king's presence, and despised Gamaliel and Karillo for abandoning their faith'.[10]

Thus does Cardozo project his own integrity, conviction, and fierce loyalty to Judaism, onto a man to whom all three qualities were alien.

THE TEXT

The Najara Chronicle occupies eight pages (fos. 75[r]–78[v])[11] in a massive Sabbatian manuscript of the late seventeenth or eighteenth century, entitled *Sefer yemot mashiaḥ* ('Messianic Times'). The manuscript was part of the 'Amarillo Collection'—Sabbatian documents preserved for two centuries or

---

[8] See the notes on Cuenque, below.
[9] Molho and Amarilio, 'Autobiographical Letters of Abraham Cardozo' (Heb.), 222.
[10] Ibid. 199.
[11] According to the Arabic numerals marked on the pages of the manuscript, 179–86.

more by the Dönmeh of Salonica, then entrusted by them in 1925 to Rabbi Saul Amarillo (or Amarilio), when they were forced to leave Salonica as part of the population exchange between Greece and Turkey.[12] Amarillo's son Abraham brought these manuscripts to Israel, where *Yemot mashiaḥ* is now manuscript no. 2262 in the collection of the Ben-Zvi Institute, Jerusalem. In 1961 he published a number of choice texts from this manuscript, the Najara Chronicle among them.[13]

The *Yemot mashiaḥ* manuscript is plainly not the autograph of the Najara Chronicle. The scribe worked from a manuscript of the chronicle that was missing one or more pages in the middle and at the end, or that was itself copied from an incomplete predecessor. In the middle of folio 77ʳ the text breaks off in mid-sentence, the words *kan ḥaser* ('here there is a gap in the text') are written in the middle of the blank space that follows, and then the text resumes, again in mid-sentence. It ends abruptly at the bottom of folio 78ᵛ, followed by the words *ad kan matsati* (literally, 'up to this point have I found'). How much of the text is lost we have no way of knowing.

I have made my translation from the text published by Abraham Amarilio, occasionally correcting it according to the manuscript.[14] There are a few transcriptional errors in the publication, which I have noted in the footnotes. But on the whole Amarilio's text is dependable.

CHRONICLE OF THE EVENTS THAT BEFELL HERE IN ADRIANOPLE, FROM THE DAY OF THE ARRIVAL OF THE WORTHY RABBI JACOB NAJARA

(GOD WATCH OVER HIM AND SAVE HIM!)

The seventeenth day of the month Shevat, of the year 'They shall sanctify the Holy One of Jacob and the God of Israel'[15] [17 Shevat 5431 = 28 January 1671]: On that night, prior to the worthy rabbi [Najara's] arrival, Amirah had a dream following upon a year and two months during which he had

---

[12] Scholem, *Sabbatai Sevi*, p. xiii.

[13] Amarilio, 'Sabbatian Documents' (Heb.). The Najara Chronicle is on pp. 254–62.

[14] I am deeply grateful to Michael Glatzer and Dov Cohen of the Ben-Zvi Institute, and Yael Okun of the Institute of Microfilmed Hebrew Manuscripts, for having enabled me to obtain a photocopy of the manuscript.

[15] Isa. 29: 23. The numerical value of the first word of the Hebrew text (*vehikdishu*, 'they shall sanctify') is 431, indicating the year 5431. The last letters of four of the following words, *kedosh ya'akov ve'et elohei* ('the Holy One of Jacob and the God'), read together in sequence, spell 'Sabbatai'.

experienced no illumination.[16] He dreamed he was falling into a very deep pit, from which it seemed to him impossible to rise. He looked up and saw his father and mother standing by the edge of the pit. They threw him a rope and brought him up from it. He was delighted by his dream, once he saw he had risen out of that pit.

On the nineteenth of the same month [30 January] his light shone forth. And on the twenty-first day of the month [1 February], this rabbi [Najara] was with him, and Amirah spoke to him of many matters. He spoke of the turban, among other things, and told him that the bulk of the Jewish people would be compelled to enter through that gate.[17] Only a very few would [Sabbatai] willingly leave within the Torah of Truth. These, however, would be inferior to the Faithful Ones who wore the turban, for these latter would attain lofty wisdom and a high rank. Yet nonetheless, unto those who believe in him and love him and whom he willingly permits to remain within the Torah of Truth—the Torah of Moses, that is—[Sabbatai] shall grant the capacity to attain the rank of the Faithful Ones who are within the Torah of Grace.[18]

[Sabbatai's] illumination grew steadily more intense up to the thirteenth day of the month of Adar [23 February]. On that day his brother came for a stay, along with four of Vani Effendi's men.[19] [Sabbatai] told his brother to come with him at once to take on the turban, for so it must be. He revealed to him whatever it was he revealed, and he swore to his brother that he had grasped during this illumination what he had not been able to grasp in any

[16] I translate the reading of the manuscript; Amarilio miscopies the word *kodem*, 'prior to', as *kodesh*, 'holy'. 'Amirah' is a standard title for Sabbatai Zevi (above, Introduction, section I). His 'illuminations' were his fits of manic exaltation. They alternated with states of depression, for which the sense of falling helplessly into a bottomless pit is an apt image (Introduction, section V).

[17] The scribe notes in the margin that some manuscripts read *tsa'ar*, 'suffering', for *sha'ar*, 'gate'.

[18] The 'turban' here, as always in the Sabbatian writings, symbolizes the Muslim religion. 'The Torah of Truth' (*torat emet*) is Judaism, 'the Torah of Grace' (*torat ḥesed*) Islam. These contrasting terms are commonly used by Sabbatian authors: Scholem, *Sabbatai Sevi*, 813, 863–4 (who derives the usage from Nathan of Gaza); Halperin, 'The Son of the Messiah', 181, and the sources cited there. Assaf, *In the Tents of Jacob* (Heb.), 243, quotes a 16th-century responsum of Moses Trani which speaks of the Ottoman empire as *malkhut ḥesed*, 'kingdom of grace', and perhaps this has something to do with the origin of the Sabbatian usage.

[19] Sabbatai's brother was Elijah Zevi, whom we have met several times in Baruch of Arezzo. (Cf. Baruch's account of the conversion to Islam of Elijah and his son, in §21 of the *Memorial*.) Vani Effendi was Mehmed IV's court preacher, and Sabbatai's patron and religious instructor after his conversion; cf. above, n. 45 to Joseph Halevi's letters, and Hathaway, 'The Mawza' Exile', 122–4. It is a little odd that Elijah should have been accompanied by Vani's men, and Scholem reverses the action so that it is Sabbatai and not Elijah who pays the visit (*Sabbatai Sevi*, 847). But this does not seem to suit the Hebrew.

illumination before it. His brother, and his [brother's] son with him, went at once to Vani Effendi's house and took on the turban. As he walked [Sabbatai] recited the verse: 'They have made Me jealous with a god who is no god, they have enraged Me', and so forth.[20]

On Purim day[21] [Sabbatai] left his brother and his [brother's] son in his house, and went to the home of the gentleman Rabbi Joseph Karillo.[22] There he recited the book of Esther, and there he celebrated the Purim feast. On the fifteenth [of Adar] he rode on a horse, accompanied by five men, and thus he passed through the city on the night of the holy sabbath.[23]

When Purim was over he went to the home of the sage Rabbi Jacob Alvo,[24] and summoned this rabbi [Najara] along with six other men. In that same courtyard was a janissary barracks;[25] and [Sabbatai] prayed there with the rabbis and welcomed the sabbath with melody and with great joy, singing aloud. He also prayed the evening service, as described. He ate his sabbath meal there that night, and after the meal he sang hymns as was his custom, until daybreak. When it was daylight he went with his serving-boy to the Portuguese synagogue, where he recited a number of petitionary prayers.[26] Many of the gentiles living around the synagogue were listening; not one raised any objection.

Afterwards he recited there the *namas* [Muslim prayers],[27] and after that

[20] Deut. 32: 21: 'they have enraged Me with their vanities. Just so, I will make them jealous with a people that is not a people, with a churlish nation shall I enrage them.' The point of Sabbatai's quoting the verse surely lies in the portion Najara forbears to quote, and the 'churlish nation' he has in mind is surely the Turks.

[21] 14 Adar (24 February), the day after Elijah's arrival. Purim is the festival ordained in the book of Esther to celebrate the deliverance of the Jews of ancient Persia from a planned massacre.   [22] See Baruch of Arezzo, *Memorial*, §25.

[23] The date is problematic. According to the calendrical tables in Mahler, *Handbuch der jüdischen Chronologie*, 15 Adar 5431 would have been a Wednesday. It would seem from the sequel, moreover, that Sabbatai spent the sabbath night after Purim indoors. Conceivably the abbreviation *shin-kuf* (*shabat kodesh*, 'holy sabbath') is an error for *shuk* ('marketplace'), and the passage originally described something like what is recounted below in a different context, that Sabbatai 'went about the city, through the marketplaces and the streets' (*ba'ir bashukim uvarehovot*). The alternative possibility, that Najara was using a calendar different from the standard Jewish calendar (below, Appendix 3), is a less likely explanation for this anomaly, for a few paragraphs later Najara speaks of 'the sabbath day, 25 Adar', and according to Mahler's tables 25 Adar indeed fell on a Saturday.

[24] Nothing is apparently known of this individual. But the family name Alvo, like Karillo, later turns up among the Dönmeh: Attias and Scholem, *Sabbatian Songs and Praises* (Heb.), 16.

[25] *Oda ehad shel jinisaros.* For this meaning of Turkish *oda* (normally, 'room'), see Iz, Hony, and Alderson, *Oxford Turkish Dictionary*, s.v. Najara's point is that, despite the proximity of the Turkish soldiers (janissaries), Sabbatai celebrated the sabbath loudly and without any shame.

[26] *Bakashot*, hymns recited in traditional Sephardi communities before the start of the regular sabbath morning prayer service.

[27] *Namas* is the Turkish word, derived originally from Farsi (so Professor Steven M. Wasserstrom informs me), for the Islamic statutory prayers. The same word, spelled more

he returned to [Alvo's] house and prayed the morning service [for the sab-
bath]. He then dined with [Alvo] in great joy, singing hymns and dancing
until past midday. He then prayed the *namas*, then the [Jewish] 'additional
service', and then the [Jewish] 'grace over meals' in a loud voice. The gentiles were watching and listening; not one raised any objection.

Then he went home, bringing with him his bejewelled copy of the
Zohar.[28] He arrived at sunset in a state of elation. When the sabbath was
done, early in the night, he declared that all the believers be summoned to
him and that everyone who believed in him must take on the turban. About a
dozen men and five women agreed to do as he wished.

The next morning he brought these people before the king. The king
was sitting in his latticed alcove,[29] the vizier and all the great men of the
empire present. [Sabbatai] took a copy of the Bible and read aloud before
them all: 'With regard to Ishmael, I have heard you' [Gen. 17: 20].[30] He
thereupon made them put on their turbans. The king sent forth an order to
provide them with a stipend,[31] but Amirah answered in a loud voice that he
did not want that. He had no wish, he said, that scoundrels should come and
enter this faith [Islam] out of desire for money and not out of conviction. He
did not want anyone to enter this faith other than with genuine conviction,
without any ulterior motive whatever.

On 22 Adar [4 March] a certain Jew came from Ipsola. At once [Sabbatai]
brought him [before the sultan?] and made him put on the turban, telling
him to go to Ipsola and say: 'Whoever wants to enter this faith, let him
come!'

---

correctly *namaz*, occurs in Israel Hazzan's Sabbatian commentary on the psalms of the midnight-vigil liturgy (fo. 111ʳ; quoted in Halperin, 'The Son of the Messiah', 209 n.).

[28] *Sefer hazohar shelo java'iri*. I understand the last word as derived from Turkish *cevahir*,
'jewellery' (originally Arabic *jawahir*), and to refer to some gorgeously bound copy Sabbatai
had made of his favourite book. (Amarilio's suggestion—'Sabbatian Documents', 255 n.—that
java'iri is a Turkish equivalent of 'Zohar' will not explain why it comes after *shelo* rather than
before.) We will see this 'bejewelled Zohar' again (below, at n. 66). I am grateful to my friend
Ms Sema Deeds for having discussed with me the meaning of this and other Turkish words in
the Najara Chronicle.

[29] Turkish *kafes*, literally 'cage, lattice, grating'. See above, Introduction, section I.

[30] Spoken by God to Abraham. The biblical verse goes on: 'I have blessed him, and I will
make him fruitful and magnify him greatly [*bime'od me'od*] . . . and I will make him a great
nation.' Even beyond the obvious allusion to Islamic power, or specifically the Ottoman
empire, this verse was much favoured by medieval Muslim polemicists, for the words *bime'od
me'od* have the same numerical value in Hebrew as 'Muhammad'. See Perlmann, *Ibn Kammuna's Examination of the Three Faiths*, 137–43; Steinschneider, *Polemische und apologetische Literatur*, 327, 364.   [31] Turkish *ulufe*.

On the sabbath day, 25 Adar [7 March], [Sabbatai] went to the [Portuguese] synagogue along with all his men and the Faithful Ones whom he had made to wear the turban. He found the congregation reciting the Shema.[32] When they reached the words, 'From Egypt You redeemed us', he told them to be silent, and he himself recited, melodiously and in a loud voice, up to the words 'You have redeemed Israel'. Many gentiles were present.[33]

Before the Torah scroll was brought out of its ark, he went up to the ark and delivered a sermon. The gist of his sermon was to convey a number of difficulties present in our holy Torah and in the sayings of our ancient sages, which could not be understood or solved except on the basis of his premises. As God privileged us to hear that sermon from [Sabbatai's] holy mouth!—as I shall say presently.[34] He went on with his sermon for something like two hours. At the end of it he read aloud from the Qur'ān, thereby conveying that the sermon's whole point was to bring the congregation into that faith [of Islam].

On the fourth day of Nisan [15 March], [Sabbatai] wrote a decree to be sent to Constantinople, to twelve men of rabbinical status, as you shall see from the text of the decree.[35] He also wrote a decree for Sofia, one for Brusa, and one for Rodosto. The messenger delayed for two days so that he might also send for the Holy Lamp, Rabbi Nathan [of Gaza],[36] who was in Iznimit.[37] As it turned out, however, the only items he sent were the decrees to Constantinople, Sofia, and Brusa, and he did not send for Rabbi [Nathan].

Amirah had told this rabbi [Najara] that his intent was to bring those he had summoned into the king's presence. There he would reveal to them the Mystery of Divinity, for so it must be. He said also to Vani Effendi that there was no one but himself who recognized the blessed Creator; and he

---

[32] The string of three biblical passages—Deut. 6: 4–9, 11: 13–21, Num. 15: 37–41—that convey the central principles of Judaism. 'From Egypt You redeemed us, O Lord our God' is the opening of one of the liturgical benedictions following the Shema in the synagogue service.

[33] May we assume they came in with Sabbatai, and were part of the reason why the congregation so docilely put up with Sabbatai's abusive behaviour?

[34] There is nothing in the sequel that would illuminate this remark. It seems a fair assumption that Najara intends to convey something like, 'As God privileged us to hear it ... so may He privilege us to see it fulfilled in the messianic kingdom.'

[35] Not in the surviving portions of Najara's chronicle.

[36] 'Holy Lamp', *butsina kadisha*, is an epithet used in the Zohar for Rabbi Simeon ben Yohai. Sabbatian writers apply it to Nathan of Gaza (Scholem, *Sabbatai Sevi*, 200 n.).

[37] 'Brusa' is modern Bursa, 'Rodosto' is modern Tekirdag, 'Iznimit' is modern Izmit (ancient Nicomedia).

expounded to [Vani Effendi] the biblical verse, 'But in this let a man take pride, that he understands and knows Me' [Jer. 9: 23].[38]

This man [Najara] went to the king and told him all these things. 'Tell him', said the king, 'that he is to make known to me God's Divinity.'[39] But to this Amirah responded: 'I cannot, until all the rabbis are gathered for whom I have sent. Then I will tell him and them together.' This man [Najara] also told the king that sometimes [Sabbatai] was in a state of illumination, sometimes not, and thus it was with the prophets who preceded him. For it is written in their books that such was the case with Joshua.[40]

Of the rabbis of Constantinople, the men for whom he had sent, there came the worthy rabbis Meir Rofé, Abraham Gamaliel, Abraham Sussi, and Sabbatai Halevi. The others held back, for the reasons mentioned in the decree.[41] (The exceptions were Rabbi Aaron ibn Hayim, who had gone to the opposite extreme[?],[42] and the worthy Rabbi Moses Alfandari, who the very week the decree went forth had come [to Adrianople] on a royal mission and was unwilling to tarry there, on account of the governmental responsibilities that had been laid upon him.) The Brusan rabbis also came: Rabbi Jacob Lodric, Rabbi Moses Yafeh, Rabbi Isaac Sardina.[43]

---

[38] The verse is quoted to a similar effect by Cardozo (Halperin, *Abraham Miguel Cardozo*, 182).

[39] Perhaps wishing to screen Sabbatai's remarks in advance?

[40] Professor Wasserstrom, who was kind enough to discuss this puzzling passage with me, suggests it may have something to do with Shi'ite traditions making Joshua into a prototype of Ali, whose relation to Moses prefigures Ali's to Muhammad. Wasserstrom (*Between Muslim and Jew*, 63–4) has noted Jewish and Islamic traditions linking Joshua and Ali, respectively, to the moon; see BT *BB* 75*a*. He suggests to me that some connection may have been made between the moon's waxing and waning, and Sabbatai's being 'sometimes in a state of illumination, sometimes not'. I do not know on what basis Scholem supposes that Jesus, and not the Old Testament Joshua, is intended here (*Sabbatai Sevi*, 848).

[41] In the absence of the decree, we can only guess what these 'reasons' were. Presumably they were not very creditable.

[42] *Sheyatsa liketseh aher*. I do not know what Najara is trying to convey, beyond (apparently) that Ibn Hayim, like Alfandari and unlike the other rabbis who chose to absent themselves, had a legitimate reason for so doing.

[43] This paragraph anticipates subsequent events. The audience with the sultan did not take place until sometime around the beginning of May (see below); the rabbis Sabbatai had summoned had presumably arrived a few days or weeks earlier. Of the rabbis from Constantinople, we have already met the highly peripatetic Rofé (above, n. 49 on Baruch of Arezzo), and will meet Gamaliel again presently. I can provide no further information on Sussi, Halevi, or Moses Alfandari. Ibn Hayim, like Rofé, was a native of Hebron; H. J. D. Azulai records (in *Shem hagedolim*) that he was a rabbi in Izmir, but does not mention him in connection with Constantinople. The three Brusan rabbis, Lodric, Yafeh, and Sardina, turn up in an anecdote of Cardozo's, who claims to have met them in 1681; see my introduction to Najara, above. Najara does not make clear what the results were of the decree to Sofia, or why Sabbatai felt compelled to dispatch another one after the audience with the sultan (below).

On the fifth of Nisan [16 March], [Sabbatai] went to the gentile archives and divorced his wife.[44] He applied to himself the biblical verse, 'Six years shall [the slave] labour and in the seventh year [he shall go out free]',[45] for on that day a full seven years had elapsed since he had married her. He made considerable effort to take his son Ishmael[46] into his custody, but she did not want to let him go. For the boy was young, and the [Muslim] laws require that a child remain with his mother for the first seven years.

On 7 Nisan [18 March], he was dining in his house with this rabbi [Najara] when who should appear but his beloved son Ishmael. Vani Effendi, it seems, had sent to the boy's mother, saying: 'Send him to be with his father!' At this Amirah rejoiced greatly. It was for this reason, he said, that he had tried mightily in days past to take the boy with him and rescue him, yet had met with no success—until this day, which was the day offering was brought by Elishama son of Ammihud, prince of the tribe of Ephraim.[47] The name 'Elishama' is [in Hebrew] an anagram for 'Ishmael'; this is an allusion to messiah son of Ephraim. 'Tomorrow', said Amirah to this rabbi [Najara], 'I wish to circumcise him, for he is now a full 3 years old. This is in accordance with the hidden meaning of the verse, "Three years it shall be to you 'uncircumcised' . . . and in the fourth year all its fruit shall be a thing holy, for the giving of praises."'[48]

So, on the eighth day of the month, he dressed his son in fine clothing and went to invite all the city's dignitaries to his circumcision. They imagined it would take place according to their custom, by which the invitation is issued one day before the circumcision. Yet as soon as he had finished inviting them, he sent immediately for this rabbi [Najara] and ordered him to bring the implements for circumcision.[49] He set up the Chair of Elijah.[50] Then he himself sat on that chair for something like an hour, enwrapped in a mantle, in a state of intense concentration.[51]

---

[44] The unfortunate Sarah. He was later to take her back, and she was to accompany him into exile to Dulcigno, and die there.

[45] Exod. 21: 2.   [46] See Baruch of Arezzo, *Memorial*, §21.

[47] Num. 7: 48–53. The sequence of offerings described in this chapter began 'on the first day of the first month' (Exod. 40: 2, 17)—that is, Nisan—and Elishama brought his tribe's offering on the seventh day.

[48] Lev. 19: 23–4, translating *hilulim* in accord with the traditional Jewish interpreters. In its original context the passage refers to a fruit tree.

[49] This sounds very much like a stratagem for keeping the Muslim dignitaries of Adrianople from witnessing his son's circumcision, while being able to protest afterwards that he had issued invitations to them all. Najara's assurances to the contrary, Sabbatai seems to have taken care that the Muslims should not observe too closely his persistently Jewish behaviour.

[50] A chair, often 'richly carved and ornamented with embroideries', set up at a Jewish circumcision for the invisible guest at the ceremony, the prophet Elijah (*Encyclopedia Judaica*, s.v. 'Elijah, Chair of'). No one but Elijah is normally supposed to sit on it.

[51] Translating *mitboded* in accord with Idel, *Studies in Ecstatic Kabbalah*, 103–69, and 'On Prophecy and Magic in Sabbateanism', 15–17.

Afterwards he rose and made the gentleman Rabbi Joseph Karillo sit as *sandak*.[52] Amirah recited the blessing,[53] '[Blessed be You, O Lord our God, King of the universe, who sanctified us with His commandments and commanded us] to enter this child into the covenant of Father Abraham.' Then this rabbi [Najara] circumcised the boy. [Sabbatai] recited the blessing of Him 'who has kept us alive' and told this rabbi [Najara] to recite the same blessing, having been privileged to perform so pious a deed.[54] This rabbi [Najara] said the blessing of Him 'who sanctified the beloved one', over the wine cup,[55] and the newly circumcised child was given the Jewish name 'Israel'.

There was a certain man present, a Jew who had apostatized years earlier, who had a 10-year-old son. The boy had not yet been circumcised, the man having vowed while Amirah was in the 'tower of strength'[56] that he would not circumcise his son except in the presence of king messiah. Amirah thereupon commanded this rabbi [Najara] to circumcise the boy, with the same blessings as before. He was given the name Ishmael.

On the sabbath before Passover [10 Nisan = 21 March], Amirah prayed in the same house in a state of great elation, adding many liturgical poems to the worship service. At the time when the Torah should have been brought forth from the ark, he took out his printed Bible and read from it. The first passage he read was the text beginning, 'This is the law of the leper on the day he is purified of his leprosy' [Lev. 14: 2].[57] He explained this as an

---

[52] The 'godfather' at the circumcision, who normally sits in a chair next to the Chair of Elijah and holds the child on his lap. (It is possible to read this sentence as meaning that Sabbatai made Karillo sit in the Chair of Elijah, which he had just vacated.) Normally, of course, the child being circumcised is an 8-day-old infant. This scene, involving a 3-year-old boy, does not bear to be imagined in too much detail.

[53] Prescribed in BT *Shab.* 137*b* for the father of the circumcised boy.

[54] 'Blessed be You, O Lord our God, King of the universe, who has kept us alive, preserved us, and enabled us to reach this day.' Maimonides rules the father is to say this blessing at the circumcision (*Mishneh torah*, 'Hilkhot milah', 3: 3); other authorities suppose he is only to do so if he himself has performed it (Karo's *Shulḥan arukh*, 'Yoreh de'ah', 265: 7, which claims that Maimonides' opinion is followed 'in the entire kingdom of the Land of Israel and Syria [i.e. the Ottoman province of Syria?] and its surroundings, and the kingdom of Egypt'). Normally the circumciser, if someone other than the father, would *not* recite this blessing. Hence Sabbatai's special directive to Najara.

[55] 'Blessed be You, O Lord our God, King of the universe, who sanctified the one beloved from the womb, inscribing an ordinance in his flesh, and sealed his descendants with the mark of the holy covenant. . . . Blessed be You, O Lord, who makes the covenant.' The Talmud (BT *Shab.* 137*b*), prescribes this blessing but does not make clear who is to say it (cf. Maimonides, *Mishneh torah*, 'Hilkhot milah', 3: 3). Normally, as here, it would be spoken by the circumciser.

[56] The fortress at Gallipoli; above, n. 93 on Baruch of Arezzo.

[57] Which would normally have been read in the synagogue, not the sabbath before Passover, but three weeks afterwards.

allusion to an evil wife, who is 'like a leprosy for her husband'.[58] Thus our ancient sages tell us the messiah's name is to be 'the White One of the master's house'—which term ['White One'] Rashi glosses as 'leper'.[59]

He went on to read the passage beginning, 'In the third month' [Exod. 19: 1].[60] This, he said, was an allusion to its being the third month of his state of illumination.[61] He commanded everyone present to stand up and to hear the Ten Commandments in trembling and dread, for that hour was just like the hour when Israel received the Torah at Mount Sinai.

He then read the entirety of the Torah portion 'Tsav',[62] and afterwards feasted in great joy. Throughout all this the windows and doors were closed. At the time of the afternoon prayer he opened all the doors and all the windows, and, although a number of gentiles were watching through the windows and doors, not one of them made any protest. When he came to the Aleinu prayer,[63] he told the turban-wearers to recite the prayer in a loud voice along with the Jews, facing eastwards as they did so, and to pay no attention to the gentiles who watched them. Thus they did.

Afterwards [Sabbatai] sat down to eat the third meal of the sabbath. He did not allow any of the turban-wearers to sit with him, but only this rabbi [Najara] and one other Jew. Then he took a full cup of wine in his hand, and he loudly and tunefully sang the hymn that begins, 'The sons of the palace who yearn'.[64] This he followed with 'A psalm of David, The Lord is my shepherd' [Ps. 23] and the blessing over the wine. Prior to the meal, and during the meal prior to the fruit course, he recited several chapters of tractate *Shabat* [of the Mishnah], and the first chapter of tractate *Berakhot*. Afterwards, at the time of the after-dinner grace, he again took a cup of wine in his hand and recited the hymn beginning, 'Let us bless Him who sustains all the

---

[58] BT *Yev.* 63*b*, *San.* 100*b*; the prescribed cure is divorce. The allusion to Sabbatai's personal situation is all too obvious.   [59] BT *San.* 98*b*, and Rashi's comment ad loc.

[60] The story of the revelation at Mount Sinai.

[61] Which began, as Najara tells us near the beginning of his narrative, on 19 Shevat. Since then less than two months had elapsed, Sabbatai presumably counts Shevat as the first month of his 'illumination', Adar as the second, Nisan as the third.

[62] Lev. 6: 1–8: 36, the appropriate Torah reading for that sabbath.

[63] A prayer recited at the close of the worship service, praising God for 'not having made us like the nations of the world . . . for they bow to vanity and emptiness and pray to a god who cannot save, while we bow to and acknowledge the King of kings of kings, the Blessed Holy One' (part of this text is censored from Ashkenazi prayer books). As recited by Sabbatai and the rest of his 'turban-wearers', the Aleinu would have been a shout of defiance—understood by them, incomprehensible to the watching Muslims—against the religion to which they had converted.

[64] A hymn for the third sabbath meal, composed by the 16th-century kabbalist Isaac Luria—normally followed, as here, by the twenty-third psalm and the blessing over the wine.

world'.[65] He then said grace in a loud voice, pronouncing each word distinctly.

That night, at the close of the sabbath, he recited the evening prayer in a most melodious fashion, and with great joy. Once the sabbath was done he went riding on a horse, taking with him some thirty of the Faithful Ones who wore the turban. In his hand he carried the jewelled Zohar book.[66] He went about the city, through the marketplaces and the streets, and all the dignitaries of the empire saw him going about with his troop of followers,[67] the book in his hand. Not one made any protest.

On the first day of the month Iyar [11 April], about eight men came from Ipsola, and he made them wear the turban.[68] On 3 Iyar he summoned this rabbi [Najara] and said to him: 'Be aware that all the tribes I have made before this were part of the mystery of the World of Chaos, the mystery of "He built worlds and He destroyed them".[69] But now I am cancelling all I have done, and now I swear this structure I am building is . . .

HERE THERE IS A GAP IN THE TEXT

. . . at the gate of the inner court, where stood the eunuchs and all the dignitaries of the empire who attended upon the king. Amirah was seated, and the rabbis previously mentioned[70] were seated beside him.

Amirah then said to this rabbi:[71] 'Do not be pained and do not be frightened. For all is in my hand.' He then took the Zohar and said to him: 'Open this book.'[72] And he opened it to this passage:

[65] A hymn composed for the grace after meals by Najara's famous grandfather, the poet Israel Najara.　　　　　　　　　　　　[66] *Sefer hazohar hajava'ir*. See above, n. 28.

[67] Turkish *alay*, often used in a military sense (but also, Ms Deeds informs me, of a wedding procession).　　　　　　　　　[68] That is, converted them to Islam.

[69] Midrash *Genesis Rabbah* 3: 7, 9: 2: 'The Blessed Holy One created worlds and He destroyed them, until He created these. He said: "This world pleases Me; the others did not please Me."' 'The World of Chaos' (*olam hatohu*) is a kabbalistic term for the system of divine potentialities preceding the current one, to which, according to the kabbalists, the strange midrashic utterance about 'destroying worlds' was intended to apply (see Scholem, *Major Trends in Jewish Mysticism*, 265–8, and *Kabbalah*, 137–40). Sabbatai is obviously comparing his own actions to God's, but it is not clear precisely what he is trying to say, or what he means by 'all the tribes [*shevatim*] I have made'. (Cf. Scholem, *Sabbatai Sevi*, 850.) It is very unfortunate that the passage is broken off, and a substantial chunk of text missing, in the middle of his speech.

[70] The rabbis who had come from Constantinople and Brusa in response to his summons; above, n. 43.

[71] Najara himself, as elsewhere in this text? Or someone else? The absence of the context makes it impossible to be sure.

[72] *Tiftah zeh hasefer*. (Amarilio, 'Sabbatian Documents', 258, mistakenly copies the manuscript's 'הפס as 'הספ.) The subjects of the verbs are left unclear, but it sounds very much as if Sabbatai has given his copy of the Zohar to 'this rabbi' and told him to open it at random.

This may be compared to a king who rejoices at his wedding, and all the people rejoice with him. He sees one man in chains.[73] He commands that man to be released, so all may be joyful.[74]

'Here is the interpretation', [Sabbatai] said. 'You are like people enchained, for you sit in this place and you are fasting. Yet you shall go forth from these chains, for anyone who wishes to put on the turban may do so.[75] And anyone who does not so desire, I will send him forth[76] in safety, just as he entered.'

Amirah then asked for water, and they brought it to him. In the presence of all the bystanders he recited the blessings before and after he drank,[77] in a loud voice and with intense concentration on the words. He also told the rabbis that all of them must drink and say the blessings.

Afterwards the Silahtar-Pasha[78] came and bade them enter, since Vani Effendi had by now arrived. The king was sitting on the throne;[79] all his intimates, the foremost men of the empire, stood to his right and his left and behind him. Amirah held his Bible in one hand, the crystal in the other.[80] He and the king were hardly three cubits distant from one another, with Vani Effendi sitting between them and the rabbis standing behind Amirah in one single line. Amirah then told the dreams to the king, along with that which the dreams revealed—their simple meaning, that is. Their esoteric significance must not be put into writing.[81]

'These rabbis', said the king. 'Why are they here?'

'These are the greatest rabbis of the Jewish people', [Sabbatai] replied. 'I

---

[73] The manuscript has *beit-nun* [*bar nash*] *yehiv bekolar*, with the printed text of the Zohar. The abbreviation *beit-beit* for *beit-nun* is Amarilio's error, as is (probably) the ungrammatical *yod* at the end of *yehiv*. (The reading of this word is not quite certain.)

[74] Zohar, ii. 207*b*. The context speaks of a man who fasts on the sabbath and is liable to punishment for this.

[75] As if Judaism were a form of imprisonment, from which the prisoner may go forth at will.

[76] Understanding *otsi'enu* for the manuscript's *hotsi'enu*. Interchange of *alef* and *heh* is common in these texts.

[77] That is, the two benediction formulas prescribed in Mishnah *Ber.* 6: 8, of which the first is recited before the act of drinking, the second afterwards.

[78] Turkish *silahtar* or *silahdar* ('weapons-bearer') refers to members of a cavalry unit, which at one point served as the sultan's personal guard. The 'Silahtar-Pasha' would be their chief, the sultan's sword-bearer. [79] Turkish *taht*.

[80] Najara seems to assume the reader will know what is intended by 'the crystal' (*habedolah*). There is surely some connection with the 'large piece of glass' (*hatikhah gedolah shel zekhukhit*) that Baruch of Arezzo represents Sabbatai as using 'to cool off his intense heat' (*Memorial*, §11). But I do not know what the object might have been, or what meanings it might have had for Sabbatai. (According to the entry for *bedolah* in Ben-Yehuda's *Complete Dictionary of Ancient and Modern Hebrew*, the word could mean 'pearl' as well as 'crystal'. The parallel in Baruch's *Memorial* points to the second alternative.)

[81] Were these dreams recorded in the missing portion of Najara's chronicle?

brought them here to debate with them, to persuade them to enter into this faith [of Islam]. For if these convert, all the Jews will convert.'

The king said to Vani Effendi: 'Ask them for their own understanding of why they have come.' Vani Effendi accordingly asked the rabbis, in Arabic: 'Why did you come here?'[82]

They answered: 'We know this man to be a great rabbi of the Jewish people. When he put on the turban [in 1666] we did not take it very seriously, given he had a reason for doing that.[83] Now, however, that we have seen how much effort he devotes to converting others to this faith, we have asked him why he does so. He answered that he would prove it from our Torah. So he has brought us here, promising to prove his case in the royal presence.'

Vani Effendi related all this to the king. 'Ask them now', said the king, 'if his arguments make sense to them, are they prepared to convert?'

To which the rabbis replied: 'If he can give us clear proof of what he proposes from our Torah, we will concede he is right.'

They spent something like two hours working these things out.[84] What a privilege it was to have witnessed it!—the great boldness with which Amirah addressed the king, the way the king conducted himself with him, and many other matters that cannot be set down in writing. The king then said to Amirah: 'Speak to them.'

'This is a subject', Amirah replied, 'that requires we be seated. It demands patience and cannot be treated while we are obliged to stand.' So the king said they should go into the Divan,[85] which they did, and they sat in the places normally occupied by the vizier and the nobles, while the king went and sat in his latticed alcove.[86]

Amirah began by raising the theological difficulties of passages like 'The Lord regretted . . . and He was grieved' [Gen. 6: 6] and other texts of that kind, until he came to the problem of 'Who is like You, O Lord, among the gods?' [Exod. 15: 11], at which point he recited the entire Song of the Sea.[87] Initially, when Amirah began raising his objections, the rabbis just listened silently. But Amirah said to them: 'Why do you keep silent? Give some answer, even though it be insubstantial, so it will not look like you are

---

[82] The implication, that the rabbis spoke Arabic but not Turkish, and the Islamic scholar Vani Effendi therefore had to be used as interpreter, is very much worth noting.

[83] Namely, to save his life.

[84] That is, negotiating the ground rules of the debate. The substantive discussion takes place afterwards in the Divan.   [85] The imperial council chamber.

[86] To watch the proceedings without himself being seen; cf. above, at n. 29.

[87] Exod. 15: 1–18. The difficulties are that the Bible attributes human feelings to God, that he appears in Exod. 15: 11 to be one god among many. Similar problems troubled the young Cardozo (Halperin, *Abraham Miguel Cardozo*, 110–11).

conceding.'[88] Every difficulty he raised from then on, the rabbis would rise to their feet and dispute with tremendous acuity, as though they were in a real yeshiva.

While this was going on, the king's nobles asked Amirah's brother [Elijah] to tell him that they had better not raise their voices too much, since the king was sitting in his alcove above them. But Amirah rebuked his brother, and said to him in Turkish: 'How can you tell me I mustn't yell in the king's presence? Don't they do enough yelling in the Imperial Divan over a lawsuit of a hundred *grossos*? Why not, when it is divine matters[89] that are at stake?'

He went on speaking even louder and more forcefully than before, in the end revealing to them the knowledge of God. The entire discussion was conducted in Spanish.[90]

Afterwards, he asked the rabbis one by one if they wanted to put on the turban. None was willing, apart from Rabbi Abraham Gamaliel and the gentleman Rabbi Joseph Karillo.[91] Amirah then said in Turkish: 'You must know you are under no compulsion. No one will kill you; no one will put you to the sword. But anyone who wants to put on the turban of his own free will, let him do so.'

(And it was the Lord's mercy he said this, for we have heard from reliable sources, who had it from the nobles who were in attendance on the king, that at the very moment Amirah spoke these words the king had commanded the executioner[92] that 'if they do not obey what Mehmed Agha[93] tells them—fall upon them!' But when he heard what Amirah said he dismissed the executioner, and the seven men who did not want to put on the turban departed safe and sound.[94])

The king then returned to his principal chamber.[95] Rabbi Abraham Gamaliel and Rabbi Joseph Karillo entered his presence, accompanied by Amirah. 'You have laboured long and hard with them', the king said to him.

'They are stiff-necked', [Sabbatai] replied. 'Their heads are hard as rock.'

---

[88] Suggesting that Sabbatai regarded this debate as an act put on for the sultan's benefit. He and the rabbis spoke in Spanish (below), no doubt with a considerable admixture of Hebrew; the sultan must have had no idea at all what they were saying.

[89] *Devari[m] elohiyim*, in the manuscript.

[90] This seems to be what is intended by *leshon la'az*. Cf. the use of *la'az* at the end of the chronicle.

[91] Cf. Cardozo's comments on Gamaliel and Karillo, quoted in the introduction to this text.   [92] Turkish *cellat* (from Arabic *jallad*).

[93] aka Sabbatai Zevi. 'Agha', literally 'chief' or 'commander', is here used as an honorific title.

[94] The 'seven' presumably included Rofé, Sussi, and Halevi from Constantinople, Lodric, Yafeh, and Sardina from Brusa (above, n. 43). Was Najara himself the seventh?

[95] Turkish *baş oda*.

'Tell me what arguments you used with them', the king said.

'I cannot tell you today', he answered, 'for I have devoted much labour to them already.'

'Well then, tell me *something* of what you said.'

[Sabbatai] recited for him in Turkish the verse, 'With regard to Ishmael, I have heard you', and so forth.[96] 'Recite it as it was written', said the king; so he recited for him the Hebrew text, with proper cantillation and accentuation. Then the two men [Gamaliel and Karillo] were made to wear the turban. 'Don't let yourself be troubled over those rabbis who would not yield to you', the nobles said to him in the king's presence. 'Just be patient. They will come.'

—And there were things that cannot be put in writing, through which Amirah's greatness may be known. He went forth in great honour, for the king loved him and magnified his splendour.

On Monday night[97] Amirah summoned those rabbis to his house, and there expatiated to them upon the subject of God's divinity. He wrote a decree that very same day and sent it to Sofia, to summon the worthy Rabbis Samuel Primo and Aaron Majar, along with the other rabbis [of Sofia?], about twelve in number.[98] On Tuesday[99] he wrote a decree summoning the holy rabbi, the Holy Lamp, Rabbi Benjamin Nathan.[100] The worthy Rabbi Jacob Ashkenazi arrived that same day,[101] while Rabbi [Nathan's] messenger delayed for about two days.

In the meantime Amirah's light vanished, and it remained concealed until 23 Sivan [2 June]. On 30 Iyar [10 May][102] Rabbi Samuel Tirmiso

[96] Gen. 17: 20; above, n. 30.

[97] Or, 'the second night'. My translation assumes that, in the missing portion of Najara's chronicle, the disputation before the sultan was said to have taken place on a certain day of the week, probably Sunday.

[98] How this decree relates to Sabbatai's earlier decree to Sofia (above, n. 43) is left unclear. On Primo and Majar (Magueres), see the notes to Baruch of Arezzo, *Memorial*, §§13, 23.

[99] Or, 'the third day' (*yom g'* in the manuscript, versus Amarilio's *yom b'*).

[100] Nathan of Gaza. Cf. above, n. 36.

[101] To judge from Cardozo's reminiscences (translated below), Jacob Ashkenazi was widely regarded in the 1670s as one of the leading intellectuals in the Sabbatian movement, perhaps second only to Nathan. Strangely, practically no information about him survives, beyond that he seems to have died not long before 1680 (Halperin, 'The Son of the Messiah', 162). Cardozo attributes to Ashkenazi one of the most memorable epigrams to be found anywhere in the Sabbatian literature, which may itself suggest why he became *persona non grata* among Sabbatai's devotees. 'I was at Edirne [Adrianople] when word arrived that Sabbatai Zevi had died at Alkum [Dulcigno]. I went to the great scholar, the Honourable Rabbi Jacob Ashkenazi, and I said to him: "Sabbatai Zevi is dead. What says Your Worship to that?" And he replied: "If Sabbatai Zevi is dead, you had best find yourself another God"' (Halperin, *Abraham Miguel Cardozo*, 280).

[102] On this seemingly impossible date, and the Gregorian equivalents given here for the dates in Sivan, see Appendix 3.

arrived;[103] on 2 Sivan [12 May][104] the Sofian rabbis arrived; and on the four-teenth of that month [24 May] Rabbi Samuel Tirmiso, after paying his respects, took leave of Amirah and returned home.

On the nineteenth [29 May], Rabbi [Nathan] came from Rodosto here to Adrianople of his own volition. He had written to Amirah prior to his arrival, begging him to treat him kindly and not force him to convert to Islam, for everyone was well aware that to convert him was Amirah's intent. (That was why [Sabbatai] had summoned him here from Kastoria[105] the year before. Yet as soon as [Nathan] had arrived, his illumination had van-ished,[106] and thus he wished to summon him now, as he had summoned the Constantinople rabbis—and even after they came the matter[107] was not brought to any satisfactory end.) Hence [Nathan] wrote, begging him not to force any such demand upon him at this time. Amirah sent him a reply, the text of which you shall presently see.[108]

On the very same day that [Sabbatai's] decree[109] went forth from Adrianople, Rabbi [Nathan] had set forth of his own accord from Rodosto, where he had been living, for Adrianople. He arrived here on 19 Sivan [29 May], bringing with him Rabbi Samuel Gandoor and Rabbi Moses Aryeh.[110] Amirah was still in his state of eclipse[111] when [Nathan] arrived. He came to pay his respects at once, on the sabbath, the twentieth of the month [30 May], in the company of all the rabbis.

They heard from Amirah about the eclipsing of his light. He told them how he remained shut away, and how this was the meaning of the talmudic allusion, 'The White One [= leper] of the master's house is his name',[112] 'leprosy' having the implication of being 'shut away'.[113] When, moreover,

[103] As far as I know, nothing further is known of this man; but see Benayahu, *The Sabbatian Movement in Greece* (Heb.), 48.

[104] Emending *uvek' lesivan* to *uveb' lesivan*; see Appendix 3.

[105] Nathan's principal place of residence, since the end of the first phase of his travels in 1669 (Baruch of Arezzo, *Memorial*, end of §20). On Nathan's whereabouts in the 1670s, see Benayahu, *The Sabbatian Movement in Greece* (Heb.), 227–30.

[106] And with it the impulse to convert Nathan to Islam. Cf. above, Introduction, section VII.   [107] Of their conversion, presumably.

[108] Not in the surviving portions of Najara's chronicle.

[109] Summoning Nathan to come see him.

[110] Gandoor had been Nathan's travelling companion for the past four years, and had been involved with the movement from its beginnings; see Baruch of Arezzo, *Memorial*, §§17 (end) and 19, and Scholem, *Sabbatai Sevi*, 213–14, 718–48, 770–81. I can provide no further infor-mation on Moses Aryeh.

[111] See above, n. 241 on Baruch of Arezzo. The word Najara uses is *he'elem*, as opposed to Baruch's *hester panim*. But the reality described is the same.

[112] BT *San.* 98*b*, referring to the messiah. Cf. above, at n. 59.

[113] *Segiruta*, literally 'shutting away', is the standard Aramaic equivalent to Hebrew *tsara'at*, 'leprosy', in the Targum on Lev. 13–14.

our ancient sages say that 'the Kingdom is destined to turn heretic',[114] they refer to the Kingdom of Heaven—to those times when he remains in eclipse, when he is in the power of the Serpents, until from the extremity of the suffering he endures he inclines towards heresy, and of his faith he retains only that single hair's breadth that distinguishes Nothingness from Being. Yet when he is in a state of illumination that single hair expands until it is as strong as a cart rope, and not even a hair's breadth of doubt remains within him.[115]

This yields the clue to the correct interpretation of the Gemara's words: 'What is the scriptural basis for this claim? "He has turned entirely white; he is pure."'[116] On Rashi's interpretation of this passage, the image and its application do not cohere, for it must be the leper himself who experiences the purification.[117] Assume [Sabbatai's] interpretation, and all becomes clear. He [Sabbatai] himself, the one who has been shut away,[118] is purified thereby and strengthened in his faith; it is as though he had died and been restored to life. The biblical verse, 'The righteous shall live by his faith' [Hab. 2: 4], may be interpreted along the same lines. The Righteous One [Sabbatai Zevi] has no life in and of himself, but only when he is strengthened [through his faith].[119]

The Men of the Great Synagogue were hinting at the same thing [when they formulated the prayer addressing God as a] 'King who puts to death

[114] BT *San.* 97*a*: 'Rabbi Isaac said: The son of David will not come, until all the Kingdom turn heretic. Rava said: What is the Scriptural basis for this claim? "He has turned entirely white [leprous]; he is pure [Lev. 13: 13]."' In its original context, this statement of Rabbi Isaac, who lived at the end of the 3rd century CE, presumably refers to the impending Christianization of the Roman empire (Avi-Yonah, *The Jews of Palestine*, 158). Sabbatai, however, uses the prooftext from Leviticus to link it to the talmudic prophecy of the 'leprosy' of the messiah, namely himself. In what follows he plainly understands *malkhut shamayim*, 'Kingdom of Heaven', to refer to himself, presumably via the kabbalistic equation of *malkhut shamayim* with the divine potentiality called Malkhut, which is linked with King David and thus with the Davidic messiah.

[115] The language of 'hair's breadth' and 'cart rope' is drawn from BT *Suk.* 52*a*.

[116] See above, n. 114. The manuscript's abbreviation *mem-kuf* stands for *mai kera* ('What is the scriptural basis for this claim?'), not, as Amarilio supposes, the talmudic tractate *Mo'ed katan.*

[117] Rashi explains the passage from BT *San.* 97*a* as follows: 'When the plague has spread through the entire skin [the biblical image]—similarly, when the entire Kingdom has turned heretic [its talmudic application]—then redemption will come.' To this Najara offers a reasonable objection. While the biblical image has only one referent (the leper), the Talmud as Rashi interprets it must apply this image to two distinct referents: the 'Kingdom' that is to become heretic, and the 'redemption' that will follow. How much more preferable, says Najara, is Sabbatai Zevi's interpretation of the passage as a reference to himself, in which the one who is 'leprous' is also the one who becomes 'pure'.

[118] *Musgar*, a technical term for a person who has developed a skin disease that may possibly be leprosy, and who is sequestered for one or two weeks until the illness can declare itself.

[119] See above, n. 90 on Baruch of Arezzo.

and brings to life and causes salvation to sprout. Faithful [are You, O Lord, to bring the dead to life].'[120] One would normally have expected the phrase 'causes salvation to sprout' to be placed first, and only afterwards 'puts to death and brings to life'.[121] But the Men of the Great Synagogue wished to imply that the Lord would perform a great work with the king destined to redeem Israel [that is, the messiah], first putting him to death and then restoring him to life—this 'restoration' being the revealing of his light and his exaltation—which in turn would effect the 'sprouting' of salvation. (The subsequent words, 'Faithful [are You, O Lord, to bring the dead to life]', speak of the general resurrection of the dead.)

Amirah went on to expand his welcome[122] remarks on these topics and others akin to them, as was his good custom: perhaps, he felt, the revelation of his light might be forthcoming from the very fact the subject was under discussion. For this was always his way. First he would proclaim his own confidence, as a sort of encouragement; then, when it should be God's will to confirm him in his confidence, this would bring about the strengthening of the exalted faith. God's light would then be revealed upon him.

He passed three days, becoming alternately stronger and weaker, until the pre-dawn hours of the fourth day.[123] Such, he told us, was always his custom: inasmuch as the revelation of his light took on particular power in the hours before dawn—this being a time of divine favour—he would at that time remain in solitary concentration,[124] and the light of the Lord would reveal itself upon him. This would provide aid and stimulus for the light of the completion of the blessed match arranged with Sarah, the daughter of Rabbi Aaron Majar.[125] But he said this matter[126] should remain concealed until seven days had passed after its conclusion.

The beginning of his illumination, consequently, was 25 Sivan [4 June]. On the fourth day he sent for us and we saw him in his beauty and power. We rabbis all fanned him with a fan, like slaves serving their master.

---

[120] From the second benediction of the Amidah, the series of benedictions, recited while standing, that constitutes the core of the synagogue service. The 'Men of the Great Synagogue', an august and probably legendary college of the 4th and 3rd centuries BCE, are traditionally credited with having formulated the synagogue liturgy.

[121] Since the messiah's coming is normally presumed to precede the resurrection of the dead.   [122] Literally 'sweet'.

[123] The dates are confusing. From what has been said so far, we would imagine the days are counted from sabbath, 20 Sivan (30 May)—the day when Nathan and the other rabbis came to pay court—and that 'the fourth day' is 23 Sivan (2 June), which has earlier been given as the date when Sabbatai's illumination returned. But the next paragraph gives 25 Sivan as 'the beginning of his illumination', and suggests that 'the fourth day' is counted from there.

[124] *Hitbodedut*; see above, n. 51.

[125] Cf. Baruch of Arezzo, *Memorial*, §23. Majar's name is given there as 'Magueres', and the present episode combined with Sabbatai's later resumption of his suit of Sarah Majar, after the death of his wife Sarah.   [126] Of his marriage to Sarah Majar, presumably.

That same day he told Rabbi Nathan to say the blessing 'creator of sweet oil' over balsam oil,[127] using the formula 'Blessed be You, O Lord, God of Sabbatai Zevi'. [Nathan], he said, was worthy to distribute the oil to everyone, inasmuch as his prophecy had come true.

On the fifth day Amirah went to visit Rabbi Asher Halevi,[128] and he sent for all the rabbis and brought them with him to his father-in-law's house, where they ate the noon meal with him. On that day he made a certain Jew wear the turban, and said: 'He is your atonement-sacrifice.'[129] On that day he made a great celebration with much loud singing—all the gentiles watching, yet none of them objecting.

On that day he seated the turban-wearing Masters of Faith in the superior places, all the rabbis in the inferior places.

On that day all the rabbis went walking with him, the turban-wearers following behind him and the rabbis behind the turban-wearers. He said to them: 'You shall make a space between one flock and the other [Gen. 32: 17], yet by no means a great distance [Exod. 8: 24].' He also said: 'I have become two camps [Gen. 32: 11].' He also said in the middle of the marketplace: 'House of Jacob, come and let us walk in the light of YHVH [Isa. 2: 5]', pronouncing the Name as written. In that marketplace he bought a lamb and brought it home with him, and they brought the kid [*sic*] before him and he said to it, 'YHVH bless you [Num. 6: 24]', pronouncing the Name as written. Each time he spoke the Name, all who were present went down on their knees and prostrated themselves, saying: 'Blessed be the Name of His glorious Kingdom for ever and ever.'[130] But on a few of those occasions, even though he had spoken the Sacred Name as written, he did not permit us to prostrate ourselves.

On the morning of the sixth day he went to the house of Abraham Meshullam. He sent for the rabbis, and he sent for this one [Najara], and they stood before him close to three hours, in fear and dread. He then warned us that whenever he was studying or singing we might look upon his face, but they[131] should not look at him when he stood silent. 'Your eyes shall

---

[127] BT *Ber.* 43*a*.

[128] I can provide no information on Asher Halevi, or on Abraham Meshullam (below).

[129] Perhaps alluding to the bizarre story in the Talmud (BT *Yoma* 23*a*), where a young priest's father pronounces these words over the still twitching body of his murdered son. Sabbatai's point seems to be that Nathan and the others need no longer fear he will force them to become Muslims, since this anonymous 'atonement-sacrifice' has taken their place.

[130] As did the bystanders in the ancient Temple, when the high priest pronounced the Sacred Name as part of the service for the Day of Atonement (Mishnah *Yoma* 3: 8). Do the speakers understand 'Kingdom' here, as earlier, to refer to Sabbatai himself (above, n. 114)?

[131] The shift of pronoun from 'we' to 'they' is in the original. I do not know if it has any significance.

see the king in his beauty [Isa. 33: 17]', he said, 'but not the king in his wrathful power.' And he said: 'When the king sits upon the throne of judgment, he scatters all evil with his eyes [Prov. 20: 8].'

He sang a number of melodies in Spanish[132] and in Hebrew. Afterwards he fanned each one of them,[133] saying as he did so: 'The spirit of the Lord shall rest upon him, a spirit of wisdom and understanding', and so forth [Isa. 11: 2] . . .

HERE THE TEXT BREAKS OFF

[132] *La'az*; cf. above, n. 90.   [133] As the rabbis had earlier fanned him.

FOURTH TESTIMONY
The Biography of Abraham Cuenque

༈

INTRODUCTION

'A PEDDLER who tramped from town to town filling his hands with the wealth of the scattered Jewish people . . . a slick-tongued rascal who caught his prey with his jaws . . . like a pig stretching out its hooves . . . like a slut spreading her legs for every passer-by, copulating with donkeys . . . '. This is how the anti-Sabbatian crusader Jacob Emden described Abraham Cuenque, in his preface to the first publication (1752) of Cuenque's sixty-year-old biography of Sabbatai Zevi.[1] Cuenque himself, naturally, had a rather different estimate of his own character: 'the faithful friend, exiled and roaming in his community's toilsome service . . . the emissary, authorized agent, scribe, and trustee of the holy community of Hebron, who sacrifices his own wishes in order to serve the wishes of others—the humble Abraham Cuenque'.[2]

Like the Sabbatian Meir Rofé, Cuenque hailed from the town of Hebron in the Holy Land. Like Rofé, he travelled far and wide raising money from the Jews of Europe for his impoverished, often persecuted community. We know the two men were acquainted, for their signatures appear together on a legal document prepared at Hebron at the beginning of 1682.[3] They shared a patron: the Amsterdam millionaire (and devout Sabbatian believer) Abraham Pereira, who had endowed the Hebron yeshiva where Rofé served as director, and to whose memory and whose sons Cuenque dedicated his book *Avak soferim* ('Scribes' Dust').[4] It would be interesting to know what they thought of each other—the learned but simple-hearted Rofé, the silky-smooth Cuenque. Like so much else about Cuenque, this is likely to remain a mystery.

[1] Emden, *Sefer torat hakenaot*, 16a–21b (31–45). The quotation is from p. 16a (31–2).

[2] From Cuenque's conclusion to the biography, translated below.

[3] Tishby, 'R. Meir Rofé's Letters' (Heb.), 127–8. The document authorizes one Jacob Halevi to act as agent collecting funds for the community's support; we may assume he was the son of the 'Joseph Halevi' who was the Hebron fundraiser in Pisa in 1669 (above, n. 4 on the Halevi letters).

[4] Published at Amsterdam in 1704; the homage to the Pereira family is on p. 5b. The book is a collection of homilies and miscellanies on the Bible; its title is derived from the mishnaic term (*Shab.* 12: 5) for the powder that scribes sprinkled over the words they had written, to dry the ink. On Pereira, see above, n. 58 on the Halevi letters.

What do we know about Cuenque's life, and the circumstances in which he wrote his (evidently untitled) biography of Sabbatai Zevi?

He speaks of himself as having been 'of tender years' when Sabbatai was proclaimed messiah in 1665.[5] The eighteenth-century bibliographer H. J. D. Azulai tells us he 'lived to a ripe old age in Hebron'.[6] We will not go too far astray if we give 1650–1730 as his dates. Again according to Azulai, Cuenque went on two grand fundraising tours and, among his other writings, composed a chronicle of his adventures abroad.[7] The chronicle was never published and now, sadly, is lost. But thanks to the meticulous research of Meir Benayahu we can reconstruct much of the outline of Cuenque's first round of travels (1684–94).[8] This is important, for it was in the course of that mission that the strange document here translated came to be written.

He began in Italy. From there he went to France (summer 1687), from there to Amsterdam, Hamburg, Frankfurt am Main, and other German towns, then to Prague and Vienna. Not yet satisfied, he continued his journeying into Poland, Russia, and Ukraine. There he braved the dangers of 'places the like of which no one before me had ever gone . . . wildernesses, lions' dens, panther-infested mountains'[9]—not to mention the jealousy of rival fundraisers, who managed on one occasion to haul him into a rabbinical court for encroaching on their territory.[10]

Wherever he went he made friends and influenced people. In Mantua he left the great Zacuto open-mouthed and gasping at his erudition and

---

[5] See text at n. 48 below.

[6] *Shem hagedolim*, bibliographical section, s.v. 'Avak Derakhim', in *Shem hagedolim hashalem*, ed. Benjacob, 209. Azulai is likely to have had reasonably accurate information on Cuenque. He was born in 1724, when Cuenque was probably still alive; from 1753 to 1758 he served as fundraiser for the Hebron community, as Cuenque had some decades earlier; Azulai's teacher Isaac Hakohen Rapoport had studied with Cuenque's nephew, Joseph Cuenque.

[7] His other writings, besides *Avak soferim*, include the unpublished homiletic collection *Avak derakhim* ('Dust of the Highways'; presumably referring to his travels) and *Minhat kenaot* ('Offering of Jealousy'). The latter is a moralizing essay on the topic of envy; Cuenque claims to have written it on board ship, presumably as a way of passing the time (*Avak soferim*, 105*b*). The title bears an eerie though surely coincidental resemblance to *Torat hakenaot* ('The Torah of Zealotry'), the book in which Emden was later to print Cuenque's Sabbatai Zevi biography. Azulai, to whom we owe the information on Cuenque's unpublished writings (now lost), makes no mention of the biography. Perhaps he was unaware of its existence; perhaps he knew of it but thought it more discreet to leave it unmentioned.

[8] Benayahu, 'The Letters of Rabbi Abraham Cuenque to Rabbi Judah Briel' (Heb.). The dates of the second tour are less clear, but certainly included the years 1703–4. 'Now he has come to us a second time', writes Rabbi Samuel Kohen Shattin of Frankfurt am Main in an approbation to *Avak soferim* (p. 2*b*), dated 25 Nisan 5463 (11 April 1703); and Cuenque speaks of having been in Amsterdam, seeing his book through to press, on 1 Shevat 5464 (7 January 1704), when he first heard the news of his friend Naphtali Katz's appointment to the chief rabbinate of Frankfurt (p. 103*a*).

[9] *Avak soferim*, 103*c*; partly quoted in Benayahu, 'Letters' (Heb.), 309.

[10] Benayahu, 'Letters', 305.

brilliance.[11] The rabbis of central and eastern Europe, including the illustrious David Oppenheim of Nikolsburg,[12] were charmed and overwhelmed.[13] In Ostrog in Volhynia, where he first arrived sometime in 1688, Rabbi Naphtali Katz became his patron, his devoted host, his lifelong admirer.[14] While he was staying in Ostrog as Katz's guest he saw—or perhaps did not see—a document purportedly written by Ishmael Zevi, the son of Sabbatai Zevi. The document impressed him deeply; or, perhaps, it made hardly any impression on him at all.[15]

On his return journey (1692) Cuenque stopped again in Frankfurt, and stayed there a rather long time. 'At the very end of his [fundraising] mission he spent seven months with us here in Frankfurt as guest of the communal dignitary, the late Rabbi Zalman Oppenheim, gatherer of funds for the Land of Israel, deeply involved in religious affairs. Thus he brought his mission to its close, winning for himself the good opinion of God and of all who knew him'—so wrote the Frankfurt rabbi Samuel Kohen Shattin, in his letter of approbation for *Avak soferim*. Afterwards, Shattin adds, Cuenque departed for Venice (in late 1692 or 1693) and thence back to Hebron.

Shattin presumably had no idea what was going on in Oppenheim's house during those seven months. If he had, he would as soon have given his approbation to Nathan of Gaza. 'This Rabbi Zalman had urgently pressed [Cuenque] to make known to the Jewish people the essential information about the Lord Sabbatai Zevi, who was claimed in the year 5426 [1665/6] to be the messiah of the God of Jacob'.[16] Cuenque coyly held back, then let himself be persuaded. 'You are most precious to me, and I value you as I would any man of great worth. I consequently bend myself to your wish, and . . . affirm, before all else, that I will write here nothing but what I have seen with my own eyes or heard with my own ears from reliable sources, worthy individuals, men of stature who meet with the approval of the intelligent.'

[11] So we gather from a somewhat patronizing letter Cuenque afterwards sent Zacuto: ibid. 301–2.

[12] Who was to become, some dozen years later, a strong supporter of (and hero to) the band of Sabbatian pietists who travelled to the Holy Land under the leadership of Rabbi Judah Hasid, there to await the second coming of Sabbatai Zevi. See Benayahu, 'The "Holy Brotherhood" of R. Judah Hasid' (Heb.), 147–57.

[13] We get some sense of the impression he made from the 'approbations'—*haskamot*, the 17th-century equivalent of blurbs—which these rabbis wrote fifteen years later for *Avak soferim* (printed on pp. 2a–3d). Rabbi after rabbi admits he has not seen Cuenque's book but is prepared to recommend it anyway. 'I know this extraordinary man and his ways, and will make the assumption he could not possibly produce anything that was flawed' (Gabriel of Kraków).

[14] The two men enthuse over one another's virtues in the pages of *Avak soferim*: Katz in his approbation (pp. 2d–3b), Cuenque on p. 103b. On Katz and his relation to Sabbatianism, see the important article by Yehuda Liebes, 'A Profile of R. Naphtali Katz of Frankfort'.

[15] See below.

[16] From the preface to Cuenque's biography by Jehiel Michal Epstein; see below.

Thus Cuenque's biography of Sabbatai Zevi came to be written, some-time in the year 1692. (This was the year, let it be noted, when witches were being hanged in Salem, Massachusetts.) When he departed for Venice, Cuenque left the manuscript behind him in Frankfurt. There, seven years later, it came into the hands of the German rabbi and moralist Jehiel Michal Epstein—already a best-selling author of devotional and moral works, already famous as an advocate for the merits of religious literature in the Yiddish vernacular.[17]

Epstein did not, as might have been expected, recoil in horror from the foul and polluted composition. Instead he reverently copied it, giving it a brief preface in which he spoke of its subject as *ha'adon shabetai tsevi*, 'the Lord Sabbatai Zevi'. This is the text that eventually came into the possession of the heresy-hunting zealot Jacob Emden (1697–1776), who published it in his compilation *Torat hakenaot*, along with a verbose and frantically hostile commentary.[18]

The first thing that is bound to strike us, in comparing Cuenque's life of Sabbatai Zevi with the earlier efforts of Baruch of Arezzo, is how vastly superior Cuenque's piece is as a work of literature. This is as we might have expected. Cuenque had a considerable reputation in his time as a *littérateur*. 'He was a great master of *melitsah*',[19] Azulai writes of him, and that is putting it very mildly. Two letters he composed[20] during his first visit to Italy made such a sensation they were copied and passed from hand to hand; they were still remembered twenty years later as masterpieces of elegance.[21] Reading the letters, one can see why. They are filled with dazzling if pointless literary acrobatics, such as entire paragraphs in which every single word begins with

---

[17] His condensed version of Isaiah Horowitz's *Shenei luhot haberit, Kitsur shelah*, was pub-lished in 1693, and went through two more editions in the next ten years; his prayer-book with Yiddish translation and explications appeared in 1697, his Yiddish *Derekh hayashar la'olam haba* ('Direct Path to a Blessed Afterlife') in 1703. See Gries, *Conduct Literature* (Heb.), 58–64. (Gries corrects the date of the first edition of *Kitsur shelah*, often inaccurately given as 1683.) According to Israel Zinberg, Epstein was 'an ardent mystic and dreamed of speedy redemption' (*A History of Jewish Literature*, vii. 219); this might explain Cuenque's appeal for him. Epstein's prayer-book, and his preface to *Kitsur shelah*, were said to contain Sabbatian allusions (Emden, *Sefer torat hakenaot*, 71b (144)). Emden blames this on Cuenque's influence, lamenting that 'the honest, God-fearing Master M. Epstein was caught in this man's net . . . .and, in all innocence, inserted into the prayer-book he published, at the end of the Aleinu prayer, a foul allusion used by Sabbatai Zevi's sect to hint at their rotten faith' (ibid. 16a (32)). It is hard to avoid the impression there is some link between Epstein's interest in Cuenque's text and the appearance in Germany, at nearly the same time, of Rabbi Judah Hasid and his followers; see below, n. 28.   [18] More on the text, and on Emden's relation to it, below.

[19] A peculiarly high-flown style of Hebrew writing, filled with complex wordplay and allu-sions to biblical and rabbinic literature. It was much admired in early modern times.

[20] To Moses Zacuto and his student Judah Briel. The letters are printed in *Avak soferim*, 103d–106b; cf. Benayahu, 'Letters' (Heb.), 300–2.   [21] *Avak soferim*, 103d.

the same letter of the alphabet, and must have given the impression that no one could possibly have mastered the Holy Tongue as this author had.

Yet Cuenque, capable of carrying *melitsah* to dizzying heights of erudite unintelligibility,[22] was also a master of lucid, elegant, straightforward Hebrew style. The Sabbatai Zevi biography is written in the latter mode. First Cuenque seduces his readers with a disingenuous pretence of objectivity; then he draws us into his story, deftly interweaving personal reminiscences with omniscient third-person narrative. These reminiscences—of Sabbatai's visit to Hebron, of Cuenque's encounter with Nathan in Gaza, of his discovery in Ostrog of a responsum written by none other than Sabbatai's son Ishmael—may be real, or they may be invented. Their effect is to make the almost unbelievable events of Cuenque's story vividly present to the reader. We feel we are there with him, experiencing the events as they occurred.

This literary skill and polish is one notable feature of Cuenque's book. Another, perhaps related, is its utter dishonesty. Normally it is difficult to tell whether an author is sincerely mistaken in his errors and distortions, or whether he is deliberately fabricating. In Cuenque's case the decision can be made with some confidence. His account of Sabbatai's exile to the Adriatic coast—which Cuenque represents as a voluntary departure rather than an exile—not only is entirely fantastic; Cuenque himself must have known it was fantastic. In Cuenque's story Sabbatai insists on going alone, leaving his wife Sarah and his son Ishmael behind in the sultan's palace. There they remain after Sabbatai's death, apparently still alive at the time of Cuenque's writing. Ishmael, 'a young man tall and sturdy as a cedar tree', has taken his father's place among the dignitaries of the sultan's court, hobnobbing with all the nobles of the empire.

In fact Sarah and Ishmael went with Sabbatai into exile, where Sarah died; Ishmael seems to have died a few years later, hardly more than 10 or 11 years old.[23] Cuenque certainly had access to much of this information: it was known as early as the autumn of 1677 to his Hebron colleague Meir Rofé, who seems to have been one of Cuenque's sources for the biography.[24] If Cuenque spins a tale about Sabbatai's last years that bears only a coincidental resemblance to historical fact, it is not because he didn't know any better. It is because historical fact played no significant part in the agenda of his writing.

---

[22] As in his preface to *Avak soferim*.   [23] Halperin, 'The Son of the Messiah', 143–219.
[24] See above, n. 3, for proof that Cuenque and Rofé were together in Hebron at the beginning of 1682, and Tishby, 'R. Meir Rofé's Letters' (Heb.), 113–14, for what Rofé knew in October 1677 about the circumstances of Sabbatai's exile. Cuenque's story, of how Sabbatai revealed the esoteric knowledge of divinity to a select group of rabbis at the sultan's court, is best understood as based on information provided by Rofé; below, n. 117.

The contrast with Baruch of Arezzo is very striking. Baruch, to be sure, perpetrates a hefty crop of errors of his own. Cuenque seems to know nothing of Sarah Zevi's death; Baruch mistakenly pre-dates it to the time when Sabbatai was still in Adrianople, before his banishment. Yet it is possible to reconstruct the path by which Baruch, for all his sincere desire to discover the truth, was led to this error.[25] His understandable confusion is in an entirely different category from Cuenque's distortions. Baruch, moreover, is well aware that Sabbatai's departure for the Adriatic coast was an exile imposed by the sultan, although naturally he tries to put the best face on it he can.[26] Not so Cuenque. It was Sabbatai himself, Cuenque assures his readers, who demanded to strike out on his own, far from the great cities of Islam. He held to this purpose, despite the sultan's grovelling pleas for him to stay.

Sabbatai's relationship with the sultan, as Cuenque describes it, is so bizarre as to provoke the question: is this for real? Can any sane human being possibly have believed that Sultan Mehmed IV 'begged [Sabbatai] to tell him what was written in the Zohar, whereat Sabbatai Zevi rebuked him: "You [gentiles] do not have the intelligence to understand such things"'— and that Sabbatai lived to tell the tale? That the sultan cancelled a hunting party at the last minute because Sabbatai Zevi told him, 'Today you have no permission to go anywhere'? It is hardly imaginable that Cuenque really believed what he was writing. What, then, would have been his motive for writing it? And who were his audience? Can *they* have believed it?

Here we are obliged to begin guessing. My guess, for what it may be worth, is this: in the course of his first fundraising mission, Cuenque came to realize that his exotic Sephardi-ness, coupled with his origins in the Holy Land, enhanced his appeal to potential patrons and donors.[27] He also discovered that part of this 'Oriental' appeal involved his proximity to the great event that had convulsed the Jewish world a generation past, the shining messianic hope that had burst forth like a supernova and then vanished. There were those among his hosts who had a fascination, perhaps half-horrified, with Sabbatai Zevi and his prophet; more than a few of them had a dim sense there was 'something more to the business' than was generally known.[28] The temptation must have been overwhelming to titillate their

[25] Above, n. 260 on Baruch of Arezzo.   [26] Baruch of Arezzo, *Memorial*, §23.

[27] This is not entirely conjecture. Cuenque's friend and protector Naphtali Katz was to admit many years later, in a shamefaced letter of apology for having given his approbation to a theological work by the notorious Nehemiah Hayon, that 'it had always been my way to show special friendship for the Sephardim, most especially their scholars' (5 Elul 5473 (27 August 1713), in Freimann, *Inyanei shabetai tsevi*, 123; cf. Carlebach, *The Pursuit of Heresy*, 120).

[28] Elisheva Carlebach calls attention to the enormous enthusiasm stirred up in Frankfurt eight years later, in 1700, by the preaching of the itinerant Sabbatian pietists led by Rabbi

curiosity by hinting that there was indeed 'something more', and that he was in a position to know what it was.

Jehiel Michal Epstein's preface, I imagine, tells what really happened. Driven half mad by Cuenque's hints, people like Zalman Oppenheim demanded that he tell all he knew. Eventually Cuenque decided to oblige them. To what extent he really believed Sabbatai Zevi was the messiah, and to what extent he found writing the biography an entertaining challenge to his creative wit—like composing a paragraph in which all the words begin with the same letter—we are unlikely ever to know. His tales of Sabbatai bullying the timid, cowed sultan may be the wish-fulfilment fantasies of a man whose livelihood depended on pleasing and impressing the wealthy. Certainly they answered to the fantasies of his audience. In Cuenque's telling they may well have felt possible, even real. In a place like Frankfurt am Main, the Ottoman court must have seemed as exotic and remote as the fairy-tale courts of the book of Daniel. Let the jealous courtiers scheme and complain to the king; anything might be achieved by a bold Jewish hero whose God was with him.

Oppenheim and the others could believe, or half-believe, that Sabbatai's 'taking the turban upon his head' was an act not of capitulation but of empowerment, akin to his intended assumption of the royal crown. They would relish Cuenque's assurance that the messianic line was still thriving in the sultan's palace, in the robust person of Ishmael Zevi. They would not ask too many questions about the document Cuenque allegedly saw in Katz's home in Ostrog, about which he seems unable to give any details beyond that it was supposed to be 'a query sent to Ishmael Zevi and his lofty response thereto, matters of great profundity'. They would trust Cuenque's 'happy ending' to his story of Sabbatai Zevi: the messiah's son lives, growing in power and influence. Even now he awaits the proper moment to step forward and complete his father's transformation of the world.

THE TEXT

Besides the two editions of Emden's *Torat hakenaot* (Amsterdam, 1752 and Lvov, 1870),[29] Cuenque's biography is represented by a manuscript, Cod.

Judah Hasid, on their way to the Holy Land to meet their messiah (*Divided Souls*, 84–5; details in Benayahu, 'The "Holy Brotherhood" of R. Judah Hasid' (Heb.), 147–57). This surely points to some pre-existing interest in Sabbatai Zevi, and some disposition to believe the hopes for redemption he stirred up might not really have been exploded after all.

[29] Emden gives Cuenque's biography the title *tofes shelishi* or *nusaḥ shelishi*, 'third version' of the story of Sabbatai Zevi (the first two being 'an abbreviated Hebrew version of Leyb b. Ozer's *Beshraybung*' and 'a Hebrew rewrite of Coenen's Dutch account, with additions from an unknown source': Scholem, *Sabbatai Sevi*, 935).

Or. 36, in the library of the University of Rostock, Germany.[30] The manuscript is written in German cursive script of the eighteenth century, and can
be dated with some precision to 1751–3.[31] It is a copy of an earlier manuscript that Emden had kept hidden among his files for 'many years', and
about 1751 decided to make public, no doubt in connection with the opening of his campaign against his *bête noire* Rabbi Jonathan Eibeschütz. Thus
he prepared the text for publication; thus he permitted the scribe of the Rostock manuscript, whose name we do not know,[32] to see and to copy a document that until then had been 'sealed away' in Emden's archive.

The *Vorlage* of the Rostock manuscript—which contained, beside
Cuenque's biography, several shorter texts relating to Sabbatianism and a
calendar of the Sabbatian festivals—passed through several hands before it
reached Emden. According to a notation by the Rostock scribe, Emden
received it from Rabbi Jonah Landsofer (1678–1712), a distinguished
Prague scholar whom the Sabbatians were later to claim as one of their
own.[33] But Emden was 15 years old when Landsofer died, and there must
have been intermediate links in the manuscript's transmission.

At some point the Cuenque biography, at least, was in the hands of the
anti-Sabbatian zealot Moses Hagiz (1671–1751). Hagiz provided for it a set
of critical annotations which are often very valuable, not least because his
father Jacob was in Jerusalem at the time of the original Sabbatian outbreak,
and was in fact head of the yeshiva where Nathan of Gaza was a student.
These annotations are recorded in small script near the margins of the
Rostock manuscript, under the title 'The Rebellious House',[34] which
the Rostock scribe seems to have devised for them. Emden prints most of
Hagiz's notes in *Torat hakenaot*, marking them with Hagiz's initials to distinguish them from his own vastly wordier comments, which tend otherwise to
swallow them up.[35]

[30]   Described by Ernst Róth in Striedl, Tetzner, and Róth, *Hebräische Handschriften*, 350–1. I
am deeply indebted to Dr Benjamin Richler of the Institute of Microfilmed Hebrew Manuscripts in Jerusalem for having made me aware of this manuscript, and to Ms Heike Tröger of
the Universitätsbibliothek, Rostock (and to Dr Elisabeth Hollander) for having made it
possible for me to obtain a copy of it.

[31]   For a detailed discussion of the Rostock manuscript, see Appendix 4.

[32]   He was not, as Róth thought (*Hebräische Handschriften*), Jehiel Michal Epstein.

[33]   Scholem, 'A Sabbatian Will from New York'; cf. the index to Yehuda Liebes's collection
of Scholem's articles, *Researches in Sabbateanism* (Heb.), s.v. 'Landsofer'. There is some confusion between the well-known Jonah ben Elijah Landsofer, who died in 1712, and his grandson
Jonah ben Mendel (Emanuel), whom Scholem speaks of as having been active around 1760
('A Sabbatian Will', 356–7). In our manuscript, at any rate, it is plainly the elder Jonah Landsofer who is intended.   [34]   *Beit hameri*, from Ezek. 2: 8, 12: 2, etc.

[35]   At one point Emden explicitly takes issue with Hagiz. When Nathan swears by God's
name that he has seen the Divine Chariot of the prophet Ezekiel, Hagiz comments: 'The
sequel demonstrates he swore vainly and falsely, in accord with how the demons deceived him,

Emden gives the impression that Cuenque's narrative is significantly incomplete, sections of it having been destroyed in a fire. This is misleading. The words missing from Emden's text can be supplied from the Rostock manuscript; the lacunae (there are six of them) turn out to be very short, never amounting to more than sixteen words. Plainly the *Vorlage* was in better condition when the Rostock scribe copied it than when Emden published it. In Appendix 4, I discuss the problems bound up with this supposed 'fire'. The reader may be assured that the text translated below is the complete text of Cuenque's biography of Sabbatai Zevi, without any gaps.

The translation is made from the 1752 edition of *Torat hakenaot*, periodically corrected and supplemented from the Rostock manuscript. Where Emden or (more often) Hagiz has something useful to say about the text, I present it in the footnotes.

 formula

The following is a copy of the text given me on Monday, 2 Av 5459 [28 July 1699[36]] by the honourable Rabbi Seligmann the Torah scholar, son-in-law of Rabbi Yokev Fann, long may he live, of the holy community of Frankfurt. He had received the text from a certain Jerusalemite named Rabbi Abraham Cuenque, from the holy community of Hebron, who had been in Frankfurt ten years ago as guest of the communal dignitary, the late Rabbi Zalman Darum.[37]

as I shall describe below.' To which Emden takes strong exception. 'Says the Zealot [*amar hamekane*, namely Emden himself]: What need have we to speak of demons? Why not just plain lunacy? Or just plain thuggishness, along the lines of the others like him who took up this craft of trying their luck and their fortune, groping in the darkness after their lucky star and the chance of profit, without one single thought to how they might be harming their brethren? How typical of those bloodthirsty money-grubbers, plotting together to grow rich off the loot of their crimes, a gang of traitors all in cahoots', etc. etc. etc. (*Torat hakenaot*, 18a (37)). The contrast between the style of Hagiz's annotations and those of Emden will be evident from this example.

[36] Which, however, fell on a Tuesday according to Mahler's tables (*Handbuch der jüdischen Chronologie*). See Appendix 3.

[37] In an approbation for *Avak soferim*, written in the spring of 1703, Rabbi Samuel Kohen Shattin of Frankfurt gives the name of Cuenque's host as 'Rabbi Zalman Oppenheim'. He and Darum are clearly the same person. I am indebted to Professor Elisheva Carlebach for the information that 'Darum' was used in this period as an abbreviated form of 'Darmstadt', and no doubt refers to Rabbi Zalman's place of origin. The Oppenheims were a distinguished German Jewish family, prominent in Frankfurt, 'producing many rabbis, financiers, and successful merchants' (*Encyclopedia Judaica*, s.v. 'Oppenheim'). They were among the strongest supporters of Rabbi Judah Hasid and his group of Sabbatian pietists, who passed through Frankfurt in the spring of 1700—some eight months after Jehiel Michal Epstein received

Now this Rabbi Zalman had urgently pressed him to make known to the Jewish people the essential information about the Lord Sabbatai Zevi, who was claimed in the year 5426 [1665/6] to be the messiah of the God of Jacob; and, consequent upon the former's urgings, [Cuenque] wrote for him a narrative concise yet complete. [. . . ³⁸] And this is the copy of it.

*The humble Jehiel Michal Segal Epstein.*³⁹

PEACE WITHOUT END, O MY DEAR BELOVED ONE! This writing of mine shall join itself to you and give you praise, by command of the King of Righteousness!⁴⁰ What you have asked of me, I shall make known to you: the absolute truth about those events that transpired long ago with regard to Sabbatai Zevi and the prophet Nathan, and all those subjects whose fame has spread, by speech and writing, throughout the inhabited world.⁴¹

In truth, I find it very difficult to set these matters down in writing. Things transmitted orally have an elusive quality. They are wanting in firm foundation, whether they dwindle and grow poor,⁴² or are abridged or expanded. Yet those things that are set down in ink on paper—especially matters like these—provoked the warning of our ancient rabbis, 'Be careful with your words!'⁴³ The writer must be a person of intelligence, complete in his knowledge, capable of setting forth his argument judiciously. Yet I—I am without human understanding, having been tossed from one place to another, a perennial exile, lacking any fixed abode.⁴⁴

the manuscript of Cuenque's biography—stirring up the most tremendous excitement (Benayahu, 'The "Holy Brotherhood" of R. Judah Hasid' (Heb.), 147–57). I cannot further identify this Rabbi Zalman, or the 'Rabbi Seligmann' or 'Rabbi Yokev Fann' mentioned in the preceding sentence.

³⁸ About a dozen words are crossed out at this point and can no longer be read. As far as I can judge, they include a date of some sort. In their place *Sefer torat hakenaot* gives the following, which certainly was not in the manuscript and which I can only assume to be Emden's original composition: 'It occurred to Rabbi Zalman on one occasion to read this text, which the Jerusalemite had composed for him, in the night-time. He was holding a wax candle, and he dozed off, and the candle fell upon the Jerusalemite's manuscript. Several pages of it were burned. At all events I have copied whatever I was able to copy, in order that the reader may discover therein its extraordinary contents.' See Appendix 4 for a fuller discussion.

³⁹ On Jehiel Michal Epstein, see above, n. 17. The name 'Segal', an abbreviation of *segan leviyah* ('member of the Levites'), indicates that his family traced its origins back to the ancient tribe of Levi.

⁴⁰ Following Rashi on Ps. 110: 4. Is the 'King of Righteousness' God, or Sabbatai Zevi (as Emden suggests in his note on this passage)?   ⁴¹ Following Ibn Ezra on Ps. 19: 5.

⁴² The language is drawn from Ps. 107: 39. I do not quite understand Cuenque's point.

⁴³ Mishnah *Avot* 1: 11.

⁴⁴ When he wrote these words in 1692, Cuenque had been travelling through Europe for the previous eight years.

Can we be sure, moreover, that it is God's will for us to probe this matter? Or are these things that are better left concealed? Can anyone know, apart from the Lord,[45] into whose hands these words written on paper are liable to fall? Perhaps he will be a wise man, perhaps a fool.[46] For these reasons and more, it would be proper for me to lift my hand and pen away from the paper, and refrain from writing.

Yet you are most precious to me, and I value you as I would any man of great worth. I consequently bend myself to your wish, and make known to you that in those days and in that time there were many shallow-minded individuals who wrote letters from place to place, concocting such lies and nonsense that one's ears would burn to hear them. They might indeed write some bit of truth, but this truth was so negligible in comparison to all the falsehood that it was as though it were entirely lacking.

Therefore do I affirm, before all else, that I will write here nothing but what I have seen with my own eyes or heard with my own ears from reliable sources, worthy individuals, men of stature who meet with the approval of the intelligent. I write what I have learned from them, and not from letters,[47] what my own eyes have seen and no one else's. I have chosen for myself the most extreme brevity and concision; and thus shall I make known to you what I have to say.

One thing more you must clearly understand. It is not my intent, in this narration that I shall lay before you, to persuade you to believe in this faith. Nor do I intend to bring you out of the faith, or to persuade you of its falsity. What I write here, as my actions shall demonstrate, is the unvarnished truth: drawn from facts that tend to confirm the faith, and also from those that tend to crumble it and refute it entirely. I will not tell you my personal opinion on this subject, for it is my own private business.

In those days, at that time [of Sabbatai Zevi's appearance], I was still of tender years, yet much involved in public affairs.[48] I witnessed the scandalous behaviour of the 'unbelieving' and 'believing' sects, each side trying to establish its own particular point of view. All this seemed to me ludicrous and contemptible. Surely it is enough for an individual to satisfy himself with his opinion; surely it is enough that he liberate himself.[49] He has no

---

[45] *Ha'adon*, perhaps an allusion not to God but to Sabbatai Zevi.

[46] Alluding to Eccles. 2: 19.

[47] Following the manuscript's *ketavim*; the editions give *ketavam*, 'their writing'.

[48] Following Targum and Rashi on 1 Sam. 17: 12.

[49] *Lehafkia et atsmo*. The language is somewhat strange, and it is not clear from what one is 'liberating' oneself. It appears, from the passages cited in Ben-Yehuda's *Complete Dictionary of Ancient and Modern Hebrew* (x. 5119*b*), that when *hifkia* takes a human object it tends to involve 'liberation' from the demands of the Torah, or from other legitimate obligations (e.g. BT *Git.* 88*b*).

need to compel others to share in his beliefs, or to deny those things that he himself denies.

And now I shall briefly tell the story.

There was a man in Izmir—Smyrna, that is—who was of the lineage of the kings of Israel;[50] his name was Mordecai Zevi. He was a simple householder, an honest and wealthy merchant with a good reputation among his fellow-merchants. In the year 5386 [1625/6] a son was born to him, whom he named Sabbatai Zevi.

The child grew till he was no longer a child. From his first maturity he was peculiar, different from other youths his age—a fact which some interpret in his favour, calling him an angel rather than a human being, while others condemn him for it as a lunatic. From first to last he would normally pronounce the Divine Name precisely as it is written, in all its aspects:[51] sometimes openly, sometimes concealing it within his chant. His distinguished contemporaries, becoming aware of this practice, protested. Yet he paid them no attention, nor did he bother himself about their criticisms.

All agree, however, that he held himself aloof from all the pleasures of this world, spurning money and eating and drinking, and human society. Daily did he torment himself, abstaining from food for almost the bulk of the year, except for sabbaths and holy days. He would go off by himself for days at a time in the mountains, or in caves or deserts, and his brothers and his father's household would have no idea where he was. Sometimes he would hide himself in Izmir, in a poor dingy room, and would spend years shut away there, appearing only at intervals. Meagrely and sparingly did he sustain himself. His brothers and his father's household were pained and embarrassed by his behaviour. Yet they could not bring him to change his ways.

In those days, certain men of stature testified that they looked frequently[52] into his room and saw him rolling about in the dust, his bed

---

[50] *Shomron* is normally used of the biblical city of Samaria. Cuenque clearly uses it to represent the classical name for Izmir; it is conceivable he originally wrote שמרנא and this was corrupted into שומרון. Hagiz, misunderstanding the subject of *hameyuḥas* as 'Samaria' and not, as grammar would require, the 'man'—'Samaria, belonging to the kings of Israel'—mocks Cuenque's alleged confusion of the biblical city with the Turkish one. Emden reinforces Hagiz's error by printing feminine *hameyuḥeset* in place of the manuscript's *hameyuḥas*, and replacing Hagiz's brief note (preserved only in the manuscript) with a long-winded exercise in misplaced sarcasm. ('Here [Cuenque] confesses to everyone what a fool he is! He is a perfect ignoramus and dolt, without any knowledge of geography . . . for what could Izmir possibly have to do with Samaria, the capital of the kings of Israel, situated in the centre of Palestine', etc. etc. etc.).

[51] Perhaps referring to the different vocalizations given to the sacred Name in the kabbalah.

[52] For the editions' *shehishkifu tadir*, the manuscript gives *shehikifu edim*, 'that they posted witnesses'.

overturned Two angels were holding him, comforting him, encouraging him. 'Shake yourself off, rise from the dust and seat yourself, O Jerusalem [Isa. 52: 2]', they were saying to him. Four angels were setting the bed upright, saying, 'O our God in heaven, raise up the fallen tabernacle of David [Amos 9: 11].'

The long and the short of it was that his brothers, and all his father's household, could no longer bear him. His peculiarities were a nuisance and a disgrace for them, they being very wealthy, practically the leaders of the Jewish community.[53] They chided him to no avail. Finally they asked him whether he wanted to go to the Land of Israel.

'I will go', he said.[54]

And so he left [Izmir], all by himself, with nothing but the clothes on his back. Neither money nor slaves nor servants did he desire from his father's household. He wandered hither and yon until he came to the Holy City of Jerusalem.

In his early days there he went to the synagogue, and, after morning prayers, sat learning with the students. They treated him with the most tremendous respect. After a few months he built himself a house in Jerusalem, called after a man named Copia.[55] In that house there was a very high room, and in that room he would shut himself away, afflicting himself with continuous fasting from one sabbath to the next.

He would begin his fast after the fourth sabbath meal;[56] that is to say, he would perform the *havdalah* ritual,[57] eat his fourth meal, and begin fasting. When Friday came, he would descend from the room. He would himself purchase whatever he needed for the sabbath—pepper, cinnamon, and the like—buying each item individually and carrying it home. This labour took him all Friday morning, until his clothing had become soaked with his sweat from all his efforts. Afterwards he would arrange for his cook all the dishes she was to prepare.

At that time a decree was issued in the province of Egypt, and [the leaders of Jerusalem Jewry] did not know where they might turn for help. There was a

---

[53] 'A damned lie! They were agents for the merchants' (Emden).

[54] 'What an impudent denial of the facts! All writers agree he was excommunicated and expelled from Izmir by his master, the late, great Rabbi Joseph Iskafa, who granted permission to anyone to shed his blood' (Emden). Rhetoric aside, Emden is right. See the Introduction, section IV.   [55] On this 'Copia', see Scholem, *Sabbatai Sevi*, 184–5.

[56] A fourth, voluntary meal that some were accustomed to eat on Saturday evening, in addition to the three statutory sabbath meals. See BT *Shab.* 117b–118a, Tosafot on BT *Ber.* 49b, Maimonides, *Mishneh torah*, 'Hilkhot shabat', 30: 9.

[57] The traditional ritual separating sacred from profane time, performed at the end of sabbaths and festivals.

high official in Egypt named Joseph Raphael, and they pondered whom they might send as their emissary to him.[58]

Sundry proposals were offered. One of the group then said, 'If it might be possible for Sabbatai Zevi to go on our mission, God will certainly grant us a favourable outcome. For the noble Joseph Raphael thinks the world of him.'

'But surely he will not agree to it?' they said.

Yet they said, 'Whatever may come of it, let us importune him. Perhaps he will agree.'

So all the rabbis, who were at the time both numerous and notable, went and spoke with him. He replied: 'I am prepared and ready. Well have you asked; timely have you spoken. I wish to depart this very day. First, however, I should like to go and pray at the Cave of Machpelah[59] in the holy city of Hebron.'

'Please', said they, 'spend the night here. Tomorrow you can go with a caravan.'

'No', he said. 'I will leave today. Do not hold me back; the Lord has already granted me success.'

That was what he did. He rode upon a horse, one man going before him, and he came to us [in Hebron] and stayed as guest of that most excellent of the scholars of his generation, the well-born Rabbi Aaron Abun of blessed memory.[60] For so he had requested before entering our sacred precinct,[61] that he should be hosted by that rabbi and only that rabbi.

[58] This is the first of the lacunae in the text of Emden's *Torat hakenaot*, which Emden blames on the fire that damaged the manuscript (see Appendix 4). In *Torat hakenaot* the first six words of this paragraph are omitted (*ba'et hahi hayetah gezerah bimedinat mitsrayim*, 'At that time . . . Egypt') and the next few words slightly altered, very much as if several words of the manuscript had been destroyed and the next few so damaged they could be read only conjecturally. The 'decree' of which Cuenque speaks is surely, as Scholem says, one of the 'recurrent extortions of the Turkish governors and pashas' who ruled Palestine (*Sabbatai Sevi*, 186–7). Cuenque seems to represent, inaccurately, Jerusalem as having been part of the Ottoman province (*vilayet*) of Egypt—a strange error for a man from Hebron. (In reality, the *sanjak*, or district, of Jerusalem, which included Hebron, belonged to the *vilayet* of Syria and was under the authority of the *beilerbeg* (governor-general) of Damascus.) He does not depict Sabbatai's mission as having been to raise the funds necessary to satisfy the government's demands—as Scholem says, no doubt correctly as far as the historical facts are concerned—but to induce 'Joseph Raphael' to intercede with the Egyptian (*sic*!) government to moderate those demands. ('Joseph Raphael' is of course Raphael Joseph; above, Introduction, section IV).

[59] The shrine at Hebron, made into a mosque by the Muslims and grudgingly shared with the Jews, where the patriarchs of Genesis were supposed to have been buried with their wives.

[60] So the manuscript; the editions give 'Abin'. Scholem supposes 'the name should read Aaron Arha, who was the grandson of one of Luria's disciples and the son of the well-known kabbalist Eliezer ibn Arha' (*Sabbatai Sevi*, 187 n.).

[61] Apparently referring to the entire city of Hebron.

This was the first time I had seen him. I was a regular visitor to Jerusalem, yet I never saw him until he came to visit us. I was awestruck at how tall he was, like a cedar of Lebanon. His face was very ruddy, a touch inclined towards swarthiness; his features were handsome, encircled by a round black beard; he was dressed in garments truly royal, and was altogether an exceedingly healthy and imposing person. From the moment he entered the sacred precinct—all the time he prayed the afternoon prayer in our synagogue, all the time he prayed the evening prayer in the Cave of Machpelah along with the crowd that had flocked after him—I could not take my eyes off him. Nor could the human mind conceive where he might have hidden away all those tears he shed as he prayed, not like natural tears, but like a vast flooding, or like streams that rush ever onward.

I spent most of that night in the vicinity of the house where he was staying, and I observed the acts he performed. All the dwellers in the sacred precinct, similarly—men, women, and children alike—found themselves unable to sleep all that night. They spent the night instead watching through the windows, peering through each crack.

He paced hither and thither through his house, which was filled in its entirety with torches, for so he had ordered. Throughout the night, until dawn broke, he recited psalms by heart in a voice that was loud and happy and joyful, most exceedingly pleasant and sweet to the ear. At dawn he went to the synagogue and prayed the morning prayer. I can attest that everything about him was such as to inspire dread, and that, among all the dwellers on this earth, he was in every way unique. I could not get my fill of watching him.

When the morning prayer was finished, about three hours afterwards, he set forth by himself in a certain direction. He was accompanied for 6 parasangs[62] by a Jew who attended him. While he was with us [in Hebron] he did not eat a bite nor did he drink any water, nor did he sleep at all, not so much as a catnap. Fasting he came; fasting he departed. To this day I never saw him again, but only twice in my dreams—one of them in Hebron, the other in the darkness of my exile.

He entered Gaza, and from there he went directly to Egypt. He was hosted by the noble Joseph Raphael, who was in great dread of him.

'Tell me what you wish', [Joseph Raphael] said to him, 'and it shall be granted you.'

He replied, 'The Jerusalem community is suffering greatly.'

'You could have written us a letter, and we would have done anything you demanded! Why did you take the trouble to journey here?'

[62] Roughly twenty miles.

'Even apart from this I would have been obliged to come here', said [Sabbatai], 'in order to meet my appointed bride who comes to me from across the seas. God has arranged matters such that I have come to fulfil two commandments in one stroke.'

'And where is your appointed bride?'

'Tomorrow', he said, 'she shall come to Alexandria on a seafaring boat. She is a virgin, and Sarah is her name.' And so it turned out.

In Damascus there lived a man named Samuel Lisbona. He was very rich, exceeding in his wealth everyone else in the city, and the Jewish community therefore made demands upon him that were unreasonable and insupportable. Realizing he could not withstand this, he left [Damascus] with his wife and children and brothers, and all the wealth he had acquired. He set out for Gaza in the territory of Judah. For the king of that land was a just king, a pious king who did not behave tyrannically.[63]

The king received him with great honour and said to him: 'My land lies open before you. Settle wherever you please; do whatever business here you like.' He dwelt there for a long time, no one giving him any trouble, and he grew richer and richer. Sons and daughters were born to him, one of them being a girl who was most perfectly lovely, yet disfigured in one of her eyes.

As the girl grew up, he did not know what to do with her. He could not possibly marry her to any man of importance, on account of her blemish. Yet to marry her to some common fellow he was unwilling. He thought the matter over carefully, and he wrote a letter to a rabbi named Jacob Hagiz—author of a commentary on the Mishnah entitled *Ets ḥayim* ['The Tree of Life']—who was at that time master of a yeshiva in Jerusalem.[64] 'I have a

---

[63] Following Rashi and Ibn Ezra on Ps. 40: 5. Hagiz scoffs at Cuenque's ignorance: there could not have been any 'king' in Gaza, since 'the great king of Turkey was ruler of both Damascus and Gaza!' By 'king', Cuenque surely intends a Turkish governor. (Cf. Joseph Karo's use of 'kingdom', *malkhut*, to designate an Ottoman province; above, n. 54 on the Najara Chronicle.) But there is still a problem: the *sanjak* of Gaza would have been subject to the governor-general of Damascus, while Cuenque seems to envisage it as a wholly distinct political unit ('the king of that land'). Cf. above, n. 58.

[64] Jacob Hagiz (1620–74) was indeed head of a yeshiva in Jerusalem, and a widely read and prolific scholar. He, and later his son Moses, were to become fierce opponents of Sabbatai and his followers. It is ironic that Nathan of Gaza should have been his student. Yet Moses Hagiz, in his note on this passage, assures us: 'This is true—he was the outstanding student of my late father . . . who certified him to be expert in the Talmud. When the event happened that made him notorious, I saw the letter that my late father wrote to Nathan his student, demanding on pain of excommunication that he tell him how he had attained this [occult] knowledge. Nathan replied that it was from a book of practical kabbalah he had stolen from the late, great Rabbi Abraham Hananiah, who had fled [MS *shebarah*] to Gaza from the plague [in Jerusalem]. There he fell ill, and commanded that he be conveyed to the city where his ancestors were buried, in the valley of Hebron. In his hurry to be going, [Nathan] stole from him the book, and used it to do those things he did.' On this passage, see Scholem, *Sabbatai Sevi*,

daughter', he wrote, 'who is most perfectly lovely, yet blind in one eye. If you should happen to have some worthy student, send him to me. I will welcome him into my household with a dowry befitting his dignity; I will provide for all his needs; he shall eat at my table and shall lack nothing of what his heart may desire.'

The rabbi considered his students, and saw among them a young man named Nathan Ashkenazi. He was a very humble man who kept strictly to himself—a man obliged to go hunting after his meals, sustained by no one apart from the Sephardi community, for he did not have anyone to look after him. This man did the rabbi select, and he sent him to Gaza to Samuel Lisbona.

The latter received him gladly. As a kind of charity he accepted [Nathan] as son-in-law,[65] and the Lord did indeed bless him for that. He led [Nathan] to the bridal canopy with his daughter; he kept all his promises to him. He fixed him up with a book-filled study where he would seclude himself, fasting much, praying much in tears.[66]

Many of the people of Gaza, respectable men who in those days dwelt there or came from other places, would come daily to visit him and speak with him. 'Won't you please tell us why you act as you do?' they said. 'Why do you spend all your time praying and weeping?[67] Why are you so much in seclusion? What means all this behaviour of yours, the like of which we have never seen?'

Finally, after being pressed day after day to speak, he said to them: 'You may be quite certain the messiah is in the world, dwelling among us. It is essential that we pray and bestir ourselves to great repentance. Let the multitudes be provided with sackcloth and ashes! For thus shall we help him to reveal his kingdom.'

This throng of people, their hearts having been touched by the fear of God, joined themselves to him. (This I heard from Nathan of Gaza

208–9; on Jacob Hagiz, and his role in the excommunication of Sabbatai in 1665 by the Jerusalem rabbis, see ibid. 199, 245–51; Carlebach, *The Pursuit of Heresy*, 19–36.

[65] The language is taken from the Talmud (BT *Ta'an.* 31*a*), where ugly girls urge prospective husbands to marry them as a kind of charity, unappealing as they may be. Clearly Cuenque does not regard Nathan as having been any great prize as a son-in-law.

[66] The second 'fire' lacuna: the text in *Torat hakenaot* omits the words *vesham hitboded vehirbah lehitanot ulehitpalel bivekhiyah* ('where ... tears'), and gives *veharbeh miyoshevei azah* ('many of the people of Gaza') as *vehirgishu bo yoshevei azah* ('the people of Gaza became aware of him'). The last two Hebrew letters of *veharbeh* and the first letter of *miyoshevei* had evidently been rendered illegible; Emden reconstructed them as best he could.

[67] The abbreviation *beit-beit-beh-kaf* (*beveit hakeneset*, 'in the synagogue'), which follows these words in the manuscript and editions, seems to have originated as a dittograph of the immediately preceding *uvekhiyah* ('and weeping'). Nathan has prayed and wept, not in any synagogue, but 'secluded' in his study.

himself.[68]) Day after day they went streaming after him. For them, his word was final.

It happened once that a group of distinguished men was sitting in his house on the eve of the New Moon[69] in their prayer-shawls and phylacteries, studying Torah and fasting, when all of a sudden the prophet Nathan descended upon them in the middle of the day. 'All of you stand up!' Nathan said to them. 'Go to the synagogue, and afterwards to the bathhouse!'

'Are we not ritually pure?' they pleaded. 'We have not been with our wives for the past three days![70] What sort of immersion do we need?'

Gently, humbly, he asked them to go; it was necessary, he told them. They rose and declared: 'We will not do it until you give us some reason.'

The prophet Nathan was deeply embarrassed. He could not keep himself from speaking. 'One of you', he said (giving the man's name), 'has just had an involuntary seminal emission.' This turned out, upon examination, to be true. They then fell a-trembling, and the fear of [Nathan] fell most heavily upon them.

It happened one day that Sabbatai Zevi returned from Egypt with his wife. As he entered Gaza, the prophet Nathan cried out with a loud voice: 'This is the saviour of Israel, the messiah of the God of Jacob! Apart from him, Israel has no redeemer whatever! Every prophecy of every prophet was spoken about him!'

Sabbatai Zevi heard about this while he was in Gaza, and he sent for [Nathan]. A great fear then fell upon Nathan, and he came trembling and shuddering, his body bowed low. And he fell on the ground before him.

'What are you saying, that I am the saviour of Israel?' Sabbatai Zevi said to him.

[Nathan] was so terrified, so beset by trembling and shivering, that he had no strength to reply. Finally [Sabbatai] said: 'I command you to stand up firmly! Speak straight out what you know about me, and who told you I am Israel's saviour!'

He answered, still shaking: 'Thus I have spoken with the Lord.' He went on to describe all the things that had transpired between Sabbatai Zevi and

[68] *Ka'asher shamati minatan azati zeh.* The manuscript puts these words in parentheses. The editions alter *shamati* to third-person *shama*, and print the words as though they were a gloss by Emden. But they will only make sense as part of Cuenque's text. On Cuenque's meeting with Nathan, see below.

[69] The editions add here *yoshevim lefanav*, 'sitting before him'. These words, absent from the manuscript, contradict what follows, which makes clear that Nathan was initially absent from the gathering.

[70] Following 1 Sam. 21: 6. I do not know how literally the number of days ought to be taken.

God, on those occasions when [Sabbatai] had secluded himself with his Creator. 'You see', he said, 'I know those things that transpired between you and God. And as for your demand that I say who told me you are God's messiah—it was God who told me, in a prophetic vision!'

He thereupon burst into prophecy. He began in the following way: 'I swear, by the great, mighty and terrible name of God, that with my own eyes and in a state of wakefulness I have seen the Divine Chariot, just as the prophet Ezekiel saw it by the River Chebar! I saw the ten *sefirot*[71] spread out before me like the ocean's waves. From the midst of them a voice came to my ears, speaking as follows: *Thus saith the Lord: Behold your saviour comes, Sabbatai Zevi his name. Like a mighty man shall he go forth, like a warrior shall he stir up passionate zeal. He shall give forth a loud trumpeting cry, mightily triumphing over his enemies.*[72] No sooner did this great voice reach me than the prophecy was inscribed before me in letters of fire. All of this I saw in a state of wakefulness, in a prophetic vision.'

All the time that he was speaking with Sabbatai Zevi there was no one else with them. It was only afterwards that Nathan the prophet revealed what he chose of the words that had passed between the two of them. As he left Sabbatai Zevi's presence the sweat streamed copiously from him; his knees shook, his limbs could hardly function together. 'What is this trembling about?' his familiars asked him. 'We've been with Sabbatai Zevi, and we had no fear or dread of him!' To which [Nathan] replied: 'If you only knew what I know, your souls would fly straight out of you the moment you looked at his face. He sets the upper and lower realms to quaking; all of the heavens shudder whenever his name is mentioned in the firmament, and all the angels tremble and say, *Holy.*[73] How might we have the strength to stand in his presence and speak to him face to face?'

Another report circulated to the effect that Sabbatai Zevi asked the prophet Nathan, 'How did you begin to experience all this?' and Nathan told him. Afterwards [Nathan] said to him: 'The prophet Elijah gave me a book that begins with you and ends at the close of the sixth millennium,[74] describing everything that is going to happen in the world.' [Sabbatai] demanded he bring him the book, which he did.

[Sabbatai] cut the first page out of the book, and returned the rest of it. 'Go to the graveyard', he said, 'and hide this [book] in a certain place where

[71] A kabbalistic term for the divine potentialities.

[72] Isa. 42: 13—referring, in its original context, to God.

[73] That is, they recite the formula 'Holy, holy, holy is the Lord of hosts, the whole earth is full of His glory' (Isa. 6: 3).

[74] From the traditional date of Creation. The sixth millennium of the Jewish calendar will end at Rosh Hashanah of the year 2240 CE.

it will be very well concealed. Keep this [first] page; you may show it to anyone you please. But all [the rest of] what you have seen written, you must
keep to yourself.'

That one page came to be well known back then, to all the outstanding
personages of the time. It begins with the words *Behold a son shall be born to
Mordecai Zevi in the Year of Creation 5386*,[75] written in a most archaic script
upon paper worn away with the passage of much time. Several times have I
seen a copy of it. I cannot remember the precise language written upon that
sheet of paper. Yet those were matters fearful and mysterious.

In those days did the prophet Nathan reveal the graves of many ancient holy
men, *tana'im* and *amora'im*,[76] in the vicinity of Gath and Lydda and Yavneh.
He would stretch himself out upon the grave and make connection [with the
holy man's spirit], and a voice would arise from the grave and speak with him
as he pleased.

Many extraordinary things were attested. I myself did not see them. Yet I
can affirm with certainty that some of the great Jewish dignitaries of that
generation would accost the prophet Nathan and beg him to tell them truly
when would come the End of Wonders,[77] that time fixed by God. 'During
the month of Nisan', he said, 'Sabbatai Zevi will rise to greatness, publicly
revealed as acknowledged messiah'—yet he did not say which Nisan he had
in mind, whether of 5426 [1666] or of 5427 [1667].[78] They asked: 'Yet perhaps, on account of our sins, some confusion may ensue?' To which he
replied: 'He is [the messiah], and no one else. Yet the time for the rebuilding
of the Temple and the ingathering of the exiles has not yet arrived.' 'When
will that happen?' they asked. And he answered: 'That matter is sealed and
concealed until the time of the end.'—All this I have heard from reliable
sources.[79]

'The sound of the trumpet grew ever stronger' [Exod. 19: 19]. 'The earth
trembled' [Ps. 77: 19].[80] And Sabbatai Zevi departed from Gaza—many

[75] From 'The Vision of Rabbi Abraham'. See above, n. 9 to the Introduction, and Baruch of
Arezzo, *Memorial*, §5.
[76] The rabbinic authorities of the Mishnah and the Talmud, respectively.
[77] The language is drawn from Dan. 12: 6.
[78] Nisan is the spring month in which Passover falls. 'What new revelation is here?', Hagiz
demands in his note on this passage. 'Our ancient rabbis have said, "In Nisan the Jewish
people were redeemed [from Egyptian slavery], and in Nisan they are destined to be
redeemed [by the messiah]"' (quoting BT *RH* 11a–b). Of course Nathan's expectation was
rooted in ancient tradition. What is 'new' is that he expected its fulfilment to be imminent.
[79] The third 'fire' lacuna, according to Emden. In fact, to judge from the manuscript, no
words are missing.
[80] *Vatirash ha'arets*, found also in Ps. 18: 8 (= 2 Sam. 22: 8), and Jer. 51: 29. (*Ha'arets*, omitted

things having happened in Gaza that are beyond the pen's capacity to relate—with a large contingent of Jews in his train.

He went to Gath, and from Gath he went to Jerusalem. There he did many deeds that seemed strange to all who witnessed them, no one comprehending his actions.[81] Word spread among the Muslims that the Jews' messiah was come, and dread fell upon them. A vast throng of Jews would assemble from each and every town and set out for Gaza, there to visit the prophet.

When it came Hebron's turn to go and seek their souls' mending,[82] I myself went to Gaza with all the rest of our community. As I stood in the prophet Nathan's presence—I having known him in the past—I shivered all over at how entirely his appearance was changed. His face was radiant as a blazing torch, the hair of his beard red-gold.[83] And his mouth—once incapable even of ordinary conversation—how it began to utter speech that set its hearer to trembling, his tongue speaking grandly! Normally it is easier for the ear to listen than for the mouth to speak. But now the reverse was the case, for one's ear had not the capacity to absorb the pure, clear speech that issued from his mouth, pronouncing literally at every instant fresh revelations, things that had not been heard since the day our faith was revealed at Sinai. Who is there among all the scholars of Israel, with any reputation for kabbalistic learning, who would not have bowed down to him and rolled in the dust at his feet?

So many people came to visit [Nathan], they had to sleep in the streets and the marketplaces and the squares, for the houses and courtyards had not sufficient room for them all. Not one word did the Jews speak among themselves; rather, they devoted themselves to fasting, one day after another, from one sabbath to the next. Young and old, lads and lasses, pregnant women and mothers all together—all of them entered [Nathan's presence]

---

from the editions, is in the manuscript.) Clearly Cuenque does not intend these statements literally. His point is that some great and incontrovertible manifestation of God's presence on earth, akin to the Sinai revelation (Exod. 19: 19) and God's appearance at the Red Sea (Ps. 77: 19, as understood by Jewish tradition), was beginning its triumphant march from its beginnings in Gaza. Cf. Cuenque's references to Sinai in the following paragraphs, and below, n. 87.

[81] 'This is a lie', Hagiz claims; 'he did nothing whatever. For my late father [Jacob Hagiz] and his court sent him a message warning him, on pain of excommunication, strictly to abstain from all his demented antics—that, if he should do any such thing, his blood would be as permissible to shed as that of a gazelle [*tsevi*] or a stag. I similarly heard from my late grandfather, the celebrated Rabbi Moses Galante, that my father used jokingly to say: "Look at this messiah, who fears and obeys my excommunication!"' Cf. Scholem, *Sabbatai Sevi*, 246–7.

[82] *Lelekh ulevakesh tikun al nafsham*. The editions omit all but the first word.

[83] Following Rashi and Kimhi on 2 Chron. 3: 6. Emden, basing himself on the portrait published in 1669 in Thomas Coenen's *Ydele Verwachtinge der Joden* (in Scholem, *Sabbatai Sevi*, facing p. ix), jeers that in fact Nathan 'had at that time no beard at all!'.

in peace and departed in peace.[84] Each group of visitors, having performed the 'mending' prescribed for them by the prophet, would prepare for themselves a joyous feast to celebrate their safe departure from that holy shrine.[85] Then, indeed, would 'the virgins rejoice in the dance, the young and the old together' [Jer. 31: 12].

The fear of the Jews fell upon the gentiles, so that they even pleaded with the Jews for their lives—a happening that beggars description!—such that if there should have been a single person in those days who entertained the smallest doubt about this faith, these tremendous events would have compelled his belief. Let it not be imagined that any occurrence like this one, or even remotely comparable to it, had ever occurred at any time in the past! Rather, just as the revelation at Mount Sinai was something extraordinary, about which Moses our Master might extravagantly declare, 'Has it ever happened that any people has heard the voice of God speaking from the midst of fire, as you have heard, and has lived?' [Deut. 4: 33]—so I shall declare, just as extravagantly: *This was something beyond the power of nature, that the Jews should have acted in this fashion in the midst of their exile, among all the nations and kingdoms to which they had been scattered beneath the heavenly dome*—in the empire of the Muslims, and most especially in the kingdom of Barbary—*without the gentiles having schemed against them to exterminate them, and to annihilate anyone bearing the name of Jew.* So should it have been, were it not for God's individual providence, and the pure divine will of Him at whose word existence came into being, by whose command it endures.[86] We are left with no choice but to bear witness to all this, to refuse to brand it a lie or to inscribe libellous compositions about the wondrous events that were done in those days, at that time.

The prophet Nathan spoke, in the full ardour of his faith: 'If only you could have such feelings always![87] Yet you must know for certain that Sabbatai Zevi will perform strange acts, bizarre acts, to such a point that all the world will come to deny his faith, and all the Jewish people will despair of him entirely. No one who maintains this faith will remain in the world, beyond one person in a town or two in a family,[88] on account of the strange deeds he

[84] Using the language of the talmudic story of the four rabbis who entered the mystical *pardes*, 'orchard' (BT *Ḥag.* 14*b*).

[85] Using the language of Mishnah *Yoma* 7: 4, which describes how the high priest would celebrate his having entered the Holy of Holies in the Temple and departed safely, uninjured by the terrible power of the divinity within.

[86] Ps. 33:9. The biblical passage goes on to say: 'The Lord nullifies the plans of the nations; He makes the thoughts of the peoples to be of no effect.'

[87] Using the language of Deut. 5: 26—yet another allusion to the Sinai event.

[88] The language is from Jer. 3: 14.

will do. Of him the prophet prophesied, "He shall be profaned for our sins" [Isa. 53: 5]—as one speaks of the "profanation" of God's name.'[89]

I myself did not hear these words. Yet many great men, the notable men of their time and also the notable men of Hebron at that time, heard him actually say these things, and not merely once or twice. It is upon their testimony that I rely.

After all these many events Sabbatai Zevi travelled to Constantinople with his wife Sarah. The land—Constantinople, that is—quivered and quaked at his arrival.[90] Numerous emissaries, men commanding respect, came forth to meet him with letters signed by all the land's dignitaries: rabbis, community leaders, and every well-placed person in the capital city. They granted him their recognition; they acknowledged his kingship and authority over them.

Then he entered into the capital, and there he performed many acts. Many people were astonished at some of his actions; others they declared to be the work of lunacy and utter madness. Astonishment grew. He issued a decree that they should no more fast on the Seventeenth of Tamuz; rather, they should celebrate it as a festival throughout the Jewish diaspora, calling it 'the Feast of Consolations'. And so they did.[91]

Afterwards couriers went forth in haste and urgency to promulgate the ruling of the king [Sabbatai]: on the Ninth of Av there was to be no fasting. Many did fast, secretly, each taking care that no one else knew about it. Those who fasted did not reveal their secret even to their own bed-partners.

At about the same time Nathan of Gaza came to Hebron, accompanied by more than three hundred Jewish followers. He had gone there to prostrate himself upon the Cave of Machpelah and to perform ritual immersions in the snow at Hebron—the reason being that it never snows in Gaza on account of the heat, whereas in Hebron snow falls most years and does not melt for several days on account of the low temperatures. What a perfectly

[89] See above, nn. 184, 190 on Baruch of Arezzo, and cf. the text below, at n. 146. Emden comments: 'The Nazarene had long preceded him with this argument; how dare [Nathan] encroach upon his territory! For the two of them are cut from the same cloth.' The observation is apt; the prophecy of the 'Suffering Servant' in Isaiah 53 had been a linchpin of the argument for Jesus's messiahship from the beginning of Christianity (Acts 8: 26–40). By understanding the key word *meholal* (53: 5) as meaning 'profaned' rather than 'pierced', the Sabbatians turned it to their own purposes. (The Lvov edition of *Torat hakenaot* mistakenly prints 'as one speaks . . . name' as though these words were the beginning of Emden's comment. They appear correctly in the Amsterdam edition.)

[90] Following 2 Sam. 22: 8, Ps. 18: 8. Cf. above, n. 80.

[91] Cuenque's carelessness is astonishing. It was the Ninth of Av, not the earlier fast of the Seventeenth of Tamuz, that Sabbatai decreed to be transformed into the 'Feast of Consolations' (Baruch of Arezzo, *Memorial*, §15; Halevi's first letter). Cuenque does not entirely ignore Sabbatai's imprisonment (see below). But he postpones it and treats it as a minor episode.

unbelievable scene that was! A hundred Jews go out to the fields together, the prophet with them, and perform their immersions by rolling around in the snow (for thus the snow immersion is to be carried out). And day after day the Muslims stand watching![92] Who can recount the wondrous deeds of God, or make known all His praise?

The most distinguished man of that time in our community [Hebron] was the master scholar, the late Rabbi Hayim Abulafia.[93] He heard about all that had been done, but declared with his holy mouth that he was not a believer; yet he would act precisely as the other Jews did, for he was unwilling to separate himself from the community.

The prophet Nathan was told of this, and was asked if he wished to call upon [Abulafia] in order to make clear to him what he had to offer.[94] 'I will go', he said. And so he went, and the rabbi received him with great honour.

'My son', he said to [Nathan], 'I have heard a great deal about you. I am not able to achieve clarity except with regard to that which I understand. Might you be able to satisfy my desire to understand all the doubtful passages in the Talmud, which my teachers were unable satisfactorily to explain?'

'Ask, my lord', said [Nathan].

So [Abulafia] queried him concerning all the talmudic passages he found difficult, and for each one [Nathan] provided at once six distinct interpretations, corresponding to the six working days of the week. He asked for a seventh; [Nathan] gave an evasive reply.

At that [Abulafia] began to walk away. [Nathan] pleaded with him:[95] 'Come back. You may hear the seventh, if you wish. But it is along kabbalistic lines, corresponding to the sabbath day.'[96] And the rabbi replied: 'Let me not seek to learn that which is too wondrous for me.'[97]

---

[92] No doubt snickering to themselves, Emden heartlessly suggests, over the behaviour of the crazy Jews.

[93] Cuenque accurately describes the position of Hayim ben Jacob Abulafia (1580–1668) within the Hebron community; see Scholem, *Sabbatai Sevi*, 358–9. One should keep in mind, reading the following account, that Nathan was then in his early twenties, Abulafia in his eighties.   [94] Literally, 'his merchandise'.

[95] The fourth and longest of the 'fire' lacunae: *Torat hakenaot* omits the words from 'corresponding' to 'pleaded with him' (*kesheshet yemei hama'aseh vayishal lo gam al perush hashevi'i vayidah oto bekaneh vayelekh mimenu vayiftsar bo*).

[96] Cuenque presumably models his narrative on the tradition that Isaac Luria 'would each day give to the halakhah six interpretations in accord with its simple meaning, corresponding to the six work-days of the week, and afterwards would provide a complete kabbalistic interpretation, corresponding to the sabbath day.' (*Sefer toledot ha'ari*, quoted in Benayahu, *The Sabbatian Movement in Greece* (Heb.), 460–1. Benayahu draws the parallel with Cuenque.)

[97] Following the injunction attributed in the Talmud (BT *Ḥag.* 13*a*), to 'the Book of Ben Sira'.

The rabbi was immensely pleased with him. 'Who teaches you this marvellous wisdom?' he asked.

'The prophet Elijah taught it to me, face to face.'

'My son', [Abulafia] said, 'can you please make sense for me of the things that are now happening, and what lies behind them?' Nathan the prophet answered with the words he had spoken to Sabbatai Zevi in response to the latter's enquiry,[98] and in addition he described to [Abulafia] absolutely everything that had transpired, from beginning to end. They spent something like half the day in private conference.

Then [Nathan] departed, and all the rabbis of the time[99] came to the rabbi to see if he had changed his opinion. 'I can attest', he answered them, 'that [Nathan's] wisdom goes beyond the powers of nature. He is certainly the object of some special providence—a holy man, moreover, and a vessel of blessing. Yet I stand by what I have been taught: I cannot believe the messiah will come in this way, for according to our inherited tradition this is not the proper manner. Still and all, I do not oppose them. I keep my thoughts to myself.'[100]

At about that time Sabbatai Zevi dispatched a decree from Constantinople, demanding that the prophet Nathan appear before him, along with a number of other men whose names were specified in the text of the decree.[101] Four men of Hebron were among those specified. At that time the above-mentioned rabbi of blessed memory [Abulafia] was beginning the study of the talmudic tractate *Ketubot* with his colleagues in the yeshiva. When the decree arrived in Hebron, he was furious his plans had been spoiled, for the [four] men from Hebron were his very favourites for their acuity and clarity of thought.

'Do not go', the rabbi said to them. 'If the king's wrath should be provoked,[102] how might I rescue you?'

[98] That is, the account he had given Sabbatai of his visionary experiences (above).

[99] Presumably, those who were in Hebron.

[100] Hagiz attaches to this sentence an intriguing note: 'Yet one's pen reveals a bit of what is going on in one's heart, even while concealing the bulk of it [read *vekhisah* for *vekhamah*], and there is enough therein to know that at heart he was a believer.' (The editions omit to attribute this gloss to Hagiz. But it is present in the manuscript, and there the attribution is clear.) It would appear from this that Hagiz was aware of some writing or writings of Abulafia, hinting at his Sabbatian belief. I have no idea what these might be.

[101] This sounds like a wildly distorted version of the summons, described by Najara (above), issued by Sabbatai from Adrianople on 15 March 1671. We shall presently see that the Najara Chronicle's sequel figures prominently in Cuenque's story.

[102] Such a convocation of the messiah's adherents, in the sultan's own capital, might well be expected to provoke the sultan's wrath.

They paid no attention to him, and some hundred and fifty men set off for Constantinople.[103]

The city was all abuzz. Complaints were made to the king. 'What is going on? The Jews are in open rebellion against you; they are choosing themselves a king!' One day the nobles of the empire forced him to look out through his window—declaring, 'You cannot even go out of your palace!'—and he saw the sea so filled with small boats that the water could not be seen. 'Believe us, our king', they said to him. 'We cannot cross the sea, because the Jews have taken all the boats. They are on the verge of seizing your crown[104] and destroying us all!'

The king simply laughed at them. 'Does it even cross your mind', he said to them, 'that the calamities of these wretched Jews will go on indefinitely? Sooner or later they are bound to be redeemed. What do you think? If the time for their redemption has indeed arrived, I will hand over to them my crown. For I am not Pharaoh, to say "Who is the Lord, that I should obey His command?" [Exod. 5: 2].'

The complaints—to tell the tale very briefly—grew ever louder, till the king was unable to silence them. He decreed that Sabbatai Zevi should go to Castillas, these being two mighty fortresses that stand at the entrance to Constantinople.[105]

Upon his going there, his fame and prestige increased dramatically. There he dwelt like a king in his palace. All the Jews did him obeisance; all their rabbis came to ask him whatever questions had perplexed them in the Written and Oral Torah. From the rabbis' donations he collected great sums of money. Seventy beautiful virgins—daughters of Jewish notables, dressed like princesses—came to serve him.[106] And Sarah [his wife] was truly like a queen.

Once more complaint was made before the king: that if he would not have this man [Sabbatai] destroyed, 'all your servants will rebel against you. For who can endure to see such things, and the vile acts that are performed in the royal court?'

So the king sent to Sabbatai Zevi, commanding that he come before him with his money and possessions. Thus he did. Three full days it took for

---

[103] It is not clear if these are 150 men from Hebron (in addition to the four who were specifically summoned), or all of the men whom Sabbatai had summoned from all the localities.

[104] A theme to be developed in what follows.

[105] This is Cuenque's version of the castle of Gallipoli (Baruch of Arezzo, *Memorial*, §11).

[106] To this intriguing detail, Hagiz adds one yet more intriguing: 'And on the sabbath he would call seven virgin girls to the Torah.' On Sabbatai's calling of women to the Torah, see above, n. 66 on Baruch of Arezzo; also Scholem, *Sabbatai Sevi*, 403–5, 670–1, and Rapoport-Albert, 'On the Position of Women in Sabbatianism' (Heb.), 216–17, 232–7.

them to bring all his possessions, and on the fourth day he himself arrived. He brought with him a chest containing many documents, and jewels such as could not be found in the royal palace.

A certain apostate Jew, close to the royal authority, was there in the king's presence. He said to [Sabbatai]: 'Be aware that this king is perfectly terrified of you. All you need to do is perform one minor act,[107] and he will seat you on his throne and you can put the royal crown on your head.'

Sabbatai Zevi answered: 'The hour is not yet come.'

'Take the turban upon your head', said the apostate.[108] 'If you do not do that, not a single Jew will survive in all the kingdom of the Turks, and the rest of the kingdoms will follow their example.'

Afterwards the king said to him: 'Are you the man whom they claim to be the messiah of the Jews?'

'So I am', he said.[109]

'Do you wish to be my friend?' [the king] said. 'For I am indeed fond of you.'

'I do so wish', he said.

The king removed the turban from his head[110] and stripped off his robes, and they dressed[111] [Sabbatai] in them. He said to him: 'This day have I appointed you to preside over the nobles who attend me in my palace.'[112]

Sabbatai Zevi was wearing his phylacteries and enwrapped in his ritual fringes, as the king could plainly see. He held a copy of the Zohar; he was dressed in priceless jewellery. The king sat beside him and asked him about the prayer-shawl and its ritual fringes, and he answered him. 'What are the phylacteries?' he asked, and [Sabbatai] gave a correct account of them. The king begged him to tell him what was written in the Zohar, whereat Sabbatai Zevi rebuked him: 'You [gentiles] do not have the intelligence to understand such things.'

[107] That is, a miracle.

[108] Cuenque deftly leaves ambiguous whether this is an *alternative* to the suggestion that Sabbatai put the royal crown on his head, or a *reiteration* of it.

[109] Contrast Halevi's account of the dialogue between Sabbatai and the sultan, in his first letter to Sasportas (above). The utter absurdity of what follows, and all the other conversations with the sultan described by Cuenque, hardly needs to be remarked.

[110] *Hesir hamelekh et hamitsnefet me'al rosho*. (So the manuscript; the editions omit *et*, and replace *me'al* with *she'al*.) The language is drawn from Ezek. 21: 31: 'Thus says the Lord God: Remove the turban and lift off the crown' (*hasir hamitsnefet veharim ha'atarah*). Jacob Sasportas uses precisely the same language in a letter written at the beginning of December 1665, describing Nathan's expectation that the sultan will 'remove his turban and lift off his crown, and place it on the messiah's head' (*Sefer tsitsat novel tsevi*, 13; cf. Halperin, 'Sabbatai Zevi, Metatron, and Mehmed', 275). Cuenque subtly represents the expectation as having been fulfilled.   [111] Understanding *laveshu* as transitive.

[112] The fifth 'fire' lacuna: *Torat hakenaot* omits *berosh hasarim ha'omedim lefanai beheikhali* ('over ... palace'), and gives the following וְהַשֵׁ״ץ as שְׁהַשֵׁ״ץ.

He had a Bible with him as well, and the king said: 'Is this also beyond my understanding?'

'Of *this*', he replied, 'you may possibly understand a little.'

The king opened the Bible and laid his finger on the verse, 'With regard to Ishmael, I have heard you', and so forth [Gen. 17: 20].[113] The king said to him: 'Tell me about this passage I have put my finger on.'

To which Sabbatai Zevi said: 'Aptly have you pointed to it—the very source of your survival! On the strength of this passage have you [Turks] achieved your empire.' He interpreted the verse to the king, expounding it for him at some length. The king could not restrain himself; his eyes brimmed over with tears.

'What is your name?' the king asked him.

'Sabbatai Zevi', he said.

Said the king: 'Now do I call you Aziz Mehmed Effendi,[114] which means "my friend Mehmed the wise".'—All this have I heard from reliable sources.

Sarah became pregnant. When her time arrived, she bore her first-born son in the king's palace. He was circumcised on the eighth day in the king's palace, in the presence of all the nobles of the kingdom and a few distinguished rabbis as well. Sabbatai Zevi wore white garments, and a prayer-shawl and phylacteries; he said the blessing over the cup, and entered his son into the age-old covenant in accordance with all the laws and ordinances [of the Torah]. He called him Ishmael, his son.

Some time afterwards, Sabbatai Zevi sent for ten great rabbis who were in Constantinople to come to him in the courtyard of the royal palace, 'for I have a secret matter to impart to you'.[115] It was then Friday; and the men

---

[113] 'I have blessed him, and I will make him fruitful and magnify him greatly . . . and I will make him a great nation.' The Najara Chronicle (text at nn. 30, 96) twice represents Sabbatai as having used this passage in his dealings with the Turkish authorities. Cuenque's story here seems to be a distorted echo of Najara's second passage.

[114] So the manuscript. The editions give the abbreviation *ayin-dalet-zayin* (*al davar zeh*) in place of *aziz*: 'On account of this do I call you Mehmed Effendi.' The one reading is clearly a graphic error for the other. It is hard to be sure which is the original—both readings yield good sense—but that of the manuscript seems preferable. Scholem mentions 'Aziz Mehemed Effendi' as a variant of Sabbatai's new name (*Sabbatai Sevi*, 681); he does not give his source for this, but he is plainly not drawing on the Rostock manuscript, of which he seems to have been unaware. Following the manuscript reading, each of the three components of the name is afterwards rendered (inaccurately) into Hebrew. In the editions' reading, the symmetry between the name and its translation is spoiled.

[115] So the manuscript. The editions have: 'Sabbatai Zevi sent word to ten great rabbis that they should be [*sheyiheyu* for *shehayu*] in Constantinople that evening, "ready to come to me tomorrow [*le'or hayom nekhonim lemahar lavo etsli*; the manuscript omits the first four words, and has *etslo* for *etsli*] in the courtyard of the royal palace, for I have a secret matter to impart to you".' The shorter reading of the manuscript seems preferable. The last sentence of the para-

who were named did as they had been told, and rose early on the sabbath day and presented themselves at the entrance to the palace gate. These were ten of those men about whom Sabbatai Zevi had written to the prophet Nathan, demanding they come with him [to Constantinople].[116]

It happened by chance that, as [Sabbatai] arrived, the king was leaving his palace to go hunting. An enormous crowd of the king's chosen attendants was already outdoors, in readiness for him. Hardly had the king gone forth, when he stopped by the entrance to the courtyard gate and saw Sabbatai Zevi standing there, ten Jews with him.[117]

'What do these Jews want?' said the king.

'I sent for them', said [Sabbatai], 'to debate with them about the religion of Moses.'

'Well, do whatever you please. I am going hunting.'

'Today you have no permission to go anywhere', said Sabbatai Zevi.[118]

So the king went back into his palace, and all his troop—more than eighty men—dispersed themselves, their plans spoiled. Sabbatai Zevi took the ten men and went into the palace, to the place where judgments were given.[119] He sat on the throne and arranged the ten rabbis in a circle before him.[120]

graph seems to imply the rabbis were already in Constantinople; and if they were in other localities, as the editions' reading seems to imply, Sabbatai could hardly have expected them to be in Constantinople that very evening.

[116] Above, at n. 101.

[117] Cf. the portion of the Najara Chronicle that begins immediately after the lacuna in the middle of the text, which also takes place by a courtyard gate. The story Cuenque proceeds to unfold is plainly based on the episode described by Najara; the resemblance is best explained if we suppose Cuenque had the details from Meir Rofé, who was a participant in the event. But Cuenque's account is also modelled on *Idra rabah*, a section of the Zohar (iii. 127*b*–145*a*) that describes how Rabbi Simeon ben Yohai gathers nine of his colleagues and reveals to them the deepest secrets of the divine essence, couched in the most highly anthropomorphic terms (see the notes that follow). I have suggested, in my introduction to the Najara Chronicle, that Sabbatai may have consciously intended a re-enactment of the *Idra*. If so, Cuenque's recasting of the story has brought out what was latent in the event itself.

[118] This preposterous exchange is surely intended to soften the historical fact of the sultan's presence at what should have been an intramural debate of Jewish scholars. The fact that Cuenque felt obliged to do this suggests that the episode, including the sultan's presence, was a widely known tradition he could not disregard without endangering his credibility. Cf. the remarks of Cardozo, quoted near the end of my introduction to the Najara Chronicle.

[119] *Mekom hamishpat*, literally 'the place of judgment', corresponding to Najara's 'Divan'. But see the next note.

[120] *Kegoren agulah* (manuscript *begoren*), literally 'like a round threshing-floor'. The language is taken from the Mishnah *San.* 4: 3, where the Sanhedrin sits 'like half of a round threshing-floor'—that is, in a semi-circle—and also from the midrash *Exodus Rabbah* 5: 12: 'In time to come the Blessed Holy One will seat the elders of Israel like a threshing-floor [i.e. in a circle] and He will sit at their head ... and they will judge the nations ... for thus it is the way of kings to sit in a circle like a threshing-floor.' (Surely it is no accident that Cuenque sets this

He began by proclaiming in a loud voice: 'It is time to act for the Lord!'[121] He asked them: 'What is this that the Torah says, "The Lord regretted He had made human beings on the earth, and He was grieved to His heart" [Gen. 6: 6]? Is He a human being, capable of regrets? Is He susceptible to grief? What about the passage, "My soul weeps in secret places" [Jer. 13: 17]?' He raised many problems of this sort,[122] then proceeded to open his discourse with a resolution of the Maimonidean problem of [our] knowledge of God.[123] 'What is this commandment', he went on to say, 'that David gave to Solomon—"Solomon my son, know the God of your father and serve Him" [1 Chron. 28: 9]? What sort of "knowledge" is this?'

After all this, Sabbatai Zevi stood up and spread his hands to heaven. 'You know perfectly well, O Lord of all', he said, 'that it is not for my own glory that I reveal what You had hidden away, nor is it for the glory of my father's

session in 'the place of judgment'.) But Cuenque also alludes here to *Idra rabah*. The Aramaic word *idra*, normally used in the Zohar to mean 'room' or 'assembly', has as its original and fundamental meaning 'threshing-floor', and it is at some *idra* in the open air that Rabbi Simeon and his companions gather for their colloquy (Zohar, iii. 127*b*; trans. in *Wisdom of the Zohar*, ed. Tishby, i. 155–8). See Liebes, *Sections of the Zohar Lexicon* (Heb.), 93–106 (Liebes points out, p. 98, that that the targumic expansion to S. of S. 7: 3 uses *idar segalgal* as the Aramaic equivalent for the Sanhedrin's *goren agulah*). Cf. Giller, *Reading the Zohar*, 90–2.

[121] Quoting Ps. 119: 126: 'It is time to act for the Lord; they have violated Your Torah.' The apparent meaning of this verse is that, when God's Torah is violated, it is time for zealots to take action. But the Talmud (BT *Ber.* 63*a*) points out that the biblical text can be interpreted with the clauses reversed: in time of emergency, when it is 'time to act for the Lord', the true servant of God will break God's law in order to do God's will. This is what Sabbatai, who has already violated God's Torah by becoming a Muslim, declares himself about to do. So, not coincidentally, does Rabbi Simeon ben Yohai at the beginning of *Idra rabah*, by quoting this very same passage from Ps. 119 (Zohar, iii. 127*b*).

[122] Similarly described in the Najara Chronicle (above); presumably these formed part of what Sabbatai actually said on the occasion. But it is worth noting that the most striking feature of *Idra rabah* is its extreme anthropomorphism, both expressed and—through Rabbi Simeon's opening recitation of Deut. 27: 15—disowned.

[123] *Pataḥ bekushiyat harambam bidiato mukhra'at*. The Hebrew is, as Emden points out in his annotation to this passage, convoluted and difficult. But it seems we must take *mukhra'at* as modifying *kushiyat harambam*, and the suffix of *bidiato*—contrary to Emden's understanding— as having an objective rather than a possessive meaning. The great medieval philosopher Moses Maimonides (1135–1204) dealt, as Emden says, with the problems raised by the doctrine of God's omniscience. He also dealt with the thornier problem of how humans are to attain the knowledge of God that is prerequisite for immortality—a long and difficult process involving, along with much else, rejection of any literal interpretation of the Bible's anthropomorphisms (see Guttmann, *Philosophies of Judaism*, 172–207). The context, and the parallel in the Najara Chronicle (text preceding n. 90), shows it is the latter that is intended here. Cardozo was also much occupied with the problem of knowing God, which he regarded as the fundamental obligation of Judaism. See the opening chapters of Cardozo's *This Is My God*, translated in Halperin, *Abraham Miguel Cardozo*; Cardozo quotes David's injunction to Solomon on p. 180.

house that I uncover Your secrets.[124] For the glory, rather, of Your great, mighty, terrible—and profaned—Name, have I sallied forth to sanctify Your name among these ten Jewish men. For I know truly that they are outstanding men, worthy of this. "And God's secret belongs to those who fear Him" [Ps. 25: 14].'[125]

At once he made them swear by God's name that, until the day of their death, they would not reveal a single word of what he was about to tell them. 'Amen!' they said.[126] Three times he warned them: 'Whoever has not understood, must ask once more.' When they were finished he said to them: 'This is the knowledge of divinity. From now on you will know who it is that you worship, and who is your God.'

The ten rabbis thereupon fell on their faces to the ground and burst out weeping. 'If only we might die this day!'[127] they said. 'It is so hard for us to depart from you!' He said to them: 'Go in peace to your homes.'

Never before had there been a day like that, when Torah was studied and its fine points debated within a royal palace. All the nobles of the kingdom were humiliated and covered their heads.[128] 'How is it possible', said they, 'to endure the ridicule that man heaps upon you and your kingdom, and upon our religion? He practises the religion of Moses right in front of you; he brings Jews into your palace and organizes a study session! What insult may you look forward to next?'

In those days the king grew furiously angry with all the kingdom's princes. 'Anyone who persists in speaking to me about this man shall be executed!' he said. 'He is no human being but an angel from heaven!' Yet they went on nagging endlessly at the king over his not having banished him;[129]

---

[124] Modelled on Rabbi Simeon's declaration at the end of his speech in *Idra rabah* (Zohar iii. 144*a*).

[125] Quoted by Rabbi Simeon at the beginning of *Idra rabah* (Zohar iii. 127*b*), and again at iii. 141*b*.

[126] The rabbis' 'Amen!' is taken from the beginning of *Idra rabah*, where Rabbi Simeon's companions respond with 'Amen!' to his quotation of Deut. 27: 15 (Zohar iii. 127*b*–128*a*). Sabbatai's insistence on secrecy was well known among his early followers. Cardozo, intensely proud of his own openness about the 'Mystery of Divinity', contrasts himself in this respect with his fellow-messiah: 'Sabbatai Zevi . . . would not even give anyone a complete exposition of the Divinity of God without an accompanying threat of excommunication. He never so much as permitted, much less commanded, anyone who had heard from him the Mystery of Divinity to reveal it to anyone else' (Halperin, *Abraham Miguel Cardozo*, 307, cf. 289).

[127] As do three of Rabbi Simeon's companions, in *Idra rabah*.

[128] As a token of shame. The language is modelled on Jer. 14: 3–4.

[129] *Amnam hayu maftsirim tamid el hamelekh al devar asher lo geresh oto me'al panav.* These words ('Yet . . . banished him') are omitted from *Torat hakenaot*, as having been destroyed in the fire. This is the sixth, and last, of the 'fire' lacunae.

and, after Sabbatai Zevi had been for a long time with the royal court,[130] he said to the king: 'I wish to depart.'

The king became very upset. 'Will you not tell me what you are lacking in my palace?' he said to him. 'Whatever you ask, it shall be done.'

'I do not lack anything', Sabbatai Zevi answered. 'But I must tell you truthfully, I cannot endure the disagreeableness of remaining here. Set me at liberty!'

'Where will you go?' the king said.

'I wish to go to such-and-such place', he said—requesting a place very far away, at the border of the empire, where there lived no Muslims but only Christians.[131]

'I should be disgraced!' the king said to him. 'Let me send you to one of the empire's great cities—to Cairo[132] or Damascus or Aleppo. I will equip you with carriages and horsemen, and there you shall be a lord and a gentleman.'

'I have no wish for that', said Sabbatai Zevi. 'It is to the place I have named that I desire to go.'

'Well, if you must', said the king, 'then take with you a military escort to serve you.'

'I have no wish for any protection. I cannot be harmed, nor do I harm anyone.'[133]

'Then take your wife and your son', said the king.

'I will not take them', said he, 'and I will go entirely alone. My wife and my son—those two I leave in your hands. I do not have the slightest wish for them.'[134]

In sum, he did just as he said he would. He set forth alone on his journey to that place, and there he remained many days.

When the eve of Yom Kippur arrived, he summoned the Christians and said to them: 'Know that tomorrow, after the noontime and towards evening, I will die. Know that when I die you must strip me entirely naked,

[130] Literally 'sitting in the king's gate', following passages such as Esther 2: 19, 21.

[131] An inaccurate description of Dulcigno, on the Adriatic coast, which Baruch of Arezzo (*Memorial*, §23 end) describes correctly as 'on the border between the territories of Islam and of Christendom', i.e. Albania and Montenegro.

[132] Understanding *mitsrayim*, like Arabic *misr*, as referring to Egypt's principal city as well as to Egypt itself.

[133] *Ein ani nizak ve'eini mazik*; so the manuscript. Emden claims to have had before him the reading *va'ani mazik*, 'and I do harm' or 'and I am a demon'—to which Emden of course makes the witty comment, 'Well did he call himself a demon!' (But *ve'eini* is obviously the correct reading.)

[134] This is pure fabrication on Cuenque's part. In reality, Sarah and Ishmael accompanied Sabbatai into his exile, where Sarah died. See the introduction to Cuenque, and above, n. 260 on Baruch of Arezzo.

and lay me down upon the sand by the seashore and leave me there. Take care that you do as I wish'—for they looked upon him as an angel, yet they did not believe him when he said he would die, but imagined he was joking with them, for he was vigorous and healthy.

The next day—on Yom Kippur, after noontime and towards evening—he passed away and was gathered [unto his soul-glory].[135] The Christians came and stripped off his clothes and left him naked, and laid him down upon the seashore; they did not neglect any detail of all he had commanded them. The following day they returned to the seashore to see what had become of him, and they found nothing there. 'Surely', they said, 'the waves of the sea must have washed him away'[136]—all this have I heard from the testimony of Jewish travellers from Constantinople; but the secret things are known only to the Lord our God.[137]

Nathan of Gaza was in Sofia, the great centre of Jewish learning.[138] When the news reached him that Sabbatai Zevi had set the Muslims' turban on his head and had dressed himself in the Muslims' clothing, he pronounced the blessing of Him 'who has kept us alive'.[139] The rabbis asked him, 'What does it all mean?' To which he replied:[140]

'These are great mysteries, hinted at by Rabbi Simeon ben Yohai in the book of the *Tikunei zohar*: "There is one who is good on the inside,[141] yet his garment is evil; this is the one whom Scripture calls 'poor, riding on an ass' [Zech. 9: 9]."[142] You may consult also the Zohar, page 533 of the section on the Torah portion 'Ki tetse',[143] concerning the hidden meaning of the figure of Esther—of whom it is written, "They divided my garments, and over my clothing did they cast lots" [Ps. 22: 19][144]—and concerning the hidden

---

[135] Following Ibn Ezra and Bahya ben Asher on Gen. 25: 8; cf. BT *BB* 16*b*.

[136] But we, of course, know the truth: he was resurrected.   [137] Quoting Deut. 29: 28.

[138] There is a grain of truth in this, in that Sofia was Nathan's second principal place of residence, after Kastoria, in the 1670s (Benayahu, *The Sabbatian Movement in Greece* (Heb.), 227–30). It is of course entirely false that he was already there when the news of the apostasy reached him; contrast Baruch of Arezzo, *Memorial*, §17.

[139] 'Blessed be You, O Lord our God, King of the universe, who has kept us alive, preserved us, and enabled us to reach this day'—uttered in gratitude for having lived to attain one or another significant milestone.

[140] What follows is mostly drawn from Nathan's epistle to Joseph Zevi (above, Baruch of Arezzo, *Memorial*, §18), or some kindred text. See the following notes.

[141] *Malka* ('king'), in both the manuscript and the editions, is an obvious error for *milegav* ('on the inside') of *Tikunei zohar*.

[142] See above at n. 188 on Baruch of Arezzo.   [143] Deut. 21: 10–25: 19.

[144] This verse is applied to Queen Esther, not in the Zohar, but in *Midrash tehilim* ('Midrash on Psalms'), at 22: 7, 27, which systematically expounds Psalm 22 in reference to Esther. The Christian use of the verse as a prophecy of Jesus (John 19: 24) may have influenced Cuenque's quoting it here, in connection with his own messiah.

meaning also of Joseph, of whom it is written, "She kept his garment in her possession" [Gen. 39: 16], and not his "clothing"—and for whom [Esther] a she-demon went as her substitute to Ahasuerus.[145]

'Isaiah also alluded to this in his fifty-third chapter:[146] "He was numbered among the sinners" [53: 12]. And it is hinted at in the Zohar on the Torah portion "Naso",[147] page 51, where the Faithful Shepherd [Moses] says that "they are quite unaware of me; among the iniquitous 'mixed rabble' I am considered as a stinking dead dog."[148] This you may consult.'

The prophet [Nathan] was very highly regarded among the [Jews of Sofia]. On one occasion the prophet was walking down the road with a band of great rabbis, and he said: 'Here, in this place, a great man from among the ancients is buried.' The prophet made a connection [with the dead man's spirit], and spread his cloak over the grave.[149] 'Listen carefully', he said to the rabbis, 'and hear what the dead man is saying.'

They heard a voice speaking from within the grave: *Sabbatai Zevi is king messiah*. It went on to speak other extraordinary things, which I do not have the strength to set down on paper.[150]

Similarly, on another occasion, he was walking with a band of rabbis in the vicinity of Livnah.[151] 'Here', said he, 'is buried a perfect saint, a great

---

[145] Zohar, iii. 276a (*Ra'aya mehemna*; I am not sure to what Cuenque's pagination refers). In the zoharic passage, Esther 'clothes' herself in the feminine aspect of divinity and thus rules over Ahasuerus and his people; it is a demon in her shape, and not she herself, who submits to Ahasuerus's demonic embraces. She is therefore compared to Joseph, who leaves only his 'garment', and not his divine 'clothing', in the grasp of the demonic seductress. In this long and convoluted sentence, Cuenque finds in the Zohar's text a hint that the messiah, like Esther, must yield his 'clothing'—or, more exactly, his choice of whether to wear Jewish or Muslim clothing—to the power of the gentiles. Nathan similarly compares Sabbatai with Esther in his epistle to Joseph Zevi, but he does not cite this passage or make this specific argument.

[146] Both the manuscript and the editions mistakenly read 'thirteenth chapter'. (The manuscript also has 'Joshua' in place of 'Isaiah'.)   [147] Num. 4: 21–7: 89.

[148] See above, n. 183 on Baruch of Arezzo. The zoharic passage (iii. 125b–126a) invokes Isa. 53: 9, '[God] placed his grave with the wicked', for which Cuenque substitutes 53: 12. Here, as above, I do not understand the pagination Cuenque uses in citing the Zohar.

[149] Scholem remarks the parallel with Isaac Luria's 'habit of discovering tombs and obtaining inspiration from the spirits of the saints buried there' (*Sabbatai Sevi*, 244–5; cf. Goldish, *The Sabbatean Prophets*, 69). The resemblance had been noted two centuries earlier by Emden, in his note on this passage. ('This is an ape's trick, to make himself out to be like Rabbi Isaac Luria! . . . If there is any grain of truth in this concocted tale, Nathan was certainly practising sorcery.')

[150] Reading *she'ein li ko'ah lehavi'em*, with the manuscript, against the editions' *she'ein yekholim lehavi* ('which cannot be set down').

[151] I cannot identify the locality intended. Perhaps the name is to be pronounced *livneh* ('birch-tree'), *levanah* ('brick'), or *levanah* ('moon'), and, in one or another of these meanings, corresponds to the name of some town in the vicinity of Sofia.

man.' He told them to look the other way. The prophet[152] spoke a certain connection-formula, and the grave opened, and he told one of the rabbis to roll away the gravestone.

When he did so, he saw the dead man as though he were alive and not in the grave. The prophet said: 'Lift up the dead man's head. Under his head there will be a pottery vessel; take from it the document that is inside.' The rabbi did so, and found a worn and ancient document in which was written: *In the year 5386 a son shall be born to Mordecai Zevi in Izmir, Sabbatai Zevi his name. He shall be king messiah for Israel, and shall perform strange and extra-ordinary deeds which will appal all who hear of them.* The rest of what was written there cannot be put on paper.[153]

The prophet told him to return the document to its place, and he did so, and the prophet told [the other rabbis] again to look away. At once the grave was sealed, and they no longer knew where it was.

On the eve of the Shavuot festival[154] he said to a band of his companions: 'Come, let's go to the graveyard.' They followed him there, and he said to them: 'Dig a grave on this spot.' 'What is this grave for?' they said to him; and he said, 'You will know presently.' And they did as he told them.

When they had finished their work, he said: 'When the festival is over, after the *havdalah* ritual,[155] I shall be gathered unto my soul-glory.[156] Carry me to this grave and bury me here.'

All who heard him grew faint and dizzy, for they did not believe this could be. Yet, in brief, they kept silent and forced themselves to say nothing, and returned to the city. When the festival ended, he performed the *havdalah* over a cup of wine and then lay down. He gathered up his feet to the bed and passed away, and was gathered to his soul-glory.[157] All Israel mourned for him, in the grave he had carved out for himself.—All this I heard from reliable sources,[158] from Jewish travellers coming from Sofia. But the secret things are known only to the Lord our God.[159]

---

[152] Thus the manuscript.

[153] Following the manuscript, *ushe'arei hadevarim lo yukhal haneyar lehakhilem.* (The editions' reading is slightly different.) The language of the supposed prophecy echoes 'The Vision of Rabbi Abraham'; see above, n. 75.

[154] The festival commemorating the giving of the Torah. It was on Shavuot of 1665 that Nathan revealed to the assembled rabbis his own prophethood and the messiahship of Sabbatai Zevi (Baruch of Arezzo, *Memorial,* §5). The account that follows here is fantasy. Nathan died in January 1680, not in June, when Shavuot would have fallen.

[155] See above, n. 57.   [156] See above, n. 135.

[157] Gen. 49: 33, describing the death of Jacob.

[158] *Kol zeh shamati mipi magidei emet.* So the manuscript; the editions omit *kol zeh* and *emet.*

[159] Quoting Deut. 29: 28, as at n. 137 above.

Sarah, the wife of Sabbatai Zevi, dwelt in the king's palace.[160] There, provided for by the king, she raised her son Ishmael. The lad grew; he took his father's place [in the royal court], spending his time among the nobles of the empire—a young man tall and sturdy as a cedar tree.[161]

I am told by reliable sources that Ishmael possessed unbelievable expertise in each and every branch of learning. Whatever unsettled problems the scholars might have, they would turn to him and he would answer every question. And this I have seen with my very own eyes: In the course of my wanderings, while I was in Ostrog as guest of the illustrious scholar Rabbi Naphtali—currently serving as rabbinic judge in Poznan—there was present a distinguished Talmud student, one Master Ephraim,[162] who was born in Ostrog but went to the great Jewish metropolis of Salonica to learn Torah.[163] He showed him [Naphtali][164] a query sent to Ishmael Zevi and his lofty response thereto, matters[165] of great profundity. This, and much else of the kind, did I see with my own eyes.

Here I shall give rest to my pen, and bring my words to their conclusion. May the Lord God of heaven give light to our gloom and shine through our darkness, and may He declare an end to our sufferings! May He gather our

[160] This statement is a deliberate falsehood. Sarah was dead by then, as Cuenque must have known, and there is good reason to believe that Ishmael died about three years afterwards (Halperin, 'The Son of the Messiah', 205–7). Cuenque wants the reader to believe the messianic line is still flourishing in the sultan's palace, ready to step forward at any time and make visible its power.

[161] On which Emden comments, with typical charity and grace: 'In fact, [Sabbatai's] offspring turned out just like him: the child of impurity [Ishmael] was laid to rot as a Muslim, and Sabbatai Zevi and all his worthless line were cut off without any survivor—no posterity or grandchild among his people, no remnant in his dwelling place. Those who come after him are shocked at his fate, his contemporaries seized with dread. This is a wicked man's just desert, to be burnt up and consumed!'

[162] The manuscript gives him the modest title *rabi*, 'Master'. The editions have the loftier abbreviation מהורר ר״מ (= מוהר״ר, 'our teacher Rabbi Ephraim').

[163] 'The illustrious scholar Rabbi Naphtali' is Naphtali ben Isaac Katz (1645–1719), who served until 1689 as rabbi of Ostrog in Volhynia, and moved to Poznan, as Cuenque indicates, in 1690 (*Encyclopedia Judaica*, s.v. 'Katz, Naphtali ben Isaac'). On this episode, see Benayahu, *The Sabbatian Movement in Greece* (Heb.), 166; Liebes, 'A Profile of R. Naphtali Katz of Frankfort', 296–7. Benayahu identifies 'Master Ephraim' as Ephraim Kohen of Ostrog (d. 1728), a scholar with strong Sabbatian connections who paid a long visit to Italy in the 1680s, bringing with him the writings of Nathan of Gaza (ibid. 117–36); Cuenque's modest description of him as a *talmid ḥakham* would perhaps cast some doubt upon this identification. What the document was that he allegedly showed Cuenque in Ostrog, we can only guess. Perhaps some schoolboy exercise of Ishmael Zevi's, inflated by Cuenque's fiction-writing proclivities into a responsum 'of great profundity'?

[164] Unless, as seems likely, we are to read *li* in place of *lo*: 'He showed me'. (The reading of the manuscript at this point is unclear. I have the impression the copyist originally wrote *lo*, but tried to correct it to *li*.)

[165] So the editions. The manuscript has *diburim*, 'utterances', for *devarim*, 'matters'.

scattered folk from the four winds of heaven,[166] and build our holy and splendid Temple! May our eyes see this and our heart rejoice!

> So speaks the faithful friend, exiled and roaming in
> his community's toilsome service, the wings of wandering[167]
> —once did he dwell in the Holy Land, in Kiriath-arba
> which is the holy city of Hebron, may it be built and
> established speedily in our days; now, with God's help,
> he returns from his mission to his former dwelling-place—
> the emissary, authorized agent, scribe, and trustee of the holy
> community of Hebron, who sacrifices his own wishes
> in order to serve the wishes of others—the humble
>
> Abraham Cuenque.

[166] The manuscript omits the first part of this sentence.

[167] So the manuscript (*bishelihut mitsvah umatsok kanfei hanedod*). For *umatsok*, the editions give *umehabek*, 'embracing the wings of wandering'.

FIFTH TESTIMONY
From the Reminiscences of Abraham Cardozo

☙

INTRODUCTION

ABRAHAM MIGUEL CARDOZO was born in 1627, one year after Sabbatai Zevi, and spent much of his long life imagining himself as Sabbatai's other half. He came from a family of Marranos, descendants of Jewish converts to Catholicism, practising and preserving their ancestral faith in secret. In 1648, at the age of 21, he converted formally to Judaism. With the spread, in 1665, of the good news of Sabbatai's advent, Cardozo conceived the idea that he had found the messiah. Not long afterwards he conceived that he *was* the messiah. More exactly, he was messiah ben Joseph to Sabbatai's messiah ben David, his own youthful profession of Christianity the perfect symmetrical counterweight to Sabbatai's late-life profession of Islam.

He was even a *tsevi*, a 'gazelle', no less than Sabbatai.[1] But unlike Sabbatai Zevi, 'who left the Jewish community and went out from Torah and holiness into the realms of the profane', Cardozo would not follow the standard 'gazelle' behaviour of looking back towards the place from which he came. He was a Jew, and a proud one. This *tsevi*, at least, would never look back towards the alien religion of his birth.[2]

Cardozo was surely the better man of the two, as well as—in so far as such a judgement can have any meaning—the better messiah. Intellectually, and perhaps morally as well, Sabbatai did not come up to Cardozo's kneecaps, and Cardozo's disconnection from reality, striking enough to the modern reader, was less severe and less destructive to those around him than Sabbatai's. Cardozo was intermittently aware of his own superiority, yet he could not cease to struggle and pine for the attention and approval of his senior partner in redemption. Sometime around the beginning of 1673 he sent Sabbatai a copy of his fledgling work of theology, *Derush boker de'avraham* ('Abraham's Morn')—a poignant gesture, intended to enlighten the

---

[1] So Cardozo proved to himself through a complex biblical argument; see the following note.

[2] 'I am the kind of *tsevi* who is always saying, "Who is like God?" and who will never, God forbid, look back to the place from which I came'—from the treatise *Derush kodesh yisra'el la'adonai* ('Israel, Holiness to the Lord'), trans. in Halperin, *Abraham Miguel Cardozo*, 263–4; original text in Scholem, 'Abraham Michael Cardozo' (Heb.), 446.

hitherto blind eyes of the elder messiah, who did not seem yet to understand how to be messiah and needed Cardozo to explain it to him. Sabbatai never replied; Cardozo was left to guess how he had responded to the treatise and the accompanying letter.[3] Years later, Cardozo met Sabbatai face to face for the first time and received from him the most heart-warming and encouraging compliments. But this was in the 1680s, after Sabbatai had died, and Cardozo had developed a talent for bringing ghosts back from the afterworld and hearing from them whatever he wanted to hear.

The story that follows, therefore, must be taken with a substantial dollop of suspicion. Cardozo recorded it towards the end of his life, some twenty years after the conversation he describes. His memory had begun to play tricks on him.[4] His report of Sabbatai's lavishly enthusiastic response to his 'long letter'—no doubt the letter that had once accompanied *Derush boker de'avraham*—has the smell of wishful thinking, perhaps triggered by some vaguely flattering remark of his informant. Yet one detail is certainly authentic: his contemptuous, dismissive attitude towards Joseph Karillo and his fellow-apostate. Cardozo defended Sabbatai's apostasy as a messianic act of self-sacrifice, corresponding to the unwilled sacrifice by which messiah ben Joseph (namely, himself) was born and raised a Marrano. As such, it was and must remain unique. For those believers who obeyed Sabbatai's demand to follow him through the 'gate' of Islam, Cardozo had the most bitter derision.[5]

His rendering of Sabbatai's parting words also feels true. I do not understand these words, any more than Karillo and his unnamed companion did; I will not attempt any interpretation. It is their very obliqueness and obscurity that gives me the sense they are genuine. Sabbatai Zevi's entire life was an enigma. It is fitting that his last known words should remain an enigma, to haunt the generations.

THE TEXT

The passage that follows is taken from the long 'autobiographical letter' of Cardozo, written shortly after 1701 and preserved in one of the manuscripts of the Amarillo Collection. I translate the text published in 1960 by Isaac R. Molho and Abraham Amarilio.[6] I have not consulted the manuscript.

---

[3] Halperin, *Abraham Miguel Cardozo*, 60–70. On the fate of the treatise, see ibid. 327 n. 8.

[4] Ibid. 385 n. 5.

[5] It is ironic that the only people to preserve and indeed venerate Cardozo's memory were the Dönmeh, the descendants of those Salonican apostates whom Cardozo had spent much of his time denouncing.

[6] 'Autobiographical Letters of Abraham Cardozo' (Heb.), 185–241. The passage translated is on pp. 217–18.

᠄᠊

... On 2 Iyar [10 May 1682] Karillo came to Istanbul, accompanied by a man of some importance who had taken on the turban at Sabbatai Zevi's behest.[7] He wanted me to tell him whether he should go to Salonica to remove the turban and return to the Jewish fold.

I said I had no competence to issue rulings on this subject, and that they should go and ask the one who had made them wear the turban in the first place.[8] To which this man—a decent fellow, not a lunatic like Karillo—responded that 'whatever Your Worship tells me to do I am bound to do, as though it were the command of Sabbatai Zevi himself'. And, at my probing, he told me the following story:

In the year 5436 [Sabbatai Zevi] sent Mullah Ali from Alkum to Edirne,[9] to summon Karillo and myself. We arrived in Alkum three days before the New Year.[10] When we entered the room where our Lord was sitting, we found him engaged in reading a long letter. When he saw us, he bade us welcome, then left us standing a full half hour while he read the letter through twice and returned to the middle of it for a third reading.

'What can that letter be', Karillo said to him, 'that Your Worship keeps reading over and over again?'

'It was sent to me'—thus [Sabbatai] said to [us]—'by a certain scholar from the Maghreb whose name you already know: Abraham Cardozo, a great man indeed.'

'As great as Rabbi Jacob Ashkenazi?' Karillo asked.

'A very great man', [Sabbatai] replied.

Then I myself said to him: 'The man, it seems, is quite an intellect! Is he then Rabbi Nathan's equal?'

---

[7] Who was this second man? In another letter, written at about the same time of his life, Cardozo calls him 'Ali Chelebi', which was presumably the name he took upon his conversion to Islam (Molho and Amarilio, 'Autobiographical Letters of Abraham Cardozo' (Heb.), 200). Was he Abraham Gamaliel, who, as Najara tells us, converted to Islam together with Karillo? But Cardozo has already mentioned Gamaliel in the same letter, some thirty lines earlier, and called him by his Hebrew name (ibid. 199). Scholem suggests the second man may be either Isaac Haver or Abraham Ohev, who appear in a letter of Sabbatai's as 'friends and colleagues' of Karillo (*Sabbatai Sevi*, 917; above, Baruch of Arezzo, *Memorial*, §25). But there is no evidence for this, and I have my doubts whether Haver and Ohev actually existed. See above, n. 284 on Baruch of Arezzo.

[8] Which, nearly six years after Sabbatai Zevi's death, was not altogether easy to do.

[9] That is, from Dulcigno to Adrianople. 'Mullah Ali', presumably a Muslim devotee of Sabbatai's, appears again as his messenger in Israel Hazzan's commentary on the midnight-vigil liturgy; see Halperin, 'The Son of the Messiah', 183–4.

[10] And thus thirteen days before Sabbatai's death.

'I told you, he is a very great man indeed.'

'Your Worship seems then to intend', [Karillo] put in, 'that he is on a par with yourself?'

He grew angry at us then. 'He is an exceedingly great man, without any peer! He will be in Constantinople; go to him, and do whatever he bids you.'

After the New Year of 5437, he took us out to the seashore with him and said to us: 'Each of you go back home.[11] How long will you adhere to me? Until you see beneath that rock that is on the seashore, perhaps?' And we had no idea what he was talking about.

So we left Alkum, and he died on the Day of Atonement, early in the morning...

---

[11] *Shuvu ish el beito*, perhaps echoing 1 Kgs. 22: 17: 'I saw all Israel scattered on the mountains like a flock without a shepherd. And the Lord said, These have no master; let each of them go back home safely [*yashuvu ish leveito beshalom*].' Is Sabbatai suggesting his followers will soon be without their shepherd? Cf. Matt. 26: 31.

ɞ

Textual Notes to
Baruch of Arezzo's *Memorial*

In preparing my translation, I consulted the following manuscripts. As far as I know, they are the only manuscripts of the *Memorial* currently available.

C   Cambridge University, Or. 804. Italian, 17th–18th century.[1]

J   Jerusalem, Ben-Zvi Institute 2264. Italian, 18th–19th century.[2]

L_1 London, British Library Add. 26959. Italian, 17th–18th century.[3] The manuscript is incomplete, and breaks off in the middle of the list of names on p. 55, ll. 2–13 of Freimann's edition of the text.

L_2 London, British Library Add. 22096. Italian, 18th century.[4] The manuscript was plainly copied by an 'unbeliever' (see below, on p. 43, l. 16), yet is a careful and faithful copy of the 'second edition' of the *Memorial*. The copyist's citation of *Kitsur tsitsat novel tsevi* ('Epitome of "Zevi's Fading Flower"') practically guarantees a date after 1757.

M_1 Moscow, Russian State Library, MS Günzberg 528. Italian, 18th century. The manuscript is incomplete; one page, corresponding to Freimann, p. 48, l. 9–p. 49, l. 27, is missing, and the scribe seems simply to have stopped writing after p. 50, l. 3.

M_2 Moscow, Russian State Library, MS Günzberg 1456. Italian, 18th–19th century.

N   New York, Jewish Theological Seminary MS 3590. Italian, 18th century—written in a really beautiful formal hand.

O   Oxford, Bodleian Library MS 2226 (Mich. 479). Italian, 18th century.[5] This is the manuscript principally used by Freimann for his edition.

W_1 Warsaw, Żydówski Instytut Historyczny LIV. Italian, 18th century. This and the following manuscript were originally in the library of the

---

[1] Reif, *Hebrew Manuscripts at Cambridge University Library*, 312.

[2] Unless stated otherwise, information on the date and provenance of manuscripts is drawn from the online catalogue of the Institute of Microfilmed Hebrew Manuscripts, Jerusalem. I am immensely grateful to Dr Benjamin Richler of the Institute for having helped me—among all his other generous acts of assistance—to access this resource.

[3] Margoliouth, *Catalogue of the Hebrew and Samaritan Manuscripts in the British Museum*, iii. 440.   [4] Ibid. 434–5.

[5] Neubauer, *Catalogue of the Hebrew Manuscripts in the Bodleian Library and in the College Libraries of Oxford*, 767.

Jewish community (Israelitische Kultusgemeinde) of Vienna, from which they were loaned to Freimann by Abraham Epstein.[6] They were brought to Warsaw after the Second World War.[7] W₁, like L₂, represents the 'second edition' of the *Memorial*, and may possibly have been the source from which L₂ was copied.[8]

W₂   Warsaw, Żydówski Instytut Historyczny LV. Italian, 18th century. The copyist was plainly an 'unbeliever' (see below, on p. 44, l. 27), who worked in a hasty and careless fashion throughout. The variants in this text are usually of no significance except when, as sometimes happens, there is specific reason to think they may preserve an authentic reading (e.g. p. 48, l. 6; cf. n. 54 on the translation).

The textual notes below refer to page and line number of Freimann's edition in *Inyanei shabetai tsevi*, 43–78.

Preface

The entire preface is omitted from J,M₁,W₂.

43.1–3 ***Memorial . . . 5436.*** This title is omitted from all MSS except O (which Freimann followed), M₂,N. The latter two MSS make it into a full title page, with the words זכרון ... לפ״ק enclosed in a frame, within which is written Ps. 126: 1–3. Arching above the frame is Isa. 60: 21–2; within the arch is the abbreviation בהנ״א (M₂; = *be'ezrat hashem natsliaḥ amen?*) or בהנו״א (N; = *be'ezrat hashem na'aseh venatsliaḥ amen?*). This is done a great deal more prettily in N than in M₂.

After 43.16 (**I would exhaust my time without exhausting my subject**), the copyist of L₂ adds the following note in parentheses, introduced by the word *hagahah* ('annotation'): 'This author neglected to indicate where you might satisfy your thirst. Go therefore, dear reader, to consult *Kitsur tsitsat novel tsevi* ['Epitome of "Zevi's Fading Flower"'],[9] where you will see the false doctrines they have imputed to the Lord our God and His Torah, which are bound to appal anyone who hears them. And a

---

[6] Schwarz, *Die hebräische Handschriften in Österreich*, 91 (nos. 141,21 and 141,21a); Freimann, p. XI.   [7] Richler, *Guide to Hebrew Manuscript Collections*, 196.

[8] Below, on p. 73, l. 19. It seems conceivable that W₁ was itself the autograph of the 'second edition'; see on p. 76, l. 7 below.

[9] An abbreviated version of Jacob Sasportas's anti-Sabbatian treatise *Sefer tsitsat novel tsevi* ('Zevi's Fading Flower'; see the introduction to the letters of Joseph Halevi), prepared by David Meldola at the request of Sasportas's son Abraham. The first edition of *Kitsur tsitsat novel tsevi* (Amsterdam, 1737) was suppressed, and nearly all copies destroyed; it was republished at Altona in 1757 by the anti-Sabbatian zealot Jacob Emden, and it is presumably to this second edition that the copyist of L₂ refers. See Isaiah Tishby's introduction to *Sefer tsitsat novel tsevi*, pp. xli–xlii.

word to the wise is sufficient.' The copyist of L₂ is clearly hostile to Sabbatianism; his motive in copying the entire text of Baruch of Arezzo, without any comments or insertions other than this one, is a mystery. Cf. below, on p. 44, l. 27.

44.7   C,L₁,₂,W₁ add, before **Though you be dispersed**, the words 'The Lord will again rejoice over you for good, as He rejoiced over your fathers', from Deut. 30: 9.

44.14   **I have no need ... this *Memorial*.** I translate the fuller text of L₂,W₁ ('second edition'; cited by Freimann in a footnote).

44.18   **From it they will learn.** L₂,W₁: 'From it they will discern truth from falsehood, and will learn ... '.

44.22   **Thus shall they merit great benefit.** L₂,W₁ add, after these words: 'Thus may it be His will, that we all be found worthy to see the Lord's salvation! Amen!' Immediately afterwards, these two MSS give the passage that Freimann prints (in accordance with the other MSS) as p. 76, ll. 9–23. The shifting of this passage from the end to the beginning of the book is one of the more significant features of the 'second edition'; see the introduction to Baruch of Arezzo, above.

44.24   *of Arezzo*. N, and possibly also M₂ and O, read פאריצו (Parizzo?) for מאריצו ('of Arezzo'). I assume this is an error; but, given that we know Baruch only as the author of this book, it is worth recording.

1. Prophecies of the Messiah's 'Concealment'

All MSS, without exception, insert the title *zikaron livnei yisra'el* after p. 44, l. 24; all except L₁,₂ begin a fresh page with this title. The MS tradition therefore clearly represents ll. 25–8 as the introduction to what follows, not the conclusion of what precedes (as Freimann prints these lines).

44.27   *may his majesty be exalted*. After the abbreviation יר"ה (*yarum hodo*), W₂ inserts between slashes: שר"י, *shem resha'im yirkav*, 'may the name of the wicked rot'. This copyist, like the scribe of L₂, was obviously unsympathetic to his subject.

2. Sabbatai's Early Years

45.10   **the true facts may be discerned.** C,L₁,₂,W₁ add: 'And if I were to write everything, I would exhaust my time without having exhausted my subject.' Cf. the end of the second paragraph of the preface.

3. The Story of Sabbatai's Bride

45.25   **church.** *Beit tefilatam*; M₂ *to'avotam*, N *beit to'avotam*.

45.29   **Put on this leather garment.** C,L$_{1,2}$,M$_2$,N,W$_1$ add before these
words, in parentheses: 'He gave her a garment of leather.'

46.4   **and the truth she spoke.** Added in C,L$_{1,2}$,M$_2$,N,W$_{1,2}$.

4. Nathan of Gaza

46.18   **Elisha Ashkenazi.** All MSS except L$_2$,W$_{1,2}$ add after Elisha Ashkenazi's
name the abbreviation נר"ו, 'may the Merciful One guard and save him',
which is used for people who are still alive. This is curious: Elisha
Ashkenazi died in the summer of 1673 (Scholem, *Sabbatai Sevi*, 895),
while Baruch is clearly writing after Sabbatai's death in 1676. Presumably Baruch was at first unaware of Ashkenazi's death. The omission of
the abbreviation from L$_2$,W$_1$ confirms that these MSS represent a 'second edition' of the book, made after Ashkenazi's death had become
known. (In W$_2$, the omission is more likely to be the copyist's carelessness.)

5. Nathan's Visions

46.34   **Najara.** Freimann gives the name, on the basis of O, as 'Nayar' (נאייר);
L$_{1,2}$,W$_1$ have נאגייר. Both are acceptable variants of the name (*Encyclopedia Judaica*, art. s.v. 'Najara'). דאייר in M$_2$,N is presumably a corruption of the former variant, אגייר in C, of the latter.

47.13   **the honourable Rabbi Meir Rofé.** In place of the rabbinic title
כמהר"ר, C, L$_{1,2}$,W$_1$ have simply ר', 'Master Meir Rofé'. M$_1$: 'the rabbi,
the physician, the honourable Rabbi Meir' (החכם הרופא כמ"ר מאיר).

47.17   **they smelled.** C, L$_{1,2}$,W$_1$ repeat the perplexing *shame'u*, 'they heard',
as in l. 8 above (see n. 47 to the translation).

47.18–19 **gave a great sigh.** So J,L$_2$,M$_{1,2}$, *anah anahah*; L$_1$, *hitane'ah anahah* (cf.
C, *hitane'ah hanahah*). Freimann gives *nah hanahah*, N,W$_{1,2}$ *hanah
hanahah*.

47.27   **Sunday, 25 Elul.** This is the reading of most MSS. As noted in the
translation, it is problematic, since 25 Elul 5425 fell on Saturday. However, M$_2$,N (and possibly also W$_1$) read בה' in place of כ"ה—that is, '5
Elul' instead of '25 Elul', which *did* fall on Sunday (16 August 1665). Is it
possible that this is the original, correct reading? (But cf. Appendix 3.)

47.34   *In the year 5386.* Freimann, following O, gives the year as 5387. All the
other MSS have the correct year.

47.35   *shall be born.* All MSS have *yivaled.*

and his name shall be called Sabbatai. These words are in L$_{1,2}$,W$_1$;
other MSS omit them.

6. From Gaza to Izmir

48.6 **Rabbi Hayim.** $C, L_{1,2}, W_1$ give the name as 'Rabbi Hayim Hayim', W_2 as 'Rabbi Hagis' (חאגיס, not חאגיז, as Freimann gives the variant in his footnote).

judge of the city. L_2, W_1 give *moshel*, 'ruler', for *shofet*, 'judge'.

48.12 **which is Aram-Zova.** Omitted from L_2, W_1

48.16 **to the home of his brothers.** $C, L_{1,2}, W_1$ 'to his home, to the home of his brothers'.

7. Strange Deeds

48.31–2 **the melodies of his hymns.** All MSS except O have *ne'imot zemirotav* (not *ne'imotav uzemirotav*, the reading given by Freimann).

49.2 **who, as we have said, had wanted to kill him.** These words, absent from Freimann's text, are added in the majority of the MSS $(C, J, L_{1,2}, M_2, N, W_1)$. All these MSS except J put them in parentheses. Cf. below, p. 63, l. 33.

49.4 **and women as well.** So $C, L_{1,2}, W_1$. C seems overall to be an eclectic text, sometimes following the readings of the 'first edition', sometimes the 'second'. (See below, on the insertion following p. 66, l. 8.) Perhaps the same is true of the incomplete L_1?

49.8 **hoped-for.** So $C, J, L_{1,2}, M_2, N, W_1$. Freimann gives 'holy messiah'.

49.17 **friendliness and affection.** W_2 adds: 'They begged [the Jews] to consider them as friends and to do them no harm, for great fear had fallen upon them.' As noted above, W_2 is a highly eccentric MS, copied freely and carelessly by an unbeliever. This is perhaps a deliberate addition, intended to make the story more grotesque and absurd.

8. The Prophesying

49.34 **Pinto.** Following C, L_2, W_1. Other MSS have פינטי for פינטו.

49.35 **Bonomo.** So, with very slight variations, all MSS.

50.2 **Simhon.** Following C, L_1; cf. Scholem, *Sabbatai Sevi*, 256 n.
and prophetesses. Omitted from M_2.

50.3 **4 Shevat 5426.** M_1 breaks off after these words.

50.25 **words of truth.** *Veha'emet* attested by nearly all MSS.

9. Constantinople: The Messiah Arrested

50.33 **is on his way here.** $C, J, L_2, M_2, N, W_{1,2}$ give *oleh* for *alah*.

10. Venice Enquires of Constantinople

51.27 **this is our proper course**. Reading *vekhakh yafeh lanu*, with C,L₂,W₁ (instead of *vekhakh yavo lanu*); cf. Sasportas, *Sefer tsitsat novel tsevi*: *vekhen yafeh lanu*.

51.33 **To those enthroned ... and so forth**. These words are found only in the MSS of the 'second edition', L₂,W₁. They are the beginning of the letter's opening flowery address to the Venetian rabbis, given in full in Sasportas.

51.34 **Rabbi Israel** (first occurrence of the name). For *harav rabi yisra'el*, L₂,W₁ agree with Sasportas's text in giving the more modest *rabi yisra'el*, 'Master Israel'. So also at p. 52, l. 1.

52.13 **as is the action taken by Rabbi Israel**. Freimann's text, which separates *vetov veyafeh* from what precedes and treats these two adjectives as modifying *ma'aseh harav rabi yisra'el*, makes good sense but has no support in the MSS. All of these, supported by Sasportas, have *uma'aseh*; I translate the awkward sentence as best I can. Perhaps we would do best to read *uma'asei*, with Sasportas, and understand this as the plural subject of the following *shelemim*. But the MSS of the *Memorial* clearly put a break between *yisra'el* and *shelemim*.

52.15 **thus speaks ... Abraham Yakhini my name**. L₁ omits.

11. The Messiah in Captivity

53.1 **Krotoschin**. This is Freimann's very plausible emendation. The MSS give קרושטין or some variant thereof, often replacing *resh* with *dalet*.

53.3 **a white robe, interwoven with gold**. L₂,W₁: 'a golden robe of white gold' (*malbush zahav shel zahav lavan*).

12. What Happens to Dissenters

53.22 **over the strange acts he had performed**. L₂,W₁ omit.

53.23 **fifty-four rabbis**. Freimann's 'twenty-four' is a misreading of the abbreviation *nun-dalet* as *kaf-dalet*. (In MS O, which Freimann followed, the *nun* and the *kaf* are very similar.) J,W₂ have the same abbreviation; L₁,W₁ spell out the number *arba'ah vahamishim*; the misreadings of C,L₂,M₂,N are explicable on the basis of this latter reading.

54.6 **Canton**. C,L₁,W₁ 'Boton' (Sasportas's reading); L₂ בנטון is presumably an error for either 'Canton' or 'Boton'.

54.9 **two worthy rabbis**. L₂,W₁ omit 'worthy'.

54.15 **divisions**. The plural is attested by all MSS except L₁, which has *yirbeh mahloket*. It is found also in Sasportas.

54.17 **Yet we, thank God, shall make the ascent**. Freimann's *va'anahnu al na'aleh* is a misreading. All MSS, O included, have ל"ת (= *tehilah le'el*) in place of *al*. Cf. Sasportas's text, which, however, corrupts *na'aleh* into *olam*. The original text of this sentence can be reconstructed as: *va'anahnu tehilah le'el na'aleh | ayin be'ayin nehezeh | beviat hago'el | uvevinyan ha'ari'el.* (*Nehezeh* for *nireh*, in C,L₁ and in Sasportas, better suits the rhythm of the jingle.)

54.19–20 **ibn Yakar . . . ibn Jamil**. Most MSS have Arabic 'ibn', not Hebrew 'ben'. Sasportas's text has 'Benjamin' for 'ibn Jamil', 'David Anigo'(?) for 'David Anaf'. Tishby, in his edition of Sasportas (*Sefer tsitsat novel tsevi*, 134 n. 10) suggests this last should be 'David Anavi', who appears in another source as rabbi in Constantinople in 1656.

54.26 **foundation of the world**. L₂ omits *yesod olam*. This is evidently a careless error, for the words are present in W₁ (representing, like L₂, the 'second edition').

54.29 **our rabbis**. Which 'rabbis' are intended? C,L₁,M₂,N read ל"זר or ל"ז, indicating the ancient rabbis of the Mishnah and the Talmud. Sasportas gives רבותינו רבני ישראל נר"ו, indicating that the 'rabbis' in question are still alive. J,L₂,O,W₁,₂ conflate the two in an impossible combination: רבותינו ז"ל נר"ו, רז"ל נר"ו, or the like (so Freimann's text). The context clearly favours Sasportas's reading.

55.2–13 **we affix our signatures**. I follow the layout of names in MS N. The MSS variously give the names in one, two, or three columns, or as straight text. The proper order of the signatures, at least as understood by the copyists of the *Memorial*, is across the columns and not down. Sasportas seems to have had a two-column text, very much like that of O, and copied down the second column and afterwards down the first.

[7] **Volesir**. Sasportas gives the name as 'Vilesid'. A 'Master Jacob Vilisid' turns up in Cardozo's reminiscences as living in Haskoy—one of the main Jewish neighbourhoods of Constantinople—some time around 1690. Quite possibly he was the son of this Joseph Volesir/Vilesid. ('The wealthy and powerful Joseph Uzziel', who plays a villainous role in the same anecdote, may have been a relative of the 'Abraham Uzziel' who appears as no. 11 on this list.[10])

[8, 14, 30] **Canarbon**. J,M₂,N have *dalet* for *resh* in all three occurrences. Sasportas gives the more plausible 'Cordon' in the first two occurrences, 'Rosanes' in the third.

---

[10] Halperin, *Abraham Miguel Cardozo*, 297, 392 n. 60.

[9] **Joseph Bon Roi**. All MSS have *bon ro'i*, here and in no. 13, except for J,O (*ben ro'i*) and W$_2$ (*ibn ro'i*). Sasportas gives 'Bon Rey'. L$_2$,W$_1$, in agreement with Sasportas, give the first name as 'Jacob'.

[19–20] All MSS of the *Memorial* corrupt these two names and conflate them into one, with the result that the list of signatories has only forty-one names instead of the necessary forty-two (see n. 103 to the translation). Sasportas gives the names as 'Israel Ya'ish' and 'Polibron[?] Yo'av'. The second name in the *Memorial* (יעץ in all MSS) is clearly a corruption of 'Ya'ish'. What may lurk behind 'Philomomeno' (J,O,N; cf. M$_2$ פילומומנו, L$_2$,W$_1$ פילומירונו, L$_1$ בנילמורונו, C בטלומוסונו) we can only guess.

[22] **Narvoni**. Sasportas gives the name, more accurately, as 'Narboni'.

[23] **Cavazon**. Sasportas: 'Cavison'.

[35] **Jehiel Alguades**. Following Sasportas; all MSS of the *Memorial* (including O) have *resh* in place of *dalet*. Ms L$_1$ breaks off after the name 'Alguades'.

[36] **Soria**. Sasportas gives the name as 'Suares'.

[42] **David Samson**. Sasportas: 'David Samson Ashkenazi'.

13. What Happens to Dissenters—Continued

55.20   **On the forty-first of the Torah's reckoning**. Freimann's reading *lema'an hatorah* is found only in the careless and unreliable W$_2$, from which Freimann apparently took it. All the other MSS, including Freimann's O, have *leminyan hatorah*. The expression is reminiscent of *leminyan beit yisra'el*, 'according to the reckoning of the house of Israel', used to refer to the counting of the Omer.[11] This will suggest that the preceding abbreviation במ"א does not stand for *bemitsvat adoni* ('by command of my lord'), as Tishby suggests, but indicates, after the preposition, the numeral '41'. The context, too, would suggest some sort of date is appropriate here.

But what is 'the Torah's reckoning'? It cannot be the Omer, since the Torah portion 'Shelaḥ', from which Num. 13: 27 is taken, was read in the synagogue on sabbath, 16 Sivan 5426 (19 June 1666). The 'week of that Torah portion' therefore would be the week ending 16 Sivan—about two weeks too late to coincide with the forty-first day of the Omer.

Or is it possible the implied subject of 'forty-first' is not 'day' but 'week', referring to the weekly readings from the Pentateuch into which

---

[11] Tishby's note to Sasportas, *Sefer tsitsat novel tsevi*, 111.

the Jewish liturgical year is divided? This might be suggested by the reading of L₂,W₁, which replace 'in the week . . . fruit' (*bes[idrat] zavat ḥalav udevash vezeh piryah*) with *vekhu* ('etc.'), as if this statement of the letter's date is a redundant extension of what precedes. This would make excellent sense of *leminyan hatorah*. Unfortunately, however, 'Shelaḥ' is not the forty-first of the pentateuchal lections but the thirty-seventh. Perhaps this hypothesis can be maintained if we suppose that Sabbatai, with his penchant for tampering with the liturgy and its calendar, had invented some lectionary division that differed slightly from the standard (cf. Appendix 3). Otherwise the meaning of 'the forty-first of the Torah's reckoning' must remain, at least for the present, an unsolved mystery.

56.5   **pen.** Literally, 'the tip of the pen' (*kets hakolmos*). All MSS, including O, have ק״ץ; Freimann's קן is an error, perhaps based on the Talmud (BT *Giṭ. 6a*).

15. The Fast Abolished

57.2   **Again the boy pulled one out.** So C,J,M₂,W₂; more concisely, in L₂,W₁.

57.17   **my spirit and my light.** All MSS except W₂ give the practically untranslatable reading *ruḥi ve'anokhi*. Freimann emends *ruḥi venafshi*, 'my spirit and my soul', in accord with W₂, and this is supported by Sasportas's text (p. 130). But it is hard to prefer the careless W₂ over the unanimous reading of the other MSS. A parallel text quoted in Sasportas, p. 78—supported by the Dönmeh festival calendar[12]—reads *ruḥi ve'ori*, 'my spirit and my light', which seems preferable to the redundant 'my spirit and my soul'. The MSS' *ve'anokhi* is an easy corruption of *ve'ori*.

16. Sabbatai Before the Sultan

58.14–16   **it having become common knowledge . . . dreadful deed there.** All MSS except J either put these words in parentheses (L₂,M₂, N,O,W₁) or in smaller script than the surrounding words (C); W₂ omits nearly all the passage.
      For *kemo shenoda*, C,L₂,W₁ have *kemo she'aḥar ken noda*, 'as became known afterwards'. J has *kemo*[13] *shehem yode'im*; M₂,N *kemo sheharei ken noda*, which I suspect is a conflation of *kemo shenoda* and *sheharei ken noda*. I further suspect that the reading of C,L₂,W₁—which, as pointed

---

[12] Benayahu, *The Sabbatian Movement in Greece* (Heb.), 288.
[13] Or *kefi*; the word is difficult to make out.

out in n. 164 to the translation, does not suit the context very well—is an error based on the reading of M₂,N (perhaps via *aḥarei ken*, which occurs in none of the MSS).

58.21   **Mehmed.** The MSS give different forms for the name. J,W₂ have מחמיד ('Mehmed'), C,L₂,W₁ מאימיט ('Me'emet'); M₂,N conflate מאימיט with a corrupt reading עֶחְעֶיד that certainly was originally מחמיד. O, followed by Freimann, gives מימיט.

17. Nathan's Journeys Begin

58.28   **him whom our Lord had called 'Benjamin'.** Placed between parentheses (or slashes) in C,L₂,M₂,N,W₁; C also puts these words in small script.

58.35   **Benjamin Halevi . . . Solomon.** I translate the reading of L₂,W₁ (the 'second edition'), which is slightly clearer than that of the other MSS, although the meaning is the same.

59.5   **as the proverb says.** For *kakh omer hamashal*, M₂,N give *vekhakh ani omer hamshel vafaḥad imo oseh shalom*, quoting Job 25: 2. I cannot imagine this is anything but a bizarre error.

18. Nathan's Epistle to Joseph Zevi

The hostile copyist of W₂ omits the entire document, summarizing it with the unhelpful words: 'as it is recorded in my notebook; you may consult that'.

59.14   **enwrapped.** Reading מעטה (*me'uteh*), with J,M₂,N, for *ma'aseh* in the other MSS. This reading is supported by Sasportas's text.

59.24   **not until.** Reading *ki im*, with Sasportas's text, for *ken anu*, found in all MSS of Baruch.

59.28   **on the Torah portion 'Naso'.** Omitted by C,L₂,W₁.

60.9   **who hold this opinion.** So all MSS of Baruch: *she'omedim basevarah hanizkeret*. Sasportas's text reads *ha'omedim behevratam keniz[kar]*, 'who stand in their company, as has been indicated'.

60.18   **Careful scrutiny . . . will reveal.** Sasportas, and all MSS of Baruch except O (followed by Freimann), read *tedakdek* and not *medakdek*.

60.22   ***Tikunei zohar.*** Sasportas, and all MSS of Baruch except O, have *besefer hatikunim*. O's בס' הפי (so Freimann) is apparently a careless error.

60.37   **and be ashamed.** Sasportas's text, and L₂,W₁, supply *veyikalemu*; other MSS of Baruch omit.

19. Nathan in Venice

61.20   **the day before Passover.** L₂,W₁, 'Monday, the day before Passover'. This is correct: the first day of Passover did fall on Tuesday in 1668.

61.25   **They then conveyed him to the Jews.** L₂,W₁ add 'in the ghetto' (using the Italian word).

62.4   **Modona.** W₂ has 'Modena'.

62.5   **Rabbi Samuel Formiggini, who was my uncle.** C,J omit 'who was my uncle'. L₂,W₁: 'my noble uncle, Rabbi Samuel Formiggini'. The MSS give various spellings for 'Formiggini': פורמיזינו (C), פורמיזן (L₂), פורמיגייסו (M₂), פורמיזין (N), פורמיזון (W₁); J is illegible at this point.

62.10   **a doltish folk and a cunning one.** L₂ omits *vehakham*. This is evidently an error—or the copyist's discomfort with the apparent oxymoron— since the word does occur in W₁.

62.11   **a Christian servant.** *Eved* ('servant'), for Freimann's *avar*, in C,J,L₂,M₂,N (but W₁ seems to have *avar*). L₂,W₁ omit *arel*, 'Christian' (literally, 'uncircumcised').

20. Nathan's Travels, Concluded

62.24   **the mission.** All MSS, including O, read *ma'aseh hashelihut*. (The copyist of N, however, accidentally wrote *hashelemut* for *hashelihut*.) Freimann's *ma'asei hashelihim* is apparently Freimann's own error, perhaps based on the Hebrew title of the New Testament Acts of the Apostles.

62.26   **Caleb Hakohen.** C,L₂,W₁ add: 'of the city of Corfu'.

63.11   **verbal diarrhoea.** For *hitrizu*, L₂,W₁ give *hiftsiru*, M₂,N *heheziru*. These may be understood as attempts to soften Nathan's disgusting image.

63.16   **the Christians.** C,L₂,W₁ read *hagoyim* ('the gentiles') for *ha'arelim*.

63.23   **[Nathan] set out ... length and breadth.** C,L₂,W₁: '[Nathan] set out for the Turkish land, travelling its length and breadth, and the land of the Morea ...'.

63.27   **Kastoria.** C gives 'Constantinople', certainly in error.

21. The Messiah as Muslim

63.30–1 **with wine and blessings recited in a loud voice.** I translate the reading of C, *im hayayin vehaberakhot bekol ram*; cf. L₂,W₁, *im haberakhot* *ve'im hayayin bekol ram*. The other MSS (and Freimann) have *im haber-akhot al hayayin bekol ram*, 'reciting the blessings over the wine in a loud voice'. But Baruch's point seems to be not that those specific blessings were recited 'in a loud voice', but that wine was part of the ceremony (which it certainly would not have been at a Muslim circumcision) and that *all* the ritual blessings were chanted loudly and without shame.

63.32 **a daughter ... named.** All MSS either leave a blank space or draw a horizontal line (L$_2$) after *shemah*. Presumably Baruch did not know the name of Sabbatai's daughter, but believed he ought to record it and left a space in his text where he could insert it. (Yet he leaves Sarah unnamed, and gives no name for any of the other women in his narrative.)

63.33 **who ... once tried to kill him.** The words *oto sheratsah lehorgo ka'asher amarnu* are omitted from J,W$_2$, placed in parentheses in L$_2$,M$_2$,N,W$_1$,[14] small script and parentheses in C.

63.34 **the pure turban.** C,J,L$_2$,W$_1$ omit *hatahor*, 'pure'.

64.1 **a sixteen-month journey.** For *shishah-asar hodashim*, C,L$_2$,W$_1$ give *shishah hodashim*: 'a six-month journey'.

the Uzbeks. All MSS have לזבעק (presumably pronounced 'al-Uzbek') except for W$_2$, which corrupts it into לובען. The reading לובעק ('Lübeck'), attributed by Freimann to W$_2$, does not exist in the MSS. The German city of Lübeck would in any case have nothing to do with Great Tartary or China.

64.2 **China.** Written קינה or קינא in most of the MSS, סינה in M$_2$,N.

64.3 **Maragheh.** So C,L$_2$,M$_2$,W$_1$: מראגא or מראגה, corrupted to מראנא in N and מרגזה in W$_2$. Freimann's reading 'Praga' occurs in J,O. Rapoport-Albert, basing herself on Freimann, identifies 'Praga' as a town near Warsaw (later a suburb of Warsaw), or possibly Bohemian Prague.[15] But Iranian Maragheh belongs at least roughly to the geographical area where the events are set; Warsaw and Prague do not.

64.4 **Rabbi Nissim.** Attested by all MSS. Freimann's emendation *harbeh nisim* ('many miracles') has no support in the MSS, and does not suit the context.

64.19 **Yitzhaki.** So all MSS (including O) except W$_2$. Freimann's reading *yitshak* follows W$_2$.

64.24 **all living creatures.** C,L$_2$,W$_{1,2}$ supply *hai* after *me'enei kol*.

64.30 **Me'emet.** L$_2$,O,W$_1$ vocalize the name with three *segols* (not *hataf segol* under the *alef*, as Freimann prints it); W$_1$ adds a *dagesh* in the final letter.

---

[14] L$_2$,W$_1$ give *katavnu*, 'we have written', for *amarnu*, 'we have related'.
[15] Rapoport-Albert, 'On the Position of Women in Sabbatianism' (Heb.), 161 n.

C writes the name in enlarged script. M₂ corrupts it into מאמיכם, N into מאמינים.

Zevi. Following the text of the letter given in the 19th-century MS *Sefer to'ei ruaḥ*:[16] *zeh hasha'ar la'adonai tsevi*. All MSS of Baruch give the full biblical verse: *zeh hasha'ar la'adonai tsadikim yavo'u vo*. Scholem remarks that the text quoted in *To'ei ruaḥ* is plainly the original.

22. The Letter of Solomon Katz

65.2   **beadle of […].** The name of the town is given in most MSS as מוויאינה, J מוויאנה, L₂,W₁ מוויאינה. Conceivably the first letter is the prefix *mi-*, in which case it is possible the name may be 'Vienna' (as suggested by Scholem, in a marginal annotation to his copy of Freimann's *Inyanei shabetai tsevi*[17]).

65.5   **Brody.** So L₂,W₁, בראד. Most of the MSS give this name in corrupted form: בדאד (M₂,N), בראר (C), כדאר (J,O,W₂).

65.8   **the Ninth to the Fifteenth day of Av.** All MSS but O read: בט' באב עד ט"ו בו ועד בכלל. O omits the *vav* of *vo*, which led Freimann to the erroneous reading עד טו"ב, 'to the Seventeenth'.

65.15   **their evil intent abandoned.** *Mera'at levavam* (L₂,M₂,N,W₂), corrupted into *mera'at levavekhem* (J), *mida'at levavam* (C,W₁), and from there to *mida'at*, with *levavam* omitted (O, followed by Freimann).

65.16   **the time is close at hand.** Following L₂,W₁, *bekarov hadavar* (other MSS, *hadibur*).

65.17   **Buda.** *Budon* (בודון) in all MSS but C, which corrupts the name into בודין. בורדן is Freimann's error.

65.27   **Denan.** דינאן, corrupted into ריבאן in M₂, ריכאן in N. W₂'s reading דנון would support Scholem's suggestion that this is the familiar Sephardi name Danon, but it stands alone in the least reliable of the MSS. The notation in Rovigo's notebook spells the name דנן.[18]

23. The Banishment of Sabbatai Zevi

66.5   **the worthy Rabbi.** C,L₂,W₁ add *heḥasid hagadol*, 'the great pietist'.

66.6   **Magueres.** Spelled מגיידיס in C, מגייאריס in N, מיגייאריס in J, מייאריס in L₂,W₁, מגיידין in M₂. O's מגייאדים (so Freimann) is an easy corruption of N's reading. W₂ gives the more familiar form מגאר.

---

[16] Scholem, 'New Sabbatian Documents from the Book *To'ei ruaḥ*' (Heb.), 49.
[17] In the Scholem Collection of the Jewish National and University Library, Jerusalem.
[18] Sonne, 'New Material on Sabbatai Zevi' (Heb.), 57–9.

66.7   **believe in him**. All MSS except C,O have *bo* after *ma'amin*.

66.8   **along with [Magueres'] brother**. C gives *ve'ahiha*, 'along with her brother'; all other MSS have *ve'ahiv*, 'his brother'. I see no good reason to prefer the reading of C, and to suppose that the reference is to Sarah Majar's brother David (who in any case clearly survived her).[19] It is reasonable enough that the girl's uncle should have been intended to accompany her.

After l. 8, C,L$_2$,W$_1$ insert the following story:

> In those days the unbelievers lodged a complaint against our Lord with the king,[20] through one of his eunuchs. 'Has not this Zevi converted and become a Muslim?' said [the eunuch] to him. 'Yet he still goes about with [Jewish] ritual fringes, wears phylacteries on his head, prays in the synagogue and keeps all the commandments, just like any Jew!' Said the king:[21] 'Leave [pl.] him to do whatever he pleases. I have no power over him.' And [the accusers] departed,[22] disappointed and angry.

This story is plainly an addition, drawn in part from the narrative that follows. It reflects the tendency, which Cuenque's hagiography carries to its absurd extreme, to represent Sabbatai as the real power within the sultan's court, and the sultan as his helpless, grovelling slave. (The Baruch of the 'first edition', for all his wishful thinking, still knew perfectly well who had power over whom.) Its presence in C,L$_2$,W$_1$ is a highly important testimony to the development of the text of the *Memorial*, as reflected in the various MSS.

24. Events in Dulcigno and Kastoria

67.12   **the name ... Rabbi Nathan**. All MSS except O (and J, which omits most of ll. 12–14 through homoioteleuton) give *shemo veshem iro* for both Sabbatai and Nathan. L$_2$,W$_1$ reverse the order of the clauses, putting Nathan before Sabbatai.

67.17   **the garb of the Muslims**. For *levush yishma'el*, L$_2$,W$_1$ have *levush tugar*, 'the garb of the Turks'. 'Their language' would then be Turkish.

67.19–20 **They recite ... benediction**. L$_2$,W$_1$: 'They recite "eternal love" and the Shema with its benedictions'.

67.23   **5736**. L$_2$,W$_1$, 5735. J gives the impression of having originally written 5735, then corrected it to 5736.

---

[19] Ibid. 61–2. Sonne's interpretation of Baruch's text seems very strained.
[20] L$_2$,W$_1$: 'the Turkish king'.
[21] L$_2$,W$_1$: 'the king answered him'.   [22] L$_2$,W$_1$: 'and he departed'.

67.24   **moḥan**. So all MSS except J (*mofan*). Freimann's *moran* is without basis in the MSS.

25. Epistles of Sabbatai Zevi

L_2, W_1 change the order of the documents, placing p. 68, ll. 6–17 (the letters to Sofia and Karillo) before p. 67, l. 36–p. 68, l. 5 (the letter to Filosoff). W_2 omits p. 68, ll. 13–17 (the letter to Karillo).

68.2   **blessed be they to the Lord**. *Berukhim hem* in all MSS except O (followed by Freimann), which abbreviates *hem* in such a way as to make it appear that *hashem*, 'the Lord', is intended.

68.10   **and the Lord of hosts is exalted in judgment**. All MSS but O give *shegavah* for biblical *vayigbah* (Isa. 5: 16). O's reading, however, is supported by the fuller text of the original document published by Rubashov,[23] and flows better in the context. I can only assume that *shegavah* is an error made by Baruch himself or his earliest copyists, which O accurately corrected on the basis of the biblical verse.

26. 'Concealment'

68.18   **5437**. The correct year is given in C,M$_2$,N. J omits the year altogether (although the following abbreviation, לפ״ק, shows it must have been present in J's source); the other MSS have 5736.

68.22   **They carried . . . their way**. L_2, W_1 omit this sentence.

68.27   **the entire house**. The MSS unanimously read *kol habayit* ('the entire house'), which makes no sense in context. Freimann's *kol hama'arah*, 'the entire cave', is his own emendation.

    Was Baruch perhaps influenced by the Zohar's account of the death of Rabbi Simeon ben Yohai (iii. 296*b*, *Idra zuta*)? In this passage Rabbi Simeon is in his house, surrounded by the other rabbis. As Rabbi Simeon dies[24] (says the narrator, Rabbi Abba), 'I did not lift up my head because the light was very great and I was not able to look. . . . All that day the fire did not cease from the house, and there was no one who came near to [Rabbi Simeon's body] because they could not, for light and fire surrounded him all that day. . . . Once the fire was gone, I saw that the Holy Lamp, Holies of Holies, had departed [*istalak*] the world.' The body is subsequently carried to its burial cave.

    The three elements of house, light, and cave are found in this narrative, as in the passage from Baruch. The 'house' plays no role in

---

[23] 'Sabbatian Documents from Aleppo' (Heb.). See n. 280 on the translation.

[24] The Zohar's verb is *istalak*; Baruch uses the Hebrew equivalent *histalek* to speak of Sabbatai Zevi's 'departure'.

Baruch's story; yet the 'light', that properly belongs in the 'cave', is transferred to the 'house' under the Zohar's influence. Otherwise I can think of no explanation for the strange reading found in all the MSS.

68.32   **saw our Lord**. C,L₂,W₁: 'gave reliable testimony that he had seen our Lord'.

68.33   **Malvasia**. Variously spelled מלוסיאה (J,M₂,N,O), מלואסיאה (W₂), מלוסיאה (L₂), מלואסיאה (W₁), מלואסיאסו (C). The variant cited in Freimann's footnote, מלמאסיה, is a misreading of W₁, where the doubled *vav* is written in a way that very much resembles *mem*.

69.1, 4   **Rabbi Nathan Benjamin**. In both lines, Freimann's edition follows the name with the abbreviation נר"ו, implying Nathan is still alive. Given that this passage seems to describe Nathan's death, this is strange indeed.

The situation in the MSS is more complicated. J,M₂,N,O,W₂ have נר"ו in both passages; C has it in l. 4 but omits it in l. 1. L₂,W₁ omit the abbreviation in both passages, along with the name 'Benjamin' (*rabi natan* for *gam heḥakham rabi natan binyamin* נר"ו in l. 1, *harav rabi natan* for *harav rabi natan binyamin* נר"ו in l. 4). On p. 68, l. 29, all MSS except C put נר"ו after 'Moses our Master'. It would seem that Baruch originally wanted to give the impression that, like Moses, Nathan of Gaza had not died, at least not in any permanent sense. He had simply 'departed', disappeared, gone to join his messiah in the land beyond the Sambatyon. In the 'second edition', represented by L₂,W₁, Baruch (or whoever was responsible for this form of the text) was prepared to acknowledge Nathan was indeed dead. Whether this is linked with the variant reading in L₂,W₁ at the beginning of p. 69, l. 1, I cannot say.

69.1   **a year or two later**. L₂,W₁: 'about a year after the departure of our Lord' (*kemo shanah aḥat aḥar siluk adonenu*, in place of *kemo shanah o shenayatim*).

69.3   **messiah of the God of Jacob**. L₂,W₁: 'messiah son of David', thereby contrasting Sabbatai Zevi with the 'messiah son of Joseph' whose story follows.

69.4   **the true and righteous prophet**. Several MSS make a major break after these words. J follows them with *tam venishlam uvda shel shabetai tsevi veshel harav natan binyamin* נר"ו ('the story of Sabbatai Zevi and Rabbi Nathan Benjamin נר"ו is done'), then fills the rest of the page with geometric designs. The page that follows begins with *zikaron livnei yisra'el* (in large formal script, centred on the page), followed by *he lakh ma'aseh biketsarah shel habaḥur yosef ben tsur mashiaḥ ben yosef* ('Here you have the story, briefly told, of the young man Joseph ben [*sic*] Tsur, messiah ben Joseph'). These words, written in large cursive script and centred on the page, replace 'Now we shall briefly narrate . . . Joseph' (ll. 4–5) of the other MSS.

N, whose layout I have followed in the translation, separates the paragraph beginning 'These are but the smallest . . . ' from what precedes by a blank space, and from the paragraph beginning 'Now we shall briefly narrate . . . ' with a decorative horizontal squiggle. Then comes another blank space, and then the beginning of the story of Joseph ibn Tsur.

M$_2$, whose readings generally accord with N's, has 'These are but the smallest . . . ' as a paragraph at the bottom of a page, followed by a triangle of dots. 'Now we shall briefly narrate . . . ' is a paragraph at the top of the next page.

Other MSS (C,L$_2$,O,W$_1$) do not separate these two paragraphs from one another with lines, spaces, or the like, but they do keep them as distinct paragraphs (none of the MSS, in other words, runs them together into one paragraph, as Freimann does). L$_2$—and, less obviously, W$_1$—leave the rest of the page blank after the 'Now we shall briefly narrate . . .' paragraph. O does much the same, but in addition marks off the 'Now we shall briefly narrate . . .' paragraph from what follows with the abbreviation תשלב"ע, *tam shevaḥ le'el bore olam* ('it is completed, praise be to God, the world's Creator'). W$_2$ gives 'These are but the smallest . . .' as a distinct paragraph, and leaves out the 'Now we shall briefly narrate . . .' paragraph entirely.

The title *Ma'aseh miyosef ben tsur* ('The Story of Joseph ben Tsur'), at the top of p. 73 of Freimann's edition, is supplied by Freimann himself.

27. The Story of Joseph ibn Tsur

73.2–3 **neither in a dream nor in a waking state.** All MSS but W$_2$ have *lo behalom velo behakits*. W$_2$ omits the first *lo*: 'in a dream and not in a waking state'. J has some odd squiggles around this first *lo*, which may possibly be intended to convey that it should be deleted.

73.3 **Joseph ibn Tsur.** All MSS but O,W$_2$ use Arabic 'ibn', not Hebrew 'ben'.

73.8 **Pakats.** All MSS, including O, have פק"ץ, not Freimann's מק"ץ. This is obviously the correct reading, since otherwise medial *mem* would appear twice in the sequence, *peh* not at all. At the end of the series, צמ"ך נ"ץ appear as two distinct words in J,L$_2$,O,W$_{1,2}$, are collapsed into one word in M$_2$, and are corrupted into צמסנ"ץ in C, צמרנ"ץ in N.

73.19 **Marrakesh, Tetuan, Salé, and other places.** Thus C,M$_2$,N,W$_{1,2}$ מרוקוס (J מרוקנס); vs. L$_2$,O *mimekom*, 'from the place of Tetuan, Salé, and other places' (so Freimann). W$_1$ writes מרוקוס in a way that is almost indistinguishable from ממקום, and I suspect this is the origin of L$_2$'s error. O's reading presumably originated in the same way, independently.

73.28   **their evil opinion.** Reading *mera'at levavam*, with L$_2$,M$_2$,N,W$_{1,2}$, vs. *mida'at levavam* (C,O; J omits the passage).

74.8   **as his tribute from the Christians.** Reading *kemas mehanotserim* (N,W$_{1,2}$; cf. M$_2$, *bemas*). The alternative reading, *kamah mehanotserim*, 'a number [of young boys] from among the Christians', is possible but awkward; one would expect *kamah* to follow *mehanotserim*, not to precede it. (The latter reading is supported by C,J,L$_2$,O. This is one of the very few cases where L$_2$ accords with the reading of other MSS, against W$_1$; cf. above, on p. 73, l. 19.)

74.11   **Rabbi Isaac Luria . . . in his writings.** All MSS but W$_2$ have *vekhuleh*, 'and so forth', at the end of this line. W$_2$: *vedok vetishkaḥ*, 'examine and you will find'; i.e. search the Lurianic writings for yourself and you will find support for this statement. Perhaps *vekhuleh* is intended to make the same point.

28. Correspondence Concerning Joseph ibn Tsur

74.12   **ibn Amram.** Arabic *ibn* ('ן) in J,L$_2$,M$_2$,N,W$_1$.

74.25   **full water-skin.** *Nod male* נאד מלא in C,J,L$_2$,W$_{1,2}$, the first word corrupted into שאר in M$_2$,N. O's *nahar male*, followed by Freimann, is an obvious error.

74.26   **come pouring out.** C,L$_2$,W$_1$ add *bekho'aḥ*, 'forcefully'.

75.10–11   **amen! . . . name!** J omits.

75.13   **for that reason.** C,O (followed by Freimann) add *vekhule*. If this is original, it presumably indicates there is more to Aboab's letter which Baruch does not intend to transcribe.

76.1   **special finery.** *Malbushim* ר"ל [*rotseh lomar*] *bigdei kavod*. For ר"ל, M$_2$,N give the interesting variant *kelei lavan*, 'white garments of special finery'.

29. Concluding Reflections

76.6   **all knew clearly.** For *yade'u bidiah berurah*, M$_2$N give *de'u bidiah berurah*, 'be clearly aware'.

76.7   **His plan.** Following C,J,M$_2$,W$_2$, *atsato* (corrupted in N,O into *atsmo*). Freimann's reading *devaro* is found only in the 'second edition' (L$_2$,W$_1$), and in W$_1$ it gives the impression of having been written on top of an erasure. Presumably Baruch's text has been 'corrected'—or, perhaps, Baruch has corrected his own text—in accordance with Jer. 23: 18, from which the first two sentences of this paragraph are drawn.

76.7–8 **surely He will show us marvels.** *Veyarenu niflaot*, found in all MSS except L₂,W₁ (followed by Freimann), which give *hu berahamav yarenu niflaot*, 'may He in His mercy show us marvels'. Baruch's original certainty, that God 'will show us marvels and speed our salvation', is modified in the 'second edition' into a pious wish.

76.9–23 **Final repentance and final redemption . . . our righteousness about to be revealed.** L₂,W₁ (the 'second edition') transfer this entire passage to the preface, into the middle of p. 44, l. 22. Cf. the textual note there. The concluding words in l. 23, 'For our salvation . . . to be revealed', occur in most MSS both here and in the preface (p. 44, l. 22); in L₂,W₁ they occur only in the preface.

76.29 **Master Joseph ibn Tsur.** L₂,W₁ omit.

76.31 **similarly.** L₂,W₁ omit, reading *veharbeh* for *vegam harbeh*, and thereby perhaps avoiding the implication that the 'prophets' Nathan and Joseph ibn Tsur are in the same category as the scholarly speculators described by Ibn Yahya.

76.34 **when God shall again settle . . . upon him.** So J,M₂,N,O,W₂, *ki yashuv adonai lehashrot*; versus C,L₂,W₁ (followed by Freimann), *ki yosif adonai shenit yado lehashrot*, 'when God shall extend His hand a second time to settle His holy spirit upon him'.

77.6 **the year 5470.** M₂,N,O, 'the year 5475'. If this reading is correct, it points to a different understanding of *ayin–tav–heh* from the one set forth in §27 above: the *heh* is treated as 5 (as it normally would be in calculations of this sort) and added on to the 470 of *ayin–tav*, the millennium being taken for granted.

77.13–15 **and the believers . . . will pay for it.** L₂,W₁ omit this entire passage, and, by omitting also the following *yehi ratson she-*, turn the pious wish of the conclusion into a prediction. ('Our eyes shall witness the King . . . we shall see our holy and splendid Temple rebuilt' etc.)

   The text of the remaining MSS is difficult. I follow the reading of C, *vekhoham shel hama'aminim ba'emunah hakedoshah vehatehorah hazot kekho'ah ha'aryeh asher hames yames*, treating the last two verbs as Hiphils and not (as in 2 Sam. 17: 10, on which Baruch draws) as Niphals (cf. Deut. 1: 28). The first word, *vekhoham* (C,O), appears in the other MSS as *uvakhem* (N,W₂), *bakhem* (J), ובבם (M₂); the last variant, meaningless as it stands, leads me to suspect an alternative reading *veliham* or *ulevavam* (cf. 2 Sam. 17: 10). For *kekho'ah* (C,N,O,W₂), J,M₂ give *bekho'ah*. For *hames yames* (C,M₂,N), O gives המס ימת (reflecting an Ashkenazi pronunciation of the *tav*?), J, W$_2$ *hemah yames*.

77.17   **Amen! so be His will**. The copyists of C and J end here with the abbreviation תושלב"ע (*tam venishlam shevah le'el bore olam*, 'it is entirely completed, praise be to God, the world's Creator'), M$_2$, N simply *tam*, 'it is
completed'.

30. Addendum: The Comments of Jedidiah Zarfatti

The addendum (77.18–78.11) occurs only in L$_2$, W$_1$. Freimann, who has
normally though not invariably[25] used O as his base text, here apparently shifts
to using W$_1$. He must have made his copy in haste. I have noted seventeen dis-
crepancies between his printed edition and W$_1$, a few of which do affect the
meaning.

77.23–4 *be'aharit* . . . **in its most exact sense**. L$_2$, W$_1$ *be'aharit daika*. Zarfatti
misquotes the Zohar's *be'aharit hayamim daika*—understandably, since
the Zohar is interested in the esoteric symbolism of 'the end of days',
while Zarfatti's interest is in the numerical value of the single word
be'aharit. Freimann, without MS support, supplies the word *hayamim*.

77.33   **Yet you may infer it** . . . **behind your laws**. L$_2$, W$_1$ *teda mimah ta'am*;
versus Freimann, *teda mah ta'am*.

78.2   **The forty-first**. L$_2$, W$_1$ *sheha'ehad ve'arba'im*; versus Freimann, *she'ehad
ve'arba'im*. (It is worth noting, though the meaning is not affected, that
the MSS have *hatikvah* in this line for Freimann's *hamikveh*, and *sheyush-
lamu* in l. 3 for Freimann's *sheyishalemu*.)

78.10   **I shall come to you like a river**. L$_2$, W$_1$ *ve'avo elekha* (L$_2$ spells *ve'avo*
without the second *vav*); versus Freimann, *ve'avi alekha*, 'I shall bring
you, like a river . . . '. Cf. Isa. 66: 12, the source of the image.

78.11   **aching everywhere**. L$_2$, W$_1$ *mazor misaviv*, a play on Jeremiah's *magor
misaviv*, 'terror everywhere' (Jer. 20: 3, 10, etc.). Freimann, reading
magor misaviv, misses the pun.

The scribe of L$_2$, whom we have already seen to be less than enamoured of
Sabbatai Zevi and his followers (above, on p. 43, l. 16), leaves after the end of the
Zarfatti text a blank verso, recto, and verso. There follows a brief text (fos.
43^r–44^v), apparently a lampoon of some sort, in praise of the ass as the most
noble of animals. The handwriting is clearly that of the copyist of *Memorial to the
Children of Israel*. Whether he is the author or only the transcriber of this text,
what moved him to include it here, and whether he intends thereby an oblique
comment on Sabbatai and the Sabbatians,[26] I cannot begin to guess.

---

[25] See above, on p. 76, ll. 7, 7–8, 34.   [26] So Margoliouth, *Catalogue*, 434–5.

ॐ

Sabbatai Zevi's Circular Letter (Nisan 1676)

Of the three versions of this letter, the one sent to Arnaut-Belgrade survives in what may be Sabbatai's own autograph copy.[1] The fuller text of the 'Sofia' version was preserved in a manuscript, apparently no longer extant, copied by Yitzhak Ben-Zvi in Aleppo in the 1930s.[2] The shorter 'Sofia' version is the one given by Baruch of Arezzo in the *Memorial* (§25).

Arnaut-Belgrade	Sofia *longer version*	Sofia *shorter version*
	Sabbatai Zevi made a serpent of silver and placed it upon the standard.	
	The day after the festival of Passover (*and Sukkot*), Monday, the twenty-third of the First of Months, whose name the Lord called Nisan.[3]	
To my brethren and friends, dwellers in Arnaut-Belgrade—	To my brethren and friends, all the faithful folk of the city of Sofia—	To my brethren and friends, all the faithful folk of the city of Sofia—
May you be privileged to see God's salvation— whoever among you is worthy of it!	May they be privileged to see God's salvation, to be eyewitnesses to His return to Zion!	May they be privileged to see God's salvation, to be eyewitnesses to His return to Zion!

---

[1]   In *Sefer yemot hamashiaḥ*, the massive Sabbatian manuscript (Jerusalem, Ben-Zvi Institute 2262) that also contains the Najara Chronicle. The text is published in Amarilio, 'Sabbatian Documents' (Heb.), 249–50; the evidence for its being an autograph is on pp. 238–9.

[2]   Rubashov, 'Sabbatian Documents from Aleppo' (Heb.).

[3]   23 Nisan 5436 = 6 April 1676. The language is modelled on Exod. 17: 15, with the name of the month Nisan put in place of the biblical *nisi* ('my standard'). The words I have italicized are apparently a copyist's note, intended to explain the allusion to Exod. 17: 15 with a further allusion to Num. 21: 9, 'Moses made a serpent of bronze and placed it upon the standard [*hanes*].' Sabbatai tended to identify himself as the 'holy serpent', and to conclude his signature with a sketch of a twisting serpent. Such serpent-signatures are used in the Arnaut-Belgrade letter, and were presumably in the original letter to Sofia as well; surely the copyist alludes to them. Why he replaced the 'bronze' of the biblical verse with 'silver', I do not know. I also do not know why he adds the inappropriate words 'and Sukkot'; cf. Rubashov, 'Sabbatian Documents from Aleppo' (Heb.), 56.

Hurry and send me a prayer
book for the New Year and
the Day of Atonement.

Thus speaks the man raised
up on high, over all the host
of heaven that are in the
heaven and over all the
kings of the earth who are
on earth—through his
nobility shall he rise up[4]—
messiah of the God of Israel
and Judah—

SABBATAI ZEVI.

From Alkum, Sunday, the
first day of the First of
Months, whose name the
Lord called Nisan.[5]

With God's help:

I am sending before you the above-mentioned angel,[6] to bring you good tidings.[7]	I am sending an angel before you to bring you good tidings.	I am sending an angel before you.
He will tell you all my honour in the Strait of the Sea,[8] and something of what he has seen.[9]	He will tell you all my honour in Egypt, and something of what he has seen.	He will tell you all my honour in Egypt, and something of what he has seen.
Be careful of him: obey him, and do not rebel against anything he tells you on my authority.	Be careful of him: obey him, and do not rebel against anything he tells you on my authority.	Be careful of him: obey him, and do not rebel against anything he tells you on my authority.

[4] Combining 2 Sam. 23: 1 with Isa. 24: 21 and 32: 8.

[5] 1 Nisan 5436 = 15 March 1676. 'Alkum' is the standard Sabbatian designation for Dulcigno.

[6] Referring back to himself? Sabbatai is the only person 'mentioned above', in the earlier section of the letter. The letter to Sofia, which lacks this earlier section, speaks only of 'an angel'. It would appear that Sabbatai has split himself, in his own mind, into the angelic messenger and the One who has dispatched him. (In the Bible, *malakh* can mean a human messenger as well as an angel. But this would be unusual in post-biblical usage.)

[7] Following Exod. 23: 20.

[8] First written *bemitsrayim*, 'in Egypt', as in the Sofia letter (and in the source of the allusion, Gen. 45: 13). The writer then crosses out *bemitsrayim* and replaces it with two words containing the same Hebrew letters, *bemetsar yam*, 'in the Strait of the Sea'; he leaves an unusually wide gap between the two words, so the reader will not miss his intent. At least on one level, 'the Strait of the Sea' surely refers to the coastal town of Dulcigno; for other possible layers of meaning, see Scholem, *Sabbatai Sevi*, 841; Liebes, 'Sabbatai Zevi's Attitude to his Conversion' (Heb.), 277–8 n. 69 (*On Sabbatianism*, 280–1 (endnotes)).

[9] Following Gen. 45: 13.

For I will not forgive your sins.[10]	For I will not forgive your sins, when God arises to judge and the Lord of hosts is exalted in judgment.[11]	For I will not forgive your sins, when God arises to judge and the Lord of hosts is exalted in judgment.
And who is a god who can save you from my power?[12] For apart from me there is no God.[13]	And who is the God who can save you from my power? For apart from me there is no God.	
But if you obey him and do all I tell you,	But if you obey him and do all I tell you,	But if you obey him and do all he tells you,
I will surely arise and fill your treasuries.[14]	I will surely arise and fill your treasuries.	I will surely arise and fill your treasuries.
Thus speaks the man raised up on high,	Thus speaks the man raised up on high, above the heights of the Father,[15]	Thus speaks the man raised up on high,
Exalted Lion and exalted Gazelle,	Exalted Lion and exalted Gazelle,	Exalted Lion and exalted Gazelle,
messiah of the God of Israel and Judah,	messiah of the God of Israel and Judah,	messiah of the God of Israel and Judah,
SABBATAI MEHMED ZEVI[16]	SABBATAI ZEVI MEHMED	

[10] Following Exod. 23: 21.   [11] Combining Exod. 23: 21 with Ps. 76: 10 and Isa. 5: 16.
[12] Dan. 3: 15.   [13] Isa. 44: 6.   [14] Combining Exod. 23: 22 with Prov. 8: 21.
[15] Combining 2 Sam. 23: 1 with Isa. 14: 14, and replacing Isaiah's 'heights of cloud' (*bamotei av*, with an *ayin*) with the very similar-sounding 'heights of the Father' (*bamotei av*, with an *alef*).

[16] In the manuscript, these three names are spaced so that 'Sabbatai' is on the right of the page, 'Mehmed' in the centre, 'Zevi' on the left. Is some kabbalistic symbolism intended?

స్

'30 Iyar'

In his chronicle of the events of 5431 [1671], Jacob Najara writes: 'On 30 Iyar [ובל׳ של אייר], Rabbi Samuel Tirmiso arrived' in Adrianople.

At first sight, '30 Iyar' seems about as likely a date as 30 February or 31 April: the Jewish calendar is structured so that the month of Iyar always has twenty-nine days. One's natural inclination is to suppose that '30 Iyar' is an error of some sort. There are several reasons, however, why this inclination should be resisted.

First, the letter *lamed*, used to indicate the numeral 30, is distinctive and not readily confused with any other letter. It is not easy to imagine any transcriptional error that would have produced this misreading—especially one so apparently implausible.

Second, Najara tells us shortly afterwards that Nathan of Gaza arrived in Adrianople on 19 Sivan, and came to pay his respects to Sabbatai the next day, 'on the sabbath day, the twentieth of the month'. According to Eduard Mahler's tables,[1] 20 Sivan 5431 would have fallen on Friday, 29 May. But now assume for a moment that Najara was working with a calendar that gave Iyar thirty days, so that 10 May 1671 would not have been the first day of Sivan (as in the standard Jewish calendar) but the last day of Iyar. 1 Sivan would then be not Sunday, 10 May, but Monday, 11 May. 20 Sivan would be Saturday, 30 May—in conformity with Najara.

Third, in the same sentence in which Najara describes Tirmiso's arrival, he says: 'on the fourteenth of that month [Sivan] Rabbi Samuel Tirmiso . . . took leave of Amirah and returned home'. By Mahler's tables, 14 Sivan would have been a sabbath—an odd day to begin a journey. On the assumption that Najara's 'Iyar' had thirty days, 14 Sivan = Sunday, 24 May. It would make perfect sense for Tirmiso to have spent sabbath in Adrianople and set out the next morning.

Now, in this very same sentence, Najara tells us (according to the manuscript) that the rabbis of Sofia arrived on 20 Sivan (ובכ׳ לסיון). We have just seen that, on the hypothesis of a thirty-day Iyar, 20 Sivan will be a sabbath, 30 May. So perhaps we have just exchanged one problem (Tirmiso's departure on the sabbath) for another (the Sofian rabbis' arrival on the sabbath)! But the date 20 Sivan is suspicious on other grounds. It breaks, without any apparent reason, the time sequence of the sentence. Tirmiso arrives on '30 Iyar'; the Sofian rabbis arrive on 20 Sivan; Tirmiso departs on 14 Sivan. The order is obviously wrong. If,

---

[1] Mahler, *Handbuch der jüdischen Chronologie.*

moreover, the Sofian rabbis arrived on the twentieth and Nathan came to pay his respects on the same day, why are these two events not juxtaposed?

It seems, therefore, we must emend ובכ' לסיון to ובב' לסיון, 'on 2 Sivan', which on my hypothesis would have been Tuesday, 12 May. The letters *beit* and *kaf* closely resemble each other; although the copyist of the manuscript plainly intended to write *kaf*, it is easy to imagine he was copying a source in which the two letters were indistinguishable. Ten lines on, when he speaks of Nathan coming to pay his respects on the twentieth, he uses the final form of the *kaf* to represent the numeral; here he uses the medial. This confirms he was copying a source in which *beit*, not *kaf*, was written.

Sabbatai's penchant for inventing new festivals, and for shifting around the dates of the current ones, was notorious.[2] I know of no direct evidence, though, that he or his followers invented a new calendar in which the months might be a day longer or shorter than in the standard calendar, and any given date a day or so off. This is a real difficulty for my hypothesis. Surely, if such a calendar had existed, one of the movement's critics would sooner or later have mentioned it?

I have no answer for this objection, and must leave the problem of '30 Iyar' without any definite resolution. I would call attention, however, to the date given by the copyist Jehiel Michal Epstein at the beginning of Cuenque's biography of Sabbatai Zevi (translated in this volume). 'Monday, 2 Av 5459'. Not only did 2 Av fall on a Tuesday that year (28 July 1699), but the Jewish calendar is structured so that it can never fall on a Monday (or a Wednesday, or a Friday). Is it possible that, by gratuitously announcing the day of the week on which he had received his copy of Cuenque's book, Epstein was communicating to those in the know that his calendar was not that of standard Judaism? Possible—but speculative. And so I must leave it.[3]

---

[2]   See the conclusion of Halevi's first letter to Sasportas. Professor Alan D. Corré, who was kind enough to discuss the calendrical problems with me by email, has stressed to me the general tendency of sectarian movements to devise new calendars setting them off from the main body of believers. Yet the absence of direct evidence for a distinctively Sabbatian calendar remains troubling.

[3]   Cf. also the problem of 'Sunday, 25 Elul 5425' in Baruch of Arezzo, *Memorial*; above, n. 51 to Baruch (also nn. 60, 203).

Notes on MS Rostock 36

1. General

The manuscript contains thirteen folio pages, of which the first and the last are entirely blank. Folio 2^r is a title page in German, folio 3^r a title page in Hebrew. The German title page contains the notation: 'This was presented to me, Joh[ann] Christoph Sticht, in 1753 by the Hamburg Jew Joseph Simon Levi Junior.' Sticht, a Christian theologian, presumably passed the manuscript on to his pupil, the Orientalist Oluf Gerhard Tychsen (1734–1818), from whose library it made its way into the collection of the Rostock Universitätsbibliothek.[1] From Sticht's notation, at all events, we learn the latest possible date for the manuscript's writing.

The Hebrew title page conveys the earliest possible date. It gives the title of the manuscript as *Sefer hamispaḥat*, 'The Book of the Scab', referring to the 'scab' designated in Leviticus 13: 7–8 as a symptom of leprosy. To this the scribe adds, as subtitle:

> . . . the inveterate leprosy, sprung from the scoundrel Sabbatai Cowturd,[2] may his name be erased from the world, in accordance with the views of his believers, blast and damn them; with annotations by the famed and illustrious scholar, Rabbi Moses Hagiz זצוק"ל, to which I have given the title *Beit hameri* ['The Rebellious House'];[3] also a version from the book *Ma'aseh tuviah* ['The Work of Tobias'],[4] a deposition taken in the holy city of Jerusalem, and the festivals of [Sabbatai's] worshippers.

The abbreviation זצוק"ל 'may the memory of the righteous and holy one serve as a blessing', shows that Hagiz was dead at the time the scribe wrote. Hagiz died in 1751. It might possibly be imagined that the title page could have been written later than the body of the manuscript; yet in the manuscript itself, on folio 5^r, the first of Hagiz's notes on Cuenque is introduced with an attribution to 'the illustrious scholar Rabbi Moses Hagiz, זצ"ל ['may the memory of the righteous serve as a blessing']'.

After the title page, on folio 4^r, there is a brief list of Sabbatian festivals, which Emden reproduces (with some variations) in a much later position in *Torat*

---

[1] Ernst Róth, in Striedl, Tetzner, and Róth, *Hebräische Handschriften*, pt. 2, 334, 350–1. The date '1753' is misprinted on p. 350 as 1783.

[2] *Tsafia*, an unpleasant pun on the name *Zevi*. [3] From Ezek. 2: 8, 12: 2, etc.

[4] Tobias Hakohen's *Ma'aseh tuviah*, published in Venice in 1707, was 'an encyclopedia dealing with theology, astronomy, cosmography, geography, botany, with medicine taking up about half of the entire work. . . . The work is also rich in historical references, e.g., on Shabbetai Zevi' (*Encyclopedia Judaica*, 'Cohn, Tobias ben Moses').

hakenaot.[5] There follows, as the subtitle promises, the Cuenque text with Epstein's preface and Moses Hagiz's critical annotations (fos. 5ʳ–9ʳ), an extract from Tobias Hakohen's *Ma'aseh tuviah* dealing with Sabbatai Zevi (to which is attached the original *Memorial to the Children of Israel*, printed at Venice in 1668; fos. 9ʳ–11ᵛ), and the text of a deposition taken in Jerusalem from one Moses ibn Habib, probably around the year 1702 (fo. 12ʳ–ᵛ).[6] The deposition, filled with all sorts of juicy and scandalous stories about Sabbatai, his followers, and his wife Sarah ('then she told him to take off her pants', etc., etc.), seems to break off abruptly, after a few words that have been very carefully crossed out and rendered illegible.[7] The scribe then writes, at the very end of the manuscript:

All this have I copied from a manuscript that was sealed away [*ḥatum*] in the archive of the illustrious scholar, the great zealot Rabbi Jacob [Emden], son of the famed and illustrious scholar Hakham Zevi Ashkenazi, זצ"ל, which he received from the man famous in his generation, Rabbi Jonah Landsofer, זצ"ל.[8]

The contents of folios 5ʳ–12ᵛ (from the Cuenque biography through the Jerusalem deposition) are printed in the same sequence, with Emden's expansions, in *Torat hakenaot*.[9] This portion of *Torat hakenaot* is clearly based on the manuscript copied by the Rostock scribe. In the same place in the text where the Rostock scribe writes his concluding note, Emden has the following:

Beyond this I was not able to copy, it was all so disagreeable to me.[10] Thus far extends the written text conveyed from the Land of Israel by a dependable messenger. The copy[11] was given to me by the illustrious scholar Rabbi Hayim Jonah, זצ"ל [Landsofer?]. May the good Lord forgive us for publishing these blasphemies, kept secret with me [*kamus imadi*] for many years, for all to read; yet He knows very well that it was for the sake of His great name, profaned through our many sins by the followers of Sabbatai Zevi's damned sect, who covertly lead the Jewish people astray,[12] that we found ourselves compelled to this...

There follows a string of abuse of Sabbatai Zevi and his followers, in Emden's typical style.

2. The Fire

In the preface to Cuenque's biography, after Epstein has said that Cuenque wrote for Rabbi Zalman Darum 'a narrative concise yet complete' concerning

---

[5] *Torat hakenaot*, 36a–b (75).

[6] Benayahu, 'A Key to the Understanding of Documents on the Sabbatian Movement in Jerusalem' (Heb.), 35–40.   [7] More on this below.

[8] On Landsofer, see the 'Text' section of my introduction to Cuenque.

[9] *Torat hakenaot*, 16a–26a (33–54).

[10] I assume this is what Emden intends by *haderekh yarat lenegdi* (from Num. 22: 32).

[11] The word *hahetek* ('the copy') is preceded by *hasaris*, printed in the Amsterdam edition in the same slightly larger, slightly raised, square script as the name 'Hayim Jonah'. *Hasaris* would normally mean 'the eunuch'. The word's presence here baffles me.

[12] Like Jonathan Eibeschütz, for example.

Sabbatai Zevi, the editions of *Torat hakenaot* have the following:

It occurred to Rabbi Zalman on one occasion to read this text, which the Jerusalemite had composed for him, in the nighttime. He was holding a wax candle, and he dozed off, and the candle fell upon the Jerusalemite's manuscript. Several pages of it were burned. At all events I have copied whatever I was able to copy, in order that the reader may discover therein its extraordinary contents.

In place of all this, MS Rostock has about a dozen words that have been carefully crossed out, so they are no longer readable (fo. 5ʳ). What these words might have been, who excised them, and why are questions that must be postponed for the time being. It is clear, however, that the Rostock text cannot possibly have contained the story of Zalman Darum's fire and the loss of some portions of Cuenque's manuscript.

Now, in those places where *Torat hakenaot* marks that some text has been lost in the fire, the text is invariably present in MS Rostock, without any indication that there is anything special or unusual about it. The 'lost' text, moreover, is very short, normally amounting to only a few words, as shown in the table below. From the last of the lacunae to the end of the text, MS Rostock has forty-two lines.

Amsterdam edition	Lvov edition	MS Rostock	Words missing	Lines since previous lacuna*
17*a*, line 8 fb**	35, line 23	5ᵛ, lines 15–16	6	44
18*a*, line 8	36, line 46	6ʳ, lines 6–5 fb	6	38
18*b*, line 9 fb	38, line 36	6ᵛ, line 4 fb	0	38
19*b*, line 20	40, line 34	7ᵛ, lines 6–7	16	43
20*a*, line 12 fb	41, line 47	8ʳ, line 7	5	31
20*b*, line 4 fb	43, line 13	8ᵛ, line 5	14	29

 * Or, in the case of the first lacuna, since the beginning of the text.

** fb = from bottom. It is often difficult to count the lines in the Amsterdam edition and in the MS because of the insertion of Hagiz's/Emden's comments within the text in a different size of script. When a passage is close to the bottom of the page, therefore, it is usually more accurate to give the line count from the bottom than from the top.

The *Vorlage* of MS Rostock was plainly complete, and its text of Epstein's preface said nothing of any fire. It is hard to avoid the conclusion that Emden himself invented the 'fire' story and inserted it into the preface, meanwhile deleting a few words here and there from the text in order to give the false impression that the manuscript was incomplete. But what possible motive could he have had for doing this? Moreover, the lacunae occur at fairly regular intervals, as may be seen from the table.[13] This is what we would expect to find if the top or bottom of a manuscript had caught fire, and the fire was quickly extinguished, but not before it had made the first or last lines of each page wholly or partly unreadable.

I can think of only one explanation that will cover the facts. The 'fire' story, as told by Emden, is essentially true, only the careless and sleepy reader was not Rabbi Zalman Darum, but Emden himself. He had already determined to publish the text of Cuenque; the Rostock scribe had already made his copy of it and departed, and presumably Emden found it impossible or inconvenient to contact him. Then came the accident with the candle. What was Emden to do? The accident could not be made to un-happen; the damaged words, few as they were, could not be reconstructed; to admit what had really happened, that through his carelessness he had mutilated a precious text, would be just too embarrassing. A little judicious fiction-writing transferred the blame to Zalman Darum, who, being dead, would not object too strongly. It is our good luck that the Rostock scribe made his copy before the accident, and not afterwards.

3. The Excisions

But what were the words originally written in Epstein's preface that someone took such care to render illegible? The curls above and below the line at the very end of line 4, compared with those of the date in line 1, suggest that here also a date may be present—perhaps the date Epstein actually copied the manuscript,[14] as opposed to when he received it from Rabbi Seligmann? Apart from this, the words are impossible to decipher.

If we ask, however, why they were crossed out, another excision at the very end of the manuscript will give us a clue. The Jerusalem deposition reads: 'If we were to try to give all the details of their blasphemies against the Blessed Holy One and His mighty Shekhinah, they could not be put in writing, inasmuch as the matters that are the secrets of the world, [Sabbatai and his followers] turn to evil purposes'—then three or four words crossed out so they cannot be read (fo. 12ᵛ, l. 27). Here, however, the excised words can be supplied from *Torat hakenaot*: *kemo talmidei* [*ḥanotsri*] ימ״ש, 'as did the disciples of [the Nazarene], may his name and memory be blotted out'.[15]

---

[13] Keep in mind that, because of the Rostock scribe's habit of inserting Hagiz's notes into Cuenque's text (in smaller script than the rest), the length of the lines of Cuenque's text varies considerably. The line counts, therefore, give only an approximate picture of the distance from one lacuna to the next.

[14] Which, if we are to take his 'ten years ago' literally, would have been some time in 1702.

[15] The Amsterdam edition (p. 26*a*) leaves a blank where I have supplied *ḥanotsri*; the blank is omitted in the Lvov edition (p. 54). Certainly the offending word was present in MS Rostock.

There is a similar erasure, though less thoroughly done, in the second of Hagiz's notes on folio 7ᵛ (l. 5). Commenting on Cuenque's story of how Sabbatai was sent to Castillas (that is, Gallipoli[16]), Hagiz says that after the apostasy the leaders of the Jewish communities requested Sabbatai be banished 'to a distant place, a place where Jews could not follow him. There [in Dulcigno] he settled, teaching the Christians [*la'arelim*, literally 'the uncircumcised'] from the Zohar in the Turkish language, until he died there'.[17] The word *la'arelim* is crossed out, though not so completely the letters cannot be made out, and *layishma'elim* ('the Muslims') is written between the lines, in a handwriting different from that of the original scribe.

I have no doubt who was responsible for these alterations. It was Joseph Simon Levi Junior, the Hamburg Jew who gave the manuscript to Johann Christoph Sticht—but not before he had gone through the text crossing out or 'correcting' anything that might be expected to give offence to a Christian. (Hagiz's sneering reference to 'teaching the Christians from the Zohar' could be taken as offensive, in an age when Christian scholars took an interest in kabbalah and might go to Jewish teachers to satisfy their curiosity.) Whatever Jehiel Michal Epstein wrote at the end of his preface—which Emden replaced in *Torat hakenaot* with the 'fire' story—must have been in this category. Beyond this, I cannot guess what it might have been.

[16] See n. 105 on Cuenque.
[17] In the editions of *Torat hakenaot* (Amsterdam, p. 20*a*; Lvov, p. 41), *la'arelim* is replaced by *lagoyim*, 'the gentiles'.

Bibliography

ABOAB, SAMUEL, *Devar shemu'el* [Samuel's Word] (Venice, 1702; repr. Jerusalem, 1967).

ALTER, ROBERT, 'Sabbatai Zevi and the Jewish Imagination', in id., *After the Tradition: Essays on Modern Jewish Writing* (New York: E. P. Dutton, 1969), 61–75.

AMARILIO, ABRAHAM, 'Sabbatian Documents from the Saul Amarillo Collection' (Heb.), *Sefunot*, 5 (1961), 237–74.

ARAMA, ISAAC, *Sefer akedat yitshak* [Isaac's Binding], 5 vols (Pressburg: Victor Kittseer, 1849).

ARANOV, SAUL I., *A Descriptive Catalogue of the Bension Collection of Sephardic Manuscripts and Texts* (Edmonton: University of Alberta Press, 1979).

ASSAF, SIMHAH, *In the Tents of Jacob: Jewish Cultural Life in the Middle Ages* [Be'o-holei ya'akov: perakim mehayei hatarbut shel hayehudim bimei habeinayim] (Jerusalem: Mosad Harav Kook, 1965).

ATTIAS, MOSHE, and GERSHOM SCHOLEM, *Sabbatian Songs and Praises* [Shirot vetishbahot shel hashabeta'im] (Tel Aviv: Dvir, 1947).

AVI-YONAH, M[ICHAEL], *The Jews of Palestine: A Political History from the Bar Kokhba War to the Arab Conquest* (New York: Schocken Books, 1976).

AZULAI, ABRAHAM, *Or hahamah* [Light of the Sun], 3 vols (Jerusalem, 1876; repr. Jerusalem, n.d.).

AZULAI, H. J. D., *Shem hagedolim hashalem* [Complete 'Renown of the Great'], ed. Isaac Benjacob (Vilna: Romm, 1853; repr. Jerusalem, 1994).

BAER, MARC DAVID, 'The Double Bind of Race and Religion: The Conversion of the Dönme to Turkish Secular Nationalism', *Comparative Studies in Society and History*, 46 (2004), 682–708.

—— 'Revealing a Hidden Community: Ilgaz Zorlu and the Debate in Turkey over the Dönme/Sabbateans', *Turkish Studies Association Bulletin*, 23 (1999), 68–75.

BARNAI, JACOB, *Sabbatianism—Social Perspectives* [Shabeta'ut: hebetim hevratiyim] (Jerusalem: Zalman Shazar Center for Jewish History, 2000).

BENAYAHU, MEIR, 'The "Holy Brotherhood" of R. Judah Hasid and their Settlement in Jerusalem' (Heb.), *Sefunot*, 3–4 (1960), 133–82.

—— 'A Key to the Understanding of Documents on the Sabbatian Movement in Jerusalem' (Heb.), in E. E. Urbach, R. J. Zwi Werblowsky, and H. Wirszub-ski (eds), *Studies in Mysticism and Religion Presented to Gershom G. Scholem* (Jerusalem: Magnes Press, 1967), 35–45.

BENAYAHU, MEIR, 'The Letters of Rabbi Abraham Cuenque to Rabbi Judah

Briel' (Heb.), *Sinai*, 32 (1953), 300–19.

—— *The Sabbatian Movement in Greece* [Hatenuah hashabeta'it beyavan] = *Sefunot*, 14 (1971–7).

BEN-YEHUDA, ELIEZER, *A Complete Dictionary of Ancient and Modern Hebrew* [Milon halashon ha'ivrit hayeshanah vehaḥadashah], 16 vols (Jerusalem, 1948–59).

BERTI, SILVIA, FRANÇOISE CHARLES-DAUBERT, and RICHARD H. POPKIN, *Heterodoxy, Spinozism, and Free Thought in Early-Eighteenth-Century Europe* (Dordrecht: Kluwer Academic Publishers, 1996).

BIALE, DAVID, 'Shabbtai Zvi and the Seductions of Jewish Orientalism', in Rachel Elior (ed.), *The Sabbatian Movement and its Aftermath: Messianism, Sabbatianism and Frankism*, 2 vols (Jerusalem: Institute of Jewish Studies, 2001), ii. 85*–110* (English section).

BIRNBAUM, PHILIP, *Daily Prayer Book: Ha-Siddur Ha-Shalem* (New York: Hebrew Publishing Company, 1949).

BLANK, SHELDON, 'The Death of Zechariah in Rabbinic Literature', *Hebrew Union College Annual*, 12–13 (1937–8), 327–46.

CARLEBACH, ELISHEVA, *Divided Souls: Converts from Judaism in Germany, 1500–1750* (New Haven: Yale University Press, 2001).

—— *The Pursuit of Heresy: Rabbi Moses Hagiz and the Sabbatian Controversies* (New York: Columbia University Press, 1990).

—— 'Two Amens that Delayed the Redemption: Jewish Messianism and Popular Spirituality in the Post-Sabbatian Century', *Jewish Quarterly Review*, 82 (1992), 241–61.

COENEN, THOMAS, *Ydele verwachtinge der Joden* (Amsterdam, 1699).

CORDOVERO, MOSES, *Sefer pardes rimonim* [Pomegranate Orchard] (Munkacs, 1906; repr. Jerusalem, 1962).

COUSINS, NORMAN, *Head First* (New York: Penguin Books, 1989).

CUENQUE, ABRAHAM, *Avak soferim* [Scribes' Dust] (Amsterdam, 1704; repr. Brooklyn: Copy Corner, 1993).

ELQAYAM, AVRAHAM, 'The Absent Messiah: Messiah Son of Joseph in the Thought of Nathan of Gaza, Sabbatai Zevi, and A. M. Cardozo' (Heb.), *Da'at*, 38 (1997), 33–82.

—— 'Sabbatai Zevi's Manuscript Copy of the Zohar' (Heb.), *Kabbalah*, 3 (1998), 345–87.

EMDEN, JACOB, *Sefer torat hakenaot* [The Torah of Zealotry] (Amsterdam, 1752; repr. Jerusalem: Makor, 1971; 2nd edn, Lvov: Michal Wolf, 1870). References in the notes give the Amsterdam edition first, followed by the page number of the Lvov edition in parentheses.

Encyclopedia Judaica. CD-ROM edition.

FALK, AVNER, 'The Messiah and the Qelippoth: On the Mental Illness of Sabbatai

Sevi', *Journal of Psychology and Judaism*, 7 (1982), 5–29.

FISHMAN, TALYA, *Shaking the Pillars of Exile: 'Voice of a Fool'*, *an Early Modern Jewish Critique of Rabbinic Culture* (Stanford: Stanford University Press, 1997).

FREELY, JOHN, *The Lost Messiah: In Search of Sabbatai Sevi* (London: Viking, 2001).

FREIMANN, AHARON, *Inyanei shabetai tsevi* [Concerning Sabbatai Zevi] (German title: *Sammelband kleiner Schriften über Sabbatai Zebi und dessen Anhänger*) (Berlin: H. Itzkowsky, 1912).

GILLER, PINCHAS, *The Enlightened Will Shine: Symbolism and Theurgy in the Later Strata of the Zohar* (Albany: State University of New York Press, 1993).

—— *Reading the Zohar: The Sacred Text of the Kabbalah* (Oxford: Oxford University Press, 2001).

GINZBERG, LOUIS, *Legends of the Jews*, 7 vols (Philadelphia: Jewish Publication Society, 1942–7).

GLÜCKEL OF HAMELN, *The Memoirs of Glückel of Hameln* , trans. Marvin Lowenthal (New York: Schocken Books, 1977).

GOFFMAN, D., *Izmir and the Levantine World* (Seattle: University of Washington Press, 1990).

GÖKBILGIN, M. TAYYIB, and R. C. REPP, 'Köprülü', *The Encyclopedia of Islam*, new edn, 12 vols (Leiden: E. J. Brill, 1960–2004), vol. v (1986), 256–63.

GOLDISH, MATT, 'The Early Messianic Career of Shabbatai Zvi', in Lawrence Fine (ed.), *Judaism in Practice: From the Middle Ages through the Early Modern Period* (Princeton: Princeton University Press, 2001), 470–82.

—— *The Sabbatean Prophets* (Cambridge, Mass.: Harvard University Press, 2004).

GOLDSTEIN, LISA, 'Split Light', in David G. Hartwell and Milton T. Wolf (eds), *Visions of Wonder* (New York: Tor, 1996), 404–13.

GRIES, ZE'EV, *The Book as an Agent of Culture, 1700–1900* [Hasefer kesokhen tarbut bashanim 1700–1900] (Tel Aviv: Hakibuts Hame'uhad, 2002); English translation: *The Book in the Jewish World, 1700–1900* (Oxford: Littman Library of Jewish Civilization, 2007).

—— *Conduct Literature (Regimen Vitae): Its History and Place in the Life of Beshtian Hasidism* [Sifrut hahanhagot: toledoteiha umekomah behayei hasidei rabi yisra'el ba'al shem tov] (Jerusalem: Bialik Institute, 1989).

GUTTMANN, JULIUS, *Philosophies of Judaism* (Garden City, NY: Doubleday Anchor Books, 1964).

HABERMAN, A. M., 'On the History of Anti-Sabbatian Polemic' (Heb.), *Kovets al yad*, NS 3 (1940), 187–214.

HAKOHEN, HAYIM, *Sefer torat hakham* [A Scholar's Torah], 2 vols (Venice, 1654; repr. Brooklyn: Copy Corner, 1992).

HALPERIN, DAVID J., *Abraham Miguel Cardozo: Selected Writings* (New York: Paulist Press, 2001).

HALPERIN, DAVID J., *The Faces of the Chariot: Early Jewish Responses to Ezekiel's Vision* (Tübingen: J. C. B. Mohr, 1988).

—— 'Sabbatai Zevi, Metatron, and Mehmed: Myth and History in Seventeenth-Century Judaism', in S. Daniel Breslauer (ed.), *The Seductiveness of Jewish Myth: Challenge or Response?* (Albany: State University of New York Press, 1997), 271–308.

—— 'The Son of the Messiah: Ishmael Zevi and the Sabbatian Aqedah', *Hebrew Union College Annual*, 67 (1996), 143–219.

HAMMER-PURGSTALL, J. VON, *Geschichte des Osmanischen Reiches*, 4 vols (Pesth: Hartleben, 1834–6).

HATHAWAY, JANE, 'The Grand Vizier and the False Messiah: The Sabbatai Sevi Controversy and the Ottoman Reform in Egypt', *Journal of the American Oriental Society*, 117 (1997), 665–71.

—— 'The Mawza' Exile at the Juncture of Zaydi and Ottoman Messianism', *AJS Review*, 29 (2005), 111–28.

HIRSCHBERG, H. Z., *A History of the Jews in North Africa*, 2 vols (Leiden: E. J. Brill, 1974–81).

HOROWITZ, ISAIAH, *Shenei luḥot haberit* [Two Tablets of the Covenant], 5 vols (Jerusalem: Oz Vehadar, 1993).

IBN YAHYA, GEDALIAH, *Sefer shalshelet hakabalah* [Chain of Tradition] (Lvov: S. L. Flecker, 1862).

IDEL, MOSHE, 'On Prophecy and Magic in Sabbateanism', *Kabbalah*, 8 (2003), 7–50.

—— '"One from a Town and Two from a Family"—A New Look at the Problem of Dissemination of Lurianic Kabbalah and the Sabbatian Movement' (Heb.), *Pe'amim*, 44 (1990), 9–20.

—— *Studies in Ecstatic Kabbalah* (Albany: State University of New York Press, 1988).

IDELSOHN, A. Z., *Jewish Liturgy and its Development* (New York: Schocken Books, 1960).

IFRAH, LIONEL, *L'Aigle d'Amsterdam: Menasseh ben Israël* (Paris: Honoré Champion, 2001).

IZ, FAHIR, H. C. HONY, and A. D. ALDERSON, *The Oxford Turkish Dictionary* (Oxford: Oxford University Press, 1992).

JACOB BEN ASHER, *Arba'ah turim*, vol. i: *Oraḥ ḥayim* (Vilna, 1900; repr. Jerusalem: Makor, 1987).

KATZ, DAVID S., 'Menasseh ben Israel's Christian Connection: Henry Jessey and the Jews', in Yosef Kaplan, Henry Méchoulan, and Richard H. Popkin (eds), *Menasseh ben Israel and his World* (Leiden: E. J. Brill, 1989), 117–38.

KINROSS, PATRICK BALFOUR (Lord Kinross), *The Ottoman Centuries: The Rise and Fall of the Turkish Empire* (New York: Morrow Quill Paperbacks, 1977).

LEWIS, RAPHAELA, *Everyday Life in Ottoman Turkey* (New York: Putnam, 1971).

LIEBES, YEHUDA, 'A Profile of R. Naphtali Katz of Frankfort and his Attitude towards Sabbatianism' (Heb.), *Jerusalem Studies in Jewish Thought*, 12 (1996),

293–305.

—— 'Sabbatai Zevi's Attitude to his Conversion' (Heb.), *Sefunot*, NS 2 (1983), 267–307; repr. in id., *On Sabbateaism and its Kabbalah: Collected Essays* [Sod ha'emunah hashabeta'it: kovets ma'amarim] (Jerusalem: Bialik Institute, 1995), 20–34.

—— 'Sabbatianism and the Bounds of Religion' (Heb.), in Rachel Elior (ed.), *The Sabbatian Movement and its Aftermath: Messianism, Sabbatianism and Frankism*, 2 vols (Jerusalem: Institute of Jewish Studies, 2001), i. 1–21.

—— *Sections of the Zohar Lexicon* [Perakim bemilon sefer hazohar] (Jerusalem: privately printed, 1976).

MAHLER, EDUARD, *Handbuch der jüdischen Chronologie* (Leipzig: Gustav Fock, 1916; repr. Hildesheim: Georg Olms, 1967).

MARGOLIOUTH, G[EORGE], *Catalogue of the Hebrew and Samaritan Manuscripts in the British Museum*, 4 vols (London: Trustees of the British Museum, 1965).

MATT, DANIEL C., *The Zohar: Pritzker Edition*, 3 vols to date (Stanford: Stanford University Press, 2004–).

MÉCHOULAN, HENRY, and GÉRARD NAHON, *Menasseh ben Israel: The Hope of Israel* (Oxford: Littman Library of Jewish Civilization, 1987).

MODENA, LEONE, *The History of the Rites, Customes, and Manner of Life of the Present Jews Throughout the World* (London: Martin & Ridley, 1650).

MOLHO, ISAAC R., and ABRAHAM AMARILIO, 'Autobiographical Letters of Abraham Cardozo' (Heb.), *Sefunot*, 3–4 (1960), 185–241.

MOYAL, ELIE, *The Sabbatian Movement in Marroco* [*sic*]—*its History and Sources* [Hatenuah hashabeta'it bemaroko: toledoteiha umekoroteiha] (Tel Aviv: Am Oved, 1984).

NASSI, GAD, 'Shabbetai Tzvi Lives—Secret Muslim Jews Await their Messiah', *Moment*, 17 (1992), 42–51.

NEUBAUER, AD[OLF], *Catalogue of the Hebrew Manuscripts in the Bodleian Library and in the College Libraries of Oxford* (Oxford: Clarendon Press, 1994).

PANZAC, DANIEL, *Quarantines et Lazarets: L'Europe et la peste d'Orient* (Aix-en-Provence: Édisud, 1986).

PERLMANN, MOSHE, *Ibn Kammuna's Examination of the Three Faiths* (Berkeley: University of California Press, 1971).

POSTAL, BERNARD, and SAMUEL H. ABRAMSON, *The Landmarks of a People: A Guide to the Jewish Sites of Europe* (New York: Hill & Wang, 1962).

RABA, JOEL, *Between Remembrance and Denial: The Fate of the Jews in the Wars of the Polish Commonwealth During the Mid-Seventeenth Century as Shown in Contemporary Writings and Historical Research* (Boulder, Co.: East European Monographs, 1995).

RAPOPORT-ALBERT, ADA, 'On the Position of Women in Sabbatianism' (Heb.), in Rachel Elior (ed.), *The Sabbatian Movement and its Aftermath: Messianism*,

Sabbatianism, and Frankism, 2 vols (Jerusalem: Institute of Jewish Studies, 2001), i. 143–327.

REIF, STEFAN C., *Hebrew Manuscripts at Cambridge University Library* (New York: Cambridge University Press, 1997).

RENAN, ERNEST, *Averroès et l'Averroïsme* (Paris: Calmann-Lévy, 1866).

RETAT, P., *Traité des Trois Imposteurs: Manuscrit clandestin du début du XVIIIe siècle (éd. 1777)* (Saint-Étienne: Éditions de l'Université de Saint-Étienne, 1973).

RICHLER, BENJAMIN, *Guide to Hebrew Manuscript Collections* (Jerusalem: Israel Academy of Sciences and Humanities, 1994).

RIVKIN, ELLIS, *Leon da Modena and the* Kol sakhal (Cincinnati: Hebrew Union College Press, 1952).

ROSS, DAN, *Acts of Faith: A Journey to the Fringes of Jewish Identity* (New York: Schocken Books, 1984).

ROTH, CECIL, *The History of the Jews of Italy* (Philadelphia: Jewish Publication Society, 1946).

—— *A Life of Menasseh ben Israel* (Philadelphia: Jewish Publication Society, 1934).

RUBASHOV, Z[ALMAN], 'The Messiah's Scribe' (Heb.), *Hashilo'aḥ*, 29 (1913), 36–47.

—— 'Sabbatian Documents from Aleppo' (Heb.), *Me'asef tsiyon*, 6 (1934), 54–8.

RYCAUT, PAUL, *History of the Turkish Empire from the Year 1623 to the Year 1677* (London: John Starkey, 1680).

SASPORTAS, JACOB, *Sefer tsitsat novel tsevi* [Zevi's Fading Flower], ed. Isaiah Tishby (Jerusalem: Bialik Institute, 1954).

SCHÄFER, PETER, *Synopse zur Hekhalot-Literatur* (Tübingen: J. C. B. Mohr, 1981).

SCHOLEM, GERSHOM G., 'Abraham Michael Cardozo: The Treatise "Israel, Holy to the Lord"' (Heb.), in *Researches in Sabbateanism*, 425–52.

—— 'The Commentary on Psalms from the Circle of Sabbatai Zevi in Adrianople' (Heb.), in id., *Researches in Sabbateanism*, 89–141.

—— 'The Crypto-Jewish Sect of the Dönmeh (Sabbatians) in Turkey', in id., *The Messianic Idea in Judaism* (New York: Schocken Books, 1971), 142–66.

—— 'The Dönmeh Prayerbook of the Izmir Sect' (Heb.), in *Studies and Texts Concerning the History of Sabbatianism and its Metamorphoses* [Meḥkarim umekorot letoledot hashabeta'ut vegilguleiha] (Jerusalem: Bialik Institute, 1982), 370–421.

—— *In the Footsteps of the Messiah* [Be'ikvot mashiaḥ] (Jerusalem: Tarshish, 1944).

—— *Kabbalah* (New York: New American Library, 1974).

—— *Major Trends in Jewish Mysticism* (New York: Schocken Books, 1954).

—— 'New Sabbatian Documents from the Book *To'ei ruaḥ*' (Heb.), in id., *Researches in Sabbateanism*, 26–53.

—— *On the Mystical Shape of the Godhead: Basic Concepts in the Kabbalah* (New York:

Schocken Books, 1991).

—— 'Rabbi David Yitshaki and his Attitude to Sabbatianism' (Heb.), in id., *Researches in Sabbateanism*, 194–202.

—— 'Rabbi Moses Zacuto's Attitude to Sabbatianism' (Heb.), in id., *Researches in Sabbateanism*, 510–29.

—— *Researches in Sabbateanism* [Meḥkerei shabeta'ut], ed. Yehuda Liebes (Tel Aviv: Am Oved, 1991).

—— *Sabbatai Sevi: The Mystical Messiah*, trans. R. J. Zwi Werblowsky (Princeton: Princeton University Press, 1973).

—— 'A Sabbatian Will from New York', in id., *The Messianic Idea in Judaism* (New York: Schocken Books, 1971), 167–75 [notes 355–9].

—— 'Where did Sabbatai Zevi Die?' (Heb.), in id., *Researches in Sabbateanism*, 77–85.

SCHWARZ, A. Z., *Die hebräische Handschriften in Österreich (ausserhalb der National-bibliothek in Wien)* (Leipzig: K. W. Hiersemann, 1931).

SHAI, ELI, *Messiah of Incest: New and Uncensored History of the Sexual Element in Jewish Mystical Messianism* [Mashiaḥ shel giluy arayot: historiyah ḥadashah uvilti metsunzeret shel hayesod hamini bamistikah hameshiḥit hayehudit] (Tel Aviv: Yedioth Ahronoth and Chemed Books, 2002).

SHAW, STANFORD J., *The Jews of the Ottoman Empire and the Turkish Republic* (New York: New York University Press, 1991).

SILVER, ABBA HILLEL, *A History of Messianic Speculation in Israel* (Boston: Beacon Press, 1959).

SONNE, ISAIAH, 'New Material on Sabbatai Zevi from a Notebook of R. Abraham Rovigo' (Heb.), *Sefunot* 3–4 (1960), 41–69.

SPINOZA, BARUCH, *Theological-Political Treatise*, trans. Samuel Shirley (Indianapolis: Hackett, 1998).

STEINSCHNEIDER, MORITZ, *Polemische und apologetische Literatur in arabischer Sprache* (Leipzig: Brockhaus, 1877; repr. Hildesheim: Georg Olms, 1966).

STRIEDL, HANS, LOTHAR TETZNER, and ERNST RÓTH, *Hebräische Handschriften*, part 2 (= *Verzeichnis der orientalischen Handschriften in Deutschland*, vol. vi/2) (Wiesbaden: Franz Steiner, 1965).

TELENBERG, AHARON, 'The Sabbatian Theology in Judah Levi Tovah's *Commentary on Genesis*' (Heb.), *Kabbalah*, 8 (2003), 151–83.

—— SHLOMO AVAYOU, and AVRAHAM ELQAYAM, 'A Translation of *Mirat bereshit tovah* from Ladino to Hebrew' (Heb.), *Kabalah*, 8 (2003), 281–368.

TEMKIN, MOSHE, 'Shabbtai Tzvi Would Be Proud', *The Jerusalem Report*, 24 May 1999, pp. 34–6.

TISHBY, ISAIAH, 'R. Meir Rofé's Letters of 1675–80 to R. Abraham Rovigo' (Heb.), *Sefunot*, 3–4 (1960), 73–130.

—— (ed.), *The Wisdom of the Zohar*, 3 vols (Oxford: Littman Library of Jewish

Civilization, 1989).

TOAFF, RENZO, *La Nazione Ebrea a Livorno e a Pisa (1591–1700)* (Florence: Leo S. Olschki, 1990).

WASSERSTROM, STEVEN M., *Between Muslim and Jew: The Problem of Symbiosis Under Early Islam* (Princeton: Princeton University Press, 1995).

WAXMAN, MEYER, *A History of Jewish Literature*, 5 vols in 6 (South Brunswick, NJ: Thomas Yoseloff, 1960).

WERBLOWSKY, R. J. ZWI, *Joseph Karo: Lawyer and Mystic* (Philadelphia: Jewish Publication Society, 1977).

—— and GEOFFREY WIGODER, *The Oxford Dictionary of the Jewish Religion* (New York: Oxford University Press, 1997).

WILENSKY, MORDECAI, 'Four English Pamphlets Concerning the Sabbatian Movement in 1665–1666' (Heb.), *Zion*, 17 (1952), 157–72.

YAARI, ABRAHAM, *Mystery of a Book* [Ta'alumat sefer] (Jerusalem: Mosad Harav Kook, 1954).

ZINBERG, ISRAEL, *A History of Jewish Literature*, trans. Bernard Martin, 12 vols (Cincinnati: Hebrew Union College Press; New York: Ktav, 1972–8). Vol. v: *The Jewish Center of Culture in the Ottoman Empire* (1974); vol. vii: *Old Yiddish Literature from its Origins to the Haskalah Period* (1975).

Index of Selected Biblical Passages

꙰

Only biblical references that are of some importance for the ideas
expressed in the texts are listed below; the much larger number of passages
reference to which is purely decorative or whose importance is
marginal have not been indexed.

General Index

𓆸

Printed and bound by CPI Group (UK) Ltd, Croydon, CR0 4YY

13/04/2025

14656579-0001